The Unknown Gulag

The Unknown Gulag

Gulag

The Lost World of
Stalin's Special Settlements

Lynne Viola

OXFORD
UNIVERSITY PRESS
2007

OXFORD
UNIVERSITY PRESS

Oxford University Press, Inc., publishes works that further
Oxford University's objective of excellence
in research, scholarship, and education.

Oxford New York
Auckland Cape Town Dar es Salaam Hong Kong Karachi
Kuala Lumpur Madrid Melbourne Mexico City Nairobi
New Delhi Shanghai Taipei Toronto

With offices in
Argentina Austria Brazil Chile Czech Republic France Greece
Guatemala Hungary Italy Japan Poland Portugal Singapore
South Korea Switzerland Thailand Turkey Ukraine Vietnam

Published by Oxford University Press, Inc.
198 Madison Avenue, New York, NY 10016
www.oup.com

Oxford is a registered trademark of Oxford University Press

Library of Congress Cataloging-in-Publication Data
Viola, Lynne.
The unknown gulag : the lost world of Stalin's special settlements /
Lynne Viola.
p. cm. Includes bibliographical references and index.

1. Peasantry—Government policy—Soviet Union.
2. Slave labor—Soviet Union.
I. Title.
HD1536.S65V56 2007
365'.45094709043—dc22
2006051397

ISBN 978-0-19-538509-0

Not even the traditional three stones mark the crossroads where they went in creaking carts to their doom.
—Aleksandr Solzhenitsyn

Contents

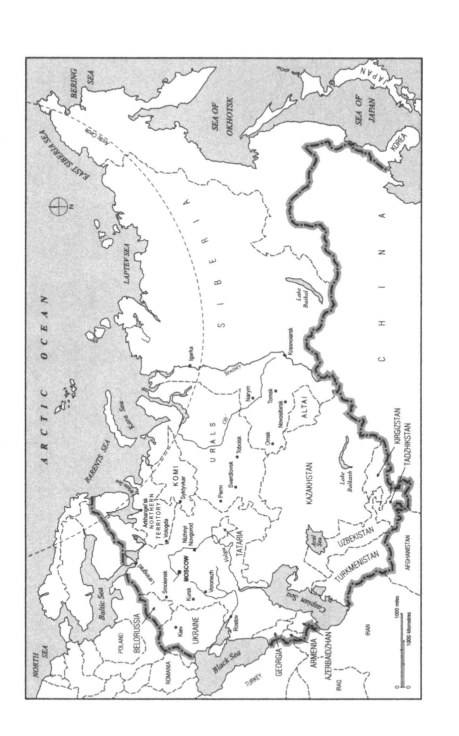

Chronology

1914–1918	World War I
8–13 March (23–28 February) 1917	February Revolution
7 November (25 October) 1917	October Revolution: The Bolshevik Party comes to power
3 March 1918	Treaty of Brest-Litovsk: Soviet Russia leaves the war
8 March 1918	The Bolshevik Party is renamed the Communist Party
16 July 1918	Murder of the Tsar's family
1918–1920	Russian Civil War; forced requisitioning employed to extract grain from the countryside
8–16 March 1921	Tenth Congress of the Communist Party and the introduction of the New Economic Policy
16 March 1921	Forced grain requisitions of the civil war era replaced by tax-in-kind, later by a money tax
March–April 1922	Stalin becomes General Secretary of the Communist Party
1923–1924	Scissors' Crisis: price imbalance between industrial and agricultural goods
January 1924	Death of Lenin
Spring 1927	War Scare
December 1927	Fifteenth Congress of the Communist Party: collectivization placed on the agenda

4 January 1928	OGPU directive to arrest private traders
January 1928	Introduction of "extraordinary measures" in grain requisitioning
July 1928	Stalin calls for a "tribute" from the peasantry
January 1929	Acceleration of repressive measures against "kulak terrorists"
April–May 1929	First Five-Year Plan ratified
June 1929	Ural-Siberian Method extended throughout USSR
June 1929	Politburo decree calling for expansion of camp system and transfer of all prisoners serving more than three years to OGPU for work in colonization and economic exploitation of far north and east
3 October 1929	Politburo authorizes OGPU and Commissariat of Justice to deal "decisively and quickly" with kulak terrorists
November 1929	November Plenum ratifies transition to wholesale collectivization; official defeat of the Right Opposition
7 November 1929	Stalin publishes "The Year of the Great Turn: On the Occasion of the Twelfth Anniversary of the October Revolution," claiming that the peasantry was flocking to the collective farms "by whole villages, volosts, districts"
5 December 1929– 5 January 1930	Politburo commission on collectivization, chaired by Iakovlev
27 December 1929	Stalin announces that the kulak will be "liquidated as a class" at the Conference of Marxist Agronomists
5 January 1930	Communist Party Central Committee decree "On the Pace of Collectivization and State Assistance to Collective-Farm Construction," officially launches wholesale collectivization
15–30 January 1930	Politburo creates commission, chaired by Molotov, for the elaboration of measures against the kulaks
30 January 1930	Politburo decree "On Measures for the Liquidation of Kulak Farms in Districts of Wholesale Collectivization"

January–April 1930	Arrests of first-category kulaks
February 1930	Deportations of families of first-category kulaks and second-category kulak families begin
2 February 1930	OGPU Directive 44/21 "On Measures for the Liquidation of the Kulak as a Class"
March 1930	Special commission under Antonov-Saratovskii to prepare statutes for special settlements (never enacted into legislation)
2 March 1930	Stalin publishes "Dizzy with Success: Concerning Questions of the Collective-Farm Movement"; temporary retreat from collectivization; peasants quit the collective farms in droves
9 March–13 August 1930	Tolmachev Commission under Sovnarkom RSFSR to coordinate special resettlement issues established
1 April 1930	Shmidt Commission under Sovnarkom USSR to coordinate special resettlement issues established
5 April 1930	Bergavinov Commission to review incorrect exiles in North begins work
Summer 1930	Families of special settlers begin trek into hinterlands
1 September 1930	Deadline for construction of special settlements
Fall 1930	Wholesale collectivization renewed; new, smaller waves of dekulakization ensue
March 1931	Bergavinov replaced by Ivanov as Northern Territory party chief
11 March 1931	Politburo establishes the Andreev Commission on kulak exile and resettlement
May 1931	Andreev Commission calls for OGPU takeover of all special settler affairs; second large wave of dekulakization begins and extends through the summer
1 July 1931	Official OGPU takeover of all special resettlement affairs
3 July 1931	Central Executive Committee decree indicating kulaks can be rehabilitated after five years

20 July 1931	Politburo declares that period of mass exile of kulaks "basically" over
Second half of 1931	Attempts to reunite exiled families with heads of households in camps
25 October 1931	OGPU issues "Temporary statutes on the rights and responsibilities of special settlers and on the administrative functions and rights of the settlement administration"
1932–1933	Mass famine
8 May 1933	Central Committee and Sovnarkom (again) end period of mass exiles
27 May 1934	USSR Central Executive Committee decree on rehabilitation of kulaks after five years
1934	Seventeenth Congress of the Communist Party: Congress of Victors
December 1934	Assassination of Leningrad Party leader Kirov
25 January 1935	Central Executive Committee decree on rehabilitation ruling that rehabilitation does not give kulaks right to leave place of exile
August 1936	First Moscow show trial ("Trotskyite-Zinovievite Terrorist Center"); Zinoviev, Kamenev, and others declared guilty; executed
September 1936	Fall of Iagoda; Iagoda replaced by Ezhov
December 1936	Stalin Constitution
January 1937	Second Moscow show trial ("Anti-Soviet Trotskyite Center"); series of key economic leaders and former Trotskyites declared guilty; executed
February 1937	Reiteration that kulaks cannot leave places of exile upon rehabilitation; NKVD address suggesting that special settlers still hostile to Soviet power be sent to labor camps for three to five years
May–June 1937	Purge of military; secret trials of military leadership
31 July 1937	Politburo sanctions order 00447; Ezhovshchina begins, continuing into 1938

March 1938	Third Moscow show trial ("Anti-Soviet Bloc of Rightists and Trotskyites"); Iagoda, Bukharin, Rykov, and others declared guilty; executed
December 1938	Fall of Ezhov; Beria replaces Ezhov
1 September 1939	World War II begins
22 June 1941	Germany invades the Soviet Union and the "Great War of the Fatherland" begins
11 April 1942	State Defense Committee directive authorizing draft of special settlers
22 October 1942	NKVD directive on emancipation of families of special settler soldiers
January 1945	Decree granting all deported kulaks the rights of Soviet citizens, but denying them the right to leave their place of exile
9 May 1945	Victory Day (V-E Day); the war ends in Europe
5 March 1953	Death of Stalin
26 June 1953	Beria is arrested
September 1953	Khrushchev becomes first secretary of the Communist Party
13 August 1954	Central Committee directive lifting all restrictions on kulaks exiled in 1929–33
February 1956	Twentieth Congress of the Communist Party; Khrushchev delivers the "Secret Speech"; beginnings of de-Stalinization
October 1960	Twenty-second Congress of the Communist Party: destalinization continues
October 1964	Khrushchev is removed from power; Brezhnev becomes Communist Party first secretary
October 1970	Solzhenitsyn wins the Noble Prize for Literature
10 November 1982	Death of Brezhnev; Andropov follows
9 February 1984	Death of Andropov; Chernenko follows
10 March 1985	Death of Chernenko; Gorbachev in power
1990–1991	Series of decrees fully "exonerating" the kulaks (and other victims of Soviet repression)
25 December 1991	Gorbachev resigns; the end of the Soviet Union

Technical Note

Several brief notes are in order to explain the changing geographical nomenclature of the regions discussed in this book as well as the complex structure of government in the Soviet Union at this time.

Geography

In 1930 the primary geographical subdivisions of the Soviet Union were union republics. Each union republic was in turn divided into regions or territories (the oblast' or krai); these regions and territories were divided into counties (okrug) in which the next subdivision was the district (raion). After 1930 and the elimination of the okrug, the district became the basic subdivision of the region or territory.

The primary geographical destinations of the special settlers were the following regions or territories: the Northern Territory, Siberia, the Urals, Kazakhstan, and the Far East. My main geographical focus in this book is on the first three territories—the Northern Territory, Siberia, and the Urals—with some greater attention to the Northern Territory. During the 1930s there were frequent changes in geographical nomenclature for each of these areas.

The Northern Territory was formed in 1929 and consisted of five counties and one autonomous region (Arkhangel'skii, Niandomskii, Vologodskii, Severo-Dvinskii, and Nenetskii counties and the Komi, or Zyrian, autonomous region). The territory encompassed a landmass of 1,122,600 square kilometers. Its northernmost regions lay just above the Arctic Circle, bordering the White Sea and the Arctic Ocean. In 1937 the Northern Territory was dissolved and broken down into two new regions, Arkhangel'skaia and Vologodskaia Regions.

Siberia encompasses an enormous landmass, stretching from the Ural Mountains in the west all the way to the Pacific Ocean. Large parts of its territories lie above the Arctic Circle, with its northernmost regions bordering the Arctic Ocean. In the south, Siberia shares borders with Kazakhstan, Mongolia, and China. In January 1930 Siberia was divided into two regions, Western Siberia and Eastern Siberia. Western Siberia consisted of nine counties (Omskii, Tarskii, Barabinskii, Slavgorodskii, Rubtsovskii, Biiskii, Barnaulskii, Kamenskii, Novosibirskii) and Eastern Siberia of ten counties (Tomskii, Kuznetskii, Khakassiia, Achinskii, Krasnoiarskii, Minuskinskii, Kanskii, Tulunskii, Irkutskii, Kirenskii), in addition to one autonomous region (Oirotiia) and two autonomous republics (Tannu-Turva and Buriat-Mongolia). In the mid-1930s Western Siberia was subject to administrative-territorial redistricting, giving rise to a series of new regions, including Omskaia and Krasnoiarskaia Regions, and somewhat later, Novosibirskaia and Altaiskaia Regions. Eastern Siberia experienced similar changes in nomenclature.

The Urals Region forms the border between European Russia and Siberia and lies astride the Urals mountain range. The Urals mountain range extends from the northern border of Kazakhstan all the way to the Arctic Ocean. In 1930 this region consisted of fifteen counties (Cheliabinskii, Troitskii, Kurganskii, Ishimskii, Sverdlovskii, Tagil'skii, Tiumenskii, Shadrinskii, Sarapul'skii, Permskii, Irbitskii, Tobol'skii, Verkhne-Kamskii, Kungurskii, and Zlatoustrovskii). In early 1934 the Urals Region was subdivided into the Sverdlovskaia, Cheliabinskaia, and Obsko-Irtyshskaia Regions.

Government

The Soviet Union was governed by a dual set of structures: those of the Communist Party and those of what is usually conveyed in English as the Soviet Government.

The Communist Party was the leading organ of power in the Soviet Union. Periodic congresses of the Communist Party (its select delegates) appointed a Central Committee (C.C.). The Central Committee convened periodically in plena at which major policy was discussed. At the summit of the Communist Party was the Politburo, which was the most important decision-making body in the Soviet Union, serving as a kind of Communist Party "cabinet." Stalin's formal position was General Secretary of the Communist Party (the head of the Central Committee's Secretariat). Each region and district had its own Communist Party committee, led by a first secretary. The Central Control Commission served as an internal party inspection agency. (The Worker-Peasant Inspectorate did the same for the government.)

The Soviet Government had within it two sets of administrative structures: the Council of People's Commissars (Sovnarkom) and the network of soviets, or councils, which existed on all regional levels. Periodic congresses of Soviets appointed a Central Executive Committee, responsible for the day-to-day management of soviet affairs on the federal level. (Similar bodies existed in the republics, and each region and district had a soviet to manage day-to-day affairs.) The Central Executive Committee appointed the members of the Council of People's Commissars. The Council of People's Commissars was the government's equivalent of a cabinet and consisted of a series of commissariats (ministries) organized mainly along functional lines. There were both federal and republic level Councils of People's Commissars.

The other institution that figures in this book is the secret police—the OGPU to 1934 and the NKVD thereafter. The secret police had offices at the federal, republic, and regional levels, as well as representation at the district level. *Polnomochnye Predstaviteli*, or plenipotentiaries, rendered in this book as chiefs or bosses, served as the leaders of the regional secret police administration.

Glossary of Terms and Abbreviations

All-Union: Federal level of the Soviet Union.

artel: A form of collective farm, featuring the socialization of most land, production, and the basic means of production; the artel was the officially accepted form of collective farm from 1930 and a less radical form than the commune, which featured the complete socialization of all land, property, and production as well as aspects of everyday life.

bania: A Russian bathhouse.

besprizornik: A homeless child.

byvshie liudi: Literally, former people (ci-devant); used to refer to pre-revolutionary economic and political elites, including lesser elites like former gendarmes, village elders, and so on.

Cheka (VChK, or Vserossiiskaia Chrezvychainaia komissiia): All-Russian Extraordinary Commission (the secret or political police from 1917 to 1922; superseded by the OGPU).

DGO: A reference to the project or the published series that resulted from it, *Sovetskaia derevnia glazami VChK-OGPU-NKVD, 1918–1939. Dokumenty i materialy* (*The Soviet Countryside through the Eyes of the VChK-OGPU-NKVD, 1918–1939. Documents and Materials*), 3 vols. (Moscow, 1998–2003), ed. V. Danilov and A. Berelovich.

dekulakization: Shorthand for the process of the "liquidation of the kulaks as a class."

detdom (plural, detdomy): Children's homes, or orphanages.

extraordinary measures: The extralegal measures employed in grain requisitioning in the late 1920s.

fel'dsher: A medical orderly or assistant.

FSB: See TsA FSB.

GARF (Gosudarstvennyi arkhiv Rossiiskoi Federatsii): State Archive of the Russian Federation.

GAAO (Gosudarstvennyi arkhiv Arkhangel'skoi oblasti): State Archive of Arkhangel'sk Oblast.

GAOPDF AO (Gosudarstvennyi arkhiv obshchestvenno-politicheskikh dvizhenii i formirovanii Arkhangel'skoi oblasti): State Archive of Social-Political Movements and the Formation of Arkhangel'sk Oblast.

GAVO (Gosudarstvennyi arkhiv Vologodskoi oblasti): State Archive of Vologda Oblast.

GPU: See OGPU.

Gosplan (Gosudarstvennaia planovaia komissiia): State Planning Commission.

GULAG (Glavnoe upravlenie ispravitel'no-trudovykh lagerei): Main Administration of Corrective-Labor Camps.

Kolkhoztsentr: Union of Agricultural Collectives; the primary agency in charge of the collective farm system and nominally under the jurisdiction of the Commissariat of Agriculture.

komendatura: A kind of headquarters or command post to administer the special settlers, organized within settlements as well as on the district and regional levels and within certain industrial concerns.

Komsomol (Kommunisticheskii soiuz molodezhi): Communist Youth League.

kulak: Literally a "fist"; a prosperous peasant who exploits hired labor; often used as a term of political opprobrium against opponents of the collective farm and other state policies.

MVD (Ministerstvo vnutrennykh del): Ministry of Internal Affairs (the secret or political police from 1946; superseded by the KGB [Komitet gosudarstvennoi bezopasnosti] in 1954).

militsiia: Regular police forces.

mir: Peasant commune or village community.

NEP: New Economic Policy.

NKVD (Narodnyi komissariat vnutrennykh del): People's Commissariat of Internal Affairs (the secret police from 1934; later the MVD).

OGPU (Ob'"edinennoe gosudarstvennoe politicheskoe upravlenie): Unified State Political Administration (the secret or political police from 1922 to 1934; superseded by the NKVD).

Old Believers: Members of a religious sect that had broken away from the official Russian Orthodox church in the late seventeenth century.

primitive socialist accumulation: A term coined by E. A. Preobrazhenskii, a Trotsky supporter, to describe the extraction of capital resources from the countryside to fund industrialization; a play on Marx's primitive capitalist accumulation.

pud: Russian weight, equivalent to 36 lbs. or 16.38 kg.

RGAE (Rossiiskii gosudarstvennyi arkhiv ekonomiki): Russian State Archive of the Economy.

RGASPI (Rossiiskii gosudarstvennyi arkhiv sotsial'no-politicheskoi istorii): Russian State Archive of Social and Political History.

razbazarivanie: Literally, squandering; an official term used to describe the peasant destruction and selling-off of properties on the eve of and during forced collectivization.

Right Opposition: The last semipublic opposition to Stalin, led by N. I. Bukharin and A. I. Rykov; the Right Opposition crystallized around the issue of extraordinary measures in grain requisitioning in the late 1920s.

RSFSR: Russian Republic.

samizdat: Literally, self-published; the underground press that developed from the late 1960s.

samoraskulachivanie: Self-dekulakization, or the state-labeled process whereby prosperous peasant households attempted to alter their socioeconomic status by selling off property, dividing their households, or fleeing the countryside.

Severoles: Northern Forestry, the economic agency in charge of the forestry industry in the Northern Territory.

shalash (plural, shalashy): A makeshift cabin constructed of branches and straw.

skhod: Village council.

SIBULON (Sibirskoe upravlenie lagerei osobogo naznacheniia): Siberian Administration of Camps of Special Designation.

Socialist Revolutionary or SR: Member of a prerevolutionary political party representing the peasantry.

Soiuzlesprom: Union of the Forestry Industry, the economic agency in charge of the forestry industry on the central level.

soviet: A council or administrative unit, found on various regional levels, from village (rural soviet) and city levels to district, provincial, and central levels.

Sovnarkom (Sovet narodnykh komissarov): Council of People's Commissars.

spetspereselentsy or spetsposelentsy: Special settlers (official nomenclature from 1930 to 1933 and again after 1944).

spetsposelka or spetsposelenie: Special settlement or village.

starosta: An elder.

TsA FSB (Tsentral'nyi arkhiv Federal'noi sluzhby bezopasnosti): Central Archive of the Federal Security Bureau (successor institution to the Cheka-OGPU-NKVD-MVD-KGB).

TSD: A reference to the project or the published series that resulted from it, *Tragediia Sovetskoi derevni: Kollektivizatsiia i raskulachivanie. Dokumenty i materialy, 1927–1939 (The Tragedy of the Soviet Country-side: Collectivization and Dekulakization. Documents and Materials, 1927–1939)*, 5 vols. (Moscow, 1999–2006), eds. V. P. Danilov, R. T. Manning, L. Viola.

TsIK (Tsentral'nyi ispolnitel'nyi komitet): Central Executive Committee (of Soviets of the USSR).

taiga: Coniferous forest lands of the far north.

troika: A committee consisting of three individuals, most often used in this book to refer to the important OGPU troikas that led mass operations of repression.

trudposelentsy: Labor settlers (official nomenclature for special settlers from 1934 to 1944).

trudposelka or trudposelenie: Labor settlements or villages.

USLON (Upravlenie Solovetskikh lagerei osobogo naznacheniia): Administration of Solovetskii Special Designation Camps.

USSR: Union of Soviet Socialist Republics.

VOANPI (Vologodskii oblastnoi arkhiv noveishei politicheskoi istorii): Vologda Oblast Archive of Contemporary Political History.

VSNKh (Vysshii soviet narodnogo khoziaistva): Supreme Council of the National Economy (responsible for all branches of industry).

VTsIK (Vserossiiskii tsentral'nyi ispolnitel'nyi komitet): All-Russian Central Executive Committee (of Soviets).

verst: A linear measure equal to 3,500 ft.

zemlianka (plural, zemlianki): A makeshift dugout or adobe cabin.

The Unknown Gulag

Introduction:
The Other Archipelago

You'll pardon my saying so, but the peasant is not yet human. . . . He's our enemy, our enemy.

—Maxim Gorky

"While my heart still beats, I will not forget the torture and suffering our family experienced."[1] These are the words of Varvara Stepanovna Sidorova. Born into a peasant family shortly after the Russian Revolution of 1917, she was a child when they came for her family. Years later, when it was safe to speak aloud about such matters, she recalled that winter night in 1930 when "they"— Varvara Stepanovna's signifier for Soviet officials—arrived at her home and, pounding on doors and windows, roused the family from its sleep. They herded the family into the bathhouse, a separate structure adjacent to the house, and began the process of what was officially called "liquidation." They took away the family's stores of grain, oats, hay, firewood. According to Varvara Stepanovna, they took everything. They even took the children's felt boots and tore the feather pillows from her mother's arms. When her parents tried to protest, "they" brandished a whip and roughly shouted, "Shut up, you kulak mug."

With only the clothes on their backs, the family was forced into a cart and delivered to the nearest railroad station. There, they met other families like their own—families with many children, families with infants, the sick, and the elderly, all thrown out of their homes, shorn of their possessions, and banished from their villages. And people kept on coming, from all the district's villages near and far. When no more could be crowded onto the station and its platforms, the families were loaded into freight trains, packed like cattle into cold, dark compartments for transport to the frozen hinterlands of the Soviet Union's far north. "This," Varvara Stepanovna said, "I cannot describe even now."

Weeks later, Varvara Stepanovna and her family arrived at their destination and were emptied out onto snow in the midst of the *taiga*, the vast and sparsely populated coniferous forests of the north. They found themselves literally in the middle of nowhere—there were no roads, no communications, and scarcely another soul to be seen apart from their fellow exiles. They were ordered to build houses, to build villages, to clear the trees. It was in this wilderness that they would reside, sentenced to what some later called "eternal exile." With minimal resources and not enough food or warm clothes, the adults in the family labored knee-deep in snow in the forest to fulfill the state's demands for timber, working desperately in their spare time to build shelter. Within a month, Varvara Stepanovna's father was dead and her mother weak from exhaustion and malnutrition. Crying "give for the sake of Christ," Varvara Stepanovna and her young siblings walked ten kilometers to the nearest village to beg for food. The family lived on the bread crusts the children collected, while the mother and eighteen-year-old brother labored in the forest.

Varvara Stepanovna halted at that point in her story, concluding that, "it has been a long time since my parents and older brothers died, but my soul still aches because of all we went through. A small child at the time, I remember a lot and can tell the truth."[2] The truth Varvara Stepanovna told was suppressed for nearly sixty years, locked in Soviet archives and buried in the memories of frightened survivors.

In 1930 and 1931, I. V. Stalin sent close to two million peasants into internal exile.[3] Entire families were condemned to be "liquidated" as "kulaks"—the Communist Party's label for supposed rural capitalists—and subjected to forced deportation to the most remote regions in the Northern Territory, the Urals, Siberia, and Kazakhstan. They were called "special settlers" (*spetspereselentsy*), a terrible euphemism cast in layers of secrecy, deceit, and human cruelty. The term cloaked the reality of their status as prisoners and forced laborers employed in the extraction of the raw materials so crucial for the Soviet Union's ongoing industrialization effort.[4] From out of the wilderness, families like Varvara Stepanovna's built special settlements (*spetsposelki* or *spetsposeleniia*), small villages, as many as two thousand in 1930 and 1931, where they lived, worked, and, in all too many cases, died.[5] This was the first mass deportation and use of forced labor of the Stalin era, coinciding with the consolidation of Stalin's dictatorship and marking the rise of the Soviet secret police as a vast economic empire and a state within a state.

The subject of the special settlements long remained terra incognita to historians. For sixty years, the topic was a state secret; even use of the euphemism of special resettlement was forbidden. Neither the word nor the world of special resettlement existed officially.[6] From the very beginning, the state decreed that this would be an un-topic, appearing neither in the press nor in published records. All the documentation on the special settlers was subject to the highest order of archival classification and would remain "top secret" until the early 1990s. It was as if neither the special settlements nor families like Varvara Stepanovna's had ever existed. Yet the special settlements laid the foundation for Stalin's infamous penal network, forming a massive archipelago within what has come to be known as the Gulag.

GULAG is an acronym for *Glavnoe upravlenie ispravitel'no-trudovykh lagerei*, or the Main Administration of Corrective-Labor Camps; as such, it designated an administrative department created in 1930 within the vast bureaucracy of the Soviet secret police. The word "gulag," however, has also become synonymous with the forced labor or concentration camps of the Soviet Union, which housed criminals, people with unacceptable pasts, regime critics, and, in general, anyone who fell into the web of Stalin's suspicion. Its inmates worked as forced laborers in forestry, mining, and construction under, often quite literally, murderous conditions. Russian scholars estimate that at its height the Gulag encompassed as many as 476 separate camp complexes, containing within them multiple smaller units.[7] The gulag population reached its largest numbers in the early 1950s with roughly 2.5 million inmates; as many as 12 million to 14 million people overall passed in and out through its gates between 1934 and 1944 alone; and no less than 1.5 million people died in the Gulag in the years between 1930 and 1956.[8]

Aleksandr Solzhenitsyn brought the Gulag to the attention of the world in the early 1970s.[9] Banned in the Soviet Union, his *Gulag Archipelago* became a classic in the West, exposing the horrors of the Gulag with a passion and a literary genius that remains unsurpassed. Yet Solzhenitsyn was unable to document that other part of the Gulag archipelago that housed the special settlers, noting eloquently that "this wave poured forth, sank down into the permafrost, and even our most active minds recall hardly a thing about it."[10]

It was only in the waning days of the Soviet Union, during the reform era of Mikhail Gorbachev, that the *Gulag Archipelago* was finally published in Solzhenitsyn's native country. With the fall of the Soviet Union in 1991, the archives began to open, gradually revealing the full horrors of the Gulag. At the same time, countless survivors stepped forward to tell their stories. Journalists and scholars, Western and Russian alike, began the arduous process of excavating the Gulag from the archives, grave sites, and living memory. In 2003 Anne Applebaum published a major new work on the Gulag, reintroducing the subject to the American reading public.[11]

The "other archipelago," however, remained largely outside the scope of these works, uncharted territory that is as opaque to outside observers today as it had been during the long years of Stalin's rule. *The Unknown Gulag* endeavors to tell the story of the special settlements and its first inhabitants, restoring a lost chapter in the history of Stalin's Gulag and documenting one of the twentieth century's most horrific exercises in mass repression.[12]

* * *

The special settlements laid the foundation of Stalin's Gulag. They housed the largest contingent of prisoners in the Soviet Union through the mid-1930s, and thereafter rivaled the labor camps in population.[13] And although the labor or concentration camp has long served as the defining institution of the Gulag, it is now clear that it was the special settlement that was first intended to house Stalin's battalions of forced laborers.

The formation of the special settlements was directly linked to the economic development and colonization of the Soviet Union. Throughout the 1920s, Soviet leaders discussed how to extract and utilize the rich natural resources located in the Soviet far north and east. The exploitation of these resources was vital to Soviet industrialization and modernization. Yet it had proved nearly impossible to maintain a permanent or even a seasonal labor force in these remote territories given the harsh conditions of life. The Soviet leadership's solution to this problem would be the formation of an army of forced laborers recruited from among the country's penal population.[14]

In 1930 Genrikh Iagoda, de facto head of the OGPU (the secret or political police), penned a memorandum articulating his vision of a new penal system that would be less costly to maintain and would serve the needs of the national economy.[15] He called for the formation of "colonization villages" of two hundred to three hundred households each that would provide a permanent labor force in forestry, mining, and other industries in remote territories, while supporting themselves through farming. Iagoda aimed in this way "to colonize the north in the fastest possible tempos" and to insure the maximum extraction of the Soviet Union's vast mineral and natural resources. Although in the end, such colonization villages would not entirely displace the camps, Iagoda's proposal envisioned the emerging order of the special settlements that would house a continuing assortment of state-defined social and ethnic "enemies" through the remainder of the Stalin years.[16]

The first inhabitants of these "colonization villages," people like Varvara Stepanovna's family, were peasant families officially labeled "kulaks." Estimates at the time placed the number of state-defined kulaks at roughly 1.2 –1.3 million households (at least 5 million people) amid a rural population of some 25 million peasant households.[17] In 1930 and 1931, three-fifths of this population fled the countryside or were forced off the land by a combination of crushing taxation and repressive measures, while the remainder were forcibly deported to the special settlements.[18] In later years, the special settlements would be replenished by other categories of people—"socially dangerous elements" from major cities, suspect ethnic groups and wartime "enemy nations" from within the multinational empire, and, on the eve of and after World War II, "socially alien" population groups from the occupied Baltic states and other bordering nations.[19]

But it was the kulaks who built the special settlements. Who were they? What was a kulak? In short, the kulaks could be defined as rural capitalists, and that was the way in which Stalin and the Communist Party sought to portray them. But the appellation was far from straightforward. The definition of the kulak was, in fact, abstract, unclear, and contested. The word itself simply and literally meant "fist." In the village setting, the term was originally a sobriquet for a "tightfisted" peasant, a village exploiter, generally a moneylender or a trader. It was paired with other negative appellations such as *zhivodery* and *miroedy*, meaning fleecers and devourers of the *mir* or village community. And this was the sense in which peasants, before and after the revolution, understood the term. Over time, however, the definition of the term lost clarity as members of the prerevolutionary radical intelligentsia engaged in debates over the issue of whether capitalism (and therefore class stratification among the peasantry) had made an appearance in the village. For those who argued it had, mainly Russian Marxists, the kulak was gradually transformed into the harbinger of village capitalism. At the very least, the kulak began to stand for the prosperous peasant, if not the village capitalist exploiter.

In the 1920s theorists attempted to pin down the definition of the kulak, using a variety of economic indicators to attempt to gauge rural social stratification and to specify exactly what type of farm constituted a kulak farm. The problem, however, was less definition than context. The peasantry was largely precapitalist, and labeling a peasant a kulak was a little like suggesting the oxymoronic existence of a "capitalist peasant." Leninist dogma dictated that the peasantry was divided among poor peasants (exploited by the kulak and allied to the working class), middle peasants (a politically wavering element and the majority of the peasantry), and the kulak. Social stratification in the village in reality was not advanced, and the application of Marxist-Leninist categories to a largely precapitalist, communal peasantry made little social or economic sense. Such categorizations distorted rural realities and obscured the fact that most village communities were both desperately poor and relatively cohesive.

The Communist Party perceived issues of socioeconomic stratification through political and ideological lenses. That meant, in practice,
that the (broadly defined) political behavior and actions of a peasant
were often equally, if not more, important in determining social status
than economic position in the village. During the collectivization of
Soviet agriculture, almost anyone could be labeled a kulak—the village
critic, the outspoken Red army veteran, peasants with large families (and
therefore greater land resources), and a host of other village authorities,
including priests, church council members, tradesmen, craftsmen, *byvshye
liudi* (village notables from the prerevolutionary regime), and even seasonal workers as well as the occasional prosperous peasant. As the state
entered into what would be a protracted war with the peasantry, the
kulak came to serve as a political metaphor and pejorative for the entire
peasantry. Peasants soon came to dread the word, understanding its
political implications and, as one official put it, "reacting viscerally to
the term."[20]

By the end of the 1920s, the state-defined kulak and his family found
themselves classified as social pariahs and subject to virtual demonization in the press. Propaganda representations created a stylized image of
the kulak. He was depicted as male, heavy-set (signifying a combination
of wealth and greed), and dressed in city-bought clothing (generally a
vest covering a polka-dot shirt). At times, he was depicted as subhuman,
with apelike depiction of his facial features. He was often posed with
a weapon (a sawed-off shotgun or a pitchfork), churches and sacks of
grain in the background, and in aggressive confrontation with poor
peasants or tractors (the latter representing Soviet power). Increasingly,
the kulak came to be stereotyped as someone less than human, as the
personification of the enemy.[21]

The dehumanization of the kulak facilitated its "liquidation as a
class," an official policy put into practice in1930. "Liquidation" meant
the "extirpation of the roots of capitalism" in the countryside through
property expropriations and the physical removal of kulak families
from the village. In theory, liquidation was to be followed (perhaps
paradoxically) by the "reeducation" of kulaks through what the Communist Party considered to be "honest" labor, meaning, in fact, forced
labor. Kulaks who could not be reeducated, those who were deemed
irredeemable—some 30,000 in 1930 and 1931—were liquidated in the
full sense of the word, with a bullet to the base of the skull.[22]

The overall results of the policy were catastrophic: tens of thousands
of people ran away and equal numbers died. Those who remained
slowly lost their ability to work due to malnutrition, exhaustion, and
the harshness of the climate and terrain. The population of the special
settlers declined steadily through the 1930s, from its peak of 1,803,392

in 1931 to 1,317,000 in early 1933, to 930,000 on the eve of World War II.[23] From 1935 on, the special settlers were eligible, on a selective basis, for rehabilitation, although they would remain tied to their exile regions until 1954 when their term of exile officially ended. They would be completely "exonerated" of their "crimes" only in 1990 and 1991, when special decrees from the Supreme Soviet and, then, the Yeltsin administration removed all culpability from the former kulaks.[24] The policy, as a whole, was not only costly in human lives, it was economically irrational, incurring far more expense for the upkeep and supervision of the special settlers, who never really became self-sufficient, than profit from their labor.[25] These were Stalin's first victims, and Solzhenitsyn was correct when he called this Stalin's most "heinous" crime.[26]

* * *

The emergence of the special settlements arose in the context of one of the most radical transformations of the twentieth century. Stalin's First Five-Year Plan (1928–1932) was an attempt to catapult an agrarian nation into modernity, an attempt to industrialize the country at lightening speed. Industrialization would be based on a "tribute" from the peasantry, to use Stalin's words. The peasantry was to pay for industrialization through taxation, the sale of grain at artificially low prices, and the provision of peasant laborers, both forced and voluntary, for the needs of industry.

The wholesale collectivization of agriculture was intended to facilitate the collection of such "tribute" by socializing the production and labor of the country's rural population and replacing the traditional village and communal land tenure with the collective farm.[27]

The liquidation of the kulak as a class—dekulakization for short— was an integral component of collectivization and vital to its realization. Dekulakization was Stalin's first great purge. It was a purge of the countryside: an endeavor to remove undesirable elements and to decapitate traditional village leadership and authority structures in order to break down village cohesion, minimize peasant resistance to collectivization, and intimidate the mass of the peasantry into compliance with the threat of dekulakization. In this way, it was used to clear the way for the creation of the new collective farm order.

Dekulakization was one part of a larger ongoing transformation in the countryside. Collectivization represented the continuation of an incomplete revolution. Following the failed radicalism of the Russian Civil War (1918–20) and War Communism, when the Communist Party attempted to replace the market with forced grain requisitioning, the 1917 revolution had ended in a kind of stalemate. The New

Economic Policy of the 1920s combined a largely socialist economy in the cities with a traditional market economy in the countryside. It was an implicit admission of the party's failure to bring socialism to the village.

This incomplete revolution had left not only a traditional economy at work in the countryside but also entrenched, though largely figurative, battle lines dividing the country. The battle lines were prefigured long before 1917. Centuries-old fissures in the prerevolutionary order served to separate town and countryside, creating two fairly distinct and ultimately antithetical cultures. The peasantry was the "domestic other," a figure "orientalized" by Populists, disdained by Marxists, and exploited by Russian and Soviet governments alike.[28] The peasantry was an internal resource to be utilized for labor, capital, and cannon fodder, and to be acted upon, molded, enlightened, and transformed. Perceived as the epitome of Russian "backwardness" and destined to disappear with the advent of a modern industrial society, the peasantry had become, already by the late nineteenth century, a major stumbling block for Russian intellectuals and economic policy makers intent on a Westernized modernization, whether that modernization was to follow a capitalist or a socialist path of development.

The Communist Party under Stalin faced the challenge of the "accursed problem" of the peasantry head-on. Besieged by a "capitalist encirclement" that was both real and phantasmagoric, and anxious to finish the revolution and the "construction of socialism," the regime attempted to compact whole centuries of Western European development into a five-year plan. In the countryside, where the vast majority of the population lived, the regime aimed at nothing less than the eradication of the peasantry as a separate and semi-autonomous cultural entity. The collective farm would be the basis for the new order in the countryside. The regime would, in one fell swoop, destroy peasant self-government through the abolition of the village council and land commune; curtail and control the peasant market; nationalize the peasant economy including trade and crafts; suppress religion through church closures and the arrest (often dekulakization) of clergy; and remove all sources of traditional village leadership and authority by way of dekulakization. The kulak became the "most implacable foe," dehumanized and abstracted, attaining a mythical and enduring status in the regime's pantheon of enemies. The cast of enemies that was engulfed by dekulakization was set at the time of the revolution and civil war: the landowner, the petty economic elite of the village, the clergy, former tsarist officials. The definition of the most implacable foe was expansive and arbitrary. The campaign to liquidate the kulak as a class was in fact an assault upon all the peasantry, a broad offensive against rural life and all that it stood for. In this sense, it represented both the final "victory" of the revolution in the countryside and the basis of Stalin's approach to modernization and the supposed construction of socialism.[29]

* * *

There was no master plan for the creation of the special settlements. Plans to exploit penal labor in the Soviet hinterlands had not envisioned the army of kulak laborers that became available as a result of collectivization. The liquidation of the kulak as a class was initially tied directly to the needs of collectivization. Precise planning for the actual resettlement and use of the kulaks came only after the violent beginning of the collectivization campaign, literally as the first contingents of kulak families were boarding the trains. In this sense, the emergence of the special settlements was contingent on the decision to embark upon the policy of wholesale collectivization.

This element of contingency, the decision to create an army of unfree laborers from dispossessed kulak families almost as an afterthought to collectivization, would have profound consequences for the fate of the special settlers. From the outset, the implementation of special resettlement policy would be shaped by a negligent, if not criminal dispatch, an almost complete disconnect between central planning and local realities, and the constant resort to repressive measures as a substitute for administrative control.

The reactive, ad hoc nature of special resettlement policy was characteristic of Stalinism. The Stalinist state was hardly the monolith of cold war legend. It was a merciless dictatorship, no doubt, but it was a dictatorship that arose within the context of a largely agrarian country and an enormous and far-flung territory. The Stalinist state operated within the confines of widespread backwardness. State structures outside the capital and major provincial cities were weakly developed. The Communist Party presence outside of urban areas was miniscule. This meant that Stalinist despotism ruled the countryside and its remote dominions through emergency mobilizations of urban cadres, the instrumental use of repression, and, at times, sheer neglect.

The weak nature of the Stalinist state does not negate the central role of Stalin. Stalin's will was decisive in drafting the policies of collectivization and dekulakization. The declassification of archival documents on these policies has made this absolutely clear. But to understand the essence of Stalinism, it is necessary to venture beyond the Kremlin walls in order to witness the full ramifications of Stalin's will. Policy came from on high, but it was enacted within a quagmire of complex provincial and local bureaucratic structures by a multiplicity of different social actors. Its reception by the special settlers' overseers as well as by the special settlers themselves further impacted upon the ways in which this disastrous policy would take shape. The result was all too often vast and nightmarish contradictions between plan and possibility, revolution and folly, utopia and reality.

* * *

The Unknown Gulag is a history of the "other archipelago" and the kulaks. It is a study of policy, its execution and its consequences, as well as a study of the internal life of the special settlements. As the story develops, it will move among a series of sometimes seemingly autonomous stages of action following its main characters: Stalin, Iagoda, and the Communist Party and secret police leaders in Moscow and the provinces; the local officials on site; and the special settlers. It will trace the evolution of the kulak special settlements from their inception in 1930 and 1931 through to the mid-1950s when the kulaks were finally released from "eternal exile." *The Unknown Gulag* documents what had remained for nearly sixty years a hidden chapter in the history of the Gulag, the peasantry, and the Stalinist state.[30]

Above all, this book is an attempt to restore the voices of a people that Stalin and the Communist Party attempted to silence, to "liquidate as a class"—the voices of people like Varvara Stepanovna. These voices have surfaced only recently. Some were long confined to the archives, only seeing the light of day after the fall of the Soviet Union. Others came out in letters, interviews, and memoirs once it was absolutely certain that the survivors were safe to tell their stories. The voices are remarkable, coming as they do from otherwise silent historical actors. They were Stalin's first victims and, along with Varvara Stepanovna, they "can tell the truth" about the lost world of the special settlements and its first inhabitants.

I

The Destruction of the Kulaks

1

The Preemptive Strike: The Liquidation of the Kulak as a Class

To advance on the kulak means to get down to business and strike the kulak, yes strike him, so he will never be able to get back on his feet again.
—Stalin

On 11 January 1930, OGPU boss Iagoda sent a memo to his top lieutenants, calling for a purge of "kulak elements" from the countryside.[1] "The kulak," he wrote, "must be destroyed as a class.... [The kulak] understands that he will perish with collectivization and therefore he renders more and more brutal and fierce resistance, as we see already, [ranging] from insurrectionary plots and counterrevolutionary kulak organizations to arson and terror. [The kulak] will and is already burning grain, murdering activists and government officials. If we do not strike quickly and decisively ... we will face a whole series of uprisings. ... By March, we must deal with the kulak, breaking his back forever."[2]

Iagoda's intelligence sources told him that the "class struggle" in the countryside was intensifying. OGPU reports of 1929 summarizing rural "counterrevolutionary activities" announced a radical upsurge in violence, mass disturbances, antisoviet agitation, and sabotage. In that year alone, the OGPU made 95,000 arrests in rural areas, claiming a vast array of enemies, including (to use OGPU wording) kulaks and counterrevolutionaries, representatives of the nationalist intelligentsia in Ukraine and the east, Socialist Revolutionaries, bandits, clergy, and former White army officers. The OGPU concluded that these forces had formed a "block," aiming to unite the "rural masses," to subvert the Red army, and to establish liaisons with allies abroad, all in preparation for an uprising against Soviet power.[3] Peasant violence was indeed on the rise. Yet it was largely a response to the escalation in state violence that had, from 1927 to 1928, become the regime's primary method of implementing its policies in the countryside. The decision to "deal with the kulak," to use Iagoda's words, grew out of this regime-initiated violence rather than "class struggle," "insurrectionary plots," or "counter-revolutionary kulak organizations."

Iagoda's call to arms came in the midst of the rapidly developing collectivization campaign, a campaign whose pace and scope had exceeded even the top leadership's expectations. Collectivization was the regime's first priority, and the striving to achieve "Bolshevik tempos" pushed the campaign to ever greater heights. Stalin and his comrades in the Politburo were anxious to see the campaign develop as far as possible by March, when the spring sowing began. Iagoda knew that timing was essential when he called on the OGPU to "deal with the kulak" by March. Yet events had rushed ahead at such an incredible pace that Iagoda could only respond with an equally rapid campaign against the kulak. There was not time to create an infrastructure to "deal with the kulak" in the aftermath of his expulsion from the village; work on the resettlement of kulak families would develop "on the fly" as one regional official put it, during the very act of deportation and resettlement.[4] All energy was directed to the tasks at hand: the decapitation of village authority structures, the destruction of all sources of opposition, and the expropriation of kulak properties for the new collective farm system. As a result, dekulakization in the first half of 1930 was largely a "confiscative-repressive" operation, featuring mass property expropriations and expulsions from the village.[5] The question of the kulaks' subsequent fate would come as a tragic afterthought to an orgy of state terror.

On the Eve

The collectivization of agriculture was to be the ultimate solution to the conundrum of the peasantry and the Soviet "construction of socialism." Collectivization was intended to socialize peasant agriculture through the creation of collective farms, in which equipment and work animals would be held in common and the land worked jointly. Peasant families would continue to live in separate homes and be permitted a small plot of land to farm for their personal needs. In theory, after paying their taxes and other obligations to the state, the collective farmers would divide the remains of the harvest. In practice through most of the Stalin era, the state would take the lion's share of what was produced, leaving peasants to live on what they managed to grow on their private plots.

By the late 1920s, when the regime turned toward rapid industrialization, the peasantry had emerged as a key resource to be tapped for the capital funding of industrialization by way of taxation, special loan levies, debt collection, and most importantly, grain for export and labor, voluntary or forced, for industry and the extraction of essential raw materials. The collective farm was intended to be a control mechanism for the economic exploitation of the peasantry. It would be far easier for the regime to gather grain from some 200,000 collective farms (the numbers of collective farms at the end of the First Five-Year Plan) than from 25 million peasant households.

Stalinist state-building required a "tribute" from the peasantry, and the Communist Party explicitly committed itself to a policy of exploitation of the countryside in the interests of state development. In his speech at the July 1928 Central Committee plenum, Stalin described the essence of the new policy:

> In capitalist countries industrialization was usually based not only on internal accumulation but also on the plundering of other countries, the plundering of colonies or vanquished countries, or on substantial loans from abroad. You know that for hundreds of years England used to drain all its colonies, from every continent, and in this way injected additional investments into its industry. . . . Our country differs from the capitalist countries, by the way, in that it cannot and must not engage in the plundering of colonies or in the plundering of other countries in general. Therefore this path is closed to us. But our country doesn't have loans from abroad either. Consequently, this path is closed to us as well. In that case what is left for us? One choice is left: to develop industry, to industrialize the country on the basis of internal accumulation. . . . But where are the sources of this accumulation? As I said, there are two such sources: first, the working class, which creates valuable output and moves industry forward; and second, the peasantry.
>
> The situation in our country with regard to the peasantry in this case is the following: it pays the state not only ordinary taxes, direct and indirect, but it also pays relatively high prices for goods from industry—that is first of all—and it doesn't receive the full value of the prices of agricultural products—that is second of all. This is an additional tax on the peasantry in the interests of developing industry, which serves the whole country, including the peasantry. This is something like a "tribute," something like a surtax, which we are forced to take temporarily in order to sustain and further develop the current rate of industrial growth. . . . This situation, needless to say, is unpleasant. But we would not be bolsheviks if we papered over this fact and closed our eyes to the fact that, unfortunately, our industry and our country cannot manage without this additional tax on the peasantry.[6]

The "situation," wherein the peasantry was supposed to serve as the primary resource for economic development, may have been "unpleasant," to quote Stalin, but from his perspective—and that of the majority of the party in the late 1920s—it was absolutely necessary.[7] The peasantry would serve as an internal colony for Soviet economic development.

The regime's designs on the peasantry, however, were not limited to economic control. Collectivization entailed not only the creation of collective farms and the remaking of peasant into collective farmer but also the implementation of a series of ancillary policies, which aimed to destroy peasant self-government and peasant markets; to suppress religion through church closures and arrests of clergy; and to remove all sources of village leadership by way of dekulakization.[8] These policies represented another side of Stalin's internal colonization of the peasantry, aimed at establishing a cultural and political hegemony over the countryside that would facilitate the taking of "tribute."

Dekulakization was an integral part of the collectivization of Soviet agriculture. Although in theory it was supposed to follow in the wake of wholesale collectivization—when socioeconomic conditions would be "ripe" for the liquidation of the kulak (meaning when the collective farms succeeded in replacing kulak farms as the main producers of grain)—in practice it most often accompanied or even preceded the collectivization campaign in 1930. It was deployed as a preemptive strike, an OGPU security operation to pacify the countryside in preparation for collectivization and the "socialist transformation" of the countryside. In addition to removing real, potential, and imaginary regime critics and enemies, it would serve to extract an army of unfree laborers for the "construction of socialism."

The prologue to dekulakization began with the grain procurement crisis of 1927/28. Peasant marketing of grain had reached a plateau due to the growth in internal grain consumption (based on higher peasant grain consumption and an increasing urban population), a dearth of manufactured goods to trade with peasants, and above all, a faulty pricing system that established relatively low prices for grain compared to industrial and other agricultural products. Given that prices for grain on the private market were far higher than what the government was paying, some peasant producers decided to withhold grain, sell it on the private market, or divert it for fodder for higher-priced livestock and dairy products. In the emergency context of a largely fabricated war scare in 1927, which pitted internal and external enemies against a Soviet Union "encircled" by the capitalist West, the withholding of grain for better times became "hoarding," while the sale of grain at higher prices on the private market was "speculation." The shortfall in grain marketing appeared to jeopardize grain export plans and consequently industrialization and defense, thereby seeming to put the nation in danger given the militarized atmosphere of the times and the widespread fears in the party of the inevitability of war with the capitalist nations. The regime's response was the application of "extraordinary measures." This was a throwback to the civil-war policy of forcible grain requisitioning. Penal code Articles 61 (failure to fulfill government obligations, including tax payments and grain deliveries) and 107 (speculation) were widely invoked against peasants, leading to a wave of fines, arrests, and property confiscations. On 4 January 1928, the OGPU issued a directive calling for the arrest of the most "malicious" (*zlostnye*) private traders. The result was the arrest of over six thousand private traders by early April 1928.[9]

At the same time, the government began an operation to siphon off all money "reserves" from the countryside, ostensibly in order to force peasants to sell their grain so that they would have the necessary disposable cash to pay increasingly onerous state taxes. New tax laws were introduced in 1928 and 1929, resulting in the exclusion of more than one third of all peasant farms (the poorest) from taxation and the consequent steeply progressive taxation of stronger peasant households.[10] As the tax press tightened, the government also launched an aggressive campaign to increase village self-taxation and to collect all arrears owed by peasants.[11] Increasingly, wealthier peasants found themselves caught in a financial vise. Failure to fulfill tax or other obligations led once again to the imposition of the dreaded Article 61.

In early 1929, the use of extraordinary measures in grain procurements gave way to the nationwide application of the Ural-Siberian method. Based on practices developed in Siberia in 1928, this "method" depended upon the rural soviet (*sel'sovet* or rural council, the lowest link in Soviet government) to divide the grain levy and other obligations among peasant households based on their socioeconomic position in an attempt to break down village cohesion and provoke class war in the village. A government decree of 27 June 1929 essentially legalized this method by granting rural soviets the right to apply Article 61 to peasants who failed to fulfill their obligations to the government. The government revised Article 61 to allow officials to assess a fine of five times the value of grain or other obligations due (the "*piatikratnoe*") on first-time offenders, to imprison repeat offenders, and to imprison and confiscate property from those whose actions were considered to be either premeditated or part of group resistance.[12]

As a result of the grain procurement campaigns of 1927/28 and 1928/29, as well as the tax press on the countryside, a de facto dekulakization was becoming a reality in the second half of 1929. Facing the excessive demands of the government, some peasant families chose what was euphemistically called self-dekulakization (*samoraskulachivanie*) in an effort to pay off government obligations with the proceeds of property sales or to alter their socioeconomic status (and consequently tax and grain obligation status) by selling off property or dividing their households. The combined results of the government's repressive actions and self-dekulakization led to large reductions in the number of state-defined kulak households in the country.[13]

By this time, the state-defined kulak and his family were under siege. Demonized in the press and scapegoated for increasing food shortages in the cities, high market prices, and "counterrevolutionary agitation" in the village, the kulak had become the most dangerous foe in the Communist Party's ever-expanding pantheon of enemies. What made matters worse was that almost any peasant could be a kulak. The party increasingly judged a peasant's socioeconomic status on the basis of his political behavior. And the cadres mobilized from the cities to work in the village were often ignorant of rural life, resulting in arbitrary definitions of kulak households based on stereotyped depictions. Peasants could become kulaks if they had large families, wore city-bought clothes, had tin roofs on their homes, or simply disagreed with the urban cadres.

The demonization of the kulak was accompanied by a series of discriminatory acts aimed against him. In 1928 the regime imposed new laws, limiting kulak access to credit and the purchase of agricultural machinery. At the end of the year, it launched a disenfranchisement campaign that revoked the civil rights of many peasants. In the first half of 1929, officials in Moscow and in the regions debated whether or not kulaks should be permitted to join the emerging collective farms. By the fall, the regime made it clear that kulaks would not be admitted to collective farms under any circumstances. At the same time, the regime demanded a purge of kulaks from all preexisting collective farms and the dissolution of any collective farm it deemed to be kulak-dominated.[14]

The regime also began to step up its campaign against peasants accused of committing "terrorist acts"—that is, acts of violence aimed against officials. There is no way to know which of these acts were actually politically motivated and which the result of drunken brawls or other types of intravillage conflicts. In the highly charged context of those times, all violence was cast in a sinister light. And by definition, a peasant who engaged in a terrorist act became a kulak.

On 3 January 1929, the Politburo proposed to the People's Commissariat of Justice that it expedite the repression of kulak terrorists.[15] That September, B. P. Sheboldaev (Lower Volga Regional party committee first secretary) and M. A. Trilessor (Lower Volga OGPU boss) enlisted the OGPU to liquidate a "Socialist Revolutionary-kulak insurrectionary group." Fifty of its supposed leaders were executed. On 2 October Sheboldaev telegrammed the Politburo with a request to allow the Lower Volga Regional party committee to punish five cases of kulak terror in grain requisitioning.[16] On the day the Politburo examined Sheboldaev's request (3 October), it issued a new directive authorizing the OGPU and the People's Commissariat of Justice to deal "decisively and quickly" with kulaks who organized terrorist acts or counterrevolutionary disturbances, and recommended execution in these cases. In special circumstances, when speed was of the essence, the OGPU could deal directly with such cases. Otherwise, OGPU measures were to be agreed upon with regional party committees and, in the most important cases, with the Central Committee.[17]

By the end of 1929, a series of regional party committees had taken the initiative to expropriate and exile *groups* of kulaks. In late June 1929, the Central Black Earth Regional party committee made the decision to exile groups of kulaks. Similar actions were taken in Tatariia in early October 1929. Other decrees to expropriate or exile large numbers of kulaks were taken in December in Ukraine, the North, Siberia, Transcaucasia, and North Caucasus.[18] In the Middle Volga and Central Black Earth Region, kulaks were exiled to the worst lands at the end of the village.[19] In the meantime, a series of republican Councils of People's Commissars and regional soviets had launched mass campaigns in the fall of 1929 aimed at the deportation of "socially dangerous elements" from border zones in Ukraine, Belorussia, the Leningrad Region, and the Western Region. This category included all types of criminals, "counterrevolutionary elements," and people with relatives living abroad, as well as "kulaks."[20]

Dekulakization, in one form or another, had begun amidst a wave of antikulak legislation and extraordinary measures. By the end of 1929, Articles 60, 61, 79, 107, and 169 of the penal code of the Russian Republic, which allowed for the arrest, imprisonment, expropriation, or exile of individuals, were applied extensively to peasants for nonpayment of taxes and fines, failure to fulfill state obligations including grain deliveries, "willful" destruction of livestock or agricultural inventory, speculation, and fraud (including the illegal sale of land and properties to avoid kulak classification).[21] On 10 January 1930, the government of the Russian Republic published a new decree on the use of exile. This decree permitted the courts to exile anyone sentenced to the deprivation of freedom for up to one year. The result of this decree would be to sanction the use of exile on a massive scale.[22]

The basic laws enabling dekulakization were in place. All that was missing was a central plan of action.

The Great Turn

On 7 November 1929, the twelfth anniversary of the October Revolution, Stalin proclaimed in his article "Year of the Great Turn" that the middle peasantry had begun to enter the collective farms.[23] The collectivization rates achieved to date had already surpassed plans from the spring of 1929 that had projected the collectivization of some 15 percent of the peasant population by 1934.[24] These projections were revised upward in the late summer and fall of 1929. First, Gosplan (the State Planning Commission) called for the collectivization of 2.5 million peasant households in the course of 1929/30. Then Kolkhoztsentr (the central supervisory office for collective farm affairs) resolved that 3.1 million peasant households would be incorporated into collective farms by the end of 1929/30.[25]

Collectivization rates increased dramatically by the fall of 1929, reaching especially startling percentages in key grain-growing regions like the Lower Volga (18.1) and the North Caucasus (19.1).[26] The momentum of the campaign in these regions provided the rationalization for Stalin's mendacious claim that the middle peasantry was flocking into the collective farms. This claim allowed Stalin to argue that if the middle peasantry—that is, the majority of the peasantry—was joining the collective farms, then the peasantry as a whole was indeed ready for collectivization. Although there was apparently some genuine enthusiasm "from below," the campaign had already begun to resort to coercion to achieve high percentages.

The crisis atmosphere that had given birth to the First Five-Year Plan defined its form and parameters. The state implemented collectivization as an act of virtual war. Violence was assumed as a necessary corollary to the revolution and as an "inevitable" result of the "class war" with the kulak. Although the actual military was minimally employed in the countryside—largely for political reasons and fears of instability among the army's peasant base—the implementation of collectivization featured the use of military practices and, to a certain extent, assumed the scale of a war, with armies of outsiders coming into the village with vast plenipotentiary powers.

The state mobilized tens of thousands of urban communists and industrial workers for the "grain front." Grain requisitioning brigades, already obsessed with attaining high percentages, were transferred en masse to collectivization.[27] Plenipotentiary rule was meant to override and overcome what was viewed as the inertia or resistance of a weak local government. Headquarters (*shtaby*) were set up on the district (*raion*) level to conduct operations. And the deportation of the kulaks was nothing if not a vast exercise in troop mobilization, substituting families for soldiers but following the basic transport and housing rules for rapid troop deployment. Collectivization would be conducted as a campaign in the full meaning of the term. Violence, arbitrariness (*proizvol*), and excesses (*peregiby*, a sanitized regime euphemism) would be everywhere, reaching nightmare proportions and sparking massive village unrest.[28]

A volatile antipeasant mood had grown in the cities, especially among rank-and-file communists and industrial workers. It was based on bread shortages, continuing news of "kulak sabotage," and long-simmering urban-rural antipathies inflamed by the regime's use of imagery from the civil war. This mood infected the grain requisitioning brigades and other, newer recruits from urban centers.[29] The combination of official endorsement, regional initiative and direction, and unrestrained action on the part of lower-level cadres together created an ever-accelerating collectivization tempo. The "success" of the regional campaigns then provided the necessary impetus for Moscow to push collectivization rates up even further, in what became a deadly and constant tug of war between center and periphery to keep pace with each other as reality exceeded plan, and plans were continually revised to register and push forward collectivization tempos.

The November 1929 Central Committee plenum formally ratified the transition to a policy of *wholesale* collectivization (meaning the collectivization of at least 80 percent of a village), leaving the specifics of implementation to a Politburo commission that would meet in December.[30] The plenum was largely an affair of consensus and acclamation. It confirmed the defeat of the Right Opposition, the last major threat to Stalin's rule and the only advocates within the party of a moderate approach to the peasantry. The plenum resolved to push collectivization forward. Although some party leaders expressed concern over the use of force and the lack of preparation in the summer-fall collectivization campaign—most notably Siberian Regional first party secretary S. I. Syrtsov; Lenin's widow, Nadezhda Krupskaia, who spoke of the disappearance of "persuasion" in the countryside; and Ukrainian delegation members S. V. Kosior and G. I. Petrovskii—most regional party secretaries expressed enthusiasm for the policy, downplaying problems and promising collectivization within twelve to eighteen months. G. N. Kaminskii, the head of Kolkhoztsentr, and V. M. Molotov, Stalin's right-hand man in the Politburo, along with a chorus of supporters, repeatedly pushed the plenum to extremes, calling for the completion of collectivization in 1930, even at one point, by the spring. Stalin responded to calls for more preparation and planning with, "Do you think that everything can be organized ahead of time?" Discussion of "difficulties" was dismissed as "opportunism."[31]

On 6 January 1930, the Central Committee published its decree on wholesale collectivization. Calling for the "liquidation of the kulak as a class," the Central Committee ordered the wholesale collectivization of the main grain-producing regions by the fall of 1930, spring 1931 at the latest; the remaining grain-producing regions were to complete collectivization by the fall of 1931, spring 1932 at the latest. Silence prevailed in regard to collectivization rates for the rest of the country. These were madly radical projections for the collectivization of a largely traditional peasantry. To make matters worse, the decree was couched in the most general of terms, omitting specific instructions and leaving the "details" to the cadres in the field—largely at the prompting of Stalin who personally revised the draft decree prepared by a Politburo commission on collectivization convened in December. Nonetheless, the Central Committee cynically warned its regional and local officials against what it called "games in collectivization"—that is, collectivization by intimidation and violence.[32]

More detailed instructions on the "liquidation of the kulak as a class" would await the formation, on 15 January, of a Politburo commission chaired by Molotov. Prior to this point, it was not entirely clear what the liquidation of the kulak meant in practice. Stalin had first used the phrase on 27 December 1929, at a conference of Marxist agronomists.[33] Following the collectivization decree's announcement of the policy, it was left to regional and local officials to determine what the policy meant in practice. As a result, the campaign against the kulak accelerated wildly from late December, creating widespread disorder in the countryside. The Molotov Commission's mandate was to work out the details of the operation and to prepare the accompanying legislation.[34]

On 30 January 1930, the Politburo approved the Molotov Commission's decree on dekulakization.[35] From this point on, kulaks were forbidden to leave their villages or to dispose of their property and possessions.[36] Property expropriations were to begin in districts of wholesale collectivization.[37] Property subject to expropriation included the means of production, livestock, homes and other auxiliary buildings, manufacturing enterprises, and fodder and seed reserves. Outside of the districts of wholesale collectivization, rural soviets were expected to inventory all kulak properties and to carry out bimonthly inspections to ensure that they remained intact. The Politburo warned that dekulakization was not to touch poor and middle peasants or the families of Red army soldiers; further, officials were to be cautious about applying repressive measures to families with close relatives in industrial employment. And no more than 3–5 percent of the peasant population was to be subject to liquidation.

The Politburo decree divided kulaks into three categories. The first was dubbed "counterrevolutionary kulak activists." They were subject to immediate arrest, to be followed by incarceration in concentration camps or, in the case of those deemed to be especially dangerous, execution. The control, or plan, figure for this category was set at 60,000 individuals. Following the arrest of the heads of households, remaining family members were subject to deportation and exile.[38] The OGPU was exclusively in charge of operations against the first category of kulak (except expropriation). The second category consisted of the remainder of the so-called "kulak activists" as well as the most prosperous farms (peasant or otherwise). This category was subject to deportation to the most remote areas of the Soviet Union. Some 150,000 families were targeted for this category, to be deported to the following regions: 70,000 to the Northern Territory, 50,000 to Siberia, 20–25,000 to the Urals, and 20–25,000 to Kazakhstan.[39] While the OGPU was in charge of the deportation process, the selection of second-category kulaks was to made by the district soviet executive committee on the basis of decisions taken at meetings of collective farmers and poor peasants, and confirmed by the county (*okrug*) soviet executive committee. Families were allowed to bring with them only the most essential of household items and farming tools and no more than 500 rubles in cash. The liquidation of the first two categories of kulaks was scheduled for the months between February and May 1930. The third and final category of kulaks—the majority—were subject to partial expropriation and resettled beyond the collective farm but within their home district. They would live in small clusters of families and serve as a local workforce in forestry, road construction, and other activities. The county and district soviet and party organs had exclusive control over this category.[40]

The momentous nature of the decree on the kulak was somewhat obscured by earlier regional decisions to take repressive action against kulaks, followed in some regions by de facto dekulakization.[41] Dekulakization campaigns had in fact begun in many places in the second half of January (if not earlier). In the Urals, mass dekulakization began in the second half of January under the slogan "better to overcount kulaks than to undercount them" while awaiting central directives.[42] In Pronskii District in the Riazanskii County of Moscow Region, the district party committee held a conference on dekulakization on 30 January, followed (according to reports) by poor peasant-led dekulakization. In fact, only five of twenty-seven districts in Riazanskii County had not begun dekulakization by this time.[43] Elsewhere in Moscow Region, rural soviets and general collective farm meetings were compiling lists for dekulakization beginning from 19 January.[44] These areas were reacting not only to Stalin's December speech and the January decree,[45] but also to the pressures that collectivization put on parts of the peasant population to sell or destroy livestock and inventory ("*razbazarivanie*") and in some cases to self-dekulakize. In those instances, dekulakization became a preemptive strike by county and district officials to avert the economic destruction wrought by *razbazarivanie* and self-dekulakization.[46] In addition, on the local level, dekulakization was increasingly found to be a useful "stimulus" for collectivization, a tool of intimidation to pressure the peasant majority into joining collective farms. As district party committee officials in Riazan put it at a January conference on dekulakization, "without deku-lakization, collectivization goes poorly."[47]

The OGPU

Iagoda and the OGPU watched in alarm as collectivization and dekulakization led to mounting disorder in the countryside. In response to reports from the Moscow Region and other areas that dekulakiza-tion was veering off the track, Iagoda sternly pronounced to local and regional officials that "we [i. e., the OGPU] lead *all* of the Union."[48] This statement was doubly significant, pointing both to the OGPU's central role in dekulakization and its growing power in the country as a whole. The OGPU's involvement in dekulakization preceded the work of the Molotov Commission; in fact, its research and recommendations served as the foundation for the commission's work. Beginning in early January, if not before, the OGPU worked as a shadow government planning the operation against the kulak and attempting to exert control over a pro-cess that was increasingly developing a logic of its own in the regions.

On 10 January, the OGPU requested its regional bosses in the North, Urals, Siberia, and the Far East to report on locations for resettlement and the numbers of kulaks that could be settled in their regions.[49] On the next day, Iagoda wrote to his lieutenants in the OGPU (E. G. Evdokimov, S. A. Messing, G. E. Prokof'ev, G. I. Blagonravov, and G. I. Bokii),[50] declaring that the kulak as a class must be destroyed by March/ April 1930. He argued that rural class struggle was worsening, and if no decisive measures were taken before the spring sowing, there would be an insurrection. It was at this time that he ordered the Secret Operations Department of the OGPU to put together a concrete plan for the liquidation of the kulaks.[51]

The OGPU based its work on the experience of the repressive opera-tions underway in the regions from late 1929. On 9 January, Iagoda received a telegram from the OGPU boss in the North Caucasus, R. A. Piliar, reporting that on 8 January the regional party committee had decided, with the agreement of Moscow, to exile 20,000 kulak farms. According to Piliar, the operation would be carried out "on the basis of the experience in Belorussia"—meaning a late 1929 campaign to deport "socially dangerous elements" from the border zones.[52] The North Caucasus Regional party committee decree included a detailed plan of exiles, established control figures per county, detailed the organization of a regional soviet executive committee commission and county and district troikas (three-person committees) to lead dekulakization under the North Caucasus OGPU, and set a timetable for expropriations (to begin everywhere on 10 February), with deportations scheduled to begin between 20 February and 1 March.[53] This decree (if not the Belorussian and others as well) appears either to have directly foreshadowed the OGPU's plans or to have served as an OGPU test case anticipating central directives. Whatever the case may be, the OGPU's communications with its regional bosses were a two-way affair, with the OGPU making direct inquiries about regional willingness to accept precise numbers of kulaks as well as regional bosses submitting their own plans.[54]

On 18 and 23 January, the OGPU issued orders to its regional bosses to prepare for the mass operation against the kulak. Coded telegram directives from Iagoda and Evdokimov ordered the regional bosses to create operative groups for the implementation of the campaign and to work out detailed plans for arrests and exiles. The OGPU noted that "The definitive directions, periods of operation, [and] quantity of exiles will be given to you in good time, after the decision of the question has been decided at the highest level."[55] The OGPU's orders and plans preceded the Politburo commission's work by almost two weeks.[56]

On 26 January, the OGPU boss of the Northern Territory, R. I. Austrin, submitted his operational plan to the OGPU. The Northern Territory estimated that it could take in 70,000 families (approximately 350,000 people). It planned to transport only able-bodied adults to their final points of destination before June, leaving the rest (including mothers with children and the elderly) in the central transit points of the North. Plans for the construction of barracks to house 80,000 to 100,000 people in Arkhangel'sk and 20,000 in Kotlas were underway. Austrin also requested 100 revolvers, 100,000 cartridges, 100 rifles, and 200 hand grenades for the operation. He indicated that each echelon of exiles would have from 2,160 to 4,200 adults with a guard of three OGPU and fifteen Red army soldiers, to travel distances ranging from 180 to 1,300 kilometers.[57] On 29 January, Urals OGPU chief G. Ia. Rapoport submitted his plans for dekulakization. His plan indicated a figure of 5,000 Urals families to be exiled with a request to increase that number to 15,000. He also noted that the operation to remove category one kulaks in the Urals had begun on 27 January—again, prior to the completion of the Molotov Politburo Commission proceedings—with the arrest of 4,685 people.[58]

On 2 February 1930, the OGPU issued its own directive (no. 44/21) on dekulakization.[59] The OGPU directive closely followed the earlier Politburo decree. Control figures in the OGPU directive were largely the same as those in the Politburo decree, with the exception of the numbers of second-category kulaks designated for exile in Siberia and

Kazakhstan. These figures were decreased by 6,000 and 20,000 respectively as a result of protests from party leaders in these regions who argued that they were not prepared to support such large numbers of exiles.[60] The OGPU's definition of first-category kulaks was more expansive than that of the Politburo and included the following (using the OGPU's terminology): the most notorious and active kulaks opposing government policy; fugitive kulaks who were hiding underground or who had joined gangs of bandits; active White guards, insurgents, former bandits, former White guard officers, repatriates, former active members of punitive expeditions (*karateli*), active members of church councils, sects, or religious associations or groups, the wealthiest peasants, moneylenders, speculators, and former landlords. The OGPU directive also broadened the second category of kulaks to encompass "local kulak authorities and the whole kulak cadre." The OGPU planned to complete the operation against first-category kulaks before the operation against second-category kulaks began. (In fact, in many regions, the OGPU had already begun arrests.)[61]

The directive was not entirely successful in bringing the dekulakization campaign under control. The center continued to cajole and threaten regional and local authorities to remember, to paraphrase Iagoda, that the OGPU led the entire Union. On 3 February, the Central Committee condemned a series of regions (Ukraine, Belorussia, North Caucasus, Lower Volga, Middle Volga, Moscow, Ivanovo-Voznesensk, Central Black Earth Region) for ignoring central directives and carrying out dekulakization in areas that were not yet designated for wholesale collectivization.[62] Two days later, the OGPU ordered its own representatives not to exceed central control figures and demanded that they halt the "races" for arrests.[63] On the same day, the OGPU suspended the expropriations of supposedly "foreign citizens," referring to ethnically non-Russian peasants whose ancestors had migrated to Russia in the previous two centuries.[64]

The confusion created by the momentum of the campaign and the lateness of the center in issuing instructions resulted in the revision of plans and conflict with regional organizations. As early as 4 February, Iagoda decreased the numbers of families scheduled for deportations in the first phase as a result of regional protest and lack of preparation.[65] And on 10 February, Iagoda simply cancelled all deportations to Kazakhstan for the next three months.[66]

On 16 February, Stalin called to task the first party secretary of the Northern Territory, S. A. Bergavinov, criticizing the North's supposed decision to take only 30,000 families instead of the planned 70,000. While Bergavinov was away in Moscow in late January, the Northern Territory party committee and its special commission on resettlement met several times to begin their planning process and had concluded that the centrally mandated construction of some 800 barracks for housing kulaks temporarily en route to exile was "unrealistic" given local budget realities. As a result, some members suggested that the North should only take 30,000 families if temporary housing was not available—hence Stalin's reference to that number.[67] Later, in March, the OGPU refused the Northern Territory OGPU boss's demand for construction materials, considering his demand to be "extremely exaggerated."[68]

A regional split developed between regions "exporting" kulaks, which wanted dekulakization everywhere, and regions "importing" kulaks (especially Siberia, Kazakhstan, and the Urals), which wanted to slow down the campaign. The importing regions called for the enforcement of policy differentials between districts of wholesale collectivization (where dekulakization was permitted) and districts without wholesale collectivization (where dekulakization was, theoretically, not permitted). These regions sought to gain some control over a campaign that was rapidly descending into chaos.[69]

Reports of violence and atrocities flooded into the center. Throughout the country, officials were dekulakizing peasant families without regard to the level of collectivization. Usurping the powers of local authorities, outsiders imposed arbitrary quotas for dekulakization, deciding who was and who was not a kulak. The dekulakization decree's instructions to rely on the rural soviet and various village activists to make these decisions remained largely a dead letter, most likely a facade of democracy that was never intended to be in the first place. Dekulakization struck widely and often arbitrarily. Poor and middle peasants found themselves reduced to kulak status. Families of Red army soldiers and industrial workers were dekulakized (in spite of the OGPU's orders not to touch them). And property expropriations turned into simple pillage and wholesale theft.

Peasants sought desperately to avoid the kulak label by altering their economic status. There was a massive sell-off of properties. The markets were flooded with samovars, featherbeds, mirrors, sheepskin coats, and clothing. Peasants and their families were fleeing in droves—hordes of refugees were camping out at railroad stations in desperate attempts to escape, some heading for the cities and industrial sites, some even crossing the border out of the Soviet Union.[70] In all, some 250,000 kulak families simply fled the countryside in late 1929 and early 1930.[71]

The OGPU perceived the chaos and disorder resulting from dekulakization as a major security threat. It feared the destabilizing effect of an influx of peasant refugees into the cities and border zones as much as, perhaps more than it feared rural instability. The OGPU directive of

2 February had included an order to secure government installations, arsenals, and grain elevators as well as to increase informer networks.[72] The OGPU directive had also ordered a reinforcement of the border guards in order to attempt to halt the flow of exiles abroad. On 5 March 1930, the Politburo directed the OGPU to purge the border zones of Belorussia and right-bank Ukraine of individuals who had been arrested for banditry, espionage, counterrevolutionary work, and contraband, as well as all kulaks regardless of the level of collectivization, stressing in particular the removal of those of Polish nationality. The directive resulted in the exile of 3–3,500 people from Belorussia and 10–15,000 from Ukraine.[73]

The OGPU was also worried about the impact that the violence in the countryside was having on the army. The OGPU decree of 2 February had forbidden the use of Red army troops in dekulakization "under any circumstances."[74] Soldiers could be deployed only in cases of insurrections and then only after careful screening by the OGPU.[75] The OGPU feared using peasant recruits to repress village disorders. The 2 February OGPU directive also ordered military authorities to review all letters sent to and by soldiers.[76] Peasants in the villages were sending thousands of letters to their sons, brothers, and husbands in the army about the atrocities in the countryside. Claiming a pronounced "kulak mood" among soldiers, Iagoda reported that relatives were not only sending letters but also coming directly to the barracks to complain and solicit support. He ordered the arrest of peasants who complained directly to the army, as well as the confiscation of letters with negative content.[77] On 1 March, Iagoda warned his regional OGPU bosses to put a stop to the dekulakization of families of soldiers.[78]

In spite of the OGPU's efforts to control the operation against the kulak, Iagoda was still forced to rely on a rural administrative structure lacking the capacity and, at times, the will to carry out such a massive endeavor. The Communist Party was an urban institution with very little real knowledge or experience of work in the countryside. As late as January 1930, there were only 339,000 rural Communist party members.[79] The rural soviets were also weak and relatively few in number, ranging from 50,000 to 55,000, with one rural soviet servicing, on average in 1929, as many as eight to nine villages. Their membership was subject to high turnover, and usually included no more than about 10 percent Communists and 6–7 percent Komsomols.[80] With the onset of the grain procurement crisis and collectivization, purges, extraordinary soviet elections, and dismissals further weakened rural administration.[81]

The local institutions of Soviet power were isolated and relatively ineffectual outposts of the state. Interactions with the village were generally limited to tax collections, army conscription campaigns, and soviet elections, which tended to be conducted like some kind of military campaign. Starting with the grain procurement crisis, the central government increasingly began to rely on plenipotentiary rule in the countryside. The plenipotentiaries were generally from the city, mobilized from the regional- or district-level apparatus, or simply volunteers from the factories. Untrained, wielding extensive powers, and animated by the continuing war scares of the late 1920s and the party propaganda linking the kulak to the foreign threat, plenipotentiaries sidestepped both the law and local organs of administration. "Socialist competition" among brigades was officially encouraged, leading to an obsession with percentages—of grain requisitioned, of farms collectivized, of households dekulakized. The plenipotentiaries approached the peasantry with crude and brutal methods based on an urban disdain for a peasantry, which both they and the state they represented increasingly came to see as kulak and counterrevolutionary.[82]

From 1928 at the latest, the OGPU had begun to "colonize" the countryside in an attempt to gain control of and familiarity with the situation on the ground. With offices in the regional apparatus on every level from the region through the district, the OGPU not only closely monitored events in the countryside but also increasingly began to "manage" the economy and politics through the use of repressive measures. To a great extent, the hard-liners in the party, beginning with Stalin and Molotov, relied more and more on the OGPU to deal with the peasantry. Yet even the OGPU had limited powers over the wide expanses of the rural Soviet Union given its own shortages of cadres.

As a consequence of an inadequate rural administration, it was perhaps inevitable that "excesses" would be widespread in collectivization and dekulakization. Although the central government in Moscow was vastly powerful, its outposts in the countryside were weak. At the same time, the collectivization and dekulakization campaigns were rooted in Stalinist methods of ruling the peasantry that grew out of semicolonial relations between the city and village. Repression became a substitute for administrative control and an acceptable, even desirable, approach to governing the peasantry.

Results

The percentages of peasant households collectivized in the USSR skyrocketed from 18.1 percent in January to 31.7 percent in February to 57.2 percent by 1 March.[83] Despite the impressive figures, most of these collective farms were little more than "paper collectives" created by intimidation and force. The violence of the campaign resulted in massive peasant rioting in the countryside, leading in some villages to the temporary fall of Soviet power.[84] Iagoda's worst fears of the consequences of not "dealing with the kulak" by March had come true. The disorders, combined with the threat posed to spring sowing, forced Stalin to publish his famous article, "Dizziness from Success"[85] signaling on 2 March a temporary retreat from collectivization. The result was a mass peasant exodus from the collective farms and a precipitous decline in collectivization percentages from 57.2 percent on 1 March to 38.6 percent in April to 28 percent in May. By the eve of the regime's next collectivization campaign in September, percentages had reached a low of 21.5 percent.[86]

There was no retreat from dekulakization. Although removals of most second-category kulak families from the village came to a temporary halt amid the general disorder in the countryside and the difficulties of moving large numbers of people in winter and spring, OGPU arrests of first-category kulaks continued. Between January and 15 April, the OGPU made 140,724 arrests (including 79,330 kulaks, 5,028 clergy, 4,405 landlords, with the rest classified as "miscellaneous"). In the second period of the operation, between 15 April and 1 October 1930, the OGPU arrested an additional 142,993 (45,559 of whom were said to be kulaks). The numbers are striking: first as an indication of the rapidity of the OGPU operation, and second in the overfulfillment of the original Politburo plan of 60,000 first-category kulaks.[87] It is almost certain that a large percentage of the "miscellaneous" elements were arrested as a result of the ongoing peasant violence in the countryside. Additional statistics suggest that the number of individuals receiving death sentences through the OGPU in 1930 ranged from 18,966 to 20,201; it is likely that the largest percentages of these sentences were imposed on first-category kulak heads of households.[88]

By early May, the total numbers of kulak families expelled from the villages and sent into exile had reached 98,002 (501,290 people). Of these families, 66,445 (342,545 people) were exiled out of their native regions, while 37,557 families (158,745 people) were resettled in remote territories within their native regions.[89] By the end of 1930, the total number of families exiled had reached as many as 115,231 (559,532 people), most ending up in the Northern Territory (46,623 families), the Urals (30,474 families), Western Siberia (15,590 families), and Eastern Siberia (12,047 families).[90] In all, as many as 337,563 families were subject to some form of dekulakization (with or without exile) in 1930.[91]

A "side benefit" of the property confiscations that accompanied dekulakization was the use of that property to pay off peasant debts and to provide a material base for the new collective farm system. According to highly incomplete information from a 4 July 1930 Commissariat of Finance report based on the dekulakization of 191,035 farms, the total value of confiscated kulak property was estimated at 111,364,400 rubles, an average of 564.2 rubles per family. Roughly 75 percent of the total was transferred directly to the collective farms. The Finance Commissariat complained that local soviet executive committees in charge of the operation were failing grossly in the compilation of statistics on expropriations. Because local Finance Commissariat officials were not directly involved in the operation, the Commissariat could make tallies only on the basis of those soviet executive committees that filed reports.[92] These figures thus provide only a very rough estimate of the value of confiscated kulak property.

The next wave of dekulakization began in the fall of 1930, as a series of regional party organizations passed resolutions to resume the removal of kulaks from the villages halted the previous spring. Not coincidentally, wholesale collectivization also resumed at this time, serving as the driving force behind dekulakization. However, the real push came at the end of the year when the Politburo called for the completion of dekulakization in all major grain regions.[93] Through the winter of 1931, dekulakization accelerated in combination with collectivization as regional party organizations planned and enacted their campaigns against the kulak. Only in late February 1931 did the Politburo intervene to take charge of the operation. At this time, it appointed A. A. Andreev, the head of the Central Control Commission and the Workers' and Peasants' Inspectorate and the former first secretary of the North Caucasus party organization, to coordinate the campaign. On 11 March, the Politburo established a standing commission on kulak exile and resettlement, chaired by Andreev with the participation of Iagoda and P. P. Postyshev, among others.[94] In the course of the next three months, the Andreev Commission drew up general plans for the next stage in the dekulakization operation. The operation was to take place between May and September 1931.[95] Increasingly, dekulakization would be uncoupled from collectivization and tied directly to industry requests for labor, so that by this time there were no longer divisions of kulaks into categories. Instead, all were slated for deportation. Statistics on the total number of families exiled in 1931 range from 243,531 families (1,128,198 people) to 265,795 families (1,243,869 people), with close to two-thirds exiled beyond their native regions.[96] More than 10,000 peasants were executed.[97]

On 20 July 1931, the Politburo declared the period of mass exiles of kulaks "basically" over. Despite this decree, exiles continued, though not on the scale of the first six months of the year, motivated by industrial demands for labor. In this same decree, however, the Politburo sanctioned decisions to exile 1,100 Kalmyk families and to draw up new plans for kulak exiles in the spring of 1932 in the North Caucasus, the Transcaucasus, and other national areas.[98] Additionally, some 20,000 to 25,000 families purged from collective farms as kulaks in 1932 would be subject to exile, not to mention the selective exiles of entire villages during the great famine of 1932–33.[99] On 8 May 1933, the Central Committee and Council of People's Commissars yet again signaled the end of mass exiles, this time in the face of regional demands calling for kulak labor totaling some 100,000 families.[100]

The total number of kulaks deported in 1930 and 1931 ranges from 356,544 families (1,679,528 people) to 381,026 families (1,803,392 people).[101] These figures do not include those peasants designated as third-category kulaks, nor those who fled the countryside. Were we to calculate in the exiles of 1932 and 1933, the total numbers would easily surpass two million (see tables 1 and 2 in appendix). Through the first half of the 1930s, the deported kulaks constituted the largest category within the unfree population of the Soviet Union; all other incarcerated categories combined equaled only one-fifth of their numbers.[102] The campaign against the kulaks was the first and would remain the single largest exile operation of the Stalin years.

Conclusion

In the violent context of the First Five-Year Plan, the countryside became a foreign country to be invaded, occupied, and conquered. By 1929 the "class struggle" in the countryside had become a domestic security issue presided over by the OGPU. Although facts stated otherwise, Iagoda consistently argued that the class struggle was worsening and that the kulak had to be removed. From as early as 1927, the OGPU had begun to involve itself in the rural economy through a series of repressive measures against private trade and agriculture. These actions had the contradictory results of decreasing the actual numbers of private traders and wealthy peasants through repressive measures, while at the same time causing violent unrest as entire villages protested against these state measures. The unrest, moreover, clearly represented all peasants, not just kulaks. Both Iagoda and Stalin blurred the distinction between kulaks and the rest of the peasantry; as a consequence the protest was "ideologized" and in practice the peasantry as a whole came to be viewed and treated as "kulaks" as politics increasingly determined class status.[103] By late 1929, the OGPU had begun to play a leading role in politics and the domestic economy, a role that would be secured with the deportation of the kulaks.

"We Will Destroy the Kulak as a Class." Soviet propaganda poster.

I. V. Stalin (Courtesy of the Memorial Society in Moscow).

G. G. Iagoda (Courtesy of the Memorial Society in Moscow).

V. N. Tolmachev (Courtesy of the Russian State Archive of Film and Photography).

S. A. Bergavinov (Courtesy of the State Archive of Social-Political Movements and the Formation of Arkhangel'sk Oblast).

R. I. Austrin (Courtesy of the Memorial Society in Moscow).

R. I. Eikhe (Courtesy of the Memorial Society in Moscow).

M. D. Berman (Courtesy of the Memorial Society in Moscow).

N. I. Ezhov (Courtesy of the Memorial Society in Moscow).

L. P. Beria (Courtesy of the Memorial Society in Moscow).

2

Banishment:
The Deportation of
the Kulaks

I had never been away from this village, not any farther than the town of
P——, where I would go to the fairs. I had never lived among any other
people but my own . . . and of a sudden I was to part from everything
and everybody I knew. . . . I tell you it was a nightmare, our trip was. We
were packed into a *teploushka* [train car] like cattle and there were so
many of us. At night we could hardly stretch out and there were women
and children who cried and just would not let us sleep. . . . And when we
got there we were herded into camps without any accommodations—
and children died, and I thought my wife and I would die, and really we
shouldn't have minded death.

—Maurice Hindus, *Red Bread*

The End of the World

Dekulakization was the first step on the road to the other archipelago.[1] It came upon the village with a deadly force, destroying
homes and communities, and tearing families apart. For many
peasants, it evoked memories of the violence and misery of the Russian
Civil War, when competing armies engulfed the countryside in an orgy
of plunder and pillage. For some, it signified the end of the world—a
calamity that could only be articulated and comprehended through the
language of apocalypse. "The kingdom of Antichrist has come," it was
said, and this fearful prophesy echoed through the land.[2] Dekulakization spelled destruction and ruin for hundreds of thousands of hardworking peasants. It was the end of an entire way of life.

N. N. Pavlov, who was exiled as a child from Belorussia to the Urals,
recalled: "One morning all the villages of the Belorussian woodlands
looked like a stirred-up anthill. All the residents, from the smallest to

the biggest, gathered at our hut to see [us] off to an unknown destination; many wailed, keened, cried. That morning, father, mother, and we two little brothers got ready to be exiled as kulaks. . . . We were only allowed to bring the clothes on our backs and a small supply of food.

"They put the four of us, dressed in homespun clothes and *lapti* [bast shoes], on a cart with two armed policemen for our guards. And just like that we left. Everyone made a fuss, cried for us along the way. The cart set off and a crowd of villagers accompanied us far beyond the [village's] outskirts.

"Indelible in my memory is our beloved Sharik running behind us. . . . The dog was gray with floppy ears. [He] followed us for a long time, sometimes running ahead, wagging his tail, looking at us pitifully. With his dog's heart, he felt a terrible calamity for us. We felt our own helplessness just like he did.

"So we left our village. The future was fully unknown, deadened by a feeling of calamity. Mother cried and loudly lamented, repeating to the local *bezdel'niki* [idlers or loafers, a pejorative used for these local activists] that our tears would not go unseen, that God sees and punishes. . . . So began our new life."[3]

A. T. Shokhireva was fifteen when her family was dekulakized. "Nothing was explained. They came and destroyed all the buildings. They took away whatever they could. . . . Our home was ruined. . . . [And] they didn't tell us where they were taking us."[4] A. M. Cherkasova, then nine, recalled, "They came with two sledges in the middle of the night, threw us all out of the hut, loaded us up, [and] took us away from the village."[5] Victor M. was thirteen at the time of dekulakization. He remembered two armed men coming into his family's house one night in December 1929. They demanded his father's papers and forced him to sign some kind of document. They stayed through the night. In the morning, they ordered the family to leave the house, taking with them only the bare essentials of life. The family watched as a boycott sign was nailed on to their fence. They were then moved into a poor peasant's hovel until March 1930 when they were loaded onto carts and taken away.[6]

In the memory of these survivors, dekulakization was a drastic and irreversible break in their young lives. The nightmarish suddenness of the experience was in sharp contrast to what seemed to them the idyll of country life. Cherkasova framed her memories with fond descriptions of her village: "My native village is Prosianyi in Markovskii District, in the Voroshilovgradskaia Region. In the middle of the village, there was a white church with gilded cupolas, surrounded by a wrought-iron fence; next to it was the school and the square where they would set up a carousel on important holidays. From the square to all sides ran streets and lanes, white huts sitting amidst green gardens."[7] I. D. Ivanov shared these memories of the good life before dekulakization: "I was eight years old in 1929 and I remember well our village Sergeevka in Troitskii District, Orenburgskaia Region. The village had just one street, stretching east to west. The street was one-sided. On that side were the houses and below were wells, ponds, streams, bathhouses, and gardens. Behind the houses were the yards, sheds, threshing barns, threshing floors, and of course the fields . . . Life in the countryside was gay, joyful, collective even though labor began from earliest childhood."[8]

Such memories of the beauty and peace of the village vied with memories of family and peasant labor. Cherkasova wrote, "I was born in 1921 into a large peasant family: grandfather and grandmother, father, mother, six aunts, and we five children. The family was friendly and hardworking. In winter we spun, weaved, in summer we worked in the fields. Father was not only a good farmer, but also a tailor, [he] sewed sheepskin coats, overcoats from homespun cloth."[9] E. I. Novoselova recalled the centrality of labor in the peasant family. She remembered rising at three in the morning in the busy season and working until nine at night: "It was hard, of course, peasant work isn't easy, but we were raised on this, [our] parents taught us from our earliest years to be accustomed to labor."[10]

Although peasant life and labor in ordinary times were never quite as idyllic as these child survivors remembered, the brutality and senselessness of dekulakization created an impression of rupture in their memory as the peasant world was turned upside down. The cadres of dekulakization descended upon the village like the troops of an invading army, threatening, destroying, stealing, and arresting. Despite attempts to weave a pall of secrecy around the policy, dekulakization was a public event in the village, resonant with the sounds of anguish, grief, shock, rage, and, from the margins of village society, an occasional cheer of victory over the "class enemy."

The cadres who came to carry out dekulakization, often city dwellers, were generally unfamiliar with local ways. Mobilized by the district party and soviet executive committees, most had been trained in the "race for percentages" that they had run during the earlier grain-requisitioning campaigns. As a consequence, dekulakization became another race, with percentages of families being substituted for percentages of grain. The cadres approached the village as if it were enemy territory, armed with varying degrees of fear, vengeance, and cultural disdain. For many, the kulak had been little more than an abstraction, dehumanized in the propaganda and caricatured in newspaper cartoons as demonic and beastly. One cadre said, "We will make soap out of the kulak," while another proclaimed, "We will exile the kulaks by the thousands and if necessary—shoot the kulak scum."[11] In Siberia, some district officials believed that the exile of the kulaks was the first step to their physical liquidation.[12] Other officials simply followed orders, fearful of the accusation of "right deviation," which blackened the records of anyone who lacked the requisite Bolshevik stamina to deal with the kulak. A minority were disgusted by what they saw. A communist and school teacher from the town of Kursk named F. D. Pokrovskii, who participated in dekulakization, wrote in his diary, "even if they are kulaks, they are people." Filatov, a communist in the Middle Volga, wrote his superiors, "I request that you remove me from this work because I cannot view all this indifferently."[13] Most, however, acted with apparent elan. As a result of ignorance forged with class hatred, inadequate guidance from above, and a policy predicated on violence, the cadres in the field committed widespread atrocities—excesses (*peregiby*) in the parlance of the times. Illegal confinements, theft, beatings, and even rape and murder accompanied dekulakization.

Dekulakization cadres frequently arrived in the dead of night, banging on doors and windows, waking terrified families from their sleep. They often began by rounding up the men and herding them into a makeshift prison in an attempt to prevent resistance, while the families watched helplessly as the cadres rummaged through their possessions, inventorying property for expropriation. Expropriation could easily become outright plunder, as was the case in the vicinity of Pskov where dekulakization was known as "the week of the trunk." In Kozlovskii County in the Central Black Earth Region, a county official instructed cadres that it was "essential to dekulakize so only the ceiling beams and walls remain."[14] An official in Rossoshanskii County, in the same region, told district officials, "The main thing is not to be afraid of excesses. There is no harm in touching the middle peasant, just don't leave any kulaks." In many places, as one official report put it, "the 'creativity' of the people [that is, officials enacting policy] surpassed by far anything in memory . . . [as] they took absolutely everything, right down to children's dirty underclothing."[15]

As a result of the "excesses" and the inevitable failure to involve the "masses" in the democratic facade of dekulakization, repression struck all manner of peasant and nonpeasant in the village, including poor and middle peasants, peasants with large families (and therefore greater land or other resources), the families of Red army soldiers and industrial workers, members of the rural intelligentsia (i.e., teachers, agronomists, doctors), *byvshie liudi* (literally former people—notables from the old regime), and anyone who dared to object. Combined with the excesses of collectivization and the ongoing assault on the church, dekulakization led to an uproar in the village. In 1930 there were close to 14,000 mass disturbances in the countryside, involving over 2 million participants, as well as more than 1,000 murders of and just under 6,000 assaults on rural officials and peasant activists. According to official statistics, close to 20 percent of all mass disturbances in 1930 arose in the face of dekulakization. And dekulakization also sparked many of the women's riots (*bab'i bunty*) that abounded in the villages at the time.[16]

Throughout the countryside, peasants resisted the dekulakization of their neighbors. Reports of peasants voting against exile or maintaining complete silence in protest at official meetings flooded Moscow.[17] In many instances, peasants, especially women, attempted to block the removal of kulaks from the village, turning out in force to surround the unfortunate families. One woman in Ukraine spoke for many when she yelled at an official, "Why are you torturing people? Where are you taking them? Why must you torture the children?"[18] In the village of Petrovka in Western Siberia, forty women, including members of the new collective farm, massed to prevent cadres from removing the kulaks and then dispersed the "kulak children" to their own homes.[19] In the village Zalesianka in Samoilovskii District, Lower Volga, fifty women gathered to block the exiles, shouting, "We won't let you exile the kulaks."[20] In many places, peasants offered the families clothes or food, sometimes even taking them into their homes when exile was not immediate. Even some collective farms helped, provisioning "their" kulaks for the journey or refusing to accept confiscated property.[21]

Peasants labeled as kulaks resisted in a variety of ways, ranging from flight and *razbazarivanie* to family divisions and divorce.[22] Some accepted dekulakization fatalistically. A Middle Volga peasant said, "I'm prepared. I've been waiting for this for a long time."[23] Some chose suicide. A seventy-five-year-old peasant in the Urals hanged himself. Fifty-year-old Marfa Alamankova, a "kulachka" (a female kulak) from the village of Pron'kino fled to her daughter in a nearby village, responding with silence when people asked why she was there. When her daughter asked her to leave, she hanged herself.[24] In Tagil'skii county in the Urals, one kulak murdered his wife and children before burning himself and his house to the ground.[25] One woman threw herself under a train rather than face the journey to the unknown.[26] Many tried, at least, to save their children. One man said, "Let them shoot us here, we are not going anywhere with our children." Shabalin, a peasant from Novo-Privol'skoe village in Western Siberia, said, "Exile me, but don't take my children. I don't want them to die."[27]

Some families would in fact remain in their villages following expropriation. The families of first- and second-category kulaks could stay with official permission, provided they were not deemed to be "socially dangerous," or if the family lacked able-bodied laborers.[28] By March, the OGPU was demanding that families without able-bodied laborers, or made up exclusively of the elderly, be left in place in light of disturbing reports from the Northern Territory and elsewhere, signaling the disastrous results of the first deportations.[29] At times, these directives were observed and the families, shorn of most of their possessions, were moved into the homes of poor peasants, who were then offered the now-vacant kulak houses. If the families did not manage to flee, exile was then postponed from the spring until the following fall or, at best, the spring or summer of 1931.

Transport

Village deportations began in February, in the dead of winter. According to OGPU instructions, ad hoc convoys of police, local communists and komsomols, collective farmers, and poor peasants were to accompany the families from the village to the collection or concentration point (*sbor-* or *kontspunkt*), where they would await transportation to their regions of exile. Small children and non-able-bodied women could ride in carts with the families' baggage. The others traveled by foot.[30] To attempt to minimize resistance from relatives and other villagers, the families were sometimes taken away in the middle of the night.[31]

All families were supposed to bring with them a two-month supply of food, which was to maintain them until they could be settled and the central government could determine whether and how central and regional supply systems might service nonworking family members.[32] They were also allowed to bring axes, shovels, carpentry tools, horse collars and harnesses, warm winter clothes and footwear, summer clothes, linens, blankets, and a small assortment of cooking utensils. The baggage allotment for each family was not to exceed 25 to 30 *puds* (900 to 1,080 lbs). Additionally, the families could keep up to 500 rubles in cash.[33] The realities of the expropriations, however, meant that few would travel with such extensive belongings. Most boarded the transport trains virtually empty-handed.

The first step on the exiles' itinerary was the collection point. Situated on or near the railroads, in some cases along river ways, the collection points were places where the kulak families were assembled in preparation for transport.[34] Military barracks and other available buildings were used for temporary housing. An OGPU-appointed commandant led the collection point operation with the aid of two assistants. The commandant was in charge of security, food, medical, and sanitary services; the reception of exiles and accounting work; and continuous communication with the OGPU. In the event of an emergency, the commandant had full authority to take all necessary measures. His most important task was to prepare the families for travel and transfer to the jurisdiction of the OGPU Transport Department and train echelon commandant.[35]

The OGPU organized registration and investigation (*uchetno-sledstvennye*) groups in each collection point. An operational official of the OGPU not lower than an OGPU county chief led the group, which also included other OGPU and Commissariat of Justice officials, all subordinated to the collection-point commandant. The groups reviewed the exiles with an eye to anything of "special interest" to the OGPU, and selected informants from the ranks of the exiles (one per thirty to fifty adults) for work in the collection points, en route, and in places of exile. Each family required two personal data cards (*lichnye kartochki*), one of which was sent to the OGPU in the event of a problem (otherwise to be maintained by the county), while the other card accompanied the family into exile.[36] At this point, heads of households arrested earlier as a preemptive measure were sometimes reunited with their families. Ivan Tvardovskii, brother of the poet Aleksandr, recalled waiting twelve days in an old military barracks for the transport to begin; on the sixth day, his father and older brother were transferred from their place of incarceration to reunite with the family for the long trip into exile.[37]

The OGPU complained about what it called poor leadership in the management of the collection points.[38] In fact, the county-level OGPU groups in charge of the collection points had had little or no time for preparations beyond the receipt and issue of formal plans, if that, given the rapidity of the operation. Cherkasova recalled being packed into a cart and brought to the collection point. "There on the square everyone moaned and cried. All around us was a guard, [they even] led us to the toilet under convoy. [Soon] our fathers were brought in under convoy."[39] Victor M. remembered arriving at the district center and being herded into a large hall with a crowd of families and a din of noise.[40] Pavlov remembered meeting up with other groups of exiles along the way to the collection points and being taken with his family to the station at Ratmirovich. "There they began to call us *spetspereselentsy*. And here was the railroad. Never having seen the railroad, we looked with great interest at the trains and train cars."[41] Undoubtedly, Pavlov's enthrallment with the railroad was not shared by his parents.

The next stage in the operation was the transport of the families to county or district towns in the regions of exile. More than likely, much of the microplanning of this phase of the operation derived from standard military procedures for troop mobilizations.[42] V. A. Kishkin, the head of the OGPU Transport Department, issued detailed instructions in a series of directives that accompanied the 2 February OGPU decree on dekulakization. The transport organs of the OGPU were responsible for all rail movement of exiles. Within the Transport Department, a central troika made up of representatives of that department, the Commissariat of Transport, and other transport agencies was given the lead operational role in all questions of transport, scheduling, funding, personnel, and so on. Road troikas made up of the heads of various agencies (including the Road and Transport Departments of the OGPU) were to establish observation and management of the loading and unloading of train echelons, including overseeing questions relating to the composition of echelons and strict adherence to the central troika's schedule. Each echelon received a number (per region, by the hundreds) and consisted of forty-four train cars (supposedly *teplushki*, or heated cars), eight baggage cars, and one fourth-class car for the command staff. Each car was to carry forty people, and to be outfitted with one stove, one chimney flue, two window frames, one lantern, three buckets (two for boiled water and one for human waste), and twenty-eight plank beds. The command staff consisted of an echelon commandant, his assistant (from the OGPU), and a guard of thirteen riflemen (including one political instructor). Riflemen received sixty ammunition cartridges per rifle.[43]

At least three hours prior to transport, each echelon commandant was to receive lists of exiles, with detailed information on family composition and age structure.[44] The commandant was instructed to send a standardized telegram to the OGPU in Moscow reporting the exact time of departure. En route, he was responsible for unloading sick exiles (if under the age of six, with the mother) and the dead. The commandant was to have a list of the informers among the exiles (including a small budget for payments) and was to keep a special log during the trip. He was also responsible for reporting on the composition and "political mood" of the echelon (particularly those from border or "bandit" areas) prior to departure. In the case of escape attempts, the guard could open fire, shooting to kill.[45]

Each train car had an elder (*starosta*) and an elder's assistant appointed by the echelon commandant. At stops, the elder and his assistant could disembark to get food and boiled water for the car's occupants. Car doors could be slightly ajar when the train was in motion. At and near stops, the car doors were to be closed, and "tightly" (*naglukho*) closed in the vicinity of Moscow. Finally, the road troikas appointed two chiefs (one for loading and one for unloading) to take charge of the technical organization of the echelons, embarkment, and disembarkment.[46]

The actual conditions and experience of transport were horrendous. The duration of travel could be as long as two weeks and more, depending upon destination.[47] Given the pillage of the expropriation process, many families were left without necessary food supplies and warm clothing.[48] On 5 March, the OGPU "categorically" ordered—in one of a series of such orders—its regional bosses to ensure that kulak families had the requisite food supplies.[49] To make matters worse, the exile contingents included children, the elderly, families without able-bodied workers, and even small children separated from their mothers.[50] On 3 March the OGPU dispatched a note to its Lower Volga OGPU chief, stating: "It is hard to imagine that eighty- and ninety-year-olds represent a danger to the revolutionary order," and that it was "completely incomprehensible" that families should be exiled without the head of the family.[51]

On 18 March the OGPU repeated its order not to exile families of first- and second-category kulaks without able-bodied family members.[52] On 20 March the OGPU wrote to its officials in districts of wholesale collectivization, ordering them to ensure that kulaks arrive with boots or else be detained in the collection points.[53] On 23 March the OGPU wrote again, saying that "despite our directives" large numbers of families continued to arrive with neither food nor money. The OGPU then announced that if all food had been "expropriated" from a family, it became the responsibility of local organizations to provide food *before* sending families into exile.[54]

Victor M. recalled traveling into exile in a freezing cattle car, with the wind blowing in through its wide wooden planks. The train car had a "*burzhuika*" stove, but it provided little warmth.[55] Pavlov remembered the experience of the transport in great detail. The train car in which he and his family found themselves had two rows of double bunks. The window was covered with bars. It was kept closed in the day time, especially near big towns. The car was full beyond capacity, forcing people to squeeze in to find room on the narrow bunks. The door to the car was bolted and, before departing, Pavlov spied armed guards on the platform through a crack in the door. When the train started, many began to cry, lamenting the fate of their lost homes and farms. The train's occupants received pails of water at the larger stations and sometimes bread and a watery soup. The latrine in Pavlov's car consisted of a bucket, screened off by a makeshift bast grille, most likely supplied by one of the travelers. The latrine bucket was emptied out at stops, leaving the car's atmosphere oppressive at most times. F. A. Rodin who was five or six at the time of the transport, recalled people holding up curtains of clothes around the latrine bucket in an awkward attempt at privacy.[56]

Soon after the train echelon left the station at one provincial town, a railroad guard spied a note on the track. The note, which may have been intended for a friendly hand to mail, eloquently described the horrors of the transport:

> We are being carried no one knows where, forty-five people in each train car; they don't let us out; there is not enough water for drinking, let alone washing; there is not enough boiled water; you can't even ask the guards to bring us snow. For what have they thrown us into this dark and stinking car which is worse than a prison. . . . If someone could look into our car, then even a heart of stone would tremble, and they [*sic*] would see such horror that even barbarians do not know. It is shameful to put infants in prison and our car is worse than a prison. There is no place to sit or lie down; for the first two days we traveled without any water and fed the children snow.[57]

Similar sentiments were wryly expressed in a letter intercepted by the OGPU from a peasant exiled to the Northern Territory. "They led us along the railroad with an honor guard, like Lenin. The only difference was that all the doors and windows were closed so that there was neither light nor air, and we almost suffocated."[58]

As the exiles neared their final destinations, there were occasional instances of resistance. On 18 March special settlers from echelon #139 in Vologodskii County, Northern Territory, refused to move into their barracks and headed back to the railroad station demanding to go home. Shots fired into the air by the commandant succeeded in turning the rebels back, though still angry and threatening to leave all the same.[59] On 19 March at 8:00 a.m., five kilometers outside Kotlas, a party of 1,500 exiles refused to be moved from the station into the settlement to which they were assigned. Someone sounded the church bell in a nearby village, and in no time 7,000 peasants gathered for a "meeting." The crowd attempted to disarm the OGPU workers. At 9:00 a.m. a special OGPU operational detachment of 2,000 troops, on skis, was called out. In the meantime, the OGPU workers on site went into hiding as the settlers and local peasants chanted "down with Soviet power." The crowd dispersed when the troops arrived. The troops surrounded the barracks, arrested the ringleaders, and posted sentries. That night the troops' barracks were set ablaze.[60]

Echelon #416 heading to Kotlas was made up of Khoperskii and Stalingradskii County Cossacks. According to a 30 March report, they were said to be in an "insurrectionary mood." A riot broke out at the time of departure. On 5 April, with the echelon already in Severo-Dvinskii County, the authorities began to prepare to separate out the able-bodied for transport to employment sites farther north, thus splitting up families. The Cossacks begged the commandant not to separate them from their families. When he refused, they surrounded the commandant's offices, cut the telephone lines, and began hurling rocks and bricks. The Severo-Dvinskii County department of the OGPU sent in 35 soldiers to put down the rebellion of 250 people, of which 25 were arrested.[61] On 6 April in the Urals, a group of 60 people from Crimea attempted to organize a demonstration to stop the movement of people further into the interior for forestry work. In all, 950 men refused to go on. A week later, 1,000 Crimeans demonstrated in front of the rural soviet, demanding to be sent to a warmer climate and given land and food. They continued to demonstrate for the next two days.[62] In the towns of Vologda and Arkhangel'sk, there were reports of kulaks "dekulakizing the dekulakizers."[63]

According to Northern Territory party chief Bergavinov, though, most exiles were pleasantly surprised to learn that they were to be sent farther onto the North in the spring, since many had expected to be shot on disembarkation.[64] Mariia Korneevna Buriak recalled her arrival in the Urals. "They transported us from Poltava for almost a month. . . . They didn't let us leave the train. We arrived in Tagil and stopped near some kind of pond where they permitted us to wash. As we washed in the pond and cleaned the children (there was no soap), a young man stood over us. He said he was our commandant, his name Eliseev. He said that we would live in Tagil until we died. Everyone cried because earlier they had told us we would only be here half a year, build a factory, and then go home."[65] Many peasants knew neither where they were going nor what they were to do once they arrived at their destination.

The actual unloading of trains occurred quickly and often haphazardly, in a matter of two to three hours, with baggage sometimes going astray.[66] On arrival, the able-bodied were separated out from the non-able-bodied (mothers with children under sixteen, the elderly) and transferred to local industries for work, while their families were kept in place temporarily or sent on to the new special settlements. Initially, this ruling applied only to the Northern Territory, following recommendations from Austrin and the OGPU. In the Urals, no temporary barracks existed, so after disembarking, all kulaks left immediately for the interior. The local population was forced to provide some 30,000 carts for transport. On 23 February, however, in view of the freezing weather, the OGPU instructed its officials in the Urals to halt further transport into the interior and to house exiles in the nearest villages. By this time, frostbite was already widespread, especially among children.[67] In the Northern Territory, kulaks remained temporarily housed in barracks or churches until weather conditions permitted transport into the interior.[68] By 19 March, 134,131 people had arrived in the Northern Territory, while 29,042 were still en route, and 70,827 awaited transport; in the Urals, 60,141 had arrived, 1,838 were en route, and 29,021 awaited transport.[69] By 10 April, the OGPU instructed all regions to keep the non-able-bodied temporarily in the towns at which they disembarked until weather conditions permitted travel.[70]

The secrecy and rapidity of the transport operation meant that despite microplanning on paper, there had in fact been little time for real preparation, especially in the winter and spring of 1930. The secretary of the Tobol'sk county party committee, one Ignatenko, summed up the situation in a frank statement to his superiors in the Urals Regional party committee: "The echelons are moving to us with such haste and with such massive force . . . that undoubtedly we were caught unprepared. Besides this, the terrible, devilish cold, going down to 36–37 degrees below zero, impeded everything."[71]

First Stop

In the Northern Territory, five echelons arrived daily from mid-February, each carrying between 5,000 and 7,000 people. Given that the county and city of Arkhangel'sk had populations of only 250,000 and 89,000 respectively, the arrival of the exiles quickly overwhelmed local officials and local resources. Bergavinov wrote to Molotov that, "even if we moved them into every village (and we cannot move children and women in winter), there would [still] be congestion [*zator*]."[72] It was expected that the kulak exile population would eventually equal some 17 percent of the territory's total population.[73] In an early February letter to M. N. Tukhachevkii, then head of the Leningrad military district, later marshall of the Soviet Union, Bergavinov wrote, "In these two months over three hundred thousand kulaks are arriving. Before navigation [opens], we must hold them, especially women and children, in Vologda, Arkhangel'sk, and Kotlas! You can imagine what sort of complicated work this is. You can't look away for one moment or there will be enormous political complications . . . the C.C. [Central Committee] looks at this especially strictly." He went on to request from Tukhachevskii permission to use empty military barracks to house kulaks. [74]

All the regions complained of inadequate planning and resources, especially for housing. Ignatenko, the county party secretary from Tobol'sk, wrote, "we are freeing literally every [building] possible and even decided to close the theatre [*kino*]."[75] Bergavinov told Stalin and Molotov that as of 17 February they had succeeded in building barracks for only 12,000 families. He pleaded for more funding, complaining that the "central organs are surprisingly indifferent on matters relating to these issues."[76]

In the Northern Territory, planning for temporary housing had only begun in late January. At a 27 January meeting of the regional party committee's commission on kulak resettlement, officials planned to survey all existing, free buildings, including churches and monasteries, as well as putting together the first plans for barracks construction. On 29 January the commission concluded that it could house 18,000 people in Arkhangel'sk city without excessive spending and an additional 50,000 in Arkhangel'skii County. At least one commission member objected, insisting that no more than 30,000 could or should be housed in the county, and succeeded in reducing the number to 40,000. Estimates for construction costs came to some 9 million rubles, even with plans for the construction of the cheapest kind of housing (*shalashy*, or makeshift straw huts).[77] In the county of Severo-Dvinskii, orders went out on 29 January to locate all possible buildings for temporary housing as well as to plan to house kulaks temporarily with the local peasant population if necessary.[78] On 31 January the regional commission completed its temporary housing plans, which included the construction of 1,200 barracks to house 150 to 160 people each, as well as housing in empty (or emptied) monasteries, churches, and warehouses. April 1 was the target date set for the completion of barracks construction— roughly one and one-half months *after* the exiles began to arrive. The commission requested that exiles from the Central Black Earth Region be brought in first to do the building, given their construction experience and familiarity with the kinds of materials found in the north (log construction).[79]

On 17 February, Bergavinov sent a telegram to Stalin and Molotov, noting that local resources were strained to the limit and pleading for financial and material aid from the Council of People's Commissars, the Supreme Council of the National Economy, the Commissariat of Trade, and the OGPU. To prevent the disruption of the operation, he wrote that he had been forced to take funds from the local budget for factory capital construction, threatening that this would hurt the plan for timber exports.[80] The OGPU had refused Austrin, the Northern Territory OGPU boss, his demands for construction materials, claiming that they were "exaggerated."[81] Bergavinov, though, could at least theoretically expect central funding for the kulak relocation operation. The OGPU was reluctant to provide funding for the relocation of first- and second-category kulak families *within* regions.[82] This meant that in areas like Siberia and the Urals, with large native populations of kulaks, expenses fell upon the budgets of the regional soviet executive committees. Siberia and Kazakhstan both resisted "importing" kulaks from other regions, given the immensity of the local problem. While Siberia theoretically could have taken in 75,000 families in 1930, when its request for some 50 million rubles for the operation was rejected, it refused to cooperate. Siberia was accused of only considering the "economic benefits" of dekulakization (i.e., kulak labor), as was Kazakhstan. In response, the OGPU was forced temporarily to halt all deportations to Kazakhstan. The OGPU was also engaged in a continuing dialogue with its Urals OGPU chief over what the OGPU considered the Urals' "exaggerated" demands for funds to pay for temporary barracks and food.[83]

Not surprisingly given this state of affairs, the conditions of temporary housing were appalling. According to inspectors from the Commissariats of Health and Internal Affairs, most temporary housing was completely unsuitable for living: dirty, cold, dark, and "colossally" overcrowded. The hastily built barracks generally lacked floors, and the inside temperature rarely rose above four degrees Celsius. There were few available kitchen facilities, and women were afraid to wash their children for fear of the cold. It was impossible to clean, let alone disinfect, clothing, and clean drinking water was a rare commodity.[84] A Commissariat of Agriculture inspector reported that on average each person had the equivalent of one square meter of living space.[85] In some places, people had less than one-tenth of a square meter—"smaller than a coffin," as V. N. Tolmachev, the Russian Republican Commissar of Internal Affairs, put it.[86]

On 19 March, a commission of People's Commissariats of Internal Affairs and Health inspectors filed a short descriptive report on temporary housing in the city of Vologda and the nearby Prilutskii monastery. The churches Pokrov and Peter and Paul received satisfactory grades for sanitary conditions and medical servicing, but were in the grip of an outbreak of measles and whooping cough among children, many of whom had complications like pneumonia. Neither church had a laundry, and clothing therefore could not be disinfected. About 3,500 people, mostly women, children, and elderly, were housed in the former exile sector of the local jail. This residence was deemed "completely unsuitable" and "dangerous," its rooms dark, damp, dirty, and cold. There was no place to prepare food. Lacking toilet facilities, human excrement was everywhere.

The commission also visited the defunct Prilutskii monastery, four kilometers outside of Vologda, where 7,000 exiles lived. People lived everywhere within the tall walls of this relatively small monastery— in the churches, administration buildings, basements—and crowding was again described as "colossal." Basement dwellings were completely dark. A general kitchen serviced the settlers, with a special kitchen for children, and the bread was deemed of "good quality." A clinic with twenty-six beds was set up on the monastery grounds and occupied primarily by children with complications from measles, mostly pneumonia. Laundry and bath facilities were insufficient to provide for even minimal hygiene. In Prilutskii monastery and elsewhere, lack of boiled water led to widespread gastrointestinal illnesses.[87]

In Velikii Ustiug, also in the Northern Territory, a political exile witnessed the horrors of temporary housing: "The kulak exiles are dispersed in the Velikii Ustiug churches and cathedrals in which they have set up four tiers of bunks. On the bunks, crowded in like herrings lie many people, side by side, back to back, youth, children in between the adults, the old, the dying with the living and the healthy, those dying from infectious diseases and those not yet touched by measles. . . . And the children are dying. From morning to night, narrow crates for children's coffins accumulate around the courtyard of the cathedral. In one day I personally counted seven coffins."[88] Another witness to the suffering of the exiles in the Northern Territory, wrote, "In the barracks, there are 250 people. It is almost dark, with little window openings here and there lighting only the lower bunks. [The exiles] prepare food outside, on camp fires. The latrine—is [just] a fenced-off area. Water— there is a river below, [but it is still frozen]. . . . The residents locked up the well: 'You will infect us; your children are dying,' and sell water in bottles. The barracks were built hurriedly in winter, and sunk with the thaw, everywhere there are cracks and drafts. That is how 25,000 exiles live in Kotlas."[89]

In Vologda, the wives of kulak men already sent into the interior wrote that "As many as 2,000 people are living in each church, in three-tiered bunks. . . . We are all ill from such bad air and drafts, and children under fourteen are falling like flies and there is no medicine for so many sick. . . . In one and one-half months, [they] have buried up to 3,000 children in the Vologda cemetery."[90] Another group of exiles in Vologda wrote, "We, together with children and invalids, were evicted from the [train] cars and placed in the forest in barracks made during the winter of beams, like a simple peasant cabin, covered with a scattering of straw and a layer of earth . . . with three-tier plank-beds; and there 180 people were settled, with [their] belongings, on an earthen floor. . . . Our husbands, some of them Red army soldiers, were driven to work right away, no one knows where. . . . Here in the barracks the atmosphere gets unbearable because of the damp wood covered with earth, the earthen floor, and overcrowding; and therefore children are starting to die. The adults feel sick. When the spring rains come, the barracks, built like a sieve and covered with earth, will begin leaking, and we will perish, together with our children and belongings."[91]

Mariia Fedorovna Abramenko, exiled to Narym, Siberia from Ukraine, recalled, "[They] took us to Siberia in winter in a freight car, unloaded us at the station Iaia, and threw us into a large barracks with bunk beds. The floor was covered with damp sawdust, [there were] strong drafts, [one] could hardly breathe. Children and old people began to die. . . . [They] piled the corpses in stacks, then took them away on horses and buried them somewhere. In our family, there were six children, three died. In April, [they] took all the exiles to Tomsk."[92] Above the Arctic Circle, in Igarka, M. Tsekhin, a former child kulak, recalled waking the first morning with his coat frozen to the wall.[93]

Central planning had not envisioned the necessity of feeding the families of exiled kulak laborers. This was, in part, because both central and local officials were more concerned with forcing kulaks out than laying plans for their use. It had been assumed that the officially prescribed (but often nonexistent) two-month food supply would tide the families over as the head of household and able-bodied family members settled into work. There the economic enterprises employing the exiles would provide workers' rations. The able-bodied would then be responsible for feeding the rest of the family. No provisions whatsoever had been made for families lacking breadwinners.

It did not take long for this state of affairs to lead to hunger. Bergavinov had realized relatively early on that he would have to feed the families of his new labor force. He made plans in late January to guarantee families food—a "hunger norm" (*po golodnoi norme*) he called it—and requested that the Commissariat of Trade send food for a four-month period until it was possible to send the families into the interior.[94] The planned food norms per person were to be 200 to 300 grams of bread per day, along with additional rations of potatoes, cabbage, and groats.[95] On 7 March, the OGPU told Austrin that the Politburo had ordered the Commissariat of Trade to transport food stocks to the Northern Territory, guaranteeing provisions for six months.[96] Yet on 28 March, Austrin reported that no decisions had been made about feeding families without laborers.[97] Bergavinov complained directly to the Politburo about food shortages, and on 20 April the Politburo instructed Anastas Mikoian, the Commissar of Trade, to check Bergavinov's report immediately.[98] In May, Bergavinov was continuing to write to Mikoian, who reportedly was not responding to telegrams about food problems. The Council of Labor and Defense then called upon the Commissariat of Trade to provide food for the exiles in the Northern Territory in ten days, simultaneously requesting a line of credit from the State Bank and additional transport ships from the Commissariat of Transport.[99] On 22 June 1930, the Council of People's Commissars finally directed "Union Fruit and Vegetable (*Soiuzplodovoshch*)" to send supplies of onions and garlic to the Urals and the Northern Territory "in view of scurvy."[100] Five days later, the Politburo ordered the Commissariat of Trade to provide supplies to the exiles from the Emergency Reserve Food Fund.[101]

Throughout 1930 the food situation was mired in interagency bureaucratic conflict, with the center continually trying to pass the buck to the regions and the regions themselves engaged in buck-passing among different agencies. In the Northern Territory and everywhere else, complaints about food supplies continued well into the summer and fall of 1930.[102] Yet even in the absence of such bureaucratic wrangling, the supply and transport of supplies on the requisite scale and the requisite time period over such enormous distances would have been beyond the capacity of the Soviet Union's bureaucracy, especially at a time when forced-pace industrialization was the country's first priority. As a consequence, hunger set in among the exiles from the outset.

The combination of poor nutrition, extreme temperatures, and unhygienic conditions soon led to the outbreak of epidemics among the exiles. Almost from the start, contagious diseases like measles and scarlet fever plagued the exiles, especially the children. Typhus and typhoid fever made an appearance, as early as April in Vologodskii and Severo-Dvinskii counties.[103] The rate of illness among exiles in the Northern Territory was five times as high as that of the rest of the population.[104] In mid-February, the OGPU had ordered its Northern and Urals OGPU bosses to take all essential measures to localize epidemic illnesses at points of exile concentration. Commissariat of Health local organs were instructed to be prepared for struggle with epidemics.[105] As of 27 February, Bergavinov was reporting to Molotov that the Commissariat of Health had sent no medicine or doctors to the Northern Territory.[106] On 7 March, Commissariat of Health and Commissariat of Internal Affairs inspectors in the Northern Territory called on their Moscow offices to send a Health Commissariat representative to unify all action. They also called for twenty to thirty doctors and the immediate transfer of the exiles out of the cities to prevent the spread of infection. The inspectors were shocked by the conditions they saw, reporting low morale, a "colossal" death rate among children, and exiles refusing even to unpack, saying, "it is all the same, they will destroy us."[107]

A Dr. Lebedev, who may or may not have been with this commission, described what he saw: "A great many dekulakized are accumulating in Vologda. . . . They will be sent on farther north, to the most distant, uninhabited and ruinous places, but they are temporarily housed in Vologda churches, the majority of which have already long been closed to believers. There they built bunks and the people are packed into the church buildings and typhus is breaking out. Horrors have begun. . . . The OGPU called me in and the chief said to me: 'If you don't liquidate the typhus—I will shoot you.' I went to one of the churches together with some OGPU men. A guard stood at the church, and behind the door—groans and cries. They opened the doors. And there I saw hell. The sick, the healthy, the dying—men, women, old people, children. And the live ones cried out and raised their arms to us: 'Water! Water!' I have seen many terrible things in my life but nothing like this."[108]

On 9 March, the Russian Council of People's Commissars organized a commission under Tolmachev to fight epidemics, with representatives from the Commissariat of Health, OGPU, and the Procurator's office. Similar regional commissions were set up in the North, the Urals, Siberia, and the Far East. The Russian Council of People's Commissars also called for "systematic" medical inspections of the transport echelons on departure, along the way, and on arrival, as well as the mobilization of Moscow and Leningrad doctors.[109] On 12 March, Bergavinov wrote the Politburo to report that an epidemic in Arkhangel'sk was not an impossibility. He warned that this would be a scandal; it would threaten export plans, and foreign ships would refuse to come into the port.[110] A 20 March report by a Health Commissariat inspector on the 24,000 exiles in Arkhangel'sk and the 20,000 in Vologda warned that here too the local population was threatened with infection if an epidemic were to break out among the exiles. He reported that the latter lived in unsanitary, overcrowded barracks without access to clean drinking water.[111] By 25 March, nineteen doctors had arrived in the Northern Territory, with ten more on the way, while the Commissariat of Health had provided 100,000 rubles (matched by the Northern Territory Soviet Executive Committee) for medicine and sanitary materials.[112]

On 6 April, the center urged the "unloading" of exiles from the city of Arkhangel'sk to prevent the spread of disease to the local population.[113] By 10 April, the Tolmachev Commission on epidemics had concluded that the measures taken thus far in the Northern Territory were insufficient and called on the Council of People's Commissars to provide another 200,000 rubles for the North, as well as the shipment of five tons of sulfur, formalin, carbolic acid, chloride of lime, hair-cutting tools, and more doctors and *fel'dshers* (medical orderlies).[114] An alarmed Bergavinov again telegrammed the Politburo for medical aid; the Politburo's response was to order him, on 27 May, "not to allow information about typhus cases to get into the press," while outlining a series of "urgent measures" to be taken to remedy the situation.[115] Tolmachev complained that in spite of ordering the OGPU to provide 1.5 million rubles to fight epidemics, nothing had yet been received in the Urals, Siberia, and the Far East.[116] Throughout the spring and early summer, central directives urged the Commissariat of Health to mobilize medical personnel, disinfectant units, and medicine for exile regions.[117] By 11 April, there were still only twenty-six doctors working among the exiles in the Northern Territory—roughly one doctor for every 10,000 people.[118]

The Commissariat of Health reported an alarming death rate among children.[119] Of the 510,096 people exiled by May 1930, 194,230 (or roughly 38 percent) were children, the youngest of whom were, along with the elderly, the most vulnerable to disease.[120] As of 11 April, the Northern Territory Soviet Executive Committee reported that 11,000 children were outpatients in hospitals in the town of Arkhangel'sk, with another 9,233 in the county as a whole. Between 31 March and 10 April, 30 percent of exile children hospitalized in Arkhangel'sk (335 children) died, while another 252 died outside of hospital. Most succumbed to meningitis, pneumonia, measles, diphtheria, or scarlet fever.[121] On 14 April, the same commission reported that 85 percent of all children in Arkhangel'sk were ill and that there was a 40-percent mortality rate among children who were hospitalized.[122] An April report on the Northern Territory offered up general figures of 3,132 exiles dead and 34,314 ill (most with measles).[123]

Little or no foresight had been given to the fate of the children. The 30 January 1930 Politburo decree on dekulakization allowed for the families of exiled and interned peasants to remain in their home district with the permission of the district soviet executive committee.[124] Other than that vague note, there was no specific reference to the plight of the children. In February, at a Central Committee conference on collectivization and dekulakization in grain-consuming regions, S. I. Syrtsov, then the head of the Russian Council of People's Commissars, interrupted a speech by I. P. Rumiantsev, secretary of the Western Regional party committee, asking what was to be done with the children of dekulakized peasants. Rumiantsev replied laconically that the issue had not come up.[125] By March, the OGPU was sending directives to its regional bosses not to exile kulak families without able-bodied members and reminding them that the 30 January decree allowed for families to remain behind with the district authorities' permission.[126] In April, the Russian Council of People's Commissars issued a general ruling that only able-bodied kulaks be sent into exile for the time being, leaving families behind. This decision was taken on the basis of "previous experience" —most importantly, the high mortality rates among the children already in exile.[127] Nonetheless, tens of thousands of children continued to accompany their parents into exile.

Nadezhda Krupskaia, an authority in education, a Central Committee member, and Lenin's widow, was appalled by what was happening to the children in the first months of resettlement. She sent the following letter to the Politburo:

> As soon as the difficult situation of the kulak children became apparent, I talked about this with Iagoda. He said measures would be taken.
> I wrote an article for *Pravda*. Com. Iaroslavskii and com. Krumin rejected it. [They claim that] the article has no facts. The article was written for the children. In my latest conversation with com. Iaroslavskii, I asked that someone write another article. There will be no article on this topic. The failure of an article to

appear in *Pravda* persuades everyone that no sort of direction has been given for the improvement of [the life of] the children of kulaks.

It is clearly essential to take measures immediately, the issue is of immense political importance.[128]

Even E. G. Evdokimov, a top official in the OGPU, admitted in a June 1931 letter to Mikoian, that "instead of preparing the children to be a future work force, they are becoming candidates for invalid status." The children of special settlers shared their parents' status legally and, to all extents and purposes, in almost every other way.[129]

Official injunctions to create "more normal conditions" for children were issued regularly.[130] In April 1930, Tolmachev wrote a letter to the Northern Territory Soviet Executive Committee Chair Komissarov, noting that "It is essential immediately to give a directive . . . about returning children under fifteen to sixteen."[131] On 13 April, the Central Committee in charge of reviewing "incorrectly dekulakized" families noted that children under sixteen exiled without adult relatives were among the categories of incorrect exiles.[132] A 20 April instruction to all OGPU regional bosses noted reports of exiled kulaks' relatives requesting to be allowed to bring the children back home to live with them. Taking into account the "difficult conditions" for children, the OGPU agreed that, with the parents' consent, relatives could take children under fourteen. The age was later revised to children under ten.[133] By December 1930, 35,400 children had left the Northern Territory.[134]

One witness described the excruciatingly painful send-off of children from the Kotlas railroad station:

> In a half hour the train leaves. Four wagons of the "Kotlas-Moscow," an unbeliev-able crowd and crush, the tears of children mixed in with the wailing of mothers.
>
> On high raised arms little ones are passed into the wagons, where the conductor catches them, risking being pushed from the footboard. . . . Older children, risk-ing being maimed, hold on to other wagons.
>
> Sanctioned by the decision "to return children to their villages" under age twelve, these are the exiled, the dekulakized, saving from death the "little kulaks."
>
> They are saving [them]—yes, since in recent weeks already up to thirty chil-dren a day have died, not being able to tolerate the conditions in which the exiles live. . . . At the post office there is a permanent queue to telegraph relatives to come. Frequently coming for children, they don't find them alive, but take away other children in the tens. In the wagon where I travelled, one old man was accompanying twelve children, another, eleven.
>
> Nursing children were taken from their mothers and sent home and therefore all night [on the train] there is endless children's crying. On the way, at the stations, it is almost unthinkable to obtain hot water and milk, since the Siberian trains are overloaded and our wagon, as attached in Viatka to the very end of the train, never gets near the station. Thus two days without hot food. Half of the children are sick—diarrhoea, coughs, measles, fever sores. What a terrible picture. And one wants involuntarily to scream together with those old people who are accompanying the dozens of children.[135]

Some parents were reluctant or simply unable to send away their children. In August 1931 a Northern Territory party committee decree instructed the OGPU "to force" the transfer of children under fourteen back to relatives.[136] In the 25 October 1931 Temporary Statutes (*polozhenie*) on the rights of exiles, parents would be ensured the right to send their children under fourteen home to relatives or friends in the village, although the journey was to be somehow paid by the families.[137] Similar provisions were allowed for elderly non-able-bodied peasants over sixty.[138]

Even onlookers were affected by the sight of the hungry and ragged families arriving in exile towns and moving into their dreadful temporary hovels, particularly when they saw the children. A group of workers in Vologda wrote to Kalinin: "We are struggling for a healthy generation, for future builders of socialism and at the same time [we] are burying children alive in the grave. Don't we know a few revolutionaries who came not only from strong peasants, but from landlords, nobles, etc. Why can you not assume that these dear children will be healthy, strong and staunch warriors for soviet power and for the construction of socialism. But we are destroying groundlessly these children, our healthy change of guard, not looking back and especially not looking forward. . . . And if you seriously think about it, what sort of benefit can come from this? If only by passing through the corpses of these children we can move closer to socialism or to world revolution . . . there is no sort of goal to go to. . . . If the parents are guilty, punish them, if it is impossible to leave the children send them into exile but let it painlessly reflect on the children."[139]

There would be nothing painless about the initial stages of dekulakization and exile. The "confiscative-repressive" nature of the policy at the outset provided no guarantees for the future; instead it simply and brutally constituted one enormous push to purge the countryside of the enemy, the kulak. As a result, the planning and administrative infrastructure of the operation continually lagged behind the desperate reality of the exiles' experience. As the exile families languished in temporary residence, the central and regional bureaucracies would begin the task of figuring out exactly what to do with the exiles. The regime would also be forced to confront some of the massive injustices of the operation.

3

No Pretensions to Reality: Forced Labor and the Bergavinov Commission

A task of this type is to a certain degree unprecedented, and so a strictly thought-out plan of measures as well as the material prerequisites—people, food, materials—had not been at the disposal of the regional committee, [which] had to decide issues on the fly.
—from a Northern Territory Party Committee
report to Moscow, March 1930

The first stage of dekulakization was repressive mayhem, centered around arrests and property expropriations, and focused on the expulsion of the kulaks.[1] There had been almost no concrete planning for what would happen to the kulaks after they were banished from their villages. Plans for the massive resettlement of the kulaks arose, to use a refrain from the complaints of provincial bureaucrats, *na khodu*, or on the fly, at the very time that tens of thousands of peasant families were already in transit or in temporary housing in the exile towns. As the disaster of the initial stages of the campaign began to unfold, Moscow slowly realized that it needed to concern itself with more than just the repressive aspects of the dekulakization campaign.

On 11 January 1930, Iagoda questioned his OGPU lieutenants as to the feasibility of organizing special settlements where the kulaks could work without guards. Three months later, on 12 April, he wrote a memorandum in which he raised the issue of "transforming the camps to a new arrangement." "Now," he wrote, "the camps are only holding pens for prisoners whose labor we use only for today. . . . We need to turn the *camps into colonization villages* without any expectation of a set period of imprisonment. The philanthropic stimulus of shortening sentences for good behavior is not only unsuitable, but even often harmful. It (this stimulus) gives the false impression of the 'correction' of the prisoners, a hypocritical kind of penance [*poslushanie*] necessary for bourgeois society but not for us."

Iagoda continued, "We need to colonize the North in the fastest of tempos." To do this, he proposed a plan in which all prisoners would be transferred to special settlements. "We will give groups (1,500 people) of selected prisoners in various regions lumber and have them build huts where they will be able to live. Those who wish can send for their families. A commandant will manage [the settlements]. The settlements will have from 200 to 300 families. In their free time, when forestry work is complete, they, especially the weaker ones, can raise pigs, mow hay, catch fish. In the beginning, they will live on rations, later [they will live] on their own account. . . . In the winter the entire population will go to forestry work or other work that we assign. . . . [And] instead of the 10–15 people who guard now the thousands [of prisoners], there will be one commandant. . . . We must do this now, immediately."[2]

In the spring and summer of 1930, Moscow finally began to address the fate of the exiles, preparing to launch Iagoda's ambitious plans for a new kind of penal servitude. By this time, however, their situation was verging on catastrophe and Stalin faced protest from within his own government. Moscow responded to the enormous atrocities of the first stage of dekulakization with the construction of a dense and overlapping bureaucracy to manage the special settlements and the admission that there had been what it called isolated cases of "incorrect dekulakization."

Planning "On the Fly"

Through most of 1930, administrative responsibility for the special settlers—both on paper and in practice—was confused and conflict-ridden. Centrally, the OGPU was the most important actor in the planning and implementation of dekulakization for first and second category kulaks.[3] The OGPU had worked with its regional chiefs in planning for the numerical size of the contingents of deportees, transport, temporary housing, and security measures, working in coordination with the Molotov Politburo Commission on dekulakization in January 1930. Beginning in late January, ad hoc commissions under the regional party committees or soviet executive committees were set up in the major exile territories to assist the OGPU in carrying out local planning for resettlement.[4] Still, the primary emphasis at this stage was operative work on deportation, rather than the much more difficult issue of what to do with the exiles once they had arrived in the regions of exile.[5]

It was only in March, as the first parties of exiles were in transit or settling into temporary housing, that a central coordinating commission on the exiles was established. Tolmachev, the Commissar of Internal

Affairs, chaired a commission on the coordination of special settler affairs. Under the auspices of the Russian Republic Council of People's Commissars, the Tolmachev Commission worked from 9 March to 13 August 1930 and included representatives from the Commissariat of Health, the OGPU, and the Procurator's office. At the same time, similar commissions were established under the soviet executive committees of the main exile regions.[6] On 1 April 1930—four months into the operation—a second coordinating commission, this one within the All-Union Council of People's Commissars, was set up under the chairmanship of V. V. Shmidt, Deputy Chair of the Council of People's Commissars and Deputy Commissar of agriculture. The Shmidt Commission entrusted all work on agriculture and "cultural and economic servicing" to the Russian Republic Commissariat of Agriculture. The Commissariat of Internal Affairs was responsible for the administration of the special settlements, while the economic enterprises employing special settler labor were charged with the actual construction of the special settlements.[7] Both the Shmidt and the Tolmachev commissions were charged with the supervision and coordination of special settlers' affairs without any clear demarcation of functions or responsibilities between the two.[8]

Despite attempts at centralization and coordination, conflict and a lack of clear lines of authority between different agencies plagued the administration of special settler affairs. Both the Tolmachev and the Shmidt commissions were constantly forced to prod, cajole, and threaten the commissariats to provide food supplies, construction materials, transport vehicles, medicines, and myriad other services. Further, the role of the omnipresent OGPU was becoming increasingly unclear. In April, Tolmachev complained that, "Up to now, there is not full clarity in this [i.e., the role of the OGPU in special settler affairs]. Where the functions of the OGPU end and where the work of the regular apparatus begins, no one knows at all."[9]

After mid-August 1930, when the Tolmachev Commission was dissolved, special settler affairs became increasingly decentralized, with overall responsibility transferred to republic-level commissariats and regional soviets. Although almost every commissariat and a variety of other republic-level agencies had some role in special settler affairs, the two primary roles belonged to the Commissariat of Agriculture for the Russian Republic (for those settlers involved in agriculture) and the Supreme Council of the National Economy for the Russian Republic (for those in industrial employment).[10] The OGPU, in the meantime, was charged with the amorphously titled "chekist (or police) servicing," while the Commissariat of Internal Affairs continued to be responsible for the administration of the special settlements and the supervision of the settlement commandants.[11] Although a Council of People's Commissars commission had begun work on a charter for the administration of the special settlements in March, as of late August this work was not yet complete and the OGPU complained that no one knew exactly what to do with the settlers.[12]

On the provincial level, the regional soviet assumed responsibility for special settler issues throughout 1930. A troika, or three-member commission, led by the regional soviet chair with representation from the OGPU and the regional land administration coordinated work on resettlement, provisions, land, and labor.[13] Responsibility for the organization of the agricultural settlement of the exiles belonged to the regional administration of migration, which worked through county-level land organs and county colonization parties and answered to the Main Migration Administration under the Russian Republic-level Commissariat of Agriculture as well as the regional soviet.[14] The forestry industry and other industries employing special settlers were responsible for all employment issues and the construction of the special settlements; they, in turn, worked through their local agencies and answered jointly to the Russian Republic-level Supreme Council of the National Economy and the regional soviet.[15] The special settlements were subordinated directly to the district soviet and its administrative department (representing the Commissariat of Internal Affairs at the district level), and led by a district soviet-appointed commandant confirmed by the county soviet and the OGPU and (in theory) assisted by one policeman (*militsioner*) for every fifty families.[16]

Throughout 1930 and early 1931, administrative anarchy and poor coordination characterized special resettlement affairs, compounding what was intrinsically a disaster in the making.[17] In a speech to the Communist fraction of the All-Russian Central Executive Committee, A. S. Kiselev inveighed against the absence of coordination and responsibility in special resettlement, warning that "[s]omeone must answer for this."[18] On 18 October 1930, in an attempt to recentralize special settler affairs, a Russian Republic Council of People's Commissars decree entrusted the jurist E. G. Shirvindt with overall observation of special resettlement business, calling upon all Russian republic-level agencies to keep him regularly informed.[19] Meanwhile, constant refrains of inadequate personnel, overstrained local resources, communication problems, and an absence of direction percolated up from the regions to Moscow. To make matters worse, the OGPU's obsession with secrecy hindered the practical work of special resettlement. The Commissariat of Agriculture was forced to request permission from the OGPU Special Department for access to classified materials concerning the special settlers. Only on 19 November did the commissariat's Secret Sector announce the declassification of issues of finance, housing, supply, land management, and agriculture. Issues relating to the actual districts of resettlement, the internal regime of the special settlements, the functions of the settlement commandants, and the employment and pay of settler labor remained classified.[20]

From start to finish, everyone and yet no one answered for the fate of the special settlers. Planning and work on special resettlement would continue to occur "on the fly" according to provincial officials, because, as a 9 April 1930 Northern Territory soviet report put it, it was impossible to plan everything in advance.[21]

Desiderata

In a 19 June 1930 letter to Syrtsov, Tolmachev wrote, "It is completely obvious that under these circumstances the employment of these hungry masses of kulak exiles is completely unrealistic."[22] It was not only unrealistic; it was still not clear exactly how and where the special settlers were to be employed. This is not to say that there was not a general idea for the use of the special settlers. There was a prehistory of discussions concerning penal labor. The fact that it was to be *kulak* penal labor was what was new.

Soviet planners faced many economic and geographic realities that the revolution of 1917 had left unchanged. The task of attracting a permanent labor force to the remote, resource-rich territories of the far north and east was a perennial problem for the Russian Imperial government. Colonization, administrative exile, and serf or penal labor were common solutions since the time of Peter the Great.[23] In the 1920s, Soviet economic planners would again look to these solutions as a means for opening up the vast natural resources of the Soviet Union.

In 1925, G. L. Piatakov, then deputy chairman of the Supreme Council of the National Economy, penned a secret report for his chairman F. E. Dzerzhinskii (who also continued to head the Soviet secret police), outlining a plan for the use of penal labor in the extraction of mineral resources in a series of remote regions above the Arctic Circle, on Sakhalin Islands, in Nerchinsk, and in Kazakhstan. The report built upon an existing legislative framework, which included as standard penal practice compulsory labor for inmates in places of detention (from 1918) and the use of administrative exile (from 1922).[24] In fact, as early as 1923, Dzerzhinskii had insisted that "we will have to organize forced labor (penal servitude) at camps for colonizing underdeveloped areas that will be run with iron discipline. We have sufficient locations and space." He also noted that "the republic cannot be merciful toward criminals and cannot waste resources on them; they must cover the costs associated with their care with their own labor."[25]

In 1928 the Commissar of Justice, N. M. Ianson, reiterated these ideas in a recommendation to utilize penal labor in the northern timber industry to stimulate the all-important hard-currency-generating timber export industry. His recommendations seemed eminently practical given the instability of peasant seasonal labor in the north and the overcrowding and expense of prisons. Moreover, Ianson's suggestions arose within the context of a fierce and ongoing institutional battle for control of the penal population being waged by the People's Commissariat of Internal Affairs for the Russian Republic (NKVD—Ianson's chief rival) and OGPU (Ianson's temporary ally). Ianson—and others—looked hopefully to the OGPU's penal system of labor camps as a solution to a variety of problems.[26]

The First Five-Year Plan pushed the issue of penal labor to the top of the agenda for Soviet planners, with Iagoda spearheading these initiatives. In April 1929, the Commissariats of Justice and Internal Affairs and OGPU jointly submitted a report calling for the creation of a network of labor camps that would be self-supporting and based on labor service. The authors of the report recommended that all prisoners serving sentences of three or more years be transferred to such camps.[27] One month later, the Politburo endorsed most of the report's conclusions and, in late June 1929, issued an extremely important decree calling for the expansion of the existing camp system, the creation of additional facilities, and the transfer of all prisoners serving more than three years to the OGPU for its work in colonization and the economic exploitation of a series of northern and eastern territories.[28] With Stalin's support, the OGPU had bested its institutional rivals and taken control of a rapidly expanding penal population and forced labor system.

Within this context, the timing of dekulakization was, in a sense, fortuitous for it was to provide the massive labor resources to fulfill the desiderata of the economic colonization of the Soviet Union's remote hinterlands. Yet there was no concrete plan on how and where to use kulak labor. As late as December 1929, the Politburo commission responsible for drawing up the legislation on collectivization still assumed that the kulaks would be used mainly as a disenfranchised labor force within the emerging collective farm order.[29] It was only on 11 January 1930 that Iagoda began to ask his OGPU associates if it would be possible to organize special settlements where the kulaks could work without guards.[30] One month later, on 11 February 1930, Evdokimov wrote to the Northern OGPU boss, Austrin, asking how the kulaks could be employed.[31]

Northern Territory party boss Bergavinov had been calling for the creation of a permanent cadre of forestry workers as a solution to the instability of seasonal labor from at least mid-1929.[32] I. D. Kabakov and R. I. Eikhe, Bergavinov's counterparts in the Urals and Siberia, shared his visions of regional development, even though neither would be quite as enthusiastic about "importing" vast numbers of forced laborers once it became clear that they would have to house and settle them in such a compressed time period. Still, there was considerable confusion over how best to utilize this seemingly endless supply of unfree labor. The earliest plans envisioned kulak labor in the North and Siberia primarily employed in agricultural pursuits, working seasonally in forestry; in the Urals and Kazakhstan, the exiles were to be used primarily in forestry and industry, while in the Far East they would work in the gold mines.[33] From the outset, the provincial leadership in the Urals was determined to "break" the kulak mentality while exploiting the exiles to maximum advantage by preventing them from engaging in any agricultural work and thereby ensuring that they were materially dependent on their industrial jobs.[34]

In the North, it was not clear what role the exiles would play in agriculture and "agricultural colonization." Initially, only about 15 percent of the exiles, mainly in the Vologda area where colonization land funds had been made available previously, were to work exclusively in agriculture. Most of the remainder of the work force would work primarily in forestry, while farming "on the side" to supplement their diet and income.[35] By 1 April, however, the Council of People's Commissars was insisting that it was "impossible" to use the kulaks as a permanent labor force in forestry; instead, they were to be settled in unchartered (neustavnye) collective farms from which they could leave for forestry work on a seasonal basis.[36]

This uncertainty continued through the summer of 1930, changing only in mid-August when, perhaps not coincidentally, the Tolmachev Commission was liquidated. At this time, the Council of People's Commissars ruled that only those settlers who were physically unable to work in forestry could be employed exclusively in agriculture.[37] The ruling seemed to fit well with the ongoing activities of most county and district party, soviet, and forestry agencies, which in any case had been "settling" exile families on lands poorly suited for agriculture, generally in the midst of the dense forests the families were to uproot.[38] By late October 1930, it was perfectly clear that resettlement in the North was to provide a year-round labor force for the forestry industry. Special settlements were to be set up near the forestry industry's enterprises. Agricultural pursuits were to be strictly supplementary for all but the non-able-bodied.[39]

This emphasis fit Bergavinov's ambitions; he had argued all along that the special settlements should be primarily for the needs of the forestry industry.[40] As he told his subordinates in the North, the kulaks "can be an enormous labor and economic factor in the development of the productive forces of the region" and "a direct economic benefit for the country and the region ... for in this way we will resolve the colonization question and surmount the sharp deficit in labor power and open up new areas of the North."[41]

By 1931, debate had ceased on the nature of special settler employment: the exiles were intended to serve as an unfree labor force for colonization and the extraction of the Soviet Union's vast natural resources. Consideration of special settlement issues from here on was linked directly to labor resource needs. According to a 1932 report on special setters working in the Urals' forestry industry, "the basic and main aim of the permanent settlement of exiled kulak families in forest areas is the colonization of underpopulated and weakly exploited forests by way of drawing in special settlers to forestry work and creating from them a permanently settled forestry labor force."[42] Although camp labor was increasingly used in these same pursuits, it was assumed to be far less costly to maintain the special settlements, given the relatively low costs of supporting their administrative structures.[43] And by deporting entire families for an as yet undefined period, the state would ensure the continuing replenishment of its labor force, while at the same time "tearing the evil" of kulakdom from its very roots.[44]

The Bergavinov Commission

Partly as a result of the "on the fly" approach and partly as the inevitable result of a policy that could only have led to disaster, the situation of the special settlers quickly deteriorated. The conditions of transport and temporary settlement of the families in the towns of the exile regions were deplorable, leading to mass outbreaks of disease and increasing numbers of death. There were not enough resources to cope with the monumentality of what Bergavinov was to call "an unprecedented task" full of "devilish difficulties."[45] In the meantime, tens of thousands of peasant exiles were writing desperate letters of complaint and submitting petitions for redress.[46]

In response, on 5 April 1930, the Politburo created a Central Committee commission, known as the Bergavinov Commission, to review cases of families incorrectly exiled to the North. Chaired by Bergavinov, its membership consisted of Tolmachev, I. G. Eremin (representing the Commissariat of Justice), and E. A. Tuchkov (representing the OGPU).[47]

At their first meeting on 13 April, Bergavinov instructed the commission on how its work was to proceed. Each of the Northern Territory's four counties, minus the Komi Republic, would be assigned a subcommission to organize the work of a series of troikas that would visit the sites of temporary residence of the special settlers. The members of the Bergavinov Commission would personally examine 3,000 to 5,000 petitions each, as well as instructing the county subcommissions during seven-day site visits (Bergavinov in Vologodskii County; Eremin in Severno-Dvinskii County; Tolmachov in Niandomskii County and some districts of Arkhangel'skii County; and Tuchkov in the city of Arkhangel'sk). Bergavinov also enlisted the services of the Northern Territory OGPU boss, Austrin, to select and verify petitions, and mobilized an additional 150 people to serve on the subcommissions and troikas.[48]

According to Bergavinov, the incorrectly exiled included elderly people deported without able-bodied family members; children under sixteen without adult relatives; teachers, doctors, agronomists, and other members of the rural intelligentsia not personally engaged in agriculture; families of Red army soldiers currently in service; Red army veterans; and poor and middle peasant families. To determine the socioeconomic status of families seeking redress, the inspectors were to ascertain a family's property situation *before* the revolution and in the period leading up to exile. They were also to investigate if petitioners had family members who had served in the White armies of the civil-war era; engaged in trade, owned mills, or operated other rural enterprises; hired labor or rented land; were former *pomeshchiki* (landlords) or kulaks; had been convicted of crimes; or (from an opposite political angle) had family working in industry or the Red army (past or present service).[49]

A little more than two weeks after its initial organizing meeting, the commission reconvened to discuss the results of its work. Of the 46,261 families exiled to the North, 35,000 had submitted petitions for redress; from these, the commission succeeded in reviewing 23,360 petitions (see table 3 in appendix).[50] The protocols of the commission concluded that 10 percent (2,341) of families had been exiled incorrectly; 12.3 percent (2,863) of families were earmarked for further questioning by the OGPU to be completed by 1 June. The commission proposed to return only 2–3 percent of incorrect exiles—those with revolutionary or civil-war service or family members currently in the army. The remainder were to be settled in the North as "free citizens with privileged conditions." The commission also requested compensation or the return of property from the counties from which the incorrectly exiled originated.[51]

The protocols of the meeting contained a counterproposal submitted by Tolmachev and Eremin. They suggested substituting all of these percentages with a resolution that read, "given that it is impossible fully to define precisely the numbers of incorrect exiles" and taking into account that some of the troikas found up to 60 percent of cases to be incorrect, "10 percent incorrect exiles is a minimal figure." Moreover, they added, it was "essential to return all 10 percent of incorrect exiles" to their homes.[52]

Tolmachev and Eremin's objections more accurately reflected the work of the subcommissions. In Arkhangel'skii County, the subcommission had determined that 28.3 percent of families were incorrectly exiled and 7.6 percent questionable; in Vologodskii County, 17 percent incorrect and 23.6 percent questionable; in the city of Arkhangel'sk, 35.4 percent incorrect and 9.8 percent questionable; in Niandomskii County, 13.8 percent incorrect and 14.2 percent questionable; and in Severo-Dvinskii County, 6.3 percent incorrect and 9.3 percent doubtful.[53] An additional summary table from the Arkhangel'sk Regional Communist Party archives provides a total of 15.9 percent incorrect exiles and 16.5 percent questionable for the entire region.[54] There is some indication that Bergavinov came into conflict with the Vologodskii County subcommission, where he was on site, revising their originally very high figures downward.[55] Finally, there was confusion in the subcommissions as to whether incorrect exiles should be returned home. The first secretary of the Severo-Dvinskii County party committee, I. A. Serkin, wrote a report to Eremin on 22 April in which, in addition to mapping out the vast challenges that the operation presented the county, noted that he had received 10,000 complaints about incorrect exiles (more than the total number of exiles in the county) and was unsure what to do with incorrect exiles. From the point of view of colonization, according to Serkin, it would be best to keep the incorrect exiles in place, but, he continued, that decision would not serve as a "decisive correction of the political line in collective farm construction" (that is, ending the excesses) and therefore it would be better to return incorrect exiles to their homes.[56]

While the commission's work was still in progress, the OGPU entered the picture. Arguably the most important actor in the actual deportation exercise, the OGPU had been concerned with the large numbers of local "excesses" in dekulakization from the first days of the operation.[57] On 28 March, before the Politburo or the Council of People's Commissars had become involved in the issue of incorrect exiles, the OGPU instructed its police bosses in the North, Urals, and Siberia to check into all complaints of incorrect exile. All poor and weak (*malomoshchnyi*) middle peasants and families of Red army soldiers who could prove their status were to be placed in separate barracks under "improved" conditions with the promise that they would be resettled (not returned) in villages with all necessary provisions. On 25 April, shortly before the Bergavinov Commission reconvened, Iagoda heard from Northern OGPU boss Austin that Tolmachev wanted to return all incorrect exiles, to which he (Iagoda) replied that they should not be returned "under any circumstances," noting that this would vastly complicate the OGPU's work. On the same day, Iagoda told Austrin that the return operation must be worked out carefully and that under no circumstances should "*makhnovtsy, petliurovtsy, savnikovtsy*" (anti-Bolshevik civil-war partisans), and other "bandit elements" be returned. Others might be returned after the commission had concluded its work and to coincide in time with the sending of other kulaks into exile.[58] In the end, the OGPU would be satisfied with the commission's (or Bergavinov's) decision to return only a small number of the incorrect exiles according to restricted categories.[59]

Before it met to discuss the commission's report on 10 May,[60] Bergavinov personally lobbied the Politburo, arguing for a downward revision of the numbers of incorrect exiles. He wrote that he could not accept the figures of 10 percent (incorrect exiles) and 12.3 percent (questionable cases) as definitive. According to Bergavinov, the commission had only reviewed the "social situation" of families, failing to take into account, for example, that many, especially from Ukraine and Belorussia, had "bandit pasts," were from border areas, or had contacts with Poland or Romania.[61] Given the OGPU's concerns to purge the countryside of "bandit elements" and to clear border areas of "social aliens," these comments surely registered positively with the Politburo. Bergavinov insisted that no more than 6 percent of families fell under the category of incorrect exiles. The "rumors" regarding the supposed high numbers of incorrect exiles, he claimed, amounted to no more than a "slander on local party and soviet organizations and through them on the policy of the party." He wrote that Tolmachev, who had come up with a figure of 44 percent incorrect exiles in Arkhangel'skii County, had arrived prepared to find excesses with his statistics predetermined. According to Bergavinov, Tolmachev had instructed the county subcommission "not to be timid" (*ne stesniaisia*) in reporting mistakes. In what amounted to a political indictment, Bergavinov concluded that Tolmachev's approach was "not only a liberal approach, but something more, which does not strengthen the position of the party in this historic cause."[62]

On 10 May 1930, the Politburo approved the Bergavinov Commission's report, accepting Bergavinov's lower figures of 6 percent (incorrect exiles) and 8 percent (questionable cases). It concurred that only Red army veterans and their families should be allowed to return home, while the rest could be resettled in the North as "free citizens with special consideration." The Politburo protocols ended with: "C[omrade] Tolmachev's proposal is rejected."[63]

A Tale of Two Men

The Politburo protocols that ratified the Central Committee Commission's report contain the shadow of a hint that not all was well in the work of the Bergavinov Commission. What had happened in the commission and why did Tolmachev, seconded by Eremin, differ with Bergavinov? Did Tolmachev represent, as Bergavinov would put it, not only "a liberal approach, but something more . . ."[64] to the policies of the Communist Party? The story of the Bergavinov Commission is a tale of two men enmeshed in bureaucratic politics and holding in their hands the fate of thousands of peasant families.

Sergei Adamovich Bergavinov was born in the Smolensk area in 1899. He joined the Bolshevik Party in 1917. He saw action on the civil-war fronts of Ukraine, at the head of a Cheka (the civil-war-era secret police) detachment. Graduating from the civil war with the medal of the Order of the Red Banner, he entered full-time party work in the 1920s, first as a party instructor and then as head of the Northern Territory party committee. In 1926, he led the purge of the Arkhangel'sk Regional party committee and was subsequently appointed first secretary of the regional party committee in May 1927. In 1929, when the Northern Territory administrative unit was created, he became its party's first secretary. He remained in that position until March 1931 when he was recalled to Moscow to serve as chairman of *Soiuzlesprom* (the Forestry Corporation under the Supreme Council of the National Economy).[65]

The thirty-one-year-old Bergavinov came to the North as a stalwart Stalin man whose first baptism of fire had been with the secret police. He was determined to lead the "socialist transformation" of the North. He set out his ambitions in a letter to Gosplan chairman G. M. Krizhizhanovskii: "Perhaps I am a passionate man who wants to take on everything immediately [and] 'wholesale' [*chokhom*]. . . . We ourselves here are going all out with hellish energy, [we] need only to find a fulcrum . . . and we will transform the economy of the entire region. . . . This [the forestry industry] is an all-union cause, and we are pioneers. . . . We will succeed gradually in turning ourselves into a wooden Donbas."[66]

Bergavinov's reference to a "wooden Donbas" drew an analogy between the resource-rich North, with its vast forests and undermanned logging industry, and the coal mining powerhouse of the Donbas in the south. All Bergavinov needed to accomplish his aims was the "fulcrum"—a steady supply of labor to colonize the North and serve as a permanent cadre of forestry workers.[67] The opportunity to attain his grandiose vision of the North came, conveniently, with the collectivization of Soviet agriculture, whose auxiliary policy of dekulakization resulted in the massive "freeing up" of what would turn into an army of unfree laborers.

Bergavinov was an active participant in the central planning operations in Moscow that determined the bureaucratic infrastructure and general contours of the collectivization and dekulakization campaigns. Commuting between Moscow and Arkhangel'sk in December 1929 and January 1930, Bergavinov first served on the December Politburo Commission on collectivization and then, from 15 January, on Molotov's Central Committee Commission on dekulakization and kulak resettlement.[68] The unrealistic planning that went on in Moscow did not sit well with Bergavinov, who complained endlessly about Moscow's inattention to "practical" problems like temporary housing and funding. At a closed meeting of his regional party committee in mid-June, he described the operation's current state as "wretched."[69] Nevertheless, Bergavinov was absolutely determined to carry through with an operation that would facilitate the creation of his wooden Donbas. Unlike Tolmachev, he never expressed any personal regret about the human tragedy that was unfolding before his eyes.

Tolmachev, however, was a very different brand of Communist. In 1930, he played a key role in the kulak resettlement operation. In addition to his responsibilities as a people's commissar, he chaired the Russian Republic Council of People's Commissar's coordinating commission on kulak resettlement, which functioned during the spring and summer of 1930.[70] He also chaired a commission on epidemics among the special settler population as well as serving as the coordinator for the regional counterparts of the Bergavinov Commission.[71] Tolmachev was arguably the most important representative of the government engaged in the resettlement operation.[72]

Born in 1886, Vladimir Nikolaevich Tolmachev was the son of teachers. An "Old Bolshevik," he joined the Social Democratic Party in 1904. He was a member of the Kostroma party committee during the 1905 Revolution. He was arrested the following year and spent the next four years in exile in the Vologda area in the North. During the 1917 revolution and civil war, Tolmachev was in southern Russia, engaged in Bolshevik Party work in Crimea. From 1922 to 1924, he was the chairman of the Kuban-Chernomorskii soviet executive committee, and from 1924 to 1928 deputy chairman of the North Caucasus Regional soviet executive committee. In 1928, Tolmachev moved to Moscow to become Commissar of Internal Affairs for the Russian Republic.[73] Thirteen years senior to Bergavinov, Tolmachev was an Old Bolshevik whose political formation had taken place before the revolution and civil war.

Tolmachev's work in the Bergavinov Commission brought him the closest to the reality of what was happening to the special settlers. Assigned to cover on-site inspections in Niandomskii County and along the railroad routes of Arkhangel'skii County, Tolmachev personally visited temporary living facilities and spoke to the deportees. It is clear from his correspondence that Tolmachev's visit to the North had a profound impact on him. Some of his experiences are reflected in a letter of 16 April that he sent to D. Z. Lebed', the deputy chairman of the Russian Republic Council of People's Commissars. He wrote, "[I] consider it absolutely urgent to report to you the first observations that I have made in my cursory acquaintance with the situation in the Northern Territory. In the entire Northern Territory, there are about 45,000 kulak families . . . from whom the able-bodied, sent off to different places of work, [make up] 36,000 people, while the remainder, that is 122,000 people, are women, children, and other non-able-bodied. They are billeted in barracks along the Vologda-Arkhangel'sk and Viatka-Kotlas railroad lines. According to information received from different local sources, 25 to 35 percent of the exiles are INCORRECTLY EXILED. Of course, these are not definitive data, based as they are on cursory observations, but they speak for themselves. . . ."

Tolmachev promised to report back in seven to ten days with more precise figures on incorrect exiles, and added, almost parenthetically, that "one could imagine" that the situation of third-category kulaks (families partially expropriated and left outside the collective farms in their native districts) was even worse. He then went on to describe the living conditions of the special settlers: "THE MOST EXTREME AND SHARP ISSUE IS HOUSING. People are billeted in 750 barracks, hastily assembled from logs. The crowding is unbelievable—there are places where each person has one-tenth of a square meter of living space in multitiered bunks (the space is smaller than a coffin). There are no floors in the barracks, the roofs are made of poles and loosely sprinkled hay and crumbled mud. As a rule, the temperature does not go above 4 degrees [Celsius]. [Everything] is lice-ridden. Along with the miserly feeding, and for many almost nothing, all this creates colossal [rates of] illness, and death among children. With the advent of spring (the second half of April, May), the earth in the barracks will melt (many [barracks] were built on marshy soil), [the roofs] will begin to leak and ALL THE POPULATION WILL STICK TOGETHER IN A MUDDY, LIVING, ROTTEN MESS."

Tolmachev continued by illustrating the consequences of the situation. He wrote that from March through the first third of April, 6,007 of the 8,000 exile children in the city of Arkhangel'sk were ill with scarlet fever, measles, flu, pneumonia, diphtheria. Eighty-five percent of all children were sick and some 587 had died. "All this indicates," he continued, "that in two–three weeks, we will be witnesses to still worse phenomena if some sort of decisive measures are not taken. Up to now the exiles have fed themselves with their own food, but now only enough is left for a few days and IF WE DO NOT ARRANGE FOOD PROVISIONS, THEN WHOLESALE HUNGER WILL SET IN. IT IS ESSENTIAL IMMEDIATELY FOR NARKOMTORG [the People's Commissariat of Trade] TO PERMIT [its] LOCAL ORGANS TO DISTRIBUTE FOOD FREE OF COST AND [provide] PROVISIONS BEFORE THE SNOW MELTS CUTTING OFF MANY AREAS." Having described in his own words his still cursory impressions, Tolmachev concluded his letter to Lebed' with what can only be described as a condemnation of the way the operation had thus far proceeded: "The plan of resettlement ... has been put together in a hypothetical way with no pretensions to reality. Up to now, they treat the exiles like dangerous criminals, keeping them in the strictest isolation. This precludes the possibility for them to use their own initiative and independence, leaving us with full responsibility for servicing them. You see, they are not crates, not cargo, but living people, primarily [people with] great initiative and practical skills. We need to give them some scope for these qualities and they themselves will manage to do a lot. . . . I greatly fear that . . . this business will miscarry." Tolmachev ended his letter by noting that he was sending the letter only to Lebed' with the instructions that the information be shared only with "those who need to know."[74]

Tolmachev also wrote to the Northern Territory soviet executive committee, pleading for it to get involved. In a letter of 17 April to S. I. Komissarov, the chairman of the Northern Territory soviet executive committee, about the plight of the families, he wrote: "Many families here do not know where their fathers [heads of households] are, it is essential to organize immediately an information bureau in order to establish contact among family members. Many families do not have *ankety* [the standardized forms that were supposed to accompany each family, listing pertinent biographical and socioeconomic information], therefore making the work of the troikas more difficult. Direct the commandant to send home children under fifteen who were sent without relatives; carry out an inspection of the ill, weak, etc. Children's provisioning is not normal. Milk is essential. . . . There is no fat [in their diet]." Tolmachev ended this letter with a plea that recurs in his letters as almost a call of desperation—a request for shoes for the children.[75]

One week later, Tolmachev wrote the regional soviet executive committee again, decrying the passivity of local soviets and branch commissariats. He argued that the district soviet executive committees had been hindered by lack of instructions and the extreme secrecy surrounding the campaign as it unfolded in OGPU hands.[76] He reiterated the necessity of organizing some sort of information bureau to aid in reuniting families, adding that the families of first-category kulaks exiled without the heads of households (who had been arrested and interned in labor camps) were "completely helpless." Tolmachev recommended substituting exile for imprisonment for these men. He also described the filth of the barracks and the widespread disease, especially among children. He noted that there were many arbitrary arrests of visiting relatives and even the carters who had transported families from their villages. He ended by repeating that starvation was imminent.[77]

Tolmachev returned to Arkhangel'sk on 28 April. The next day, he met with Bergavinov and the other commission members. There was heated disagreement at this meeting. Tolmachev, supported by Eremin and possibly even Tuchkov,[78] objected to the low findings put forth by Bergavinov without any apparent statistical foundation, and argued that it was not possible to specify the exact numbers of incorrect exiles given the enormity of the excesses and in light of the fact that some troikas had concluded that up to 60 percent of families had been incorrectly exiled. Tolmachev also argued for the return of *all* families who had been incorrectly exiled.[79]

In the meantime, Bergavinov had somehow managed to obtain a copy of Tolmachev's letter to Lebed'. Bergavinov was appalled. He viewed Tolmachev's dissent as a direct attack on party policy and used the letter to argue his case with the Politburo that Tolmachev had arrived ready to conclude high percentages of incorrect exiles and had "slandered" local party and soviet organizations.[80] Bergavinov's attack fed directly into Stalin and the OGPU's own designs to marginalize Tolmachev and to push the Commissariat of Internal Affairs out of penal affairs.

The conflict between Bergavinov and Tolmachev was played out against the backdrop of a much larger conflict in Moscow, a struggle between Stalin and the Politburo, on the one side, and the Council of People's Commissars, on the other. In this struggle, Bergavinov represented the Communist Party and Tolmachev, the Council of People's Commissars. According to the historian Ronald Suny, "Stalin pushed hard for the end of any duality between party and state" in the early 1930s, seeing the latter as an obstacle and self-perceived counterweight to the party.[81] In fact, Stalin's conflict with state institutions had more to do with the prominence of leaders associated with the Right Opposition within the Council than with any concern with duality per se, representing Stalin's ultimate consolidation of power over party and state.

The Right Opposition had been the last real political challenge to Stalin. Led by such Communist Party luminaries as Nikolai Bukharin and A. I. Rykov, it opposed the spread of repression in the country-side in 1928 and 1929, pushing for moderation and balance in economic development. Although Stalin soundly defeated the Right at the November 1929 Central Committee Plenum, a number of its former members and sympathizers continued to serve in the All-Union and Russian Republic Councils of People's Commissars. Rykov held on to his position of chairman of the All-Union Council of People's Commissars until the end of 1930. His deputies, A. P. Smirnov and V. V. Shmidt, the head of the Council's commission on special settlers, were also loosely connected with the Right. Tolmachev himself was considered part of a supposed "Rykov school."[82] In addition, a series of other important officials working in the Council of People's Commissars (Russian Republic and All-Union) would be accused of "antiparty" activity in the next few years. These included Syrtsov (the chairman of the Russian Republic Council of People's Commissars), as well as Tolmachev and Smirnov.[83]

However weakened, the Council of People's Commissars managed to act as a counterweight to the Stalinist majority in the Politburo through much of 1930. This was evident in the struggle between the OGPU and the Commissariat of Internal Affairs (Tolmachev's institutional base) over the control of the prison population. It was evident in the struggle within the Bergavinov Commission. And it would be evident later in 1931, when the OGPU took over all special settler affairs from the Commissariat of Internal Affairs.

Stalin despised Tolmachev for his independent views, seeing him as an advocate of the Right Opposition. He refused to appoint Tolmachev chairman of what became the Bergavinov Commission because he viewed him as too "liberal."[84] More ominously, in September 1930, Stalin called Tolmachev "rotten through and through."[85] With the blessing of Stalin, the OGPU assisted in Tolmachev's defeat at the Bergavinov Commission and in government affairs as a whole. By the fall of 1930, the OGPU succeeded in pushing Tolmachev's Commissariat out of special settler affairs. In December 1930, the Commissariat was liquidated.[86] At the same time, both Rykov and Tolmachev lost their positions within the government. Molotov, a Stalinist stalwart, was appointed to be the new chairman of the All-Union Council of People's Commissars, thus putting the government firmly under Stalin's control. The story of the Bergavinov Commission then is more than a parable about a struggle between the dictates of Moscow and the dictates of conscience. It formed a part of the backdrop of Stalin's consolidation of power and the aggrandizement of the OGPU.

Bergavinov and Tolmachev, however, did have something in common. Both resented, in Tolmachev's words, Moscow's "hypothetical" reality, its intricate planning exercises conducted "on the fly" and moored to little more than a grandiose and ideologically-inspired road map in social engineering. Moscow conducted this exercise in mass repression less as a precise surgical operation aimed at incision and transplant than as a military campaign. Moscow issued orders, directives, and threats, and relied on an inefficient and underdeveloped regional administrative machine to wage the war. The cost of this disconnect was a human tragedy of enormous proportions.

Bergavinov and Tolmachev's mutual concern for the practical realities of the special resettlement operation divided over their motivations. Bergavinov looked upon the special settlers as labor, as a "muscle force," to use a term commonly bandied about at the time, to build his wooden Donbas.[87] That, in part, explains his obsession with not returning most categories of incorrect exiles. His civil-war experiences in Ukraine may also partly explain why he was so persistent in arguing for lower percentages of incorrect exiles. (Iagoda also served in Ukraine during the civil war.) According to Bergavinov, there were relatively few "mistakes" among the Ukrainian contingents, who accounted for the lion's share of the Northern exiles. Moreover, those who came from "bandit" stock, especially from border areas, represented a danger for Bergavinov regardless of their socioeconomic status. Tolmachev, in contrast, did not view the settlers as labor, or even simply as kulaks and enemies, but as families and people with "great initiative and practical skills." In fact, in an 11 July 1930 letter to his boss, Syrtsov, Tolmachev argued that the use of kulak labor was "only of secondary significance"; instead, the basic aim was to isolate the kulaks and prevent them from further struggle against the collective farm order.[88] Even after his Council of Commissars coordinating commission was liquidated in August 1930, Tolmachev maintained an interest in the plight of the settlers, carrying on a regular correspondence with Syrtsov on these matters.[89]

The Northern experience of special resettlement was an unmitigated disaster, one that led Moscow to rescind its support for Bergavinov's ambitions and sharply lower the numbers of special settlers destined for the North in 1931. Bergavinov himself was recalled to Moscow in March 1931, where he worked for a short time in the Supreme Council of the National Economy as chairman of the Forestry Corporation. Later that year, he became first secretary of the Far Eastern Regional party committee, serving in that post until his dismissal in 1933, under murky and less than auspicious circumstances. By 1934 he was a delegate to the

Seventeenth Party Congress, listed only as a representative from the Central Black Earth Region, and in 1936 he was reported as heading the political department of the Main Administration of the Northern Sea Route. Tolmachev, whose Commissariat was liquidated at the end of 1930, worked in 1931 as the head of the Main Roads and Transport Administration and was also a member of the Russian Republic Council of the Economy. Accused of oppositional activity as part of the so-called Smirnov, Eismont, and Tolmachev antiparty group in late 1932, he was publicly castigated at the January 1933 Central Committee Plenum, expelled from the Communist Party, and sentenced to three years in prison. In 1937 he was rearrested and, along with Bergavinov, executed as an enemy of the people.[90]

In the end, both the regional and human interests that Bergavinov and Tolmachev attempted to represent ran counter to Stalinist centralization and plans for the special settlers. The deportation of the kulaks was first and foremost a police operation aimed against supposed class enemies and ideological foes. Even with the best of intentions, no commission could have corrected the "mistakes" of the policy. Mistakes instead were the hallmark of the policy, without which it could not have been implemented. At best, this kind of commission was used to offer up scapegoats and serve as propaganda for Moscow. Given these realities, planning "on the fly" and brutality were natural accompaniments to policy. And they would continue into the next stage of the operation, the building of the special settlements.

4

Pencil Points on a Map: Building the Special Settlements

At present we are in such a place that one could not dream of.
—from a special settler's letter intercepted by the OGPU

In a memorandum of 23 April 1930, I. A. Serkin, secretary of the Severo-Dvinskii County party committee, wrote to his boss Bergavinov in Arkhangel'sk that "in the beginning, when the issue of resettlement first arose, many of us did not think out to the end and did not imagine all the complexities of the issue."[1] No one had carried out the necessary studies of land and soil conditions, and some of the land tracts mapped out for the settlers were uninhabitable, completely inaccessible and located on marsh land or in dense woods. Geographical surveys were urgently needed, but on-site work was impossible with snow blanketing the terrain. The land tracts would require an enormous amount of work to create even the most elementary conditions for planting. Serkin warned Bergavinov that it would be unrealistic to expect any income from the special settlers' agricultural pursuits in the first year.[2]

Serkin also warned that the county's economic enterprises—in this case, the forestry industry—were completely unprepared to build the special settlements where the settlers and their families would live and from which a large part of the able-bodied population would commute for seasonal work. The forestry industry instead complained, "we haven't received special funds," "there are no building materials," or there were "no directives" on how to proceed, all of which were true but needlessly formalistic from the point of view of a Serkin or a Bergavinov. Although the majority of able-bodied settlers were now at or near their final destinations, there were still no special settlements: the forestry agencies had not begun work on their construction. To make matters worse, there were shortages of skilled carpenters, tools, and an almost complete absence (apart from lumber) of building materials. Serkin warned Bergavinov that it was possible that they would have to take the "extreme measure" of removing able-bodied settlers from forestry work until September in order to work on the construction of the special settlements. Otherwise, he wrote, "this business with resettlement could lead, without exaggeration, to catastrophe."[3]

Serkin's letter was by no means unusual. The story he told was unfolding all over the Soviet Union, as the first parties of special settlers arrived in the interior. These consisted, mainly, of the able-bodied males who had been forcibly separated from their families in the exile towns. They had come to begin the actual work of raising the special settlements out of the still-frozen earth and found themselves caught up in a bureaucratic nightmare that fully matched the horrors of their surroundings.

In the Northern Territory, they traveled in groups of 500 to 1,000, under convoy and mainly on foot. They marched between 20 to 50 kilometers a day, for anywhere from eight to twenty-five days, stopping to rest only at night.[4] "The first twelve days," one man wrote of the experience, "we had to go on foot for up to 45 versts [approximately 48 kilometers]. Many fell. . . . There were searches on the road and they took our money, sat us down in the cold, simply tortured everybody."[5] Their destinations were, in most cases, 100 to 300 kilometers away from the exile towns where their families languished.[6] If their first stop was a logging camp, they generally found preexisting workers' barracks used earlier by "free" peasant seasonal labor. If they ended their journey at the as-yet-hypothetical special settlements, they might, in the best of cases, live temporarily with peasant families if a village was nearby. In most cases, they made do with hastily erected makeshift abodes—zemlianki or shalashy—to shelter them from the elements of the extreme northern winter.

"We are in the tundra, 200 versts [214 kilometers] from Arkhangel'sk, where there are only samoedy [aboriginals]," wrote one special settler to relatives back in his native village. "Our work is very hard. We work around the clock and rest for only four hours, earning only a piece of bread, and we are very bad off, truthfully I will not survive, we see only forest and water. Any other kind of life we don't see. We don't know when it will be over. . . . If you can manage to send some kind of documents, then I can try to leave since there is no kind of guard over us and many have run away."[7]

The OGPU regularly intercepted letters like this one, desperate pleas for help, often pleas for documents—documents with which to escape, documents to "prove" one was not a kulak, or simply blank or fake documents to save one's life. "Send documents," one man wrote, "what kind is not important, [it is not important] that it is in my name, only that it comes from the rural soviet. . . . You can get that kind of document from somebody, perhaps somebody who is leaving and no longer needs it, but it is essential for me."[8] The constant refrains of this ghostly trail of pleas for help were death and despair: "Don't let us die from hunger," "Hundreds of souls are dying from starvation," "Each day we expect death," "The end is near."[9]

These men had come in advance of their families to begin the construction of the special settlements and what they saw filled them with dread for their own fate and the fate of their families. "They tell us that they will transport you here to us," wrote one young man to his family back in a Northern Territory exile town. "No matter what, don't come. We are dying here. Better to hide, better to die there, but no matter what, don't come here."[10]

Pencil Points on a Map

"The plan of resettlement . . . has been put together in a hypothetical way with no pretensions to reality."[11] That was Tolmachev's diagnosis of the situation. It was only at the end of January that the Molotov Politburo Commission had suggested the formation of a new commission to "concretely" work out where the kulaks would be resettled and how they would be employed.[12] Several days later, similar commissions were set up in the provinces. In the Northern Territory, OGPU boss Austrin chaired the commission, which soon ordered its county party committees to deliver plans for a series of resettlement issues within *five days*, a typical and characteristic bureaucratic devolution of responsibility.[13] Elsewhere, coordinating commissions (other than the OGPU) on resettlement only arose in March and April.[14]

As a rule, the special settlements were intended to be located in the same general, remote territories as labor camps, with plans for the size of populations tied directly to labor and security needs.[15] County- and district-level agencies (party, soviet, economic enterprises) were to choose exact locations for the settlements, working in coordination with "colonization parties" under the jurisdiction of the regional land management and migration administrations, which, in turn, reported to the Main Migration Administration under the Russian Commissariat of Agriculture.[16] The colonization parties began their work in February, just as the first groups of male settlers were making their way into the interior.[17] They attempted, whenever possible, to locate the settlements on lands previously prepared for "free" migration.[18] In most cases, however, the settlements would start off as little more than pencil points on a map, made by an official hard pressed to find places for his region's "native" and "imported" kulaks.

In the Northern Territory, the provincial migration administration managed the early colonization efforts.[19] County-level colonization parties led settler work on the ground from February through May. These parties were responsible for research and preparation of land tracts for the special settlements, and recruited their staff from the county land apparatus.[20] In Vologodskii County, the staff consisted of twenty-five people: seventeen land surveyors, four hydraulic engineers, two road engineers, one land survey inspector, and the head of the party. On 18 April the deputy chairman of the county land apparatus, Tret'iakov, submitted a report on the work of the colonization party. His plans were based on the original calculation of the impending arrival of fifteen thousand families.[21] The settlers were to go mainly to the northeastern and northwestern parts of the county. The colonization party needed to select land tracts—up to 124[22]—with a total of 149,805 hectares (370,018 acres) that could support agriculture pursuits. The party decided first to redistribute colonization tracts that had been cleared and prepared in earlier years for use by free migrants. As for the rest, Tret'iakov wrote that the selections of these tracts would be completed first, given the urgency of the assignment, and "corrections" would undoubtedly be introduced later.[23]

In Severo-Dvinskii County, colonization work proceeded poorly. Here the colonization party chose to place settlers not on agriculturally suitable lands but in areas closest to the center of forestry work and in unsettled regions as far as possible from population points. They mapped out their forty-two land tracts on paper, without any work on the ground. As a consequence, some of the tracts proved completely inaccessible, many located on marsh lands.[24] As early as May, the regional commission on the kulaks censured Severo-Dvinskii County for its choice of land tracts, telling it to select less remote areas.[25] As of mid-July, the colonization party would still be looking for land for half of the settler families.[26]

It ordinarily took about four years to prepare lands for new (free) settlers, yet only three to four months were allotted for these tasks in 1930.[27] What this meant, among other things, was that the settlers themselves would have to prepare the land tracts.[28] They would spend their first two years of exile simply clearing land—in addition to working in forestry and other industries—in the midst of dense woods.[29] In many cases, later "corrections" to the colonization parties' initial work would result in the removal and transfer of entire settlements. The colonization parties received endless blame for this state of affairs; they, in turn—along with everyone else—blamed the economic enterprises.

The economic enterprises employing special settlers were responsible for the construction of the special settlements.[30] Yet in the Northern Territory—and undoubtedly elsewhere as well—it was only at the end of June that the economic enterprises (in this case, *Severoles*, or the Northern Forestry Agency) signed contracts with the colonization parties clarifying issues of responsibility and jurisdiction.[31] As late as September, Tolmachev complained to the Russian Republic Council of People's Commissars that the economic enterprises had done nothing and asked the Council to intervene.[32] In Severo-Dvinskii County, Serkin ordered his party organization to take direct control of construction matters.[33]

The deadline for the completion of the construction of the special settlements was set for 1 September 1930.[34] The enormity of the task was well beyond the capacity of any single agency, let alone the economic enterprises, which had other plan-related priorities. Housing construction was only the most immediate and obvious goal of construction. Plans for settlements of necessity included the construction of auxiliary buildings like storage facilities and barns, administration buildings, bathhouses, stores, and, in time, schools, clinics and hospitals, post offices, and registry offices (ZAGS). The region also had to install telephone and telegraph lines and import from outside the region security personnel (from the OGPU and the Commissariat of Internal Affairs), medical personnel, agronomists, veterinarians, skilled carpenters, and teachers. Apart from lumber, the forestry industry had to bring in all building materials and tools from the outside, while supplying (with the agricultural agencies) manufactured goods, food, horses, cows, and agricultural inventory in the first couple of years. A rudimentary system of banking, credit, and tax collection would be required as well. All these tasks took place in remote, virgin lands, accessible only by boat, small cart, or on foot for a part of the year, given weather conditions. The regional authorities "mobilized" tens of thousands of boats and carts from the local population just to get the settlers to their settlements, never mind the transport of food, supplies, and building materials.[35] The costs were phenomenal, estimated in the tens of millions of rubles.[36]

Nevertheless, schedules were imposed on local agencies with little real hope of fulfillment. In Siberia, a schedule outlined work for every month from February through September 1930. In February, the colonization parties were to choose suitable locations for the special settlements; building materials, food, and other supplies were to be readied for transport; and housing construction was to begin. In March, the supplies would be sent into the interior; road construction and work on medical facilities would begin, continuing into April when the authorities would start to move the settlers into their new settlements. In May, work on building roads would continue and work on clearing land was to begin. In June, all families were to have been transferred. Between July and September, all work was to be completed, including roads and maps of the new settlements.[37] In Vologodskii County, there was an exact schedule for every phase of housing construction, starting with the erection of the walls on 1 July and ending with the completion of stoves and roofs by 20 August.[38] Similar schedules were designed elsewhere, and everywhere they fell obscenely short of completion.

Complicating matters further, the center flooded the regions with madly overdetailed plans, blueprints, and building specifications. The organization and construction of the special settlements was centralized throughout most of the country in 1930, with minimal variations, usually determined by employment needs, local land quality, and agricultural requirements. The settlements were to be set up in isolated areas, usually at least 10 to 50 kilometers from the nearest *sel'sovet* or district soviet.[39] In Siberia, the OGPU forbid special settlements to be built within 150 to 200 kilometers of the border.[40] The average size of the settlement was to be 100 to 200 families (500 to 600 people), with twelve to fifteen houses, a size far larger than most peasant villages in the exile areas.[41] Log houses were each to contain eight families in the Northern Territory, sometimes fewer elsewhere. Each person received four meters of living space, with a maximum of twenty square meters per family. The dimensions of each eight-family house were to be 24.5 × 9.40 × 3.5 meters with a total area of 991.08 meters. Each house was to be separated from the next by not less than 30 meters, allowing for clear observation by the local commandant. In Vologodskii County, there were detailed plans for the construction of bathhouses (*banias*). There was to be one bathhouse per settlement, each 70 square meters long, divided into two parts, one for dressing and one for washing. They were expected to be used by up to 200 people each ten-hour day. Plans were also made for the construction of barns (one per eight families) and storage facilities (one per eight families).[42]

In addition, each family was to receive an allotment of land: 5 hectares (about 12 acres) in the Northern Territory, 10 in Siberia (5 for those working full time in industry), and 2.5 in the Urals where special settlers were to be made dependent upon their industrial employers. The total amount of land apportioned to the settlers was close to 1.5 million hectares (about 3.7 million acres).[43] The settlers themselves faced the gargantuan task of clearing and readying this land for crops.

The Shmidt Commission called for the requisition of some 5,000 horses for the special settlers in the Northern Territory, Siberia, and the Urals. Although they were to be used mainly in agricultural and construction work, the horses' first job would be to transport food and supplies into the interior.[44] Along with horses, the central government would transport other kinds of livestock as well as seed grain for the settlers. Tools and agricultural inventory were also requisitioned—over 18,000 plows, 145,000 scythes, 145,000 sickles, 87,000 pitchforks, and so on.[45] There was a terrible irony to this process given the recent expropriation of the settlers' own livestock, tools, and other belongings.

Plans were also made for the construction over time of medical facilities and schools. In 1930, these plans remained vague, with calls for the Commissariat of Health to "mobilize" doctors from Moscow and Leningrad.[46] In mid-June 1930, the Tolmachev Commission recommended putting off the construction of schools until the following year, given the demands of housing construction.[47] The following year, on 6 June 1931, the Commissariat of Education would call for the introduction of universal education for special settler children, ages eight to eleven, and the construction of one seven-year school for every nine thousand people by 1932.[48] Like the plans for housing, plans for medical and educational facilities would take far longer to implement than the bureaucrats in Moscow imagined.

The central government extended five million rubles credit to the special settlers to set up their farms, also freeing them from all taxes and other government levies until at least 1 January 1934.[49] The all-union budget was to pay for the settlements through 1930, transferring that responsibility to the regional soviets in 1931.[50] Special settler laborers were to be provisioned the same as other workers.[51] However, the economic enterprises were to garnish 25 percent of their wages to pay for the costs of administration, in addition to deducting 1–2 percent for "cultural and educational" expenses.[52]

Tolmachev was right to call attention to the hypothetical nature of special settlement planning. The reality was that this operation was an enormous endeavor, and it was taking place at the same time as the forced industrialization and collectivization of the Soviet Union, vast projects with higher priority and also requiring extensive capital, labor, and resources.

Bureaucratic Quagmire

"To this time, we don't even know how many special settlers there are in the district," complained the Totemskii District (Vologodskii County) party secretary in early July 1930.[53] At about the same time, thousands of miles away in Siberia, the secretary of the Tomsk County soviet executive committee said, "They exiled about 10,000 Siberian kulak families to us. . . . What is happening in the districts where the kulaks were sent, we still don't know. We have now sent out a special expedition. . . . What the situation of these kulaks is, we don't know."[54]

The situation of the kulaks was, in fact, proceeding "wretchedly," to quote Bergavinov.[55] Everywhere, the resettlement project was mired in bureaucratic confusion, conflict, and sheer overload. In the Northern Territory, the forestry industry initially refused to participate in the construction of the special settlements, withholding funds and materials and claiming that this was the OGPU's responsibility.[56] In Siberia, migration agencies complained to the All-Union Commissariat of Agriculture that they had received no directions on "special colonization" despite written requests.[57] In Totma (Vologodskii County), the director of the forestry agency along with a group of engineers wrote a letter to the migration agency "demanding" construction plans and blueprints. They complained in a second letter that they had received no plans about how and where to build the special settlements. They also reported inadequate supplies of materials and personnel as well as the very poor living conditions of the special settlers.[58] In the meantime, regional authorities in Siberia and the Urals pleaded with the Council of People's Commissars to convince the OGPU to assume financial responsibility for the resettlement of "native" first and second category kulaks.[59]

M. A. Korenev wrote a series of letters and reports to his superiors in the Severo-Dvinskii County soviet executive committee about his experiences in special resettlement work. When he arrived in early April in Cherevkova, he immediately went to the district party committee secretary, who told him, "I don't know anything [about special resettlement]. Go to the RIK [district soviet executive committee]." Korenev then proceeded to the RIK, where he was told that they needed him for some other work, claiming he was now in their jurisdiction and therefore under their authority. Korenev refused. He wrote that the district agencies had done nothing in special resettlement work and no one would assume responsibility for construction. In the meantime, the special settlers, many from the Middle Volga, had limited supplies of food, up to 65 percent had no shoes, no one had money, and almost one hundred people had run away. Further, only 5 percent of the settlers were working in construction, the rest having been conscripted to attend to the timber rafting. And there were no materials for construction, except for lumber. Korenev ended the second of his missives, writing, "I am sitting here now and receiving nothing from you, no sort of instructions. I don't know what to do or how to do this or how to carry out the construction plan. . . . Nothing and no one means anything here."[60]

The secretary of the Severo-Dvinskii County party committee, Serkin, complained that the district agencies related to work on resettlement "formally," without any "critical evaluation" of the land tracts on which the settlements would be situated.[61] The protocols of his county commission on resettlement read like a saga of disaster with one "catastrophe" after another, ranging from food supplies to medical services to transport.[62] In mid-July, Serkin complained that no one was controlling the work of the forestry industry in resettlement and called on the party to take direct control. By this time, he had begun to issue the first of a never-ending series of reprimands (*vygovory*) for unsatisfactory work to officials in agencies dealing with the special settlers.[63]

Serkin also noted the tendency for the forestry enterprises to refuse to release special settlers from forestry work for work in settlement construction.[64] This was a problem that was occurring everywhere, given the conflict of interest which the economic enterprises had between their short-term economic interest in fulfilling plans and the long-term interests of settling and therefore acquiring a permanent work force.[65] The Northern Territory soviet executive committee had ordered that 60 percent of all settlers be assigned to work in settlement construction.[66] Yet the Northern Forestry Agency contract called for the settlers to spend 192 days a year in forestry work.[67] According to the head of the OGPU in the Northern Territory, not only were the economic enterprises reluctant to part with their kulak labor; the settlers themselves often ran away from settlement construction because in forestry work they were at least provided with rations.[68]

On 19 June, Bergavinov declared that the situation with resettlement was "clearly threatening . . . a break of this most important political measure of the party." He placed the blame squarely elsewhere—on central organs that had failed to fulfill the party decisions.[69] However, three days earlier, his own party committee had issued a special decision on the course of resettlement in Arkhangel'skii County, writing that the colonization parties and economic enterprises were "criminally disorganized" and not fulfilling the directions of the county and district party committees.[70] The fact of the matter was that the central government had presented the regions with a next to impossible task. In these circumstances, everyone was to blame, but most of all the central institutions that had devised the policy in the first place.

The bureaucratic and administrative quagmire of special resettlement was augmented by inadequate personnel and resources, perennial features of the Soviet Union's rural undergovernment. The regional migration agency had a staff of thirty-six and the Northern Territory OGPU had a staff of eighty-one. As early as January, Northern Territory OGPU boss Austrin began pleading for an additional seventy-nine staff members, almost a doubling of his force, to prepare for the impending flood of exiles.[71] At that time, the regional party committee also demanded that Moscow cease sending criminals into administrative exile in the Northern Territory.[72] The regional branch of the Commissariat of Internal Affairs was only able to provide one commandant for every five thousand settlers as of April despite the fact that the Shmidt Commission had called for a commandant to lead each special settlement. By the end of the year, the situation had improved in the Northern Territory with a total of 184 commandants for the North's then 189 special settlements.[73] The situation in Siberia and the Urals was no better, in some cases worse. And the enormous expanses of territory covered by the special settlements magnified further the inadequacies of the rural administrative infrastructure.

Once the construction of the special settlements had begun, other problems came to the fore, most notably the problem of an insufficient number of skilled carpenters. There were, of course, peasants with carpentry skills among the special settlers. In the Northern Territory, Bergavinov had explicitly requested that the Central Black Earth kulaks arrive first because of their carpentry skills.[74] However, this recourse was not particularly effective, because the settlers were expected not simply to replicate their village homes but to construct complex multifamily structures, for which they had no experience. Furthermore, the many Ukrainian peasants, who constituted over 40 percent of the peasants going to the North, had no experience whatsoever in working with log construction in their native villages.[75] A Vozhegodskii District (Vologodskii County) forestry construction engineer reported in June that without the aid of hired carpenters, the houses would not stand. He personally thought that plans for simpler homes were essential but did not dare take any initiative lest he be accused of sabotage.[76] As a result of these problems, the economic enterprises of the Northern Territory were forced to "mobilize" free carpenters from elsewhere in the region to work in the special settlements. And there were never enough of them.[77] As of 1 January 1931, a report from the Northern Territory indicated that 220 free hired workers were engaged in housing construction.[78]

In addition to the shortage of skilled workers, there were shortages of carpentry tools and building materials (apart from lumber).[79] The OGPU summarily rejected the Northern Territory OGPU chief's requests for construction materials, calling them "extremely exaggerated."[80] A similar exchange occurred between the Urals regional OGPU and the central OGPU.[81] There were also severe shortages of horses for hauling materials at construction sites and transporting building supplies into the interior.[82]

The enormous expanses of land and distances involved in the operation were a planner's nightmare. Virtually everything except lumber had to be brought in from the outside. Many of the settlements were completely inaccessible for a large part of the year, and then only accessible by small boat or on foot. In the Northern Territory, this problem, in theory, necessitated a nine-month food reserve, an impossibility given the lack of funding, transport vehicles, and storage facilities.[83] As a consequence, food was always in perilously short supply, leading to outbreaks of scurvy as well as malnutrition, from the outset.[84] In June, the Politburo ordered the Commissariat of Trade to provision the Northern Territory and the Urals from the central emergency grain reserve.[85] On paper, settlers working for the economic enterprises were to be given the same food norms as free workers, although the OGPU admitted that "in cases of difficulties provisioning can be lower."[86] The norms for settlers engaged in physical labor were in theory 2,027 calories, including from 300 to 500 grams of bread, 20 grams of groats, 6 grams of sugar, and 75 grams of fish per day.[87] Given limited food reserves, these norms were not filled in most cases, especially for those assigned to work in settlement construction. And in these isolated places, there was often nowhere to buy food in those few instances when settlers had managed to hold on to some of their rubles.

Under these conditions, the construction of the special settlements proceeded very slowly. While the bureaucrats blamed each other and especially the economic enterprises for this state of affairs, the economic enterprises blamed the special settlers themselves, accusing them of a lack of discipline and insubordination.[88] Words like "lazy," "hostile," and "anti-Soviet" appear regularly in reports about the settlers' work activity.[89] Inadequate numbers of foremen and on-site commandants to supervise construction only exacerbated the situation. In a special settlement in Vozhegodskii District, in the Vologda area, a hired foreman arrested a "saboteur," described also as a "problem element," for "disorganizing work," but the mostly absentee commandant rehired him, claiming that he was needed at the work site. According to this report, the commandant's actions reduced the foreman's authority in the eyes of the kulaks, although, at the same time, the report accused the foreman of an "extreme lack of tact"—yelling, threatening, and cursing the settlers.[90] In some areas, the settlers refused to work; one report even claimed that there were "strikes" in the Urals. The cause of these work stoppages was almost invariably hunger.[91] In one such case, a foreman wrote to a series of officials, pleading for food for his workers, who, he feared, were otherwise likely to quit work and leave.[92]

The special settlers worked under desperately harsh conditions in the spring and summer of 1930, facing hunger, illness, endless work days, and, at times, cruel bosses. One settler in the Vologda area wrote, "They treat us very bad, they consider us counterrevolutionaries . . . they threaten to shoot us for the smallest insubordination. It is impossible to describe all the horrors."[93] Another settler, farther north, wrote, "Here they beat us horribly. On the 21st of May in the night we thought we would all die. They beat us with revolvers while we slept. The commandant broke one man's skull. This is how they treat us in Arkhangel'sk. There is no defense from anyone. We will likely perish here."[94]

The September deadline for the completion of the construction of the special settlements was not met anywhere. In the Northern Territory, only 118 of 3,974 planned houses were ready by this time.[95] By the end of 1930, only 39.8 percent of the houses planned for the Northern Territory's 189 special settlements were finished.[96] In the Urals, where the OGPU chief complained about not having a "full picture" of resettlement because of "insufficient information," only 50 percent of housing was complete by November 1930—and this was still before the much larger wave of exile to the Urals in 1931.[97] Everywhere, the settlers would resort to makeshift abodes or, in the rare instances when it was possible, residence with peasants in neighboring villages.[98] In the meantime, life would only become more difficult as the families began to arrive in the special settlements in the summer of 1930. And the situation grew worse in the course of the fall as the next waves of the dekulakized were sent into exile.

The Arrival of the Families

Although some families had been sent directly into the interior the previous winter, before the authorities called a halt to this practice, most began to arrive in the summer of 1930.[99] The transport of the families and their generally meager possessions was described as "catastrophic." Shortages of transport vehicles meant that literally tens of thousands of carts and small boats had to be "mobilized" from local populations.[100]

As a rule, families from the same village were settled together.[101] Some attempt was made to settle "native kulaks" with "imported ones," in order to teach them local ways. In the Northern Territory, two to three families of native kulaks were placed in each special settlement.[102] In the Urals, the regional authorities asked Moscow for permission to resettle 250 native kulak fishing families in special settlements to act as "instructors" in organizing fishing collectives.[103] Most faced long weeks with inadequate or no shelter; those who could be were quartered with peasants in nearby villages, sometimes, ironically, within vacated and empty kulak homes.[104]

Irina Fedoseevna Korostelkina, who was deported to Narym from Altai in 1930, recalled, "we were put on an open barge, packed in like sardines in a tin, for a month. It rained frequently, pouring above with nowhere for cover. From time to time, we approached the shore, [and] a part of the people were unloaded and then we went on again farther north." Irina and her family were soon left off in the middle of a dense and dark forest. "We were surrounded by taiga, as I now recall. Mama said, 'Look children—there's a hole in the sky.' But we didn't understand and asked her, 'Where is the hole?' In the first months, hundreds of children and old people died. I remember everything—I was nine years old then."[105]

Ekaterina Sergeevna Lukina, exiled to Narym from Krasnoiarsk somewhat later, also remembered her first days in the special settlement. "In the beginning we lived in shacks made from birch bark, then people began to build wooden huts. [They] gave us meager rations.... We children scavenged clay from which our parents built stoves. [They] gave us six kilograms of flour a month.... We were weak.... People began to swell and die. [They] buried them without coffins, in collective graves, which grew every day."[106]

Mariia Fedorovna Abramenko, exiled from Ukraine to Siberia, recalled "[They] took us to Mogochino. [We] lived on the banks, without any shelter. Mama left to work at a sawmill." Then one day, "a barge swung into the banks" bringing her father and the other men who had been initially sent elsewhere for work. They traveled on together along the Suiga river, arriving in a place with only three barracks, all without roofs. "[Our] parents began to work, to build the barracks— papa sawed logs into blocks, mama sanded [them], and we children helped when we could. Mosquitos ate us alive. [Our] legs and arms [turned] to bones...."[107]

The first settlers to arrive in Igarka, a tiny settlement beyond the Arctic Circle, also arrived without their men. They came ashore in a "wild and desolate" place. The women built the barracks. When the men arrived, they divided the barracks with partitions into four rooms, one per family. Olga Chernousova remembered sitting up in her bunk at night, before the building was subdivided, and gazing in wonderment at the little sparkling lights given off by the kindling each family used for light during the long polar nights.[108]

Many families had been separated from their men at the outset of dekulakization. In some cases, this separation was temporary as the men were sent elsewhere to work or held in temporary detention after dekulakization. In the case of first-category kulak families, the situation was still more serious. These families had lost their men to execution or internment in labor camps. Tolmachev was the first to write about this, noting that these families, some lacking any able-bodied members, were completely helpless. He recommended substituting exile for imprisonment.[109] In early June 1930, the OGPU ordered the release from labor camps of first-category kulaks whose families were in the Far East.[110]

Generalized rulings on such families in other regions would be delayed into the second half of 1931 when efforts were made to reunite families.[111] In the meantime, the families of men who had been exiled alone in the spring of 1930—the so-called *odinochki* removed from border areas in Belorussia and Ukraine—were also being reunited with the heads of their families. Some 2,000 families from Belorussia and 14,500 families from Ukraine whose heads of household had been considered especially "socially dangerous" made the journey to their new homes in the fall of 1930.[112]

From the moment they arrived on the empty land tracts designated as settlement sites, all special settlers worked, from children to the elderly. T. I. Evseeva, who was exiled as a nine-year-old with her family to the Perm region, recalled, "The first months we lived in a *shalash*. After several days, they sent us to work. We walked eight kilometers to clear taiga to plow fields. Everyone had to work: both men and women, even children and old people worked in felling trees. . . . Despite the hard work, they fed us poorly. We were hungry from the first months. Bread, rationed, was never enough. . . ."[113] Viktor M., who was thirteen at the time, remembered working in the construction of the special settlements alongside the adult men.[114] N. N. Pavlov also worked in construction, as a carpenter, and he remembered that he "worked a lot" for "ahead of us lay winter."[115] At the end of July, in the Northern Territory, orders were issued for all settlers to be employed in special settlement construction, from thirteen- and fourteen-year-olds to the elderly.[116] In October 1930, 36,672 settlers, roughly one-third of all settlers, were occupied full time in construction in the Northern Territory.[117]

Young Pavlov remembered those days as a time of hunger: "For food, they gave out only 200 to 300 grams of bread for adults and 100 grams for nonworkers. There was no other food. In the summer, we ate mushrooms and other gifts of nature. My little brother and I managed to catch fish and this helped to improve our beggarly existence for a while."[118] Because there had not been time to plant, the special settlers were almost entirely dependent on the government for food. Very few had reserves left by the summer or money with which to make purchases if that was even a possibility. The Central Union of Consumers' Societies (*Tsentrosoiuz*) declared in August that it had exhausted all its reserves and would not send any more food or manufactured goods out to the settlements without a special government directive. At this time, it was still not clear who was to support families without able-bodied laborers; up to now, they had fallen through the cracks, existing—poorly —on local resources. An "opinion" expressed in August at a Moscow meeting on special resettlement was that the special settlements themselves should support these families.[119]

A sign nailed to the roof of a house in a special settlement in Ledengskii District in the Northern Territory read "Death settlement— don't come here to live." In this district, as of mid-September, only 3 percent of housing was complete, living conditions were terrible, and the commandants were described as "drunken."[120] In Chekuevksii District, also in the Northern Territory, conditions were similar. Only one house had been completed by mid-September. Moreover, people were said to be dying every day—mainly due to exhaustion, festering ulcers, and hunger.[121] Reports of scurvy were frequent and cases of typhus were on the rise.[122] Children and the elderly suffered the most, experiencing the highest mortality rates and accounting for thousands of deaths despite the April directive on the return of children and the elderly. In some places, only laborers received rations, necessitating the division of a single ration among an entire family.[123]

Some of the land tracts provided for the special settlements proved to be completely uninhabitable.[124] As of July, the colonization party in Severo-Dvinskii County was still looking for suitable lands for more than half the county's families.[125] In other areas, the authorities were removing and relocating entire settlements. To make matters worse, the country underwent a major territorial-administrative redistricting in mid-summer 1930, which led to the elimination of an entire layer of provincial government—the county (*okrug*) level. Fortunately, at least in the Northern Territory, the county-level colonization parties were retained for the time being given the urgency of their assignments.[126]

Mortality rates were staggering by the end of the year. In the Northern Territory, the OGPU reported 21,213 deaths. The special settler population there was already in decline, since 35,400 children had been sent back to their villages and 39,743 mostly adult males had run away (of whom 15,458 were still at liberty).[127] Everywhere there were reports of high mortality among children.[128] The chaos of resettlement and the still-fluctuating numbers of special settlers prevented an accurate accounting of the death toll for the country as a whole, but there is little doubt that in 1930 the mortality rate in the Northern Territory was the highest of all, given the large numbers exiled there and the disastrous conditions encountered in attempting to settle so many people in such a short period of time. This state of affairs would contribute to Bergavinov's downfall in March 1931. Moscow condemned the Northern Territory in no uncertain terms, claiming that Bergavinov took in the kulaks enthusiastically and then did nothing to settle them. Now, according to Moscow, they could no longer be used as a workforce. In response, Bergavinov threatened that he could not fulfill the timber plan without more workers and even argued that the plan in the Northern Territory was "unrealistic." Nonetheless, in 1931, the

Northern Territory's exile plans would be drastically cut to 10,000 families, as a result of which it would cease to be the main destination for kulak exiles.[129]

Conclusion

The first phase of special resettlement determined in large part the future direction of important aspects of the policy. Geographically, the generalized north would remain the primary destination for kulak special settlers, but the next wave of kulak exiles would flow in an easterly direction toward the Urals, Siberia, and Kazakhstan and away from the Northern Territory.

There would be no rethinking the human dimensions of the policy. The need to rid the countryside of the kulak remained a paramount goal. If anything, antikulak convictions strengthened in 1931 and the year witnessed a numerically larger deportation than in 1930, this time without the subdivision of kulakdom into categories of greater and lesser evil. And the need for kulak labor had not diminished.

In the meantime, the first waves of special settlers had arrived in the most isolated and forbidding regions of the Soviet Union, devoid of any kind of governmental or economic infrastructure. They had been transported and deposited in the exile zones with relatively little forethought or preparation. While the bureaucracy moved slowly, reluctantly, and inefficiently, the settlers started the work of raising the special settlements. Under extremely inauspicious conditions, the kulak settlers would begin life and labor within the regimen of the special settlements.

II

Life and Labor in the Special Settlements

5

The Penal-Economic Utopia: "Reforging through Labor"

They liquidated you as a class. Understood?
—Ivan Tvardovskii, former special settler, recalling a frequent
refrain of the bosses

I remember that when the women were working and began to cry and the tears began pouring out, [they] would sing one of the couplets from the thirties exile years: 'Sick of cold barracks, sick of bed bugs, sick of working in the Urals' forests.'" This was one of I. S. Olifier's childhood memories. As a twelve-year-old, he watched his mother and the other women work day and night, while the special settlement's commandant stalked the village on horseback, whip in hand.[1]

The commandants and work bosses in charge of the special settlers viewed them as little more than a "muscle force" to be exploited mercilessly in order to fulfill the plan. In their minds, the kulak workforce was infinitely replenishable as a result of both the exile of entire families—labor reproductive units—and the continuing deportation of peasants through the first half of the 1930s.[2] According to an official in the Northern Territory, "there was practically a directive that the sooner the special settlers die, the better."[3]

The plan was all that mattered. Output and production indicators took precedence over human lives, over any consideration that the special settlers were, as Tolmachev had written in 1930, "not cargo, but living people."[4] The "socially alien" status of the workforce, their dehumanization and castigation into the role of "class enemy" predetermined relations between special settlers and their overseers. Local officials in charge of the special settlers were not necessarily ideologues or even true believers. Yet Communist ideology and the mind-set that went with it pervaded the world of officialdom, underlying and shaping attitudes and human relations. Ideology was most evident in everyday practice. Local officials responsible for the special settlers were true "company men," working for the extended interests of a state that was undifferentiated from its economic concerns and sharing its general worldview on questions of enemies, labor, and the plan. And, if in 1930 there were still visions of the "reforging" and "reeducating" of the kulak, especially the young, by 1931 and after these visions would all but vanish.

The Special Settlement Regime

On 24 August 1930, an OGPU memorandum noted that work on statutes (*polozhenie*) for the economic employment and internal administration of the special settlers had begun in March and "was ongoing." In the meantime, the memorandum concluded, no one knew exactly what to do with the special settlers.[5] The "ongoing" nature of the work on the statutes reflected the haphazard approach to kulak policy apparent from the outset. Policy itself was indeed an ongoing affair as the liquidation of the kulaks as a class evolved in the course of 1930 from a purely repressive police operation into a policy of colonization and forced labor. In fact, it was only in the late spring of 1930 that the term "special settler" made an appearance, replacing or complementing the kulak modifier.[6]

The attempt to construct an administrative blueprint for the special settlements was both the Stalinist bureaucrat's response to the reality of disorder and an endeavor to create an entirely new set of institutions to control, regiment, and remold an "enemy" population within a village setting. In Moscow as well as in the capitals of the main exile regions, committees of jurists and policemen were busily engaged in outlining a vision of the special settlements. This exercise in planning was, in a sense, a kind of mythmaking. Special settlement planning in 1930 was socialist realism in another context. It represented an "imagined future"—laid out in endless plans, reports, memos, figures, tables, graphs, and budgets—superimposed on the present-day realities of the Soviet hinterlands.[7] It was planning grafted onto chaos, a projection of communist visions of order onto the disorder of a reality of the regime's own making.

In March 1930, the Council of People's Commissars created a special commission under V. P. Antonov-Saratovskii, a leading jurist, to prepare a set of statutes for the internal order, administration, and economic organization of the special settlements. The commission completed a preliminary draft of the statutes in the second half of June; following detailed revisions—many apparently at the hand of Tolmachev[8]—it was sent on in mid-July to the Central Executive Committee and the Council of People's Commissars as a draft decree.[9] The draft decree was never enacted into legislation, but instead replaced in early October 1930 by a series of Central Executive Committee and Council of People's Commissars decrees outlining the rules of order, employment, and administration for the special settlements.[10] These decrees remained in force until the OGPU took over all special resettlement operations in 1931 and introduced what was to remain a temporary statute for the special settlements through the 1930s.[11]

The special settlements were not to replicate the peasant village; on the contrary, they were intended to break down and replace traditional peasant structures, social patterns, and sources of authority. In the process, both Moscow and the bureaucrats in charge of the resettlement operation made use of a combination of practices—penal, military, and traditional—to create the world of the special settlements.

The actual organization and construction of the special settlements were prescribed, on paper, to the smallest detail. Blueprints for standardized multifamily housing units, having nothing in common with typical peasant homes, were sent down to the special settlements from on high. Moscow dictated the exact dimensions of space in the special settlements: the size of rooms, kitchens, and stoves, as well as the dimensions of auxiliary structures like bathhouses, barns, and sheds, and the space between homes. Further, the special settlements were to be situated in isolated areas, thereby segregating the socially dangerous from the socially healthy. The size of the special settler population was set according to labor and security needs; this meant in most cases from one hundred to two hundred families.[12] The central organizing principles of the settlements were standardization, transparency, and the regulation of space, all demanded for the creation of an institution pliable to control and observation—the kind of "panoptic" effect Michel Foucault has described as typical of modern penal institutions.[13]

The special settlements of a given district were subordinate to a district or divisional *komendatura*, the administrative headquarters for special settler affairs within a given district or branch of industry. Each special settlement was to have its own administration led by a commandant. The commandant's word was the law. Within the special settlements, the population was forbidden to assemble without the permission of the commandant and, in general, had no right to any kind of self-government. Special settlers could not leave the territory of their settlements or even relocate within them without the commandant's permission. Visits of friends and relatives were subject to strict control. Nonspecial settlers could live within the territory of the special settlement only with official permission.[14]

When necessary and strictly as an expedient, perhaps even natural response, tradition was invoked in the ordering of the special settler population. Commandants divided the population into sectors, appointing a *starosta*, or elder, for each sector, who was aided by several assistants confirmed by the commandant. The term "elder" was a traditional appellation for a subaltern leader, whether in the context of the village, prison, or school, and it had no relation to the actual age of a person. The elder's duties, in addition to full-time employment in the special settlements, included the fulfillment of all of the commandant's orders; the provision of information on escapes and disorders; regular head-counts of the population; the observation of rules of hygiene for the settlement and individual homes; the transmission of all complaints from the settlers to the commandant; and the announcement of the commandant's orders.[15] In some areas, a system of collective responsibility (*krugovaia poruka*, another term familiar to peasants from tsarist times) was introduced to try to stem the massive flight of settlers from the settlements. Special settlers had to sign a collective responsibility agreement, and one elder or *desiatnik* (a kind of foreman) for each ten households was responsible for monitoring the movement of settlers and for reporting escapes and escape plans to the commandant.[16] In effect, the commandant was charged with the formation of a new hierarchy of leaders to be selected from the most "loyal" settlers and, whenever possible, from the supposedly more politically malleable youth.[17] This was an attempt—ironically punctuated by the use of traditional statuses and practices—to elevate some at the expense of others, in the process altering traditional, and especially generational, loyalties.

The commandant was responsible for the whereabouts of all settlers at all times. He was also responsible for ensuring that both industrial employers and special settlers fulfilled all their respective obligations as specified in their labor contracts. The commandant had the task of reviewing all complaints and requests from settlers; if he could not resolve them, he was to redirect them to an institution or higher organ that could. The commandant answered for the political and social order of the special settlement, including all matters of hygiene and protection of state and collective property.[18]

For violations of order (quiet, hygiene, use of state property), work truancy, and drunkenness, the commandant could either fine (up to five rubles) or place under arrest (up to five days) the offending special settler. For "systematic" violations of this type, the office of the divisional or district *komendatura* could apply fines (up to ten rubles) and arrest (up to ten days). For more serious crimes, the commandant could transfer a settler to the jurisdiction of the Commissariat of Justice or the OGPU. Under no circumstances were settlers to be deprived of their ration as a means of punishment (a clear indication that this practice was in fact employed as punishment).[19]

The statutes of the Urals Regional soviet, published in April 1931, offered a still more detailed scheme of punishment in four ascending stages: warnings; transfer to more difficult work; exile to a more distant place; and, finally, transfer to a punishment team (in addition to a series of possible fines). Settlers in punishment teams received no wages and obtained their food "*iz obshchego kotla*" (literally "[eating] from a common bowl"). They worked a ten-hour day, were forbidden to write letters, and were under a twenty-four-hour guard.[20]

The special settlers also had a series of defined rights. In theory, if they observed the laws and worked "honorably," they were eligible for full rehabilitation of all civil rights five years from the time of exile. Children had the right to go to school on the same basis as "free children." Special settlers had the right to organize—with the commandant's permission—cultural-educational circles; the unlimited right to receive newspapers and literature published in the USSR as well as correspondence, packages, and money gifts; and the right to send children under fourteen and non-able-bodied elderly home to relatives or friends.[21] Special settlers were also allowed by statute to marry free citizens, without the latter losing civil rights (or the former gaining them).[22] By 1932, special settlers could organize voluntary societies in the settlements, provided that these societies had no potential for military training. Any kind of physical culture that could turn into preparation for military preparedness was forbidden, and settlers were not allowed to receive military literature of any kind.[23] In individual special settlements, the commandant could add or subtract from the rights of settlers according to whim. One commandant, for example, required special settlers to obtain a pass (*propusk*) to go to the baths.[24]

Finally and most importantly, all able-bodied settlers were required to be engaged in socially useful work, either within the settlements or for the industries that contracted their labor.[25] Exceptions occurred only with the sanction of a special medical commission that determined whether a settler could be exempted from work on the basis of health considerations.[26] The non-able-bodied were generally employed back in the settlements in agricultural or artisanal work. The industries that employed the special settlers did so on the basis of special contracts that they signed first with the Commissariat of Internal affairs and later with the OGPU.[27] The industrial concerns were responsible for the maintenance of their labor force. They were expected to provide housing, provisions, medical assistance, maternity care, and educational facilities for the special settlers and their families. The length of the work day and the provision of free time were to be similar to that of the free workforce.[28]

The industrial concerns were to pay their special settler laborers the same salaries as their free laborers minus deductions for the costs of their administrative upkeep, which ranged over time from 25 percent to 15 percent (from October 1931) to 5 percent (after January 1932).[29]

Labor was intended to transform the kulaks. Special consideration was given to youth, who were encouraged to take leadership positions at work and in the special settlements. Along with socialist reeducation in schools, literacy groups, and various types of circles, labor was meant to redeem and transfigure the kulaks, molding them into socially useful laborers, able and willing to participate in the great Bolshevik project of communist transformation.[30]

The disjunctures between Moscow's and the regional capitals' plans for the special settlers and the reality of their existence never achieved the perfection of order and control intended. Reality was vastly different —untidy, unmanageable, and shaped more by geographical, economic, and cultural realities than by Moscow's seeming omnipotence. Beyond the center, Moscow's "omnipotence" was a paper reality, an intricate utopian blueprint that remained a wish projection, if not a rationalization for disorder and an abnegation of responsibility. In spite of rhetoric and ideology, the special settlers' primary dictate became, by 1931, economic, or to be precise, economic-penal. What on paper was a penal utopia for isolating and reforging social enemies became in fact little more than a shoddily constructed institution of forced labor. By 1931, any remaining visions of the penal utopia would simply evaporate in the face of local realities and the harsh desiderata of the Gulag. As the OGPU put it in an August 1931 memorandum, "they [the special settlers] consider themselves condemned to eternal rightlessness [*bespravie*]."[31]

At Work

On 8 July 1931, the Andreev Commission met to review the "claims" (*zaiavki*) for kulak labor that were pouring into Moscow from industries all over the Soviet Union. In response to the chaos of the first year of the special resettlement operation, the Politburo had created, in March 1931, the Andreev Commission to administer all kulak operations. Dominated by high-level representatives from the OGPU, including Iagoda, the commission's task at its 8 July meeting was to farm out kulak laborers to key industries experiencing deficits in their labor force. The commission doled out kulaks in quantities of hundreds and thousands of family units to the forestry, mining, coal, and other industries of the Urals, Siberia, Kazakhstan, the Far East, and elsewhere.

Rarely were requests for kulak labor turned down. The exception was the Northern Territory where the forestry industry's request for seventeen thousand additional families was rejected "as a result of the problems in the use of special settlers," meaning the disastrous first year of special resettlement in the North.[32] In general, however, the allotment of kulak families (on paper) was effortless work, as easy as any other allocation of raw materials for Soviet industry.

By this time, forestry work had become the predominant form of employment for the majority of special settlers. OGPU data on 1,427,539 people (or 324,665 families) exiled in 1930 and 1931 indicated that the largest numbers were employed in forestry work, followed by employment in agriculture, coal and peat production, and mining for nonferrous metals and gold (see table 4 in appendix). Included in these numbers were also families employed in the giant construction projects of the First Five-Year Plan: 9,935 families (40,426 people) at Magnitogorsk, 681 families at Sinirstroi, 1,538 families at Tagilstroi, 1,170 families at the Nadezhdinskii Factory, and 4,617 families at Kuznetskstroi (as of late summer–fall of 1931).[33]

In the Northern Territory, Western Siberia, and the Urals, the basic occupation of special settlers was forestry work. In the case of the Northern Territory and Western Siberia, special settlers worked in agriculture on the side. In the Urals, according to an early 1930 regional soviet executive committee resolution, the special settlers were supposed to be rendered materially dependent on their industrial employers in order to prevent them from ever creating their own farms again. Except for special settlers living in the northernmost zones of the Urals, very few in fact continued to do any farming, apart from occasional work in kitchen gardens. In Eastern Siberia and the Far East, special settlers worked primarily in the gold and platinum mines, while in Kazakhstan, they worked in copper mines and other local industries.[34]

Kulak laborers and their families lived in the special settlements (renamed, after 1933, trudposelenie or "work settlements") from which they traveled to their jobs in the forests, mines, and fields.[35] In some cases, especially in the Northern Territory and in Western Siberia where forestry work dominated, laborers could be assigned to work anywhere from forty to one hundred kilometers away from their settlements, and they sometimes had to go without seeing their families for months at a time.[36] In other cases, special settlers were allocated to work at the giant stroiki, or construction sites of the First Five-Year Plan, like Magnitogorsk, the White Sea Canal, and Kuznetskstroi.

The industrial organs, which submitted claims for kulak labor, played a central role in the fate of the special settlers. The OGPU contracted out special settler laborers to industry.[37] For the duration of the contract, the industrial organs were responsible for all aspects of the material upkeep of their charges, but by and large they treated them like a cheap and replenishable army of laborers to be exploited to the full. Like unfree labor everywhere, the special settlers were judged solely by their capacity to work. In the Urals, special settlers were defined exclusively according to their ability to work. They were divided into five groups: group A—able to perform any kind of physical work; group B—able to perform light physical work; group C—incapable of physical work but able to work in and around the special settlement in various seasonal activities (gathering mushrooms, berries, etc.) and in handicrafts; group D—incapable of work; and group E—children under sixteen.[38]

On paper, kulak laborers were entitled to the same remuneration, benefits, and rights as free workers performing at a similar skill level, minus salary deductions to cover the costs of their administrative and penal upkeep.[39] The length of the workday and other work norms were to be governed by the same labor legislation that set the terms of labor for free workers. Legislation relating to the protection of child labor and female workers was also to be enforced. The Commissariat of Social Services was to provide support for those without families and incapable of working (e.g., invalids, the elderly, orphans).[40]

The reality of the special settlers' labor experience had little in common with Moscow's paperwork. Because the plan was everything, because Moscow dictated impossible production tasks, and because industries and local bosses believed they had an inexhaustible source of labor, the special settlers were treated as another form of raw material, as chattel. Decisions about their lives and employment increasingly were linked directly to industrial priorities. Individuals, families, and even entire settlements could be relocated at a moment's notice as economic needs changed.[41]

The special settlers were subjected to grueling work regimens. Their bosses routinely violated central directives on the length of the workday and on work norms. Almost everywhere, bosses raised the output for their laborers, sometimes to twice that expected from free workers.[42] The Urals OGPU boss complained that such norms were simply impossible to fulfill.[43] In the Far East, the regional soviet executive committee claimed that even the most experienced free workers would not have been able to fulfill the norms assigned to special settlers.[44] According to a May 1931 report from Urals OGPU boss G. Ia. Rapoport, all special settlers regardless of age were forced to work in the forests. Twelve-year-olds and the elderly alike were given norms of 2 to 2.5 cubic meters of logs. (The average work load for grown men in the free labor force was 3 cubic meters per day.) As a consequence of such impossible expectations, special settlers had no choice but to remain in the forest day and night, suffering exhaustion and frostbite. Otherwise, they risked the loss of their rations or punishments ranging from fines to incarceration.[45]

A. K. Rodionova, a special settler in Siberia, recalled that she would be "up at four and to work at six. The plan was three cubic meters of wood. If you didn't fulfill it, you didn't go home—they wouldn't give you your rations."[46] In a letter smuggled out to relatives in Canada, special settler Franz Warkentin echoed Rodionova's statement: "All men over eighteen years of age were to work in the forest. Here we were forced to cut trees from early morning until late at night in snow a meter deep. If you completed 50 percent of the required work, you received 50 percent of your food ration."[47] The eight-hour workday was never observed. Inspection teams reported eleven- and twelve-hour workdays as the norm with no days off.[48] In the Northern Territory, bosses were said to dismiss the very idea of an eight-hour day, arguing that they needed special settlers to work at least eleven hours.[49] Doubtless, most worked far more than this.[50]

Rules regulating the labor of children, minors, women, the elderly, and the non-able-bodied were also routinely violated. According to directives from August 1931, minors under sixteen were not to be employed in industry; exceptions were allowed only with a doctor's certificate and then only if the minor was over fourteen. Fourteen- to sixteen-year-olds were to have a four-hour workday, and sixteen- to eighteen-year-olds a six-hour day. In agriculture, children under twelve were not supposed to work at all.[51] In fact, as a report on special settlers in Kazakhstan noted, children's labor was used "almost everywhere . . . equally with adults and without time limitations."[52] Iagoda complained that the same norms for healthy men were applied to minors, pregnant women, and the non-able-bodied.[53] A report on the Urals also noted that norms were not differentiated by gender or age.[54]

Special settlers often worked without a day off. When bosses in the Northern Territory were forced to grant their workers a day off, they held back their rations for the day.[55] Many special settlers went for long periods of time receiving no pay whatsoever. As was the case throughout Soviet industry during the First Five-Year Plan, there were often long delays in paying workers. In the case of some special settlers, these delays could extend for up to two years. In addition, industrial officials frequently refused to pay special settlers anything while they were building their settlements. By September 1931, more than one million rubles in back pay was owed to special settlers in the Northern Territory.[56] When they were paid, their salaries were generally pitifully small because they were based on the fulfillment of impossible norms. In the Far East, for example, daily wages of special settlers rarely exceeded one ruble twenty kopeks, a small fraction of the average working salary.[57] There were also reports of women being paid less than men for the same work and women on pregnancy leave being refused wages and rations.[58]

Partly as a result of their exploitation as forced laborers, partly as a result of the continuing neglect and negligence of the industrial organs, the special settlers' material conditions remained abysmal. In the Northern Territory, only 50 percent were housed in permanent shelters by June 1931. The forestry industry was reluctant to allow their workers "time off" to build the special settlements. The Gulag administration had to order its Northern Territory OGPU chief to force industry to fulfill its contractual obligations for the use of the special settlers.[59] The situation was similar in the Urals, where only some 50 percent of housing was complete by the end of 1931.[60]

The problems of inadequate housing were compounded by poor nutrition.[61] The food situation of most special settlers was dire, threatening malnutrition if not outright starvation. The OGPU reported special settlers starving in 1931 in the Northern Territory, the Urals, Kazakhstan, and Siberia. Cases of scurvy were widespread.[62] In Tavrsinskii District in the Urals, 70 percent of special settlers were ill with various stomach disorders, mainly dysentery, from eating what were euphemistically labeled in official documents "food surrogates" (e.g., grass, roots, bark). In Kytlymskii District, also in the Urals, 9,989 non-able-bodied special settlers had received no food for a year and were, according to an OGPU report, "systematically starving."[63] In the Northern Territory, mothers reported feeding their infants black bread because they had no breast milk.[64] In some areas, as a result of these conditions, epidemics of typhus flared up in the summer of 1931. Mortality rates among children were highest.[65] Officials everywhere reported able-bodied workers in decline and, correspondingly, non-able-bodied and dependents on the rise.[66]

As a consequence of these conditions, the OGPU carried out a series of inspections of the provinces in the summer of 1931. In the Northern Territory, the OGPU concluded that no one was interested in the fate of the special settlers except the OGPU. A commission dispatched from Moscow visited nineteen special settlements between 6 and 16 August and concluded that neither the party organs nor the Northern Forestry Agency had fulfilled their obligations. "Normal housing" for special settlers was nonexistent; instead of the required four meters per person, they received on average one and one-half meters per person. There were no schools or medical facilities, and rations were very low. Children everywhere were pale and sickly, and many were forced to take part in hard labor. The non-able-bodied received nothing. Scurvy was widespread. According to the commission, the industrial organs were only concerned with reaching day-to-day production goals and had no interest in creating a permanent work force from the special settler population.[67]

The story was similar elsewhere. In the Urals, a commission headed up by N. I. Ezhov, Stalin's secret police chief during the terror of the late 1930s, reported that special settlers were "found in difficult material conditions"; they were owed large amounts of back pay, had no money for food, and were forced to sell their belongings to feed their children. According to the report, "Thanks to such horrendous conditions, the forestry industry cannot in future receive real results from its labor force of special settlers."[68] In Kazakhstan, where an army of some fifty thousand special settler families had only just arrived, the situation was reported to be "disastrous." Here the industrial organs were "completely unprepared for the special settlers' arrival and unable to guarantee even minimal living conditions."[69] As a result, some 13–15 percent of the settler population died.[70] In fact, the Russian historian, S. A. Krasil'nikov, has suggested that rates of death and illness among special settlers in 1931 may very well have exceeded those of 1930.[71]

Conditions of life for the special settlers who worked on the giant construction sites of the First Five-Year Plan were scarcely better. At Magnitogorsk, for example, as of early October 1931 there were 10,000 special settler families (42,462 people, of whom 15,000 were under the age of 14). Only 14,185 of these people worked; the rest were dependents, thus making this an extremely expensive work force to maintain. The special settlers here lived in four different sectors of the site, either in tents or general barracks where living space amounted to roughly 1–1.5 meters per person (vs. 2–3.3. for free workers). Bathhouse facilities were sparse, and it was impossible to feed everyone given the inadequate number of spaces available in the collective dining rooms. Approximately 80 percent of all children were said to be ill; in the three months leading up to the report, death rates for children amounted to 591 children under three years of age; 174 under eight; and 10 in the eight to fourteen age range, for a total of 775 deaths. The able-bodied in Magnitogorsk were said to receive the same rations as free workers, but the non-able-bodied received far less. The special settlers here worried about the coming winter and especially about the fate of their children.[72] Meanwhile at Kuznetskstroi, where close to five thousand families (22,077 people) would be settled in the summer of 1931, the district party committee secretary and Kuznetskstroi director desperately attempted to forestall the arrival of the special settlers, pleading that it was impossible to prepare housing and organize food and medical services in such a short period of time.[73]

Although there were other regional party and industrial organs that foresaw the immense difficulties of "receiving" this enormous labor force,[74] they had little choice but to accept their new-found workers—both as a result of pressure from Moscow and pressure to fulfill the plan. Most industries, unlike some of the regional party organizations, welcomed this new source of cheap labor. They looked upon the special settlers as a short-term, stopgap measure to cover labor deficits, often ignoring the need to build up infrastructure to retain these workers as a permanent labor force and always resenting the special settlers' "dependents," as they were called, for the huge material burden they in fact were. And if the OGPU and Moscow constantly interfered in this state of affairs, it was not out of humanitarian concerns but the need to maintain a permanent supply of labor in the Soviet hinterlands.

Reforging

Although it soon became clear that labor was the paramount goal of the kulak deportations, the regime, or some part of the regime, consistently spoke of the need to reeducate the kulak. Labor was meant to be the first step toward such a reeducation, toward the reforging of the kulaks.[75] Yet the kind of labor that the special settlers performed was not sufficient, on its own, to transform the kulaks, except perhaps to bring about untimely death. Moreover, the regime had doubts about the ultimate "transformability" of the adult kulak population, supposedly raised in the spirit of individualism and petit-bourgeois enterprise.

For that reason, the regime placed its main emphasis on kulak youth and a Soviet education. Soviet schools, particularly those built specifically for the special settler population, were to be the primary tools for reforging the kulaks. Politics and ideology were among the chief concerns in the education of special settler children. The children were to be prepared for participation in the construction of socialism and communism. They were to know that they had "every possibility" to enter the ranks of socialist society and that the authorities differentiated between them and their parents.[76] Instructions to teachers proclaimed that "the task of the schools is to separate the children from the ideological influence of their families, to break up families, to raise children in a communist spirit, and to develop in them a hatred for the enemies of Soviet power."[77] The children were to be taught a "hatred for the kulaks," based on the official history of the "kulak exploitation" of the "toiling masses."[78] The ultimate goal was to teach the children the "skill" of collective labor and the "instinct" of socialism, so that they could become "equal members" of Soviet society.[79]

And so, with the noise of such platitudes in the background, party, police, and education officials in Moscow set out to create a network of schools for the other archipelago. From the start, the central authorities had assured special settler children of their right to an education.[80] In locations where there were nearby villages with preexisting schools, special settler children were to be admitted on an equal basis with the village children.[81] Elsewhere, the industries utilizing special settler labor were to take charge of the construction of schools.[82] The regional outposts of the Commissariat of Education were responsible for the administration of the schools.[83]

On 6 June 1931, the Commissariat of Education issued a directive announcing plans to introduce universal education for special settler children, aged eight to eleven, in the 1931/32 school year, and to develop in 1932 one seven-year school for every three settlements.[84] The actual construction of schools proceeded very slowly, mirroring in even slower motion the pace of the construction of the special settlements themselves. According to Iagoda, by January 1932, 22,242 (40 percent) of 55,774 special settler children were in elementary schools in the Urals; 14,500 (41 percent) of 35,000 in Western Siberia; and 6,300 (49 percent) of 13,000 in the Northern Territory.[85] Victor M., who was thirteen at the time of his family's deportation, later recalled that not until 1933 could he and his siblings go back to school. And because the school was in another village, they were forced to live apart from their family while they studied.[86] Mariia Fedorovna Abramenko, who was exiled to Narym from Ukraine in 1930, remembered that a local school opened only in 1935: "My sister and brother went to study, but I couldn't or else there would be no one at home to manage things" while her parents worked.[87]

Conditions in the schools were very poor. Students and teachers worked in abject poverty. There were shortages of everything—pencils, paper, books, desks, and chairs.[88] The school buildings themselves were often cold, stuffy, and poorly lit. In some cases, the classroom doubled as the teacher's living quarters.[89] A Politburo directive of December 1935 claimed that little about these conditions had improved through the early 1930s and ordered that an inspector be put in charge of special settler schools in order to establish "systematic control."[90]

It was also exceedingly difficult to find teachers willing to work in the isolated and far-flung special settlement schools. The Commissariat of Education had initially planned to have four teachers per school, two of whom could be special settlers.[91] It then "mobilized" 424 teachers, of whom no more than 60 percent actually showed up for work. The regime had little choice but to turn to adult special settlers to staff the schools and, ironically, to "reforge" their own children.[92] In the Urals, as of early 1932, 42 percent of teachers were special settlers, while they made up 80 percent of teachers in the Northern Territory and 70 percent in Western Siberia.[93]

The OGPU had little faith in the political loyalties of the teachers, mobilized and special settler alike. An April 1932 OGPU circular warned that teachers in special settlement schools must be carefully screened in order to remove those who violated the "political line." The circular also called, irrationally, for the removal of all special settler teachers.[94] Similar calls to remove special settlers from teaching would be repeated in 1936.[95] Attempts to mobilize urban teachers and komsomol members were largely unsuccessful.[96] In consequence, the OGPU and other agencies continually complained about the politics and quality of teaching in the special settlement schools. Most teachers in the North were reportedly quite young, had completed only a seven-year school education themselves, and were weakly prepared, according to a Commissariat of Education report. And, the report continued, although most of these young teachers worked well, some retained what was described as an "alien ideology."[97] In Plesetskii District in the North, teachers were said to teach in the style of the old church teaching, stressing memorization and recitation.[98]

Whether special settlers or not, the teachers lived under terrible conditions, more or less on par with the surrounding population. When and if they were paid, special settler teachers earned less than half of what the mobilized teachers were supposed to receive.[99] According to Northern OGPU boss Austrin, in the third quarter of 1932, mobilized teachers began resigning because of worsening material conditions.[100] Although famine prompted this situation, it is clear that the hardships in the lives of teachers in the special settlements forced the state increasingly to rely on special settlers as teachers. Beginning in 1936, every attempt would be made to send special settler youth to teacher training colleges so that they could come back to the settlements to replace their less-trusted parents.[101]

The schools for reforging kulak youth suffered the same fate as the penal-utopia of the special settlements. Theory could not be translated into practice. The schools were criminally underfunded and understaffed. The ultimate irony was that reforging in the schools was left in the hands of the "class enemy" for want of another alternative. In the context of the remote Soviet hinterlands, reforging became little more than a hollow facade. Children lived under the same conditions as the adults, within the confines of a special settlement regiment in which the only real law was the commandant's will.

Soviet Company Men

Kuz'ma Larukov was the commandant of a special settlement in the Komi Republic. In a rare photo from the early 1930s, he sits posed atop a horse in full commandant regalia—belted soldier's great coat, high leather boots, pointed Budyonnyi cap, and sidearm. Set against a backdrop of snow, Kuz'ma appears larger than life, dwarfing a log home and several people in the distant background. In another photo—this one with his family and the family of another commandant—he is no longer larger than life but rather appears ordinary, austere, with a plebian look about him and his plain wife and children in their Sunday best. He looks like a poor man, likely a hard man, behind his official persona as a special settlement commandant.

Other photographs of commandants tell a similar story. At work, the commandants invariably are dressed in military or chekist (police) attire—tunic-neck shirts, leather belts and straps for side arms, on horses or in their offices, figures designed to intimidate. In unofficial settings—at rest in Sochi in 1937, for instance—they appear as ordinary Soviet workers of proletarian or peasant background. In other words, the company men of the special settlements seemed little different from the average Soviet man.[102]

To their subordinates, however, they *were* Soviet power, emissaries of a dreaded, all-powerful state. F. A. Rodin's memory of his commandant, one Kitaev, was of a man who "always wore leather boots and carried a lash in his hands."[103] Rodin was a youngster at the time of his exile, and his comments, like those of other special settlers who survived, generally reflect a child's perception. Evgeniia Alekseevna Griaznova, for instance, remembered her commandant as "very, very strict." His name was Petr Petrovich Pystin, and the children made up a secret tongue twister around his temptingly alliterative name.[104] L. I. Ermolina remembered that the commandant's word was the law for the youth of her special settlement. "The commandant decided where we could go to study after finishing school [in the special settlement]. Those who were good and disciplined could leave for Tiumen or Tobol'sk to study; those who were truant or had been in trouble in general could not go on to study. The commandant registered marriages—he himself decided whether or not to let you get married."[105] Another former special settler, A. K. Rodionova, recalled, "The commandants Penizhin and Izhmaev acted like beasts."[106]

Gerbert Emmanuilovich, an ethnically German "kulak" special settler, recalled, "We had different commandants. The first, from Chernysh, Andrei Alekseevich Ul'ianov, mocked us, threatened us with his pistol. Once he tied an old man to a post. For such arbitrariness, he was tried [in court]." He continued, "Another, also a Chernysh *muzhik* [colloquial for peasant], Ivan Andreevich Serditov, was kind, merry. We respected him. He loved to say, 'When the boss comes, the worker should take a break.'"[107] Gerbert Emmanuilovich was not alone in having mixed memories of his commandants. Ivan Tvardovskii wrote that his commandant was a young, kind man, but noted all the same that they were not allowed to address him as "comrade."[108] Ekaterina Sergeevna Lukina, who was exiled to Narym, remembered, "The settlement was called Mogil'nyi, but when the commandant Smirnov came, he renamed it Smirnovka." She continued, "When Nikitin became commandant instead of Smirnov, it became easier to live. He was compassionate to people. [He] let us go eight kilometers to a village where we could exchange goods for food . . . he renamed the settlement Novyi Vasiugin [after the nearby river]. But by this time, scarcely half of the exiles remained—Novyi Vasiugin stood on bones."[109]

"The commandant's power was unlimited in the taiga conditions of those times," recalled Olifier, a former special settler who had been exiled to the Urals as a child.[110] Like the other children who held onto memories of their commandants, Olifier remembered the commandant as the supreme authority in the special settlement. His word was law and could determine whether people lived or died. But while most of these former special settlers retained childhood memories of the external trappings of the commandants' power—military bearing, horses, whips, brutish behavior, and so on—Olifier was correct in his adult conclusions of the "taiga conditions"—lawless, ungoverned, wide-open expanses far from the reaches of Soviet power—that allowed the commandant virtually unlimited powers.

The commandants and work bosses who ruled over the lives of the special settlers held enormous responsibilities, far too onerous for men of limited background. Like their charges, they were cut off from the rest of the world for months at a time. And they were always at risk if they did not fulfill the economic plans dictated to them from above. Most often, they were caught between the terrible contradictions that had plagued special resettlement policy from the outset: the pressures of settling and creating a permanent labor force versus the immediate and short-term need to throw this labor force into work in order to meet plan expectations. The result of these contradictions meant that the company men were caught in a vise between the OGPU, which needed the special settlers for its emerging economic empire, and the industrial and party organs, whose main concern was the immediate fulfillment of the plan.

The commandants were poorly prepared for their position of supreme authority in the special settlement. Apart from a few three-week preparatory courses offered in some regions,[111] the commandant was to rely on his military or chekist (secret police) background—along with an assumed "revolutionary instinct." In the first year when the Commissariat of Internal Affairs was still largely in charge of operations, some commandants had prior experience working in the prison system;

from the summer of 1931, the OGPU endeavored, often unsuccessfully, to mobilize chekists from the reserves as well as to recruit communists and soldiers whenever possible. Given the isolation and hardships, it was not easy to fill these positions. In Siberia, the OGPU placed newspaper advertisements to try to entice former chekists to apply; in the event, only about 15 percent of lower-level workers in the special settlement administration here had any background with the secret police services.[112]

Commandants were expected to be physically strong, energetic, and ready for action (*boevoi*); they were to be enterprising (*smetlivyi*) and preferably communists with a military background;[113] and they appear to have been mainly male.[114] Most were young, under thirty, and few had more than a primary education, if that. In Siberia in the early 1930s, 56 percent of commandants came from peasant backgrounds, while 30 percent were of working-class origins. Here, just over one-half were Communist Party members.[115] In the Northern Territory, roughly two-thirds of the commandants were members of the Communist Party.[116]

To complicate matters, high turnover and personnel shortages plagued the administration of the special settlements at all levels of the regional hierarchy.[117] In Western Siberia in 1933, there were 1,237 administrative personnel (at all levels of the command hierarchy) to administer some 326,992 special settlers.[118] At about the same time, there were only 328 people working in the Urals regional *kommandatura*.[119] Given the general conditions, there was little incentive for commandants to remain on the job. Payment of salaries was frequently irregular; most commandants lived no better than their charges.[120] Chances for career advancement were slim; in Siberia, for example, about half of all commandants could expect some sort of promotion, but generally not more than one rank up the commandant hierarchy.[121]

"It seems to me," quipped Western Siberian party chief Eikhe in 1931, "that the OGPU should publish, not only for the commandants but for dissemination among all special settlers, instructions laying out what rights commandants have and don't have. For example, [special settlers] go to the commandant for permission to get married and [they can] say, for whatever reason, I won't permit you to marry. This smells of abuse. And there are many such instances."[122]

Eikhe was certainly aware that such instructions had been published by central and regional authorities, if not exactly for dissemination among the special settlers.[123] What Eikhe had in mind was as much the inability or unwillingness of commandants to observe rules as the absence of clear guidelines on every aspect of special settler administration. As Eikhe and his superiors in Moscow well knew, given "taiga conditions," most commandants ruled by repression, arbitrariness, and simple lawlessness, traditional Russian remedies to rural undergovernment made worse by the socially "alien" status of the subject population. Living in isolation from the world for months at a time, lacking telephone or telegraph communication with their superiors, and faced with the terrible demands of both the survival of their populations and the fulfillment of economic goals, the commandant's power was in effect unlimited and could descend into arbitrariness if not outright criminal behavior. As was the case of Smirnovka/Novyi Vasiugin, the special settlement had the potential to become the personal fiefdom of the commandant.

The worst of such arbitrary and lawless behavior surfaces in party disciplinary and legal records. Providing an "adult eye" to complement the children's perspective, these records confirm the more brutal aspects of the special settlement regime. Doubtless, they represent only the tip of the proverbial iceberg of lawlessness, most often coming to light with attempts by the OGPU to scapegoat lower-level officials. Generally speaking, though, authorities were reluctant to press their subordinates too severely, given the dire shortages in administrative manpower in the special settlements.[124]

The most frequent charges brought against commandants and other company men were corruption, mismanagement, and the abusive treatment of special settlers. "Systematic drunkenness," or alcoholism, a perennial scourge of lower-level Soviet officials, appears as the most common stated underlying cause for violations.[125] But commandants could also be fired simply on the basis of "systematic drunkenness," "systematic drunkenness with special settlers," "systematic group drunkenness," "aimless shooting in an intoxicated state," and, in general, "debauchery."[126] Given that drunkenness served as a major cause for the individual purging of Communist Party members through the early 1930s, the frequency of this charge is not remarkable.[127] What in other contexts might be viewed as a weakness became, however, a defining attribute of the behavior and abilities of Soviet company men working in the special settlements in the 1930s.

"Lack of discipline," "*grubost'*" (or rude behavior), and social degeneracy (*bytovoe razlozhenie*) were also accusations brought against company men. Social degeneracy could mean anything from the illegal employment of special settlers as domestic help, to mutually agreed sexual relations between bosses and special settler women, to sexual abuse and rape.[128] Lack of discipline and *grubost'* were generally accompanying modifiers for behavior that ranged from "tactless relations to special settlers" to illegal incarceration, beatings, and murder.[129]

Commandant Malygin presided over a special settlement in the Pinezhskii District in the Northern Territory. He was accused of "tactlessness" in his relations with special settlers. In the spring of 1931, he was arrested for arbitrarily arresting special settlers and incarcerating them in the bathhouse for work truancy.[130] Commandant Mitevskii from Vologodskii County was arrested and sent off to the OGPU for what was described as "full counterrevolutionary *proizvol* (or arbitrariness)." Mitevskii was a "systematic drinker." According to reports, he beat up special settlers, carried out sexual assaults on several women, embezzled money and property from his laborers, and imprisoned people for periods ranging from seven to thirty days. Several special settlers served as witnesses in his investigation. It turned out that the district officials knew exactly what was going on and indeed were Mitevskii's regular drinking partners. The special settlers informed the OGPU that there was "lots of wild shooting" in the course of these drinking bouts.[131]

In the Syktyvkar region of the Komi Republic, commandants Beznosikov and Pigulin were fired and then arrested for a series of crimes. Both "speculated" in flour and other food supplies most likely intended for their special settlers. Both slept with special settler women. Beznosikov was said to drink collectively with his laborers, while Pigulin was charged with hiding special settler "deserters" as well as refusing to send for medical assistance for a sick settler who later died as a result. Both cases were sent on to the OGPU.[132]

In the Urals, there was a case against a commandant for attempting to force a seventy-two-year-old woman to participate in the timber rafting; when she refused, he shot her. Another Urals commandant brutally beat a special settler and imprisoned him for leaving work. The settler died that day, as did another settler who had been tossed into a freezing river. The OGPU indicated that these were not isolated instances of abuse.[133]

In April 1932, the OGPU sent a memorandum to all regional procurators discussing the "alarming" number of cases against commandants and indicating that it was taking steps to check all commandants. The OGPU ordered procurators to "take seriously" the issue of defending special settlers.[134] At about the same time, an OGPU circular ordered the removal of all commandants with criminal records of any kind, an order that more than likely remained a dead letter.[135]

It is important to note once again that the OGPU was not acting out of humanitarian concerns when it initiated these cases against commandants. It shared the company men's prejudices regarding the special settlers, not to mention their criminal tendencies. The OGPU, however, had a broader perspective—that of the long-term interests of Soviet economic development and colonization as well as the interests of its own emerging economic empire. The Soviet company men worked within a smaller universe.

Soviet company men filled a power vacuum in the Soviet wilderness under extraordinarily difficult circumstances and in an epoch when history—or Stalin and his Politburo who saw themselves presiding over history—had no time for the suffering of individuals. "You can't make an omelet without breaking eggs" and "when the forest is cut the chips fly" were two sayings popular in the political lexicon of the Soviet First Five-Year Plan period. What this meant was that the agents of Soviet power had free rein to get the job done—whatever it may have been— consequences be damned. There was no room for "moral absolutism" or "rotten bourgeois liberalism." If the company men were agents of Soviet power, the special settlers were little more than tools to be exploited in the greater interests of history.

This mentality shaped the world in which the Soviet company men lived and worked. It empowered them both literally and figuratively. The implementation of special resettlement policy, especially in the early years, had created a vortex of unlimited power in which men of very limited background and ability found themselves dealing with what the state pronounced to be its "most implacable foe," the chief enemy of the day, the "socially alien" kulak. They brought with them their own cultural prejudices and fear as well as rudimentary organizational or security skills learned in the army or Cheka, which only served to compound revolutionary-historical intransigence with the brutal ethos of the Russian Civil War.

The special settlers were expendable. In fact, the state had calculated a "planned loss" of some 5 percent of the special settler population as an "acceptable" loss.[136] Soviet company men accepted (and often overfulfilled) the notion of a planned loss, in some instances even stockpiling coffins or digging graves in advance in an otherwise rare display of Soviet efficiency.[137] Soviet company men especially resented the "dependents" of able-bodied special settlers, often referring to them as "ballast."[138] They were not people but an unproductive burden that needed to be housed, clothed, and fed at "company" expense. They were a stopgap measure to fill the labor deficits of the most crucial "fronts" of the First Five-Year Plan.[139]

To make matters worse, most company men believed what they heard about the kulak; many had grown up in the countryside and recalled the village and the kulak—whatever he may have stood for in their memory and understanding—with hate. They knew, or believed they knew, that the kulak exploited the laboring peasantry mercilessly, that kulaks were, to quote Lenin, "avaricious, bloated, and bestial," "the most brutal, callous, and savage exploiters," "spiders," "leeches," and "vampires," determined to subvert Soviet power.[140] In their minds, the kulak had been transformed into an abstraction, a repository for the projection of all the bitterness and cruelties of the old (and sometimes present) order. Like other enemies in the generic and collective meaning of the term, the kulak had been dehumanized. The kulak (if not the entire peasantry) had been transformed into an object, the infamous "other" of the Bolshevik Party, to be put to work, dominated, subjected to Communist "reeducation," and mercilessly exploited.

Such ideological fervor, real or simply paraded, manifested itself among many Soviet company men in their dealings with special settlers. In Narym, for example, local officials said of the special settlers, "This kulak, this is our enemy," to which Eikhe replied, "Of course to say that the special settlers are our [nash] people, one cannot. They are our enemies." Nevertheless, Eikhe held out the possibility that these enemies could be remolded by the joint efforts of the party and OGPU.[141] For others, remolding was not an issue for discussion. "We need to kill and destroy the lot of you," the senior foreman Ragushniak, a Communist Party member, yelled at his special settlers in the Urals. Another official in the same area told recent arrivals from the Kuban, "we will destroy the people from Kuban, no one will live to return." Here special settlers were punished by incarceration in unheated cells. Anyone could arrest a special settler and order such punishment—the commandant, the foreman, even brigadiers. In some cases, such confinement led to death, in other cases, to loss of the ability to work.[142] In Siberia, some officials looked upon deportation as the first step to the "physical liquidation" of the kulaks.[143] In Kytlymskii District in the Urals, company men were heard to say of their special settlers, "they must be beaten like dogs," "such parasites should be put to death."[144]

In other cases, it was less ideological fervor, per se, than the everyday realities of survival that determined the behavior of company men. In late August 1931, an OGPU commission arrived in Arkhangel'sk to begin an inspection of the special settlements of the Northern Territory. The commission's members were surprised by the "unfriendly" reception they received from V. I. Ivanov, who had replaced Bergavinov as party chief in the spring of 1931. Ivanov dismissed the commission's inquiries, telling them, "Here we have party committee members' children dying. One of the members of the party committee bureau lost two children. Our cadres in the north live under terrible conditions and yet you want to talk about the kulak!?"[145] Doubtless, Ivanov spoke for many company men lower down the chain of the command, who could barely eke out an existence for themselves and their families, let alone lose sleep over the material conditions of a socially alien work force.

The precise mix of belief, cynicism, fear, and hatred among company men is not easy to disentangle. But at some level, they were Stalinists oblivious to individual suffering for the sake of the collective. True believers coexisted with (and shaded into) cynics intent on maximizing production and overfulfilling plans, men of great ambition and determination, as well as, less frequently, the occasional sadist who viewed the special settlement as a personal domain or fiefdom. Others may have felt fear or pressure to toe the line. And their actions were contingent upon the "taiga conditions" that shaped their relations with the special settlers.

Not all of the company men were sadists, true believers, or drunkards. The archives yield scattered cases of commandants and work bosses who attempted to aid or shield their workers. Sergei Kladykov, a commandant in the Urals, asked in wonderment when he first surveyed his enemy work force, "What kind of kulaks are these?!" He was promptly arrested.[146] Ivan Vasil'evich Gagarin, a union official, wrote a strongly worded complaint to the Nizhne-Tagil'skii procurator, telling of widespread hunger among the families of his laborers and the embezzlement of their food supplies. He told the procurator that he had attempted to enlist the aid of the local secret police, but was told that special resettlement affairs were none of his business and was even threatened with arrest if he pursued the matter further.[147] Others made extraordinary efforts to secure food and other necessities for their laborers, or appealed to superiors and the OGPU for assistance, often at considerable personal risk.[148]

Kuz'ma Larukov may well have fit into any of these categories of company men. Time and circumstance placed the Kuz'mas of the world of special settler officialdom in their positions and determined their behavior. Before the revolution, Kuz'ma would likely have lived and worked for most of his life in the village in which he was born, venturing out only for his military service and trips to town. The war and revolution changed all of that, hardening men like Kuz'ma and giving them vast responsibilities and vast powers. By the time of the First Five-Year Plan, Kuz'ma and his colleagues had become a part of Soviet power, agents of history for whom the end justified the means.

Conclusion

The reality of the special settlements in the early 1930s was that there was little room for the reforging through labor and education that some in the party and OGPU envisioned. The special settlers lived within a militarized penal system devised to eliminate all traces of their former existence and to remind them on a daily basis that they were enemies destined to toil for the state until the end of their days. The "taiga conditions" in which the special settlements arose permitted Soviet company men to wield vast and unlimited power over their charges.

Stalinism abounded in contradiction, if not outright hypocrisy. The seeming contradictions between the intricate (however belated) planning for the special settlements and actual reality, between the ethos of reforging and the brutal conditions of life and labor of the children were typical of Stalinist rule. The modernist social engineering that took place in Moscow had scant relation to the primitive conditions of the hinterlands or the regime's actual capacity to translate plans into action. There was, moreover, often an inverse correlation between the degree of intricacy in planning and the state's capacity to implement the plans. The detailed blueprints of special resettlement policy were little more than a Communist projection of order and modernity superimposed upon chaos. They were fiction—socialist realism in another form.

Similar contradictions appear in the actions of the company men. On the one hand, they were exemplars of the system sharing a Stalinist mentality; on the other hand, many, if not most, of them regularly flouted the law. Once again, the contradiction is seeming rather than real, representing the essence of Stalinism. Stalinism cannot be reduced to pure ideology. Instead, its essence lay in praxis—that is, the ways in which ideology came together with reality. In this sense, Stalinism was tantamount to ideology and prejudice translated into practice within the context of "taiga conditions"—weak administrative structures and the primitive conditions of a far-flung agrarian country. Stalinism was lawlessness constrained and empowered by ideology. The lawlessness of the company men served a purpose: it got the job done. Only when it threatened to imperil the long-term economic interests of the regime, or when scapegoating could serve a useful political purpose, did Moscow step in with reprimands, party expulsions, dismissals, and, on rare occasions, arrest and imprisonment.

The result was a situation that gave rise to the worst possible atrocities. In the late summer of 1931, the OGPU would describe this situation as "outrageous" (*bezobraznoe*). The disastrous implementation of the policy was leading not only to skyrocketing costs and the decline of the special settler population but also to disorder and security threats. This set the scene for the OGPU takeover of 1931.

6

Flight and Rebellion:
The OGPU Takeover

Comrades, [they] say that we have no organs occupied with these issues
[kulak resettlement]. [We] need to put before the C. C. the issue of
someone occupying themselves with these matters. [We] need coordination so they can say that the OGPU is concerned with this and the
Commissariat of Internal Affairs with that. Someone must answer for all
this.
—A. S. Kiselev, a member of the Central Executive Committee

In May 1931, a special Politburo commission declared that "In view
of the outrageous use of the special settler labor force and the disorder in their material conditions," all special settler affairs were
to be transferred to the jurisdiction of the OGPU.[1] In the Northern
Territory, where the largest contingent of special settlers came in 1930,
the mortality rate was "not less than 15 percent."[2] In the Urals, which
would surpass the Northern Territory in 1931 as the region receiving the
largest numbers of exiles, an August 1931 OGPU report noted, "Thanks
to the outrageous conditions in the forestry industry, we cannot in
future achieve real results with the special settler labor force."[3] In the
meantime, tens of thousands of special settlers had attempted to escape
or were still on the run. And in the summer of 1931, a series of revolts
in the special settlements would rock the provinces, arising, to use
the refrain of 1931, as a result of the constant "outrage" of the special
settlers' existence. This security threat, more than any other factor, led
to the OGPU takeover of July 1931.

As early as July 1930, at a conference on escapes from the special
settlements, the OGPU expressed alarm at the ever-rising numbers of
escapes and declared the situation to be out of control.[4] Nonetheless,
the Council of People's Commissars and the Commissariat of Internal
Affairs continued to be responsible for special resettlement into the

spring of 1931, with some greater devolution of authority to the Commissariat of Agriculture, the Supreme Council of the National Economy, and the regional soviet executive committees.[5] The OGPU still held some vaguely defined responsibility for general observation and for maintaining "pressure" (*nazhim*) on industry to uphold its responsibility for the special settlers.[6] In fact, in a November 1930 memorandum on escapes, the OGPU told its regional bosses in Eastern Siberia and the Urals that they were *still* responsible for security "despite the transfer of jurisdiction of the kulak operation to the offices of the Commissariat of Internal Affairs."[7] Conflict and ambiguous lines of demarcation of authority between the OGPU and the Commissariat of Internal Affairs continued throughout 1930.[8]

To make matters worse, preparations had begun for the resumption of dekulakization. In the fall of 1930, the OGPU had orchestrated the exile, mainly to Siberia and the Far East, of some 36,000 kulak family members from Ukraine and another 1,880 from Belorussia to join their heads of households who had been exiled alone the previous spring. Plans for the 1931 dekulakization operation, which would numerically exceed that of 1930, began shortly thereafter. In its 20 February 1931 protocols, the Politburo called on the OGPU to prepare in the coming months for the exile of 200,000 to 300,000 families.[9] At this same Politburo meeting, Andreev was placed in charge of all matters relating to dekulakization and exile, leading the following month to the formal creation of the Andreev Commission, charged with supervision of all operations pertaining to special resettlement.[10] By May 1931 the Andreev Commission would reduce the numerical plans for exile, mainly in response to the lack of preparation in Kazakhstan, the region originally slated to absorb the largest numbers of exiles (some 150,000) in 1931. In the end, according to OGPU statistics, as many as 265,795 families (or 1,243,860 people) would be resettled in 1931, including 95,544 in the Urals, 54,360 in Western Siberia, 14,508 in Eastern Siberia, 49,455 in Kazakhstan, 11,648 in the Northern Territory, and 5,778 in the Far East.[11] In the meantime, in May 1931 the Andreev Commission had formally made the decision to transfer all special resettlement operations to the OGPU, effective from July.[12] No doubt the dismissals of Tolmachev as head of the Commissariat of Internal Affairs and of former Right Oppositionist Rykov as head of the Council of People's Commissars at the end of 1930 facilitated the transfer of operations from the Commissariat of Internal Affairs and soviet state apparatus to the OGPU.[13]

The primary reasons for the transfer of operations to the OGPU were security and the need to keep the special settler labor force alive. The OGPU charged the soviet, party, and industrial organs with neglect of the special settlers; short-term interests in fulfilling the plan led to a willful disregard for their physical survival. The OGPU set its sights on what it called the *permanent* settlement of the special settler labor force as a cornerstone of its newly emerging economic empire in the Gulag. The OGPU was equally alarmed by the escalating numbers of escapes; tens of thousands of special settlers were fleeing to the cities and industrial sites or home to their native villages. Within the special settlements, there was also disturbing news of a variety of so-called counterrevolutionary activities. The OGPU blamed "negative" moods and "antisoviet" activities in the special settlements on the continuing "outrages" in the provinces, which it perceived to be a major security threat and to which it was determined to put an end.

Flight from Chaos

The OGPU was fully aware of what it called in its reports the "mood" of the special settlers. Through its censorship practices and network of informers in the field, the OGPU attempted to track the mood and opinions of the special settlers. According to a December 1930 special report on the Northern Territory, there was, rather unsurprisingly, an overwhelmingly "antisoviet" mood among the majority of exiles. They compared their situation with prison and believed that they would all die from hunger. One special settler was quoted as saying, "Whether we build [homes] or not, it's impossible to live in this dense forest, we will die all the same." Another said, "They forced thousands of people here like convicts, they torture [them] and do with them as they please, even forcing them to work without bread."[14]

Some pinned their hopes on the outbreak of a war that would lead to the overthrow of the Soviet government. An intercepted letter from one exile included the following wishful thinking: "America demands that the USSR quickly send home all the dekulakized and exiled or it will take other measures." In another letter, a special settler wrote, "Now soon there will be war. They've declared a mobilization. The government won't last long since foreign governments want to intervene and stop the violence over people." Rumors of war were everywhere in the special settlements.[15]

The OGPU listed examples of the exiles' "hatred" for the existing order. One was quoted as saying, "I promised my dying daughter that I would murder fifty communists. For this I am guarding my health." Another said, "We must protect our health and wait for the time when we can get even with them for everything." Still another was quoted as saying, "Our patience will soon be exhausted. But all the same they won't reeducate us and we will never forget that they took all our property from us." The OGPU also noted that there were "conversations" about organizing revolts and bandit gangs. One elder said, "If we hadn't been such fools, we would never have suffered so, but would have organized to resist."[16]

Active, organized resistance was, in fact, seldom an option given the conditions and isolation under which the special settlers lived. More common were various kinds of labor actions: strikes, work stoppages, refusal to work. These were reported in all regions and generally had as much to do with hunger, exhaustion, and inadequate clothing as with resistance.[17]

Flight was by far the most common recourse for able-bodied men, women, and youth. It was in fact such a common response to the desperation of their situation, especially in the early years, that some feared that in time only the elderly and women with children would remain in the special settlements.[18] People left alone, in groups, or in entire families. Over the decade of the 1930s, it became more difficult to remain at liberty, but in the earlier years less than half of escapes ended in an arrest or return. As of February 1931, the OGPU claimed that close to 72,000 special settlers were in flight.[19]

Escape was not an easy choice, for as one special settler wrote, it could "tear apart" a family.[20] But many families had no choice. From the very first days, flight became a major problem for the authorities. The majority of escapees were male. The decision to separate the able from the nonable was responsible for many initial flights from the interior, as men ran to rejoin their families in temporary residence in an effort to save them. The OGPU also complained that the return of children facilitated flight because the children required adult accompaniment to return home.[21] Flight was made more possible by the fact that manpower was insufficient to guard the exiles.[22] The terrible conditions of exile would guarantee that flight became a chronic headache for the OGPU.[23]

Families who were forced to make the difficult decision to send their children home could not always rely on official procedures of return. Some children left alone or with adult accompaniment, taking the route of illegal flight. The parents of N. N. Pavlov (whom we met earlier as he traveled into exile) decided to send him home to relatives. "But since I couldn't run from exile alone, I had to run together with a woman who was getting ready to run from exile and whose village was six km. from ours. . . . So I ran together with this woman whose last name I no longer remember." Pavlov recalled the railroad stations crawling with guards looking for escaped exiles, as well as his difficult journey home. "My circumstances worsened. My fellow traveler left me, saying that my parents gave me too little money and that she could not feed me on this money . . . ." So Pavlov was left on his own to complete the journey to his village. He earned money for food at one of the railroad stations, by getting tips for carrying passengers' bags. Finally, a driver offered him a ride home to his village. Having heard Pavlov's story, he refused to take any money.[24]

A. M. Cherkasova recalled, "Hunger began, people began to leave in families or alone, my older brother left, writing a note that we should not look for him, we did not see him again. . . . Father sat home in the winter, he couldn't work because of asthma, in the spring, he also left."[25] T. I. Evseeva, born in 1921 and exiled with her family to Perm from the Nizhnyi Novgorod area, remembered that "they fed us very badly. [We] began to starve in the first months. The bread given out as rations was not enough. . . . Many, not being able to handle this kind of life, resolved on desperate acts: [they] consciously maimed themselves or tried to run away home. [They] ran away at any time of the year—in winter and in summer. But not many reached home, many people died unknown."[26]

Ivan Tvardovskii wrote in considerable detail about his family's experience of flight. The Tvardovskii family's story was not exceptional among the stories of special settlers. What was exceptional was the fact that Ivan's elder brother was Aleksandr Tvardovskii, the renowned Soviet poet and editor of the flagship progressive journal of the Khrushchev thaw era, *Novyi Mir* (or *New World*). In 1931, Ivan and his family were exiled from Zagor'e in Smolensk to the Urals. They were put to work in forestry, "harvesting" and floating logs.

Ivan recalled how easy it was to leave the special settlement, since, he noted, there were no guards or security. In fact, Ivan and his elder brother Konstantine escaped from their settlement three times. The first time Ivan was caught and simply sent back to the settlement—without an escort of any kind. The second time he was put to work in a local factory after being caught near a railroad station. When Ivan and his brother fled the factory—despite what he described as quite tolerable conditions there—they were soon apprehended by the OGPU. Eventually they found themselves in a labor camp in Perm, set up for kulak escapees, where conditions were very bad. After a month in the camp, they were sent—again without a guard—back to their family in the special settlement.

Ivan and his brother stayed in the special settlement from January to April 1932. Only his mother, a sister, and his youngest brother were still there. His father had fled with another brother, thirteen-year-old Pavel, some months earlier while Ivan and Konstantine were still in flight. In April, Ivan left once again, this time on his own. He spent the next months working in a series of jobs without documents and riding the trains illegally with other runaway kulaks. At one railroad station, a kindly man approached Ivan and, after inquiring about what had happened to him, gave him money for a haircut and a bath. As it became more and more difficult to live and work without documents, Ivan acquired a set of forged documents. With these he found work in Nizhnyi Novgorod. Eventually, he left his job. With genuine documents newly acquired from that job, he set off. He had a series of odd jobs, including, ironically, a job with the OGPU. (An OGPU labor contractor recruited him and a crowd of other idle hands for temporary work from a railroad station.)

While Ivan was in Nizhnyi Novgorod, his father visited him. (Ivan had sent his address to a third party, an aunt.) He told Ivan his own escape story. He left in the summer of 1931 with Pavel. They traveled back to Smolensk and sought out twenty-one-year-old Aleksandr who was living there as a student and budding poet. (Aleksandr had been living independently from his family from before the time of their dekulakization.) Aleksandr was a member of the Komsomol at the time. In spite of his family's fate, he was a true believer in communism. His family had written to him for help from exile. He responded:

> Dear Family! I am neither a barbarian nor a brute. I ask you to stay strong, be patient, and work. The liquidation of the kulak as a class is not the liquidation of people, still less of children . . . I cannot write you . . . do not write me. . . .

When his father and younger brother arrived at his door pleading for assistance, Aleksandr sent them away, offering only to pay their way back to exile. He renounced his family as "enemies of the people" and had no more contact with them until 1936, the year he published his epic poem, "The Land of Muravia," and won the first of his three Stalin prizes.[27]

In the meantime, Tvardovskii senior lived as a fugitive, regularly sending money to his wife and younger children back in the special settlement. In late 1932, he returned to the Urals and brought his family out of exile. They lived in the forest for weeks. Eventually, he found work in a state farm under the assumed name of Tarasov, passing himself off as his wife's "second husband." In 1936, Aleksandr attempted to reconcile with his family, helping them to move back to Smolensk. As the mounting terror claimed three of his brothers-in-law, the father fled once again, this time to the Kuban.[28]

Mariia Solomonik also fled. She was a child when her family was exiled to Narym in Siberia. Her father was separated from the family en route into exile. He escaped, again with little initial effort since security was, in fact, minimal. He traveled some 800 kilometers back to his home village. There he managed to obtain false documents for himself and his wife. With the help of neighbors, he assembled the necessary supplies to make the return journey into exile to bring out his family.

Once in Narym, Mariia's father led the family, along with a group of young women (probably also separated from their menfolk), out of exile, traveling only at night. Most of the group was soon captured when they approached a river clearing for fresh water. The family got away and sought help from an Old Believer[29] living in the forest who had recently lost all his children to smallpox. He promised to help on the condition that the family leave their eldest daughter with him. Despite the mother's hysterical reaction to this proposal, the father reluctantly agreed. After resting at the Old Believer's home, they left. Within a few hours, the father settled the family in the forest and went back to retrieve his daughter.

Eventually the family (including the daughter who had been left behind) was caught and imprisoned in a barn, full of thieves and criminals, eight to ten kilometers from Tomsk. The father was held separately under conditions that allowed him to work as a driver hauling vegetables in Tomsk. The family meanwhile awaited transport back to Narym in the spring. While working in Tomsk, the father met sympathetic people who agreed to help him save his family. He secreted his daughters from the makeshift prison in vegetable sacks, and soon the family was back on the road, this time on the way to the mines outside of Stalinsk where there was a pressing need for workers. There they stayed, living in hiding and moving from time to time. Mariia's father would be arrested twice more. Only after 1934 did the family succeed in living in relative peace. Still the OGPU kept tabs on her father, placing him on a special registry list of suspect elements.[30]

Neighbors

The borders of the special settlements were porous; just as special settlers could get out, others could get in. Archival records and memoirs alike testify to peasants traveling thousands of kilometers to try to save their relatives with food, money, and falsified documents, or at least to bring the children out of exile. This, and evidence of escaped heads of households sending money back to their families in exile or struggling to rescue them, bears witness to the enduring cohesion of the peasant family.[31] According to the OGPU, the continued support of friends and relatives often facilitated escape. The villages were deluged with letters from their former neighbors now in exile. The exiles wrote individually and collectively to relatives and friends, as well as to their former rural soviets and land societies, requesting assistance, documents, and the rescue of children. One exile in Vologda wrote to his brother, "Dear Brother, come here, take our little ones . . . save our two children," while another wrote, "Save us, as you can, please Uncle F., do everything you can."[32]

In Ukraine, according to the OGPU, a "movement" developed for the return of kulaks in thirty-two counties, supposedly spearheaded by relatives receiving alarming letters from exiles. Family members and friends sent petitions, delegations, and even involved their rural soviets in their efforts to help.[33] Friends and relatives came in relatively sizeable numbers to the regions of exile in attempts to save loved ones or bring children home. They did so at great risk, given the OGPU's propensity to arrest suspicious-looking characters approaching the exiles. (Even the peasant carters who originally transported the exiles had been subject to arrest.)[34] In July 1930, the OGPU reported that in the Northern Territory, it had turned back 2,225 visiting relatives, from whom it confiscated 376 fake documents and 152 blank documents. Soon after this, the OGPU put a halt to such visits, at least as long as the exiles were still in temporary residence.[35]

Kulaks who succeeded in making their way back to their native villages often had the support of their fellow villagers, at least in the first months when the villages were still in turmoil from collectivization. In one Middle Volga village, a crowd of two hundred women blocked the removal of runaways, seizing those under arrest and moving them to their own homes.[36] In the village Belova in Barabinskii District, Western Siberia, the rural soviet attempted to arrest a kulak who came back from exile. A Red army soldier named Starkov who was on leave in his village mobilized a crowd and demanded the release of the kulak, claiming he had been incorrectly dekulakized. The kulak was released to the crowd but rearrested the next day. Starkov again gathered a crowd as well as starting a petition. In the end, both Starkov and the kulak were arrested.[37] A group of eight kulaks in Pokrovskii District, Rubtsovskii County, Siberia, returned home, shot to death the activist who had dekulakized them, and then burned his home down, killing his wife, a grown daughter, and her two children.[38] Some kulaks returned to their villages and took back their homes and property from the collective farm.[39] In the summer of 1930, the Siberian OGPU chief gave an order to arrest returning kulaks "without publicity" (that is, as quietly as possible) to avoid peasant protest in their defense.[40]

It was not only relatives and fellow villagers who helped the special settlers. Although evidence is relatively sparse on the relations between special settlers and local, indigenous populations, there is more evidence of locals aiding settlers and declining to search for escapees than there is evidence of locals assisting the state.[41] In those rare cases when there was a nearby village, young special settlers made the journey there to beg. Pavlov remembered crying, "Dear people, give for the sake of Christ."[42]

It was the all-too-visible injustice of their circumstances that led to support for the exiles. How widespread that support was cannot be measured, although sources indicate numerous examples. A. T. Shokhireva, born in 1915, recalled arriving in a village called Pavda in Tagil'skii County in the Urals. "The local residents mocked us in a good-natured way," she noted. "We didn't look like kulaks at all. They thought that kulaks should be [dressed] in gold and silver."[43] Elsewhere in the Urals, there were reports of local peasants meeting the exiles with bread and salt, a traditional village greeting. Here, there were also reports of large crowds of peasants surrounding the exiles and plying them with food and other necessities.[44] An exile in the Northern Territory wrote, "On such rations one cannot live. The only salvation is the countryside. Each day, someone runs to the village for food. The villagers do everything for us, all for nothing, they will not take money from us."[45] Of course not all peasants sympathized; some took advantage of the exiles' plight, selling them food and goods at inflated prices, while others were inhibited by fear.[46]

As a sixteen-year-old, Anna Ivanovna Selivanova was exiled from her native Saratov village to Komi in the far north. She recalled, "We began to starve immediately. We lived in a makeshift cabin. We cooked food on a fire and dried our clothes by the fire." When spring came, Anna's father decided to send her and a neighbor's daughter to look for a village where they could get help. "We walked 75 kilometers before we reached a village. Mezhog was its name. There we met a woman who was shepherding a cow. We asked for shelter for the night. She boiled a pot of potatoes for us, gave us bread and let us spend a night in the hayloft. The woman's name was Marina. She was a Komi but spoke Russian. We knitted a pair of mittens for her son, a soldier. Marina kept us to live with her for a while. Other women started bringing us work, too. We knitted socks and mittens. For Easter, following Marina's advice, we went begging along the village. We each gathered up bags of dried rusks. Then we got ready to go back to our families at Udorskaia. Again 75 kilometers by foot. Father told us that the people were good there and one could live there. Father, mother, and I went back to Mezhog. There were no collective farms there yet. We began doing all kinds of peasant work for the householders. Thus we lived till the winter. Then father decided to escape and go home. We were stopped in the village of Irta. Father managed to get away, but we women were detained. They put us in a bathhouse and then herded us to Iarensk. There we also sat in a bathhouse, but there were no guards. We [escaped and] went away again to Mezhog, to Marina. We sometimes took care of children, sometimes

Prilutskii Monastery (Vologda) in 1998 (author's photo).

NKVD montage on special resettlement (Courtesy of the Institute of History, Russian Academy of Science, Siberian Branch, and Dr. S. A. Krasil'nikov, from the album *Sovetskii Narym* [1936]).

началось...

Special settlers being transported to Narym by barge (Courtesy of the Institute of History, Russian Academy of Science, Siberian Branch, and Dr. S. A. Krasil'nikov, from the album *Sovetskii Narym* [1936]).

Special settler family in Narym (Courtesy of the Institute of History, Russian Academy of Science, Siberian Branch, and Dr. S. A. Krasil'nikov, from the album *Sovetskii Narym* [1936]).

Special settlement in Narym (Courtesy of the Institute of History, Russian Academy of Science, Siberian Branch, and Dr. S. A. Krasil'nikov, from the album *Sovetskii Narym* [1936]).

Special settlement in Narym (Courtesy of the Institute of History, Russian Academy of Science, Siberian Branch, and Dr. S. A. Krasil'nikov, from the album *Sovetskii Narym* [1936]).

Kuz'ma Larukov, special settlement commandant in the Komi Republic (Courtesy of fond Pokaianie).

Kuz'ma Larukov and unknown commandant with their families (Courtesy of fond Pokaianie).

A Group of special settler commandants on holiday in Sochi, 1937 (Courtesy of fond Pokaianie).

Special settler orphanage in Narym (Courtesy of the Institute of History, Russian Academy of Science, Siberian Branch, and Dr. S. A. Krasil'nikov, from the album *Sovetskii Narym* [1936]).

Special settler orphanage in Narym (Courtesy of the Institute of History, Russian Academy of Science, Siberian Branch, and Dr. S. A. Krasil'nikov, from the album *Sovetskii Narym* [1936]).

Ivan Tvardovskii at his home in Zagor'e, outside of Smolensk, in 1998 (author's photo).

Ivan and Mariia Tvardovskii at their home in Zagor'e, outside of Smolensk, in 1998 (author's photo).

did the laundry, and sometimes knitted—they paid us only with food. Father sent a letter in Marina's name saying that he was in Kotlas. In the spring, Marina took me to the boat and dressed me Komi style: a red kerchief, a broad skirt, and a tight blouse. I arrived at Kotlas with only 15 kopecks in my pocket." [47]

Anna Ivanovna and doubtless many others survived due to the help of villagers like Marina.

The Security Threat

The prevention of escapes presented the main security issue in the special settlements. The statutes specified that special settlers could leave their villages only with the commandant's permission. The visits of friends and relatives were subject to strict control. Nonspecial settlers could live within the territory of the special settlements only with official permission. [48] The control of the extraneous population was intended to eliminate the possibility of escape. In some regions, the special settlers themselves were enlisted in the prevention of escapes. Collective responsibility was introduced in the settlements to stem the tide of escapes, and elders were called upon to monitor the movement of all settlers and to report escapes and escape plans to the commandant. [49] In addition, the OGPU attempted to create a network of informers within the special settlements. These were individuals who had been selected at the collection points, just prior to transport to the exile regions. [50] In the Urals, there was supposed to be two informers for every fifty families, one-half of them to be recruited from among the supposedly more politically reliable youth. [51] In the Northern Territory, as of late summer 1931, the OGPU claimed that there were 4,000 informers among the exiles, but complained that no work had been developed with them. [52] In the Urals, connections with informers were also lacking. In the Kalatinskii District only 16 of 24 informers were active; in Cherdynskii District, 59 out of 149 informers were in contact with the OGPU; and in Chusovskii District, there were contacts with 139 of 153 informers (5 had fled). [53]

The Stalinist regime was terrified of social disorder, and the continuing mass escapes from the special settlements represented some of its worst fears. The authorities were afraid that runaway kulaks would not only spread "counterrevolutionary agitation" in town and country about their experience but also join the "cadres" for banditry, which was widespread at this time in Siberia and several other regions. [54] They feared as well the "infection" of factories, cities, and new construction sites. [55] As a result, the OGPU and regular police began to make widespread arrests. In Siberia, OGPU boss L. M. Zakovskii ordered rural soviets to check the documents of all newcomers and to hold them if they looked "suspicious." He also ordered the urban police to be on the lookout.[56] In Vologda, the OGPU was said to have become "overly suspicious," arresting all sorts of people (some 3,153) with no connections whatsoever to kulaks, but lacking proper documentation.[57]

In the towns, kulaks were reportedly registering at employment offices and, with the help of networks of zemliaks (peasant seasonal workers from their home districts) and fake papers from their rural soviets, finding employment in industry. The OGPU ordered its regional chiefs to strengthen operative work to find these kulaks, increasing surveillance of night lodging, seasonal workers' dorms, tea houses, railroad stations, and especially Peasant Houses (the doma krest'ian, which provided social and legal services to peasants in many cities). They were also to strengthen their work with the trade unions that, following the Politburo 30 January 1930 decree, were supposedly carrying out a purge of individual kulaks from industrial enterprises.[58] An OGPU memo of 3 April 1930 to its regional chiefs would note an ongoing purge of towns from counterrevolutionary elements fleeing from the countryside, while it simultaneously decried arbitrary arrests of ordinary peasants lacking proper documentation and demanded stepped-up surveillance and informant work among zemliak networks and in the towns in general.[59]

The alarming dimensions that flight assumed prompted the OGPU to convene a special conference on the issue in July 1930.[60] At that time, the OGPU ordered its regional bosses to strengthen informant work as well as to institute a system of collective responsibility. OGPU regional chiefs were told to "involve" and offer material incentives to the local population in tracking runaways and finding out how and where kulaks were obtaining fake documents.[61] The OGPU regional authorities were ordered to take "decisive" measures to prevent returns to the village, organizing special checkpoints at railroad stations and warning exiles of the dire consequences of escape. Recaptured kulaks were to be sent back to their places of exiles or on to yet more remote places; if they succeeded in reaching their home villages, they were to be treated as first-category kulaks; "counterrevolutionary elements" among the escaped were to be tried by the regional OGPU tribunal and sentenced either to internment in a labor camp or execution.[62] In practice, however, given the magnitude of escapes, most runaways, especially women and young people, were simply sent back to their special settlements or, at worse, sent on to more distant places of exile.[63]

Meanwhile, escapes skyrocketed as desperate settlers, mainly men and boys, attempted to flee.[64] In the Northern Territory alone at this point, twenty-five OGPU operative groups were working on the capture of runaways.[65] The cottage production of false documents in towns like

Vologda made it relatively easy to assume a new identity.[66] Fake documents were reportedly sold to special settlers for twenty to twenty-five rubles each.[67] In Nadezhdinskii District in the Urals, a person described only as a "recidivist" was arrested for having in his possession twenty-eight blank documents with the insignia of various city institutions, including six blank forms from the city branch of the OGPU. The documents were so professionally done that the OGPU could not tell the difference between the falsified and the authentic documents.[68] The OGPU reported in July that thirty to forty people were escaping each day in the Urals.[69] Here, flight was facilitated by the fact that kulaks in some counties received work books that identified them only as seasonal workers with no hint as to their special status.[70] Elsewhere, according to the OGPU, there were "wide networks" composed of special settler fugitives who had escaped earlier and now sought to aid new escapees to find work and housing.[71]

By the end of the year, OGPU statistics would claim that 16.4 percent of all exiles were in flight or had fled. Although this figure undoubtedly incorporated multiple escape attempts, the numbers were still staggering. A total of 71,859 escapes had occurred (39,743 in the Northern Territory, 9,666 in the Urals, 21,000 in Siberia, 50 in the Far East, and 1,400 in Kazakhstan); of these, 33,110, or 46 percent of the total, had been recaptured. Kulaks in the Northern Territory who were recaptured were either returned to their special settlements (17,590), sent to a labor camp (3,100), or held for further investigation (3,595).[72] By October 1931, the number of escapes had risen to 101,650.[73]

Flight would continue to be a problem even after the OGPU took over all special settler operations in the summer of 1931. The number of those in flight would, in fact, reach its height in 1932 and 1933, the years of famine.[74] The reality of the special settlements was that their boundaries were porous; only geography and climate could bolster repressive measures in keeping the special settlers fixed to their place of exile. In the meantime, the fluidity of this population created havoc in the cities and parts of the countryside, feeding into regime fears of social instability. Mass escapes from the special settlements played no small role in the expansion of the secret police's powers in the early 1930s as it struggled against social dislocation, rampant crime, and "class enemies" in a series of repressive purging campaigns that would form an important part of the backdrop to the mass operations of 1937 and 1938.[75]

Rebellion

While the majority of special settlers could do little or nothing to alleviate their plight, short of fleeing or seeking assistance from relatives, conditions had become so dire by the spring and summer of 1931 that a series of uprisings broke out in special settlements in the Urals, Siberia, and perhaps elsewhere as well, further adding to the OGPU's fears.

In March 1931, a party of exiled kulaks from the Western Region (around Smolensk) arrived in the Petropavlovskii timber camp in the Urals. Most of the settlers already working at the camp had come from the Kuban in 1930. The new exiles confronted horrendous conditions. The Kuban kulaks were literally starving. They faced crushing work norms. Even children and the elderly were forced into the forest. Many of these people could no longer work. At the same time, the local officials were described as "sadists." They locked up people who would not or could not work in unheated rooms without food. There were reports of torture, rape, and murder; a mass grave was dug in full view, so that the settlers would know their ultimate fate.

The new arrivals were shocked. They made contact with other exiles from the Western Region in the immediate area and began to plan an escape. In the second half of April, they arranged the murder of an especially brutal guard, using this as a pretext for action. Immediately, a group of some three hundred families left the settlement, moving slowly along the railroad tracks toward the nearest town. The local railroad workers provided what assistance they could. Before long, however, OGPU troops arrived and, in an undisclosed manner, halted the exiles' flight, arresting fifty-three "ring leaders."[76]

Four other "incidents" (*vystuplenie*—a regime euphemism for various types of protest or disturbances) took place in the Urals in June 1931, involving from two hundred to two thousand special settlers in actions more clearly akin to riots, the traditional Russian *bunt*, and including violence against property and persons. Each was suppressed by OGPU troops. Although these four incidents were clearly sparked by hunger and extreme conditions, they were also facilitated by the arrival of new contingents of special settlers, whose community cohesion was still intact.[77]

The influx of new settlers also catalyzed the Parbigskii uprising in Narym, Siberia. The uprising began on 29 July 1931. About 200 special settlers armed with fifteen hunting rifles, clubs, and axes surrounded the commandant's offices in one of the area's special settlements in an attempt to disarm officials. The ensuing shoot-out left three special settlers and one Soviet official dead. By the next day, the rebel forces had grown to some 350 people. They took control of several special settlements (Krylovka, Bakchar) and attacked the Parbigskii special settlement regional headquarters (*kommandatura*), which controlled some 33,000 special settlers. In Krylovka, the band "mobilized" all men between the ages of eighteen and fifty. According to OGPU reports, the band marched under the slogans, "Down with Communists," "Long Live Free

Trade," and "Long Live the Constituent Assembly" (the last a reference to the suppressed national assembly of 1917, which had been elected on the basis of universal suffrage just prior to the Bolshevik revolution.)

On 31 July, the rebels moved on to the Galkinskii special settlement regional headquarters but were met en route by an OGPU detachment, which dispersed the band. According to the OGPU reports, most of the "mobilized" returned voluntarily to their special settlements. The most active rebels, under the leadership of a man named Morev, continued to resist. In the end, seventy-nine rebels were killed and, depending on the source, from one to four and possibly more were killed on the Soviet side. In addition, sixty-three hunting rifles were seized, which the rebels had gotten from local hunters (who on several occasions had aided the rebels) and from Soviet offices. The revolt, which went on for almost a week, paralyzed soviet and party organs throughout the region.

The circumstances surrounding the Parbigskii revolt were similar to the Petropavlovskii "incident." The special settlers were all fairly recent arrivals from southern Siberia, who had relocated with their fellow villagers and drew on these community bonds in their rebellion. The conditions they encountered in the special settlements were terrible: there had been no salt for over a month; there was not enough bread; and the water supply was contaminated. Many people were ill. Everyone lived in rough, makeshift shelters. Many of the families were of first-category kulaks, whose heads of households were in the camps. Women demanded the return of their menfolk, pleading that they could not build housing without them. Official reports described the Parbigskii revolt as a hunger riot (*bunt*) and a "counterrevolutionary insurrection."[78]

The rebellions of the spring and summer of 1931, combined with the demoralization of the special settlers and skyrocketing rate of escape, placed in stark relief the "outrageous" conditions in the special settlements and highlighted the OGPU's security fears. Since the summer of 1930, the OGPU had expressed concern about inadequate security measures in the special settlements. When an explosion shook the Chernogorskii mines in Western Siberia, the regional authorities' first reaction was to purge the mines of supposedly kulak workers, although investigations would later prove that the explosion was not the result of an act of sabotage.[79] The Western Siberian authorities' reaction, however, was indicative of the anxieties felt in the provinces and in Moscow. When rebellion broke out in a series of special settlements in the spring and summer of 1931, it was clear that the administrative infrastructure had to change. The rebellions marked a turning point in special resettlement policy. This roughly coincided with the transfer of operations from the state apparatus to the OGPU and inaugurated a series of new policy initiatives aimed at ameliorating the conditions of the special settlers in an effort to preserve them as a permanent labor force.

The OGPU Takeover

The OGPU officially took over all special resettlement operations on 1 July 1931. The Politburo's decision to transfer full control to the OGPU was determined by the massive chaos and disorder of the first eighteen months of the special resettlement operation. It was also a natural political outcome of institutional rivalries within the government and of Stalin's increasing reliance on the OGPU in the administration of the state and economy. With Iagoda at its helm, the OGPU took control of the special settlements, placing them under the jurisdiction of the Gulag administration. Henceforth, the special settlements became one of the foundation stones of the Gulag.

The OGPU administered the special settlements through its Gulag bureaucracy in the form of a Department of Special Settlements (*otdel spetsposelenii*). Regions with large special settler populations had their own Department of Special Settlements under the OGPU regional offices. Depending on the size of the region, there also may have been district headquarters, as well as production headquarters, which worked on the sites where kulak labor was employed. At the base of the structure was the OGPU-appointed settlement commandant.[80]

On 20 July 1931, the Politburo issued a directive stating that the mass exiles of the kulaks had been fulfilled and that, in future, exile from areas of wholesale collectivization would occur only on a case-by-case basis.[81] At the same time, the Politburo requested that the Andreev Commission appoint someone to inspect employment and material conditions in all special settlements.[82] Within days, the Andreev Commission issued a directive calling attention to the "completely inadmissible situation" of the special settlers working in the forestry industry in the Urals, the Northern Territory, and Siberia and ordered reprimands for top industry officials. It also strongly criticized the ferrous metal and gold industry, enlisting G. K. Ordzhonidikze, the chairman of the Supreme Council of the National Economy, to intervene personally to sort out special settler affairs.[83] Finally, the Andreev Commission created a new commission, dominated by the OGPU, charged with settling and maintaining the special settlers as a permanent labor force.[84]

"With the aim of the full employment of the special settler work force and their settlement in exile," the Andreev Commission and the OGPU initiated a series of reform efforts designed to secure the special settlers as a permanent work force.[85] Salary deductions for special settlers were reduced from their original 25 percent to 15 percent, and the industrial organs were once more instructed to establish the same work norms for special settlers as for free laborers employed in similar work.[86] The Andreev Commission ordered the provision of 240,000 hectares (nearly 593,000 acres) of land for the special settlers' farming needs (84,000 hectares [207,480 acres] for grain crops and 156,000 [385,320 acres] for garden crops). The commission instructed the Commissariat of Agriculture to issue 11,330 rubles worth of seed and 5,400,000 rubles worth of agricultural equipment to special settlers. The Commissariat of Supply and a series of regional agencies were instructed to provision them with 20,000 horses, 33,000 cows, 8,300 pigs, and 150,000 rubles worth of poultry. In all, the sum of 40 million rubles was authorized for permanent settlement in what amounted (at least on paper) to a "repropriation" of the kulaks.[87]

Special settlers were henceforth allowed to obtain at their own expense or with the aid of special credit, a horse, cow, goat, pigs, sheep, and poultry. The Andreev Commission revoked the decisions of local organizations that had forbidden those special settlers working in industry from having garden plots. Special settlers were now allowed to build their own individual family houses without limitations on their patterns or sizes. Further, the industrial organs were still obliged to house special settlers working for them.[88]

On 26 October 1931 Iagoda wrote to Rudzutak, who replaced Andreev at the head of the Politburo commission on kulak resettlement, noting the "absolutely unacceptable" situation of the special settlers in 1930 and 1931, created "as a consequence of the absence of even minimal concern about them from local soviet organs and the economic agencies employing them." Iagoda demanded that by winter, the special settlers be guaranteed permanent housing, schools, and hospitals. He reiterated that provisions, pay, and the working day for special settlers should be the same as that for free workers.[89]

A flurry of directives surrounded the late summer/early fall 1931 reform efforts of the Politburo and OGPU. The OGPU issued orders to open up postal outlets (22 August), savings banks (24 August), registry offices (26 October), and a network of trade warehouses, communal dining halls, and bakeries (10 November).[90] M. D. Berman, deputy head and later head of the Gulag administration, issued directives to establish an educational system within the special settlements.[91] The Commissariat of Education issued instructions to develop in 1932 one seven-year school for every nine thousand special settlers. It also ordered the opening of a network of reading huts and centers for the "liquidation" of illiteracy (for adult education).[92] To pay for this, an additional 1–2 percent was to be deducted from special settlers' salaries for "cultural-educational" costs.[93]

Similar plans were made concerning the construction of hospitals and clinics to serve the special settler population. Berman described the situation here as "highly unsatisfactory," resulting in high mortality and the physical disablement of special settlers.[94] Plans were made to build one hospital for every 22,500 special settlers, each with two doctors and five staff members, as well as one sanitary director and assistant for every 50,000 people. Additional plans were made to mobilize 135 doctors (including 27 for Kazakhstan, 53 for the Urals, 17 for Western Siberia, 15 for the Northern Territory, and 13 for Eastern Siberia) and 754 *fel'dshers* (or medical orderlies).[95]

New directives were also issued concerning children and the elderly. According to temporary statutes issued in October, all special settlers had the right to send children under fourteen and non-able-bodied elderly to friends or relatives back in their native villages.[96] This decision was temporarily overturned by the Gulag administration in December based on the reasoning that "conditions had improved" and such transfers should be allowed only in exceptional cases.[97] By January 1932, however, Iagoda overruled the Gulag administration, reinstating the October 1931 rulings on the return of children and the elderly.[98]

The OGPU also issued instructions to free kulak heads of households (category-one kulaks and those arrested during the rebellions of 1930) from labor camps—provided they were not a "social danger"—and to reunite them with their families in exile. (The preliminary sanction of the OGPU was required in each case.) This measure was intended both to alleviate the suffering of exiled families without male heads of households as well as to try to stem flight.[99] At the same time, the OGPU again turned its attention to the fate of kulaks "incorrectly exiled" and ordered that their situation be "clarified."[100]

On 25 October 1931 L. M. Kogan, then the head of the Gulag administration, issued the "Temporary Statutes on the Rights and Responsibilities of Special Settlers and on the Administrative Functions and Rights of the Settlement Administration."[101] These statutes served to codify the rights of special settlers to medical services, education, social insurance, and the same labor conditions as "free workers," as well as strictly defining their labor obligations and restricting their movement. The statutes would remain in force through the 1930s.

Conclusion

Despite the OGPU takeover and attempts to stabilize the special settler workforce, little would change in the short term. By December, the Commissar of Justice, N. V. Krylenko, was complaining that the situation was still "unsatisfactory." The procurator's office was deluged with reports about the "unplanned" use of special settler labor, abysmal material conditions, epidemics and continuing high mortality rates, and the abuse, often violent, of special settler laborers.[102] To make matters worse, plans were in progress to remove all special settlers from centralized provisioning and to make them reliant on local resources.[103] Life for the special settlers would only worsen with the approach of the great famine in 1932 and 1933.

The realities of the special resettlement operation remained largely impervious to reform. Inadequate planning, material scarcity, corrupt or criminal commandants, a deadly climate, and vast geographical distances served as the primary context for the resettlement operation. In the end, repression would be the only real mechanism of control. Stalinist governance, high and low, had no administrative recourse but coercion to exert its control over the far-flung and undergoverned territories of the Soviet Union. Given these realities, the OGPU was the only institution capable of administering the special settlements, which, starting in 1931, became an official archipelago of the Gulag.[104]

7

Hunger unto Death:
The Famine of 1932/33

Hunger—this is not only a feverish dream about food, but a brutal nightmare of fear.
                    —I. S. Olifier, former special settler

I have traveled around the villages and found the situation to be extremely grave.[1] With few exceptions, the entire population is so emaciated that about 30 percent can barely walk due to hunger-related edema. Mortality for the month of March was as follows: special settlements Sapych—11; Emel'stan—1; Vezh—3; Vuktil'—21; and almost all [deaths were] a result of famine. . . . The death is easy—they simply fall asleep and never wake up. . . .

"Because of insufficient rations, people are eating birch bark, silage, leaves, and even cow dung. . . .

"The children are sick, anemic, many are swollen with edema. Vuktil' is the worst in this respect, since there are over two hundred children there. . . . All of the able-bodied are so weak that they sometimes cannot even rise from their beds. . . .

"The number of patients at the hospital grows every day—all suffering from emaciation and in need of a high calorie diet. The amount of milk per village is very limited, and whatever milk is available is taken by the commandants in Pevk and Sapych for their own consumption.

"It is essential to take some sort of measures in order to improve the situation of the settlers, since mortality has increased in April—thus, for example, in Vezh seven people died in a week."[2]

This report, dated 9 April 1933, was written by the Vezh special settlement doctor for the chairman of the Komi soviet executive committee, whose name, perhaps aptly, was Tarakanov (or, "of the cockroaches"). What the doctor described was a snapshot of the famine in the special settlements, a quiet offshoot of the mass famine that consumed large parts of the Soviet countryside in 1932/33, taking with it in the process as many as five to seven million lives nationwide.[3]

One special settler—the son of a kulak who claimed to be a civil war veteran—wrote to the central authorities that 75 percent of the population in his locale were swelling up from hunger. He pleaded with them to investigate, arguing that "the center doesn't know what is happening locally."[4] The center knew. Reports not just of hunger, but of full-blown famine circulated through every level of government.

"We special settler women of Talaia settlement write to you with a request. We receive a [bread] norm of 5 kilograms a month which is not enough and we are forced to eat grass. Many of us have nursing children, but we have no breast milk." That petition came from a group of sixty-four women living in Ivdel'skii District in the Urals.[5] In the Northern Territory, a doctor who had been posted to work with the special settlers since July 1930 wrote in 1933 that roughly one-half of the special settler women in his purview had ceased to menstruate due to anemia and emaciation. Exhaustion and hunger had led to such a state, according to the doctor, that "there occur very drawn-out deaths—today you see a down-and-out person, and by the evening you find out that he died. He goes to work, and they carry him from the forest barely alive and he dies in the night."[6] Another doctor in the Northern Territory wrote that six hundred special settlers were starving in Vozhegodskii District and warned that they would die if no one came to their assistance. He wrote that the special settlers looked "awful": they sat, not moving, with shining, yellow eyes.[7] In Western Siberia, a public health official reported that five- and six-year-olds looked like old people; they no longer played and hardly moved at all.[8] The regional OGPU sounded the alert everywhere, warning of famine and the death of entire families in the special settlements. As one OGPU official put it in a letter to the head of the Northern Territory forestry industry, "The situation is so catastrophic that the failure to take quick measures to set straight the food issue will lead to the fall of labor discipline and a sharp drop in work rations."[9]

Moscow knew. And like the OGPU official just quoted, the regime chose to allow life and death to take a back seat to the plan. The "food issue" concerned officials only to the extent that it affected productivity or state security. The famine was the natural conclusion of the disasters of collectivization, dekulakization, and merciless grain levies; it was minutely observed and publicly ignored by a regime and a dictator that viewed the peasantry as less than human, as raw material to be exploited to the maximum. The "construction of socialism" was an end to justify any means, and the cause of the imagined collective came before that of individuals and families.

The already perilous conditions within the special settlements eased the work of the famine. Contrary to the cliché, the famine did not rage. It was silent and unmoving. People died quietly, alone in their houses, alone on country paths in search of nonexistent help. And like millions of other victims, the special settlers died unofficial, classified deaths. Moscow dictated official silence about the famine. It denied both the famine's existence and its victims, a denial that would last almost as long as the Soviet Union itself.[10]

The Unfolding of the Famine in the Special Settlements

By early 1932, Iagoda was optimistic that conditions in the special settlements had improved in comparison to the dire situation of the previous spring and summer. In a lengthy report, dated 4 January 1932, he voiced his confidence in the OGPU's new management of the special settlements and its ability to turn the special settlers into a permanent source of labor for the Soviet hinterlands. Still, he noted, some issues remained "unsatisfactory."

The "unsatisfactory" issues continued to center around housing construction, food supply, and public health. In the Urals, where supposedly "enormous strides" had been taken in housing, 97,734 families had permanent dwellings while the remaining 32,333 families continued to live in a variety of makeshift abodes. In the Northern Territory, roughly 25,000 people remained in temporary shelters while 131,313 had permanent housing. The supply and transport of food continued to be a problem in all exile regions, especially affecting those working in forestry, although Iagoda pointed to progress in the clearing and planting of new lands. There was a grave shortage of doctors and other medical personnel. In some places, like Vologda in the Northern Territory, the government had opened special three-month courses to train special settlers in elementary health care. Cases of typhus and typhoid fever continued to surface in the Northern Territory, the Urals, and Siberia.[11]

Little had actually changed since the OGPU takeover of 1931. Despite Iagoda's relatively optimistic prognosis, famine was already in sight throughout the zones of exile. As early as September 1931, a Central Control Commission report noted that "Interruptions in food supply in the Urals manifest themselves like a kind of system. Periodically, the kulak exiles live through literal famine and are forced to survive on various surrogates. As a result of systematic starvation, mass cases of stomach disorders and edema have developed."[12] In the Northern Territory, where, "as a rule not one settlement within the Northern Territory forestry industry's control had a cow," rickets were widespread among children and, by December, typhus had reached epidemic proportions.[13] In one place, local authorities arbitrarily declared the size of special settlers' rations "classified," refusing to allow even the Central Control Commission representatives access to such information.[14]

A Commissariat of Justice report of late December 1931 echoed many of these concerns, pointing to serious problems in slow and inadequate housing construction, unhygienic living conditions, and typhus epidemics, which in the Northern Territory were spreading to local populations. According to this report, some 15,000 special settlers in the Northern Territory were either invalids or "decrepit elderly," and in areas where typhus had reached epidemic proportions such as Lenskii District, two to three corpses were removed from the settlement daily.[15]

Conditions for epidemic were in fact ripe everywhere. In addition to their weakened physical state, special settlers faced unsanitary living conditions and often had limited access to sources of clean water. In Western Siberia, recently constructed bathhouses could only accommodate one third of special settlers. In the Urals, the special settlers still awaited the construction of some eight hundred wells.[16] In the Northern Territory, the majority of special settlers had no access whatsoever to clean water.[17] The Politburo commission on the special settlers, now under Rudzutak, was well aware of these circumstances, concluding in January 1932 that sanitary conditions were "unsafe" and that in the Northern Territory, Kazakhstan, and the Urals there were "enormous nests of infection," especially of typhus and smallpox. Already, according to the commission, mortality rates had become "significant," particularly among children under eight, in some areas reaching 10 percent in the course of a month.[18] In fact, in many areas typhus developed into epidemic proportions in the winter and early spring months of 1932.[19]

The Rudzutak Commission created a series of special commissions in the Northern Territory, the Urals, Kazakhstan, and Siberia to lead the "struggle" against epidemic illnesses. The commission also ordered additional food rations for the weakest children under eight. It dispatched one hundred portable disinfectant chambers (for delousing) to the provinces and ordered a wagonload of soap for the Northern Territory. Up to 350 additional medical personnel were ordered "mobilized" to the affected regions.[20] In the North, the regional party committee announced that April and May would be devoted to the "struggle for cleanliness."[21] In the Urals, there was an "operational plan for the struggle with epidemics" in the special settlements, calling for the "liquidation" of typhus by 15 March 1932, the "full liquidation" of smallpox by 15 April 1932, and the liquidation of typhoid fever by 1 May 1932.[22]

In spite of such artful planning, the reality was that there were simply not enough qualified medical personnel to deal with the epidemics. In the Urals, only 73 doctors, 285 *fel'dshers* or medical orderlies (217 of them special settlers), and 33 clinics were in place to serve more than half a million special settlers.[23] In the Northern Territory, there were 12 doctors, 112 first-aid posts, and 6 clinics for some 211 special settlements.[24] Doctors mobilized from Moscow and Leningrad to exile zones failed to show up at their assigned posts in roughly one out of every four cases in the fall of 1932, undoubtedly due to their horror at the prospect of working in the special settlements.[25]

In the meantime, the food situation of most special settlers, especially those employed in forestry, continued to deteriorate. Because of nationwide shortages, regional and local authorities began to lower the food rations of the families of special settlers.[26] Everywhere there were major "interruptions" in the supply and transport of food. Frequent calls for nutritional supplements for the children had little if any effect.[27] In June 1932, the Gulag administration issued a circular ordering its agents to "mobilize" all special settlers—especially those not wholly utilized in production, the non-able-bodied, and children—to pick mushrooms and berries for feeding special settlers and for trade.[28] In July, it authorized special settlers to sell or slaughter livestock they had acquired on their own (that is, not through government loans) and to sell surplus produce on the market.[29]

At about the same time, Iagoda wrote to Kaganovich, telling him about the "threatening nature" of the "food situation" of those working in forestry and the growth of famine-related epidemics.[30] Iagoda's note prompted a series of Politburo directives calling for the Commissariat of Supply and the Commissariat of Forestry to look into provisioning.[31] In September, the Politburo instructed the Council of People's Commissars to allot close to 7,000 rubles for provisioning special settlers in the Northern Territory from the Council's reserve fund.[32] That these measures were too little and too late is apparent from attempts in the fall of 1932 to scapegoat officials in the Forestry and Supply Commissariats for the misappropriation of grain reserves in the exile zones.[33]

The perilous conditions of 1932 set the stage for 1933, when full-blown famine consumed the territories of the other archipelago. In the Northern Territory, famine became an ongoing reality as early as the fall of 1932. Here the lion's share of special settlers worked in forestry, the sector hit hardest by food and transport problems. The provincial OGPU documented the unfolding of the famine in the Northern Territory in frank and startling detail. The head of the Northern Territory OGPU, Rudol'f Ivanovich Austrin, and his deputy, Avgust Petrovich Shiiron, conducted an extensive correspondence internally within the OGPU and with other agencies and other levels of government, charting the course of the famine.

Austrin and Shiiron were fairly typical chekists. Both were born in 1891 into humble working-class families in Latvia. Neither had more than two to three years of formal education. Following his father's example, Austrin entered into revolutionary activities in 1905, joining the Bolshevik party in 1907, and working as a typesetter while leading party work in several districts until his arrest in 1915. Shiiron's biographical trail begins in 1919, when he became a member of the Bolshevik party. Both began their careers with the Cheka during the civil war—Austrin in 1918 and Shiiron in 1919. Austrin rose up through the ranks in the 1920s, receiving his post as head of the Northern Territory OGPU in 1925. Shiiron joined him in the North in 1930. Together they led the Northern Territory OGPU through the First Five-Year Plan, and the famine and its aftermath.[34]

Neither man was particularly suited to his position as herald of famine and advocate of the special settlers' physical survival. There is no clear evidence that either man was motivated by humanitarian concerns, although their reports are distinguished by the horror and anguish they detailed. Like Iagoda in Moscow, it is most likely that Austrin and Shiiron were motivated in their scrupulous reporting of the famine by urgent concerns of security and the survival of the OGPU's unfree work force. Unlike Iagoda, however, they had no illusions about the local situation or the OGPU's ability "to set right the situation" with the special settlers.

On 9 August 1932, Shiiron wrote to the Northern Territory soviet executive committee protesting the regional supply department's decision to lower the bread rations for nonworking members of special settler families.[35] The supply department had first raised the issue of lowering the rations from 300 to 200 grams of bread in the summer of 1932. Shiiron protested in early July, convincing the regional soviet to reconsider the issue.[36] In his 9 August communiqué, Shiiron wrote that the reduced ration was "insufficient." He told the soviet executive committee that the supply department refused to change its position, justifying its decision with reference to a recent regional soviet executive committee order to decrease the bread rations of office employees to 200 grams. Shiiron argued that at least office workers had ways to compensate for the decreased rations. He warned that making the same change for the special settler families would lead to unrest, which would "complicate the political situation."[37]

On 3 September 1932, Shiiron wrote another letter, this time to the secretary of the regional party committee, Ivanov, telling him that the food supply situation of the special settlers, particularly of their families, was "sharply worsening," bordering on famine in some areas, as a result of the region's generally deteriorating food stocks. Consequently, special settler workers were running away or refusing to work in what Shiiron described as massive numbers.[38]

Discussions about rations and "food difficulties" (an official euphemism for the famine) continued in internal memoranda until 19 November when the regional soviet executive committee held a special conference on food supply issues. There, the executive committee pledged to continue to provision special settler families, but requested food aid from Moscow, warning that the region would not be able to feed the families with local resources after the first of December.[39] On 23 November, Ivanov wrote to the Central Committee in Moscow that "in spite of our many requests to central organizations" to provision the special settlers, the issue was still not resolved. He repeated that food would run out on 1 December if Moscow failed to act.[40]

On 9 December 1932, Austrin wrote to Ivanov to tell him that the special settlers would have to be removed from the region's supply system. The chairman of the regional soviet executive committee, G. K. Priadchenko, had returned from Moscow on 6 December with news of the center's refusal to supply "this category." On the next day, Austrin gave orders to look for other ways to provision the special settlers. Austrin went on to say that he "refused" to lower the rations of non-able-bodied special settlers whose families had no working members, arguing that they had been "guaranteed" by the Commissariat of Supply. Moreover, he wrote, 33 percent of them were children and they would undoubtedly die without rations.[41] On 17 December, the regional party committee resolved to leave the rations for this category of special settler unchanged.[42] The actual impact of this ruling, however, would be largely meaningless.

Less than a week later, on 21 December, the Supply Commissariat in Moscow ordered the lowering of monthly rations for special settler families after the first of January, from 9 to 5 kilograms of flour, 1.5 to .8 kilograms of fish, and .9 to .3 kilograms of sugar. Ivanov immediately protested this decision, pleading with the Central Committee to reverse the Supply Commissariat's order. He told the Central Committee that the families had no reserves to fall back upon—their harvest was 68 percent lower than the regional average and most lived far from collective farm markets. Worse still, according to Ivanov, the consequent flight and labor turnover was already hurting the timber plan.[43]

By February 1933, typhus and typhoid fever epidemics were in full swing through the Northern Territory, along with widespread outbreaks of scurvy.[44] At the same time, it was becoming frighteningly clear that the number of able-bodied special settlers was rapidly declining. According to a report from early March 1933 on special settlers working within the Northern Territory's forestry industry, only about 30 percent were able-bodied and some 25 percent of families were without breadwinners.[45]

Already in late February and March 1933, reports from Vozhegodskii District indicated that the special settlers were "under the immediate threat of starvation." They were ill and unable to work. Individuals, especially children, had begun to wander through the countryside seeking out villages where they could beg for food.[46] In Plesetskii District, in March, the chairman of the district soviet executive committee wrote to the regional soviet executive committee that large numbers of special settlers were suffering from edema. There had already been cases of death here, and many no longer were able to work. He reported that special settlers were fleeing, that theft and even murder for a piece of bread were on the rise, and that one case of cannibalism had been reported.[47]

In March 1933, Shiiron penned a report for Ivanov, describing the full horror of the situation in the special settlements. The special settlers' harvests had failed dismally. Incidents of flight were increasing. Special settlers were begging all over the region. Reports of attacks on special settlers for theft in the already hungry villages had reached Arkhangel'sk. Special settlers were eating dead horses, dogs, and cats. In Ust-Vymskii District, women, with their children in tow, had besieged the commandant, threatening to break into the warehouse if they did not receive bread. In Kargopol'skii District, the commandant had given up trying to stem the nightly flights of entire families. One special settler robbed and murdered a fellow settler upon his return with the settlement's bread supply. Shiiron concluded with a plea for an increase in rations for the families and for a special supplement for the children.[48]

On 16 March, Shiiron again wrote to Ivanov, telling him that "people are swelling up from hunger in entire families." Children's rations were down to 170 grams of bread per day. Their parents had no recourse but to send them away to beg. When one commandant tried to stop children from begging, the children told him that they would stay if he gave them bread, "but for now we are hungry and want to eat." Shiiron reported one special settler saying, "They brought us to the forest and did not feed us, but torture us with hunger, besides which they gave us a small parcel of land upon which nothing can grow and from which we can expect nothing."[49]

It was not only the OGPU that was writing. The head of the Northern Territory Control Commission and Workers' and Peasants' Inspectorate wrote his superiors in Moscow to tell them about the famine in the Northern Territory. His report included death rates—237 in November 1932, 248 in December 1932, 551 in January 1933, 347 (incomplete) in February 1933—a total of 1,383 deaths. He also warned that special settlers were leaving the work sites in groups of fifty to one hundred and that included even the best workers (the "shock workers" or *udarniki*) among them. He wrote that the soviet executive committee had created a special commission to improve the food situation but that local supplies were limited and the situation would only continue to deteriorate without help from Moscow. He ended his letter by pleading for food aid from central stocks and for special supplements for the children.[50]

As famine spread, security worries came to rival concerns over the loss of labor. On 8 May 1933, the chairman of the Kotlas District soviet executive committee wrote to his regional counterpart, Priadchenko, about the widespread tramping and begging of special settlers through the Northern Territory. The situation was especially dangerous just outside the city of Kotlas. Collective farmers in large numbers were deserting their work floating timber in order to return home to protect their property.[51] In some places, the special settlements were becoming ghost towns.[52]

On 11 May, Ivanov took the step of contacting Stalin directly. He told him that of the 120,170 special settlers working in the Northern Territory, more than 41,000 were children under sixteen, and an additional 19,000 were unable to work. He said that the general picture for the majority of the region's special settlers was one of hunger, famine, and particularly high death rates for children. He begged Stalin for an additional 17 million rubles, an increase in children's bread rations from 165 to 300 grams, and the transfer of 45,000 families out of the region. His request for the removal of the families was a clear admission of defeat.[53]

The situation remained unchanged. Within a month, on 10 June 1933, Austrin lashed out in frustration at Ivanov, telling him that there was "full anarchy, no system, no planning, no control, and no responsibility in the industrial organs' management of the special settlements, from top to bottom." The special settlers' material conditions continued to get "worse and worse." Over all, wrote Austrin, the numbers of working special settlers had declined by over 22,000 between September 1932 and May 1933. In the same time period, 20,666 special settlers had fled, and an additional 31,634 had been caught fleeing. He gave the figure of 12,609 deaths for the period from 1 September 1931 to 1 May 1933 (3,624 for 1 September 1931 to 1 January 1932; 7,291 for 1 January 1932 to 1 April 1933; and 1,694 for April 1933).[54] A late 1933 postmortem report on the famine in the Northern Territory prepared by the region's health department for the Russian Republic Commissariat of Health would offer even higher mortality figures: a total of 14,896 deaths in 1933 (2,865 in the first quarter; 5,796 in the second quarter; 4,911 in the third quarter; and 1,324 in the fourth quarter).[55]

Conditions began to improve only in the late summer of 1933. First, in August, the OGPU increased the size of the land allotments for special settlers to a minimum of two hectares (about five acres) per person, larger when conditions permitted, in an attempt to stimulate garden farming.[56] Then, in November, Moscow raised the food rations for special settler families back to their pre-1933 levels.[57] Moscow also extended seed loans at this time.[58]

The Northern Territory was not exceptional in its experience of famine. Other areas of special resettlement suffered the same cataclysmic conditions with the same lethal results. The Russian scholar, V. N. Zemskov has estimated that a total of 241,355 special settlers died in 1932 and 1933 (89,754 in 1932 and 151,601 in 1933).[59] Escapes in these regions also skyrocketed in these years. In the Urals, 55,983 special settlers fled in 1933, in Western Siberia, 49,718. According to nationwide statistics compiled by the OGPU, escapes reached 207,010 in 1932 (with 37,978 returning) and 215,856 in 1933 (with 54,211 returning), thereby surpassing even the mass flight of the first two desperate years of special resettlement.[60]

In the end, Moscow levied some small measure of blame for the famine. In the Northern Territory, special settlers were actually accused of attempts to create "mass famine."[61] When it was not the special settlers themselves to blame, it was the industrial concerns that employed them and were responsible for their upkeep.[62] But these were only scapegoats for the famine; the industrial concerns neither created nor controlled the mass famine that consumed the special settlements in these years. The famine was the natural and predictable consequence of the Stalin regime's policies on the peasantry and on special resettlement.

Within the Famine

"[We have] a dispensary with three beds; the medical orderly is poorly qualified and negligent in his responsibilities. He allowed corpses at the cemetery to be buried under [only] 15–20 centimeters of earth. Now, no one can enter the cemetery because of the stench. Corpses were also dumped into a silage pit. The medical orderly was ordered to rebury the corpses . . . [but] under Commandant Sakharov they were not removed but simply covered up with more earth. After my arrival, I ordered the corpses to be removed. There was also five to six corpses in the silage pit. I decided not to remove these but instead ordered the entire pit covered with about a meter of earth. I decided not to dig up those corpses because the pit was full of water and the stench unbearable. . . . Now we are removing corpses from graves which were only superficially buried and where the coffins are visible. I have not, however, ordered reburial for graves buried under 30 centimeters. . . ."[63]

The current commandant of the Sapych special settlement where the cemetery stood wrote this report for his superiors on 25 June 1933. According to an earlier (April 9) report, famine had taken eleven lives in March; two cases of typhoid fever had been recorded; and the commandant (presumably the former one, Sakharov) had stolen the settlement's milk for himself.[64] The commandant of Sapych blamed the scandal at the cemetery on the former commandant as well as on the medical orderly, who happened to be a special settler. As usual, scapegoating devolved downward.

The report on the Sapych cemetery evokes the lived experience of the famine—the death, the stench, the crude and contemptible attempts (literally and figuratively) at cover-up. The corpses resurfaced. In the same way, the voices and actions of the famine's victims continually resurface.

"I heard that they freed us a long time ago, but that the local authorities are keeping us here to make us work. We all must run away or they will starve us to death." This exclamation was recorded in a special OGPU report on the "political mood" of the special settlers. The OGPU counted it as one of several categories of rumors that were sweeping the settlements. Rumors of freedom, local deceit, and famine, accompanied by calls to quit work and flee, circulated everywhere. Ever-present rumors of war and foreign intervention also increased, whether as wish projection or a way to legitimate flight and work stoppages. News of famine elsewhere in the countryside, as well as news of the workers' strike and rioting in Ivanovo-Voznesensk, circulated through the special settlements.[65]

Rumors were spread by letters from friends and relatives back in the settlers' native villages.[66] They were fueled, as well, by the vast mobility within the exile territories. In addition to the massive numbers of special settlers on the run at this time, there was widespread tramping and begging throughout the countryside.[67] It was often the children who were sent begging. In the process, they too served as heralds of famine. Olifier recalled that, "In order for our family not to die from hunger, I, as the oldest of the children, begged for alms at local villages [within a 25 kilometer radius], crying out, 'Give bread or whatever you can, for the sake of Christ. Good people, give for the sake of Christ, neither food nor drink has passed my lips for two days.'"[68]

Talk of famine ran thick through the exile territories. In addition to the noise of rumors and the tramping and the begging, special settlers wrote about the famine in letters home and in letters of petition to the authorities. "I cannot consider myself guilty for being born into the family of a kulak; in this I have no control and there are many in this situation," wrote special settler F. M. Lobod to the Politburo on 22 August

1932. "You need only come and have a look at the resettlement villages—75 percent of those remaining (many took off and many have died) are swelling up and the reason is famine. One sees this picture: young people tramping everywhere to beg or even steal bread . . . and, on the way, they fall and die."[69] Special settler P. A. Babin who worked in the Pokrovskii mines in Nadezhdinskii District in the Urals, wrote the regional party committee about the conditions of the families. He wrote about the paltry bread rations and how the special settlers "went about stealing from each other." "Hunger does not wait," he continued. "The commandant will not give us passes to leave the mine. . . . We ask you not to let us die. . . . There are honorable people among us."[70] The medical orderly, Gololobov, working in a special settlement in Komi wrote to the district health authorities that "the situation at present in our settlement is very sad. In view of the situation with rations, little children and the elderly are starving. . . . What is to be done?—write, there are no rations. In the dispensary, we have two patients, but there is nothing to feed them. . . . Please send us rations, otherwise the matter will turn out sadly. . . ."[71]

Elsewhere, the famine retained visibility through the very actions of the special settlers as they attempted to fight for their survival. Along with massive flight and tramping, theft and work stoppages increased at this time. Special settlers were reported stealing from one another and from the already strained and hungry collective farmers in the exile territories. In some places, it had become dangerous to go out at night.[72] In other places, special settlers refused to work without proper rations for themselves and their families. In one special settlement outside Kotlas in the Northern Territory, the settlers rioted when the authorities refused to issue them credit for bread.[73]

These kinds of activities not only left behind traces of the famine but also unnerved the OGPU and local authorities. The OGPU smelled the scent of counterrevolution behind the desperate acts of the special settlers. In the Northern Territory, the OGPU claimed to have discovered a "counterrevolutionary wrecking and insurrectionary" organization that aimed to break the timber harvest; seventy-one people were arrested. In the Urals, the OGPU claimed that it had liquidated nine "counterrevolutionary groups" with a total of seventy members. In the Far East, the OGPU unearthed five such groups with forty-one members.[74] Whether as an exercise in scapegoating or as a desperate attempt to silence the symptoms of the famine, the OGPU supplemented its scrupulous reporting on the famine with an analytic cloak of conspiracy, its preferred rationalization for problems and threats.

The OGPU would not, however, succeed in silencing the special settlers. Ekaterina Sergeevna Lukina, exiled to Narym in Siberia, recalled,

"We were weak. . . . People began to swell and die. [They] buried them without coffins, in mass graves which grew every day. . . . [The commandant] was very brutal, when [they] divided the rations, some, swollen from hunger, shoved in their mouths pieces of moldy bread and they were beaten. Soon they died. Only those who could work got rations, the rest were doomed."[75] A. S. Nagdaseva described the hungry years of her exile in the Urals: "Especially difficult were the years 1932 and 1933. Hunger, cold in the barracks. Bread and other products were rationed—in a miserly fashion. Mama cut up the bread into little squares, [we also had] barley kasha and soup with nettles. . . . My sister slept more and more. My mother talked and cried—'she'll die from hunger'. . . . Illnesses began, especially typhus. There was even a typhus barracks. People went there either swollen or emaciated. Many died . . . the little ones most."[76]

Olifier remembered the famine well, its stark and tragic impact: "1933 began. Famine. Daily undernourishment, difficult work, bad clothing and shoes, frost did its damage. For the people it remained only to die. And [they] died. . . . The local authorities gradually cut the bread rations. People ate grass. . . . The clothing was inadequate, and on our feet were 'birch boots'—lapti. To avoid freezing, we had to move endlessly, but strength was exhausted and people gradually languished and died." He continued, "In the summer of 1933, my stepfather died—Aleksei Emel'ianovich, the father of my brother Andrei and sister Galia. He was buried in an inhuman way. Dead from hunger convulsions, without a proper burial, cross, and inscription where one could bring flowers, where one could bow down. [He] was simply hidden in the ground, [half covered] with rocks, as if a buried piece of wood. There was no one to bury him—those who could were at work, and those who remained in the settlement had no strength."[77]

The survivors noted that the people whom Soviet sources labeled non-able-bodied and who some of the bosses called "ballast"[78] were the most vulnerable during the famine. Special settlers who could work had a fighting chance at survival, thanks to the rations provided at the work site. For those in the non-able-bodied category, the chances of survival diminished. And even when people worked, it was impossible to fulfill the required work norms. In Western Siberia—and elsewhere—the OGPU issued an order to differentiate the size of rations according to the percentage of the norms filled.

Olifier described the consequences of such policies in the Urals.[79] "At the time [1933], she [Olifier's mother] worked in the forest collecting pine resin. In one hand [she] carried a pail into the taiga, in the other was a wooden stick—a scraper, and so [she worked] from early morning until late at night. All day she walked from pine tree to pine tree, never attaining the 12 kilogram norm. The resin ate at her hands, face, hair. Even teenagers worked. Only in individual cases of weak, sick, emaciated men, women, youth were they freed from work in the collection of sap, from work in the timber harvest, and transferred to light work—removing tree stumps, cutting wood. . . ."[80]

As a result of the impossible work rations and the lack of bread for the infirm, it was mothers of young children, invalids, the elderly, and the children who suffered most. The category of non-able, moreover, continually grew as workers lost their strength and ability to work and as children were orphaned by the death or flight of a working family member.[81] The center urged the Commissariats of Public Assistance, Health, and Education to take charge of living arrangements for invalids, elders, and orphans, but generally with poor results due to underfunding and neglect.[82] Mass transfers of children and the elderly back to their native villages, temporarily suspended in late December 1931 when the OGPU believed it had turned the corner on material conditions, resumed in the summer of 1932.[83] In the Northern Territory, about 1,200 elderly peasants helplessly awaited transfer to special homes for the aged.[84] The Gulag administration instructed all regional OGPU chiefs to organize special colonies for families without breadwinners where the aged and infirm could be employed in crafts and light work.[85]

There were frequent calls for and attempts to arrange special feeding for the children. In some cases, additional rations or meals were provided in day cares or schools when there were such institutions.[86] Nonetheless, the conditions of children, according to a member of the Northern Territory's children's commission in May 1933, had "sharply worsened" during the winter and spring. "According to the conclusions of doctors," the report stated, "the overwhelming majority [of children] are extremely emaciated and require food urgently. Under the influence of hunger, the children are stealing oats from the stables and boiling them into kasha. They steal produce from the cooperative stores and bread from each other. . . . The numbers of deaths have grown by two to three times. . . . Such a completely inadmissible situation is paralyzing all measures in the region [concerning] the social and cultural reeducation of the children, and threatening to grow into a catastrophe."[87]

Starvation trumped reeducation in any case, and the catastrophe was present rather than pending. Perhaps no situation was as tragic as that of special settler children left orphaned by the famine. According to OGPU statistics from early January 1932, there were already a total of 4,453 orphans in the special settlements, only 2,007 of whom had been sheltered.[88] The famine would provide a steady supply of new orphans to replace those who moved into the orphanages and those who died.

The OGPU viewed the increasing numbers of unattended and orphaned children as a security threat, recalling the mass *besprizornost'* (the phenomenon of homeless, vagrant children) that had accompanied other upheavals in the past, most notably the Russian Civil War.[89] A November 1933 Gulag administration directive described the situation of the orphaned children as "no longer tolerable," leading to "parasitism" and begging.[90] A February 1933 report from the Northern Territory claimed that a "significant" proportion of the region's special settler children were left on their own, leading to the threat of mass *besprizornost'*.[91] The OGPU continually pressured the regions to move these children into orphanages.

The orphanages, however, rivaled the special settlements in their negligence and corruption. Both funding and beds were in short supply.[92] The orphanages were universally overcrowded, filthy, and mismanaged. Children in Komi orphanages slept two to three to a bed (even those who had tuberculosis) or on the cold floor.[93] An October 1933 report on a special settler orphanage in the Syktyvkarskii District revealed the nightmarish conditions of the children warehoused there. The orphanage had been set up in an old and poorly winterized five-room building. It housed ninety-three children, ranging in age from three to fifteen. The building was dirty, unhygienic, and dark (there were shortages of lamps and kerosene). There were only twenty-five beds, so the children had to sleep two to a bed as well as in the corridors and dining hall. Most used their outer clothes for blankets. The children all had lice. They went to the bathhouse only once a month and had no change of underwear. Only about one third of the children attended the local school; the rest had arrived after the school year began and were refused entry. Consequently, they had nothing to do, so they busied themselves with begging to supplement what the report described as inadequate rations. This report, penned by the Komi OGPU, thoroughly condemned the conditions at the orphanage, but OGPU officials could do little to improve the situation. The Komi OGPU managed to move some of the children elsewhere, bringing the population down to a still-too-high figure of sixty-five; it provided a change of underclothing, eight more beds, two tables, seven chairs, and orders for the children to be taken to the baths once every ten days. The Komi OGPU also fired several of the attendants.[94]

A procurator's report on the Sol'nychegodskii orphanage and several other children's homes in and around Kotlas described roughly similar circumstances. When inspectors arrived at the Sol'nychegodskii orphanage, the caretaker claimed not to know the whereabouts of all the children—some were out, some had been taken by relatives. The orphanage was overcrowded, filthy, and provided grossly inadequate food for its inmates. Twenty-five to thirty children had died during the winter of 1933. The inspectors even discovered the corpses of two children hidden in the barn. According to the report, the caretaker had made a deal with the local cemetery guard to bury these and the other children secretly, with multiple bodies to a grave, most likely so that these little "dead souls" could be kept on the books and the orphanage could continue to collect their rations. Perhaps he did this for the benefit of the remaining children, perhaps for his own enrichment. Whatever the case, the caretaker was arrested and sentenced to a three-year prison term.[95]

The head of the Komi OGPU, one Andreev, personally carried out an inspection of four orphanages in the Ust'-Kuloma District where more than two hundred special settler children were housed. Deeming them "highly unsatisfactory," Andreev wrote, "As a result of bureaucratic criminal administration, the orphanages have been turned into nests of infection. For example, in the Seregovo orphanage the following has been discovered: the orphanage is designed for forty people, but fifty-five children of different ages (kindergarten, preschool, and school age) are being brought up there; there are no beds in the orphanage; the mattresses are not stuffed; the children sleep on the floor. There are lice all over the blankets; many children suffer from itching; syphilis infection is suspected; however, the children receive no medical examinations or treatment. There is dirt on the premises, various parasites have multiplied all over the place. The children's nutrition is poor and usually consists of water with cabbage and porridge without butter; sugar is almost never supplied. The orphanage has not been receiving firewood; the rural soviet does not provide horses to deliver firewood. The situation is identical in the other orphanages."

Andreev charged the district officials with disregard and neglect, claiming that these officials were fully aware of conditions in the orphanages. Some 15,000 rubles set aside for the orphanages had been spent elsewhere and the cooperative stores had refused to provide food and supplies. Andreev ended his report in an unpromising but customary manner, pledging to organize a committee for a "careful inspection of all the shortcomings at the orphanages" and promising to determine "the liability of those at fault."[96] It is likely that the OGPU report had little effect, leaving conditions in the orphanage to improve, if they did, only as the general material conditions in the region improved.

Veniamin Makarovich Kurchenkov, exiled as a child from Altai to Narym, recalled his experience as an orphan. He remembered when the "mass death" began: "In the majority of families, there were many children and the horrible suffering cut down the children first. The mothers suffered no less, not being in any condition to save their children. Whole families died out. In the settlements Gorodetsk, Palochka, Suiga, and Protochka, from seven thousand, eight hundred exiles only two thousand remained living after two years." He continued, "From the eleven in our family, seven died in one and a half years. In the orphanage where I lived, there were about two hundred children, all orphaned children of 'kulaks.' In each room of the orphanage hung the slogan, 'Thank you, beloved Stalin, for our happy childhood.' There weren't any miracles in the life of the children for which they should be grateful to the *vozhd'* [the leader], especially since he 'made them happy' by leaving them without fathers and mothers."[97]

The children paid for the "sins of their fathers" long after their parents were dead. Many did not survive, although no statistics are available to even estimate the mortality rates in the orphanages during the famine. But the children who did survive would not forget the famine. In the end, the corpses did not stay hidden.

Conclusion

In a 5 April 1934 memorandum to Iagoda, M. D. Berman, the head of the Gulag administration, wrote that, "in the majority of cases the material conditions of life [in the special settlements] are worse than in the [labor] camps."[98] By this time, the special settlements had been renamed "labor settlements" (*trudposelenie*) as new categories of inhabitants, in particular a large influx of urban "social aliens" entered the other archipelago. The Gulag administration itself had been reorganized from the "Main Administration of Camps" to the "Main Administration of Camps and Labor Settlements."[99]

The famine had taken its toll. The population of the special settlements declined from 1,317,022 in January 1932 to 1,072,546 in December 1933 to 973,693 by December 1934. The decline in the numbers of special settlers was mainly the result of death and flight. At the same time, some 339,327 new exiles joined the "kulak" contingent of 1930 and 1931: 71,236 in 1932 and 268,091 in 1933.[100] The new exiles included more "kulaks"—those purged from collective farms or repressed for "sabotaging" spring sowing during the famine, and those who had fled dekulakization or the special settlements to work in industry. They also included new categories of inhabitants as the OGPU first carried out a purge of "social aliens" from the cities and, then in 1934, carried out an additional urban purge following the assassination of the Leningrad party chief, S. M. Kirov.[101]

On 8 May 1933, the Central Committee and the Council of People's Commissars issued a directive ordering the cessation of mass exiles of peasants. The official justification for this directive was the "victory of the socialist order in the countryside." The so-called victory would still allow for the exile of an additional twelve thousand peasant families, but all other exiles were supposed to occur only on a case-by-case basis.[102] This directive would mark the end of the special settlements as exclusively peasant ("kulak") institutions. Henceforth, other categories of exiles —first, the city dwellers and then increasingly the ethnic categories that came to dominate the special settlements—would begin to join the kulaks in the other archipelago.[103]

The famine was a turning point in the history of the special settlements. Although the center resorted to its usual scapegoating of lower-level officials, Iagoda would, in fact, suffer something of a defeat in 1933. The experiment with self-supporting penal institutions was anything but cost-effective; the OGPU had not succeeded in turning the situation around. Yet, intent on maintaining his labor force for the OGPU's growing economic empire, Iagoda had proposed the exile of two million additional people for 1933. His plan was to make the special settlements the central and defining institution of the Gulag. Given the general context of famine and what Austrin had called anarchy in the management of the special settlements, the Politburo rejected Iagoda's proposal. Stalin had grown frustrated with the costs involved in special resettlement. At the same time, regional officialdom resisted additional mass exiles in light of the regions' strained budgets and food reserves, and the continuing chaos in employment and living conditions.[104] Western Siberian party chief Eikhe complained directly to Stalin in February 1933 that the plan to send 100,000 new special settlers to his region was "completely unrealistic, understandable only to those comrades . . . who know nothing about the conditions of the north." He went on to say that they would need 30,000 to 35,000 horses to move those people, which in turn would lead to the destruction of the horses and therefore damage the spring sowing and forestry work.[105] In the end, Iagoda would get a "mere" 268,091 additional "kulak" bodies for the other archipelago, certainly a far smaller number than he requested, but a sizeable contingent all the same. The arrival of these newcomers only exacerbated the desperate situation.[106] The special settlements continued to be an immense archipelago of the Gulag. But from this point forward, the labor camps began to rival the special settlements in size, function, and importance, becoming the defining institution of the Gulag.[107]

8

The Second Dekulakization: Rehabilitation and Repression

They will never allow us to be equal, and they never will believe that we've forgotten and forgiven everything. We are damned, from now until the end of our lives.
—from the diary of A. S. Arzhilovskii, former special settler released in 1936 and rearrested in 1937

Although the other archipelago would not in the end displace the labor camps so synonymous with Stalin's Gulag, Iagoda and the NKVD (the OGPU's successor from 1934) were determined to maintain their unfree work force and to prevent the release of the kulaks from captivity.[1] In 1935, kulaks who had completed five years of exile (the 1930 contingent) and had proven themselves "honorable laborers" loyal to the regime became eligible for "rehabilitation"—that is, they could be accorded full legal and voting rights. Iagoda urgently sought to forestall the consequences of such an action. In a 17 January 1935 letter to Stalin, he wrote, "I consider it expedient to enact an amendment to the USSR Central Executive Committee decree of 27 May 1934 in which it must be indicated that the rehabilitation of the rights of labor settlers does not give them the right to leave their place of exile."[2] Iagoda considered it "politically undesirable" for the settlers to return to their home villages and warned of the consequent damage to "colonization."[3] Iagoda's fears were based on a January 1935 report he had received from Berman, head of the Gulag administration, which detailed that only 25 percent of those rehabilitated had remained in the settlements, while a large part of the newly rehabilitated kulaks had flocked home to their villages or to the cities. Berman strongly advised against "mass rehabilitations" and recommended that in future rehabilitated kulaks be confined to their place of exile and not accorded the right of free movement.[4]

As a consequence of Berman and Iagoda's intervention, Stalin ordered the revision of earlier legislation (from 1931 and 1934) on kulak rehabilitation, penciling "exactly" in the margin of Iagoda's letter.[5] The new 25 January 1935 Central Executive Committee decree would read: "The restoration of the civil rights of exiled kulaks does not give the kulak the right to leave his place of exile."[6] Yet in spite of this decree, tens of thousands of kulaks would continue to flee the settlements—rehabilitated or not—joining those who had already left or fled illegally in the first half of the 1930s. Further chaos would ensue when the new Stalin constitution of 1936—the "most democratic in the world"—granted, on paper, equal rights to all citizens. At that time, entire families would claim their supposed new rights and leave, necessitating NKVD intervention to ensure that the special settlers remained in place.[7] The porousness of the other archipelago and the fluidity of its population led to increasing anxieties among the leadership, further fueling fears of the existence of a "fifth column"—this one with kulak reinforcements—planning to subvert Soviet power from within. This irrepressible dynamic would flow directly into the "Great Terror," when the so-called "second dekulakization" (code-named "mass operation 00447") began.

The Calm before the Storm

Following the devastation of the famine, the special settlements entered a period of relative stabilization. From its 1930/31 highpoint of 1,803,392 to 1,317,022 in 1932, the population of the special settlers declined to 1,072,546 in 1934, 973,693 in 1935, and with an increase due to births and new contingents, upward to 1,017,133 people living in a total of 1,845 settlements in 1936.[8] In 1935, for the first time, births (26,122) surpassed deaths (22,173).[9] And although flight would continue, escape rates in 1934 were only 40 percent (87,617) of the 1933 highpoint (215,856), 20 percent (43,070) in 1935, and 12 percent (26,193) in 1936, with a far larger percentage of fugitives recaptured or voluntarily returning.[10] However, the seas of the other archipelago remained in motion, to borrow Solzhenitsyn's metaphor, as new, smaller contingents of officially designated kulaks continued to arrive in exile, making up for some of the population losses of 1932/33.[11]

In a letter to Stalin and Molotov dated 9 July 1935, Iagoda was moderately optimistic. He noted that some 445,000 people lived and worked within 1,271 unchartered agricultural collectives, with a total acreage of 368,000 hectares (908,960 acres). Kulak families who had been exiled in 1930–32 to Narym and Northern Kazakhstan had become, by 1934, "fully self-sufficient" in grain and vegetable production, even participating in state requisitioning levies on the same basis as the "free" population. Livestock production continued to languish, mainly as a result of the dearth of fodder in earlier years. Unlike the agricultural collectives, the special agricultural colonies that housed kulak invalids were still far from self-sufficient; Iagoda recommended that they be exempt from all taxes and collections in kind for another three to four years.[12]

While some 41 percent of special settlers worked in agricultural collectives, 640,000 worked in industry (383,000 in heavy industry, 179,000 in forestry, 78,000 in light industry and transport). According to Iagoda, their families were able to produce enough vegetables for their own needs. As the years had progressed, and especially after the famine, more families were employed in industry, and within industry, fewer families were occupied in forestry.

In his November 1935 report to Iagoda, Berman provided further details about conditions in the special settlements in the northern zones of Western Siberia. Here, 81 percent of settlers worked within agricultural collectives. Berman claimed that they were all self-sufficient in grains and vegetables, even boasting a surplus crop of 1,250,000 puds of potatoes.[13] As elsewhere, livestock cultivation lagged behind. For every two families in these territories, there were .64 horses, 1.2 cattle, and 1 pig. The settlers had also managed to construct 236 schools (serving 29,169 students), 19 orphanages (for 3,058 orphans), 15 hospitals, 2,226 bathhouses, 146 disinfection chambers, and 34 first-aid posts. The average housing space per person was 4.2 square meters, if the figure can be believed, a quite healthy size given Soviet norms, although this number did not take into account the 12 percent of settlers still living in makeshift abodes (*zemlianki* or *shalashy*). Despite frequent cases of malaria (7,145 in 1934, 4,493 in 1935), mortality had reached "normal" levels, with births (2,401) surpassing deaths (1,926) in the previous six months. For all these supposed accomplishments, Berman requested a series of special awards for those "chekists" who had served five years on the special settlement "front." Nevertheless, he also requested an extension of the special settlers' debt payments to 1938.[14]

Even in the hard-pressed Northern Territory, regional leaders claimed that the situation in the special settlements had stabilized after the terrible devastation of the early years and the famine. NKVD boss Austrin noted in a July 1934 report that the kulak settlers of the North had fulfilled the spring sowing plan by more than 100 percent.[15] The regional party committee then concluded that such an achievement would guarantee self-sufficiency for the settlers. It is sobering to note, however that in the 179 special settlements of the North, the population had withered from its highpoint of 285,609 (58,271 families) in 1930 and 1931 to 76,732 people (25,491 families) by the fall of 1934.[16]

Everywhere the government encouraged special settlers to buy their own homes, providing credit for materials or offering them the old eight-room collective homes at "discounted" prices.[17] The state also endeavored to reward the best kulak laborers (the *udarniki*, or shock workers) with goats, pigs, and cows, while extending debt repayments, canceling some debts altogether, and exempting some settlers from the obligatory state requisitions of farm produce that plagued the collective farms.[18] All of these efforts were aimed at keeping the special settlers permanently in their place of exile, regardless of rehabilitation. Berman, for one, firmly believed that the kulaks would stay put only if they were economically secure.[19]

Life in the special settlements continued to be bleak, bureaucratic optimism notwithstanding. Those "kulaks" resettled in 1933, in perverse retaliation for the famine, lived in desperately hard conditions.[20] Those worst off were the families who still worked in forestry.[21] In early January 1935, Iagoda wrote directly to Sergo Ordzhonikidze, Commissar of Heavy Industry, about the terrible conditions of forestry workers in the Sverdlovsk Region, where as many as one half had died or fled in three and one-half years of exile.[22] Iagoda based his complaints on a report from the Sverdlovsk NKVD chief, I. F. Reshetov, who had written, "I have no confidence that the remaining exiles will settle permanently if the forestry industry fails to take necessary measures." In Sverdlovsk, there continued to be chronic salary delays, food supply interruptions, and housing problems. The NKVD had had to take the drastic step of "liquidating" some sixty "prospectless" (*besperspektivnyi*) special settlements because of their remote location.[23] The Forestry Commissariat shifted the blame for this state of affairs on to their subordinates, the timber trusts that directly administered the special settlements, claiming that the trusts "still had not complied with rules on the employment of the special settlers" and that the very difficult material circumstances threatened the settlers' retention as a permanent workforce. Forestry officials in Kazakhstan came in for the biggest share of criticism: the Forestry Commissariat and the Gulag administration ordered the removal of all special settlers from Kazakhstan's forestry trusts and the criminal prosecution of its leadership, adding that such criminal prosecution was also underway in the North and in the Urals.[24]

Throughout the Northern Territory, the NKVD was liquidating or merging special settlements considered too remote or economically unviable, or whose populations had diminished to the point of unsustainability. In part, these actions derived from the "theoretical planning" of the early days when special settlements were chosen as "pencil points on a map." In Leshukonskii District, for example, the special settlement "Vyborgskii," established in 1930, had been planted on sandy and marshy lands where it was simply "impossible to work." In four years, the people of Vyborgskii had managed to plow only eighteen hectares (44.5 acres) of land. NKVD official Shiiron proposed the transfer of Vyborgskii's 133 families to a special settlement in another district.[25] Transfers also occurred in other special settlements in the North where it was concluded that "there were no prospects for improvement."[26]

The NKVD did not limit its criticism to the forestry industry. A 1935 report by deputy NKVD boss Prokof'ev for Ordzhonikidze discussed the situation of the 60,000 people working for Kuzbas Coal. Most of the 24,500 able-bodied special settlers here worked in mining or forestry. According to Prokof'ev, Kuzbass Coal and the administrators of its individual enterprises paid not the least attention to even the minimal needs of their special settler work force. Some 25,000 special settlers lived in dugout shelters and in "inadmissibly unhygienic conditions."[27]

Despite these chronic problems, Iagoda and the NKVD emphasized progress. NKVD officials in the field even went so far as to propose further normalization in the everyday administration of the special settlements, transferring economic and cultural work to the soviet apparatus while maintaining the NKVD administrative regimen of the *kommandaturas*.[28] In July 1935, perhaps anxious to relieve the NKVD of some of this vast and unproductive burden, Iagoda broached the matter with Stalin and Molotov. He suggested that such a partial transfer of administrative duties could occur in 1936, by which time most of the special settlers would be rehabilitated.[29]

In response, the Politburo set up a special Council of People's Commissars commission, chaired by D. Z. Lebed' (deputy chairman of the Russian Republican Sovnarkom), to examine this possibility. Along with recommending debt relief and exemption from state agricultural requisitions, the commission followed Iagoda's advice and proposed a transfer of economic and cultural matters to the jurisdiction of the soviet and commissariat bureaucracies. In the end, the commission's recommendations were not confirmed, dying a quiet death in the filing cabinets.[30]

Although it is not entirely clear why the suggestions of the Lebed' Commission were not enacted, there is evidence that resistance to the transfer of the special settlers from the NKVD to the regular government bureaucracy arose in the provinces. Western Siberian party chief, Eikhe, wrote to Stalin and Molotov arguing that the transfer of some administrative measures from the NKVD to the soviet apparatus was "untimely at present."[31] Eikhe was especially concerned about the possibility of assuming responsibility for the unchartered agricultural collectives that covered so much of Western Siberia. He, and likely other regional leaders in similar circumstances, would attempt to forestall this measure for the next two years.[32] Given the continuing fluidity of the special settler population and the upcoming rehabilitation process, it surely appeared dangerous to Stalin to lessen the NKVD's grip on any part of the other archipelago. In the end, fear trumped possible administrative reason, and the need to keep the special settler population in place became the paramount concern of Stalin and the NKVD alike.

Rehabilitation

The special settlers had been sent into exile by administrative or extra-judicial fiat, with no particular term set for their sentence. The first mention of a possible temporal demarcation of their time in exile had come at a meeting of the Andreev Politburo Commission on 15 May 1931. At that time, the Andreev Commission proposed that kulaks be eligible for rehabilitation after five years in exile.[33] The Central Executive Committee subsequently enacted a decree to this effect on 3 July 1931, which read (in part): "In the course of five years from the time of exile, [kulaks] can receive civil and voting rights if they prove that they have ceased their struggles and show themselves [to be] honorable laborers."[34] A little over a month later, on 6 August, the Andreev Commission proposed that kulak youth be eligible for rehabilitation upon reaching the age of majority (eighteen).[35]

When Stalin heard of this proposal, he was furious. "There is no need for any law by the Central Executive Committee on restoring the rights of certain former kulaks ahead of schedule. I just knew that the jackasses among the petty bourgeoisie and the philistines would definitely crawl into this mousehole," he raged in a 30 August 1931 letter to Kaganovich.[36] Dekulakization had been aimed at the entire kulak household, not just heads of families. This, after all, to quote Solzhenitsyn, "was the nub of the plan: the peasant's seed must perish together with the adults."[37] The "hereditary" essence of kulakdom had been politically implicit from 1930. For Stalin, the son did indeed answer for the father, and all kulaks were enemies of Soviet power.[38] The issue of early rehabilitation, however, would not go away easily, whether as a result of the activities of Stalin's "jackasses" and "philistines" or the simple but desperate necessity to provide some incentive for special settlers to work under impossible conditions.

From the outset, no one was quite sure how to handle legal matters pertaining to the special settlers, which as late as July 1931, according to the Gulag central administration, remained "undefined."[39] Back in November of 1930, the Procurator was reporting that petitions were flowing into regional OGPU offices from special settler families concerning issues of legal status. Among the most asked questions were:

1. Could "kulak daughters" marry free citizens living outside of exile?
2. Could children who had reached the age of majority break with their parents and leave the settlements?
3. Were elderly peasants allowed to leave exile to live with other relatives who had not been repressed?

The response of the Procurator was to remind his regional colleagues that dekulakization was of the entire family, not just the head of household. Children could not therefore alter their status. Daughters could marry as they pleased, but their legal status would remain the same and they would have to remain in exile. Children born to special settlers while in exile shared their parents' legal status.[40]

Similar questions continued to arise in the provinces. In early 1932 Northern Territory party chief, Ivanov, wrote directly to Stalin, requesting permission to rehabilitate twenty to thirty kulaks who had "proven themselves." He told Stalin that rehabilitation could "play a large role in the sense of more full and better use of the labor of thousands of kulaks" by offering them "realistic perspectives for the future." What Ivanov had in mind was the use of early rehabilitation as an incentive to stimulate labor productivity.[41]

Economic necessity competed with political intransigence in keeping the issue of early rehabilitation alive. As a consequence, piecemeal legislation emerged to enable some special settlers to attain rehabilitation prior to the end of the five-year period denoted in the July 1931 legislation. In February 1932 the Central Executive Committee revised the legislation, adding an amendment that held out the possibility of early rehabilitation for exemplary kulaks.[42] Two months later the Central Executive Committee presidium enacted a decree on the partial rehabilitation of exiled kulaks, especially youth, who had demonstrated their loyalty through shock work. The Central Executive Committee enlisted the regional soviet executive committees to compile lists of candidates based on OGPU recommendations. These rehabilitations were to coincide with celebrations of May Day and, according to the OGPU, were primarily "for show."[43]

The Gulag administration also called for early rehabilitation in selected cases—again primarily of young people. In August 1932 the Gulag administration launched preparatory work on rehabilitation in connection with the upcoming fifteenth anniversary of the October Revolution.[44] By the following spring, the Central Executive Committee had managed to pass legislation that allowed the rehabilitation of kulak youth upon reaching the age of majority—precisely what Stalin had so objected to in 1931.[45] In August of 1933, the OGPU ordered the liberation of families of Belbaltlag (White Sea-Baltic Sea Canal Labor Camp) prisoners who had proven themselves as shock workers.[46] In the meantime, special settlers working in the gold and platinum industries had their terms of exile reduced from the standard five years to three years, most likely due to the horrendous work conditions in the mines.[47] A new Central Executive Committee decree of 27 May 1934 replaced this piecemeal legislation, setting out the terms of rehabilitation for those who had worked honorably and had "ceased their struggles with Soviet power."[48]

On the eve of the completion of the five-year term for kulaks exiled in 1930, some 8,505 special settler families (31,364 people) had been rehabilitated. Only about a quarter of these families subsequently remained in the special settlements. The rest left, some for their home villages, some for the cities.[49] Those rehabilitated before 1935 had been issued passports without restrictions, and it had not been spelled out where they could live.[50] A 1931 Western Siberian regional soviet executive committee decree indicated that kulaks who were rehabilitated could return home.[51] The 1933 liberation of the Belbaltlag prisoners specifically indicated that their families could leave the special settlements.[52] According to the Gulag administration's own legal council, special settlers rehabilitated according to the legislation enacted in 1932 through 1934 had not been subject to any limitations on where they could live.[53]

These were the circumstances that led Berman and Iagoda to seek Stalin's intervention in fixing the special settlers to their place of exile. On 25 January 1935, the Central Executive Committee passed an amendment to its 1934 legislation on rehabilitation that forbade rehabilitated special settlers to leave their place of exile.[54] The punishment for breaking this law was arrest under Article 82 of the penal code, a charge used against anyone fleeing a place of incarceration, which carried a sentence of up to three years' imprisonment.[55]

In 1935 and 1936, 115,676 special settlers were rehabilitated (among them, 53,479 in Western Siberia; 12,982 in Sverdlovsk Region; 6,424 in the North; 4,639 in Eastern Siberia; 2,516 in Omsk Region; and 2,368 in Krasnoiarsk Region). Added to previous rehabilitations, this brought the total numbers of rehabilitated special settlers to some 147,040 by 1936.[56] It is clear from this data that rehabilitation was anything but wholesale, instead limited to those special settlers who passed muster with the NKVD. When the head of a household was rehabilitated, so was his entire extended family. Rehabilitation of an adult male who was not the head of household extended only to his immediate family.[57]

Special settlers who had ever escaped were denied all possibility of rehabilitation.[58]

In 1936 the new "Stalin Constitution" restored, in theory, civil rights to all groups previously disenfranchised by the 1917 revolution. The new constitution proclaimed the victory of socialism in the Soviet Union and celebrated the proletariat's victory over its class enemies, the bourgeoisie and the kulak. Henceforth, according to the constitution, only two classes remained: the proletariat and the collective farm peasantry, two supposedly nonantagonistic classes, along with the intelligentsia (not a class but a "stratum").[59] The constitution was heralded as the "most democratic" in the world, but was in large part a propaganda weapon aimed at convincing the domestic audience of the success of the First Five-Year Plan and at winning Western supporters in the face of the growing fascist threat in Europe.

The constitution inevitably begged the question of the legal status of the kulak. The constitution implied that the kulak was no more and that everyone, presumably including the special settlers, enjoyed the same civil rights. This was the context in which Stalin pontificated that "a son does not answer for the sins of his father," meaning that children would no longer be ascribed to the same class category as their parents. Few, however, took him at his word.

The NKVD reported that the new constitution was fueling all sorts of speculation and rumors about the end of the special settlements. Many special settlers viewed the constitution with distrust, cynically but reasonably concluding that the "constitution is not for us." Others, believing it foretold the liquidation of the special settlements, prepared to leave. Some simply planned to leave regardless of what the constitution portended, claiming "we are now citizens with equal rights." In Western Siberia, kulaks who had fled earlier and had been living in the area illegally reportedly approached the authorities for documents, arguing that "according to the new constitution we are citizens with equal rights."[60] Even the local authorities were uncertain about what the new constitution meant for the special settlers. The Tatar branch of the NKVD inquired about the status of fugitive special settlers who wanted to live in their former villages.[61] And as late as 1942, there were reports of commandants in the Novosibirsk Region who thought that the special settlers were free to work and live as they chose because of the Stalin constitution.[62]

The Stalin constitution only served to make the legal situation of the special settlers more ambiguous and more glaringly unjust. It sparked a new exodus from the special settlements. The NKVD reported illegal returns of kulaks to their home villages.[63] Although flight was drastically down compared to earlier years, the NKVD still recorded 26,193 cases of flight in 1936 and 27,809 cases in 1937.[64] In the Urals, there were reports of officials issuing "all kinds of documents" to special settlers without any indication of their status. As a result, the NKVD later forbade the issue of any documents to special settlers.[65] Those rehabilitated after 1935 were not issued passports—with the notable exception of kulak youth leaving the special settlements temporarily for study or work.[66]

If in 1935 and 1936 the NKVD believed that rehabilitation would stimulate labor productivity and had some results to prove it, by 1937 the situation would change drastically. In February 1937 the NKVD wrote to the Council of People's Commissars, the Central Committee, and the USSR Procurator about the constitution's implications for the special settlers. The prospect of wholesale rehabilitation was unacceptable and politically dangerous. The NKVD suggested instead that special settlers still "hostile" to Soviet power be sent to labor camps for three to five years, leaving open the possibility of a kind of second dekulakization.[67] At about the same time, Nikolai Ezhov, the new NKVD chief, and Andrei Vyshinskii, the USSR Procurator, ordered the Council of People's Commissars and the Central Committee to leave in force the 1935 amendment forbidding rehabilitated special settlers from leaving their regions of exile.[68] In the context of the rapidly deteriorating internal political situation in the Soviet Union, the porousness of the other archipelago led Stalin and the NKVD to see kulaks everywhere. And where there were kulaks, according to the dominant mentality of the times, there was the threat of subversion.

The Second Dekulakization

"My parents were peasants, both illiterate, [they] couldn't even sign their own names.... [They] took my father away in 1937 as an enemy of the people. He was a tireless laborer, knew only his family and work. In childhood, [he] had been an orphan, in his whole life he never hurt a soul. How was he an enemy? To whom?" This is how Ekaterina Sergeevna Lukina, an only child, remembered 1937. Lukina, it may be recalled, had been exiled to Narym and lived in the special settlement Novyi Vasiugin, which, she wrote, "stood on bones."[69] A. M. Cherkasova, who was exiled to the Urals as a child, wrote, "And then 1937 passed through our settlement.... Late at night ... the OGPU came, searched, and took away father. In the morning, we found out that they had taken many. They held the arrested under guard at the school.... We didn't see father again."[70] In polar Igarka, former special settlers remembered the "raids" of 1937 and 1938, when they took away the fathers. One of the

Chernousov sisters eventually managed to track down her father in the camps, where, she said, he had turned into a "walking skeleton."[71]

O. Burova, who with her family had been exiled from the Rostov-on-Don area to the Urals in 1930, remembered when they came for her father. "On 25 August 1937, the day of the arrest, father left to work the night shift. That day we had cut wood together. He was sad when he left and embraced the children. I was awakened that night by the sound of footsteps. Several people walked down our long corridor. They knocked on our door. A guard led father in. . . . The search began. They sat father at a distance [from us] and did not allow him to speak. Mama sat with my youngest sister on her knee. They didn't find anything. They told my father, 'gather your things.' Father turned around at the door and said, 'Children, I am guilty of nothing.' My sister cried and mama stood stone-faced." Burova's father was put in prison, where he was allowed to receive packages and even several visits with his wife. After that he disappeared and Burova, who was fourteen at the time, found out that he had been sentenced to ten years without the right to correspond. "I wrote in those years to Stalin and Beria, asking about my father. In 1943, an NKVD worker-acquaintance told me not to write—otherwise I'd end up with my father." In 1947 Burova learned that her father had another ten years tacked on to his sentence. Then in 1957 she learned that her father had died in 1943 from a heart attack. At that time, he was formally rehabilitated. It was only in the years of *perestroika* that Burova found out the truth—that her father had been executed on 4 October 1937.[72]

The "fathers" were taken away in 1937 and 1938, at the height of what has come to be known as the "Great Terror." According to official statistics, in those two years alone, the NKVD arrested 1,575,259 people, leading to 1,344,923 convictions and 681,692 executions; by early 1939 well over 2 million people were imprisoned within the labor camps, colonies, and prisons.[73] The terror has primarily been associated with the notorious Moscow show trials, in which Zinoviev, Kamenev, Bukharin, Rykov, Iagoda, and other luminaries of the Communist Party were sentenced to death; the midnight braking of the Black Maria and the infamous "knock on the door" that captured the horror of intelligentsia memoirists; and the decimation of party, government, and military elites in numbers beyond imagination. Yet the largest numbers of victims of the terror were not members of the elite. "Mass operations," targeted against specific national and social categories of the population, resulted in the arrests of hundreds of thousands of ordinary people.

The special settler men (and no doubt women, though in smaller numbers) who were caught up in this campaign of terror were targeted as part of NKVD order 00447, a mass operation aimed at—to use the

official parlance—"former kulaks, criminals, and other anti-soviet elements."[74] Order 00447 had been justified—after the fact—in entirely
fictional terms by accusations made at the Moscow show trials, most
notably at the March 1938 trial of the so-called "Anti-Soviet Bloc of
Rightists and Trotskyites," which featured Bukharin, Rykov, and former
NKVD boss Iagoda, among a cast of some twenty-one former Communist
dignitaries. The state procurator, Vyshinskii, charged the defendants
with a battery of crimes, ranging from the assassination in 1934 of
Leningrad party chief S. M. Kirov and the poisoning of Maxim Gorky
to espionage work for Japan, Germany, and England and active plans
to overthrow Soviet power and murder its leaders, most importantly
Stalin. The mass base of the bloc's supposed intended counterrevolutionary activities included a host of "bourgeois-national" groups, various prerevolutionary elites (*byvshie liudi*), and the always infamous and
never-disappearing kulak.[75]

These accusations were rooted in the notion that "kulaks," whatever
that word may now have meant in truth, continued to represent a
colossal threat to Stalin and the Communist Party. They were viewed
as part of a potential "fifth column," which could rise up against the
Soviet regime in the event of war. Molotov admitted this, when, many
years later, he said, "1937 was necessary. Bear in mind that after the
Revolution we slashed right and left; we scored victories, but tattered
enemies of various stripes survived, and as were faced by the growing
danger of fascist aggression, they might have united. Thanks to 1937
there was no fifth column in our country during the war."[76]

Although this threat was little more than a paranoid and politically
useful delusion, it grew phantomlike out of the reality of the chaos of
official policy on the kulaks. During the initial dekulakization campaign
in 1930, some 250,000 kulak families had fled their villages to escape
their fate.[77] Escapes from the special settlements were in the hundreds of
thousands.[78] The piecemeal rehabilitations of the first half of the 1930s
set loose yet another wave of "former kulaks." The more restrictive
rehabilitation of 1935 and 1936 may have penned the kulaks into exile
"forever" (*navechno*), but did so on the basis of the acknowledgment, at
least officially, of their now equal rights with the rest of Soviet society.
There is little doubt that this partly free population of former kulaks
haunted Stalin and served in his mind as the army for the dreaded fifth
column so widely feared by a regime born in the throes of civil war.[79]

Mass operation 00447 was a part of the so-called "*ezhovshchina*" (the
time of Ezhov), named after the new NKVD chief, Nikolai Ezhov. Ezhov
replaced Iagoda in September 1936. Initially demoted to the relatively
lowly position of Commissar of Communications, Iagoda was arrested
only in March 1937. He then found himself in the dock as a defendent

at the third of the great Moscow show trials along with Bukharin and Rykov. He was sentenced to execution. Although the circumstances surrounding his fall are still not entirely clear, the ruinous development of the special settlements could not but have abetted his fall from Stalin's grace. His plans for self-sufficient penal colonies based on family labor had never justified themselves, proving both costly and at times disastrous. And although the costs in human—kulak—lives would not have upset Stalin, the economic costs, the chaos, and the fluidity of this suspect population surely helped to turn him against Iagoda.[80] It was no coincidence that within months of his appointment as new secret police chief, Ezhov reiterated that rehabilitated special settlers were forbidden to leave their place of exile and that those still hostile to the regime be re-arrested and sent to labor camps. With Iagoda's fall, Ezhov reversed the reform trends of the mid-1930s and decisively returned to a more repressive course in regime dealings with the special settlers.

The ezhovshchina, however, was a misnomer.[81] Ezhov was dependent on Stalin for his position and powers; by late 1938 when the terror was winding down, he would no longer be needed. He would be replaced by Lavrentii Beria as NKVD chief, and then arrested and shot. The ezhovshchina therefore could more aptly be labeled the stalinshchina with all consequent connotations of responsibility and ultimate control. The sequence of events leading to order 00447 makes this abundantly clear.

On 17 July 1937, Western Siberian NKVD chief, S. N. Mironov, reported the discovery of what was described as a vast counterrevolutionary organization intent on spying for the Japanese and preparing an armed overthrow of the Soviet government. According to the NKVD, the organization's base consisted of exiled kulaks living in Western Siberia. Close to 3,000 individuals labeled "kulaks" and special settlers were indicted in this case from a total of 4,526 people. The Politburo responded to the unearthing of this supposed conspiracy by ordering the formation of a troika (consisting of Mironov, Eikhe, and the regional procurator Barkov) to expedite the investigation and by ordering the death sentence for all "activists" involved in the organization.[82] The troikas, used in earlier campaigns of repression—most notably in dekulakization—were military-like tribunals, consisting of the regional NKVD chief, party boss, and procurator, which had vast powers to order arrests. They would form the operational backbone of the mass terror throughout the country, issuing 688,000 criminal sentences in 1937 and sentencing 681,692 people to be shot in 1937 and 1938.[83]

Stalin seized upon this pretext of a vast counterrevolutionary conspiracy in Western Siberia to issue a directive that lay directly behind order 00447. On 2 July 1937, he personally signed a Politburo protocol calling for a telegram to be sent to the regional party apparatus on the subject of "antisoviet elements." It informed them that "A large part of the former kulaks and criminals exiled in the past from various regions to northern and Siberian districts, and then at the end of their period of exile returning to their home territories—are the primary ringleaders of all sorts of antisoviet and diversionary crimes both in the collective farms and the state farms and in transport and other branches of industry." The Central Committee then ordered its regional party and NKVD apparatus to register (*vziat' na uchet*) all returning kulaks and criminals in order that "the most hostile of them be immediately arrested and shot" and the "less active, but still hostile elements" be sent into exile. The telegram concluded by asking the regional apparatus to report in "five days" the composition of troikas and the numbers of people to be shot and exiled.[84]

The next day, Ezhov followed up on Stalin's directive, ordering the regional NKVD chiefs to register all kulaks and criminals who had returned to their home territories upon the end of their sentences or who had escaped from camps or special settlements. He told his underlings to complete two lists—one for the "most hostile elements" subject to arrest and execution, and the other for the "less active, but still hostile elements" subject to exile. Ezhov gave the regional NKVD five days to report back with the numbers for each category and promised to issue a directive indicating when the operation would commence.[85]

On 30 July 1937, NKVD deputy M. P. Frinovskii sent Stalin's personal secretary, A. N. Poskrebyshev, a copy of order 00447 for Politburo confirmation.[86] Officially entitled "The operation to repress former kulaks, criminals and other antisoviet elements," the order began with the following preamble:

> Investigative materials from the cases of antisoviet organizations have established that a significant quantity of former kulaks, [—those] earlier repressed, [those] hiding from repression, and [those] escaped from camps, exile, and labor settlements [—] have settled down in the countryside. Many clergy and members of sects [and] former participants of antisoviet armed uprisings who were earlier repressed have [also] settled. Almost untouched are significant numbers of former members of [prerevolutionary] political parties . . . and also formerly active participants of bandit uprisings, white punitive detachments, repatriates, etc.
>
> A part of those elements listed above have left the village for the city and have penetrated industrial enterprises, transport, and construction.
>
> Besides them, there are in the villages and cities significant numbers of criminals —cattle and horse thieves, repeat offenders, robbers, etc., who have completed their sentences, escaped from prison, or are hiding from repression.[87]

The task of the NKVD, to quote from the order, was "to destroy in the most merciless way possible all of this band of antisoviet elements." The operation was to begin on 5 August in most parts of the country and to conclude in four months.[88]

The order set out numerical quotas by region for each category of the repressed, based on the figures submitted by the regional NKVD chiefs. The first category, consisting of the "most hostile," came to 75,950. These individuals were subject to immediate arrest and execution. The second category—those "less active, but still hostile"—came to a total of 193,000 and were to be sentenced to eight to ten years in labor camps. The total numbers to be repressed in this operation came to 268,950 with the largest numbers in the Moscow Region (35,000), Western Siberia (17,000), Leningrad Region (14,000), Azovo-Chernomorskii Region (13,000), Belorussia (12,000), and Sverdlovsk Region (10,000). Operation 00447 targeted an additional 10,000 from within the labor camps. Border regions, major cities, and areas of exile were hit hardest.[89]

Order 00447 described the categories of "kulak elements" to be arrested:

former kulaks who had returned to their villages after completing their sentences and continued to lead active antisoviet, subversive activity

former kulaks who escaped from camps and labor settlements and also kulaks who had hid from dekulakization, [and] who engaged in antisoviet activity

former kulaks and socially dangerous elements who participated in insurrections, or fascist, terrorist, and bandit organizations, and who, having served their sentences, hid from repression, or escaped from incarceration, and have renewed their antisoviet, criminal activity.[90]

Also included were "the most active elements" from former kulaks currently held in prisons, camps, and special settlements who continued to lead "active subversive work."[91]

The Politburo confirmed order 00447 on 31 July 1937. At this time, it also outlined the fate of the incoming (category 2) camp population. The 00447 contingents were to be employed in Gulag construction projects, the construction of new camps in Kazakhstan, and forestry work. The Politburo instructed the Forestry Commissariat to transfer to the Gulag entire land tracts for the organization of forestry work camps.[92] Those arrested but not executed were to provide the new brawn for the labor camps' expansion of 1937/38. They would continue the work of "colonization" and the extraction of raw materials for Soviet industry and military efforts, but now primarily from within the camps rather than the special settlements.

The population of what is familiarly known as the Gulag (camps, labor colonies, prisons) mushroomed in these years. The burgeoning labor camps now rivaled the special settlements (or at least the "kulak" contingent of the special settlements), overshadowing what Iagoda had planned as self-supporting penal colonies of prisoners and their families.[93] The special settlements had proven far too costly and unproductive, partly as a result of their size and location, partly as a result of the "ballast," to use the jargon of the local bosses, that the families represented. It seemed now to be far more cost-effective to exploit the labor of able-bodied men and women, without their families, within the rapidly developing camp system.[94] Yet, the "kulak" still formed the bulk of this new army of unfree laborers flowing into the camps.

The appellation of kulak had lost any residual socioeconomic meaning by this time, retaining only a political content that could be molded according to regime needs. In addition to the tens of thousands of officially designated kulaks among the ranks of the new labor camp population, order 00447 absorbed individuals who had been charged with counterrevolutionary crimes in the countryside in the early 1930s, such as those who had participated in the mass rebellions of those years, and a host of other past and present rural inhabitants, including "recidivist" criminals, petty village criminals, urban hooligans, and former members of the popular, prerevolutionary Socialist Revolutionary political party. In short, the peasantry continued to pay the highest price for the "triumphs" of Soviet power under Stalin.[95]

Operation 00447 swept through the labor camps and special settlements, as well as through the countryside and cities.[96] Although documentation is scant and impressionistic, special settlers who were children in the late 1930s later recalled their parents and neighbors being taken away to be shot or moved to the camps. According to the Russian sociologist V. N. Zemskov, as many as 46,215 special settlers were convicted in 1937 and 1938, or about 17 percent of all "kulaks" rounded up in the operation.[97] There is no evidence of any particular logic to the dynamics of 00447 within the other archipelago. It is likely that the NKVD made arrests in 1937 and 1938 in the same way that the OGPU before it selected locations for the special settlements—fulfilling quotas designated on paper from afar, in Moscow and in the regional capitals. What is clear are the regional dynamics of 00447. The greatest impact of repression was felt in exile zones like the Urals and Western Siberia, home to large special settler populations but also to the labor camps, which in many cases still housed those designated as first-category kulaks back in 1930 and now subject to resentencing.

As a final coda to operation 00447—and indeed to the great terror as a whole—the NKVD turned in upon itself. Although some regional NKVD leaders like Austrin fell along with Iagoda in 1937, most would see their careers, and usually their lives, ended with the dismissal of

Ezhov in late 1938 and his arrest the following spring. At this point, Stalin slowed down the course of the terror, turning Ezhov into a scapegoat for "excesses" and replacing him with Beria. The purges were extended through the ranks of the NKVD and Gulag administration, bringing down, among others, those who had been most important in implementing special settlement policy—Berman, Firin, Pliner, Kogan, and others. They were now labeled "enemies of the people" and charged with, among other crimes, enriching the kulaks at government expense and setting up special settlements dangerously close to the borders. With the purge of the Gulag leadership on charges that can only be described as perversely ironic, the entire administrative structure of the special settlements was shaken to its core.[98]

9

Tearing the Evil from the Root: War, Redemption, and Stigmatization

What I saw and lived, that is what I learned.
—Valentina Timofeevna Slipchenko, a former special settler

Sooner or later all the same Soviet power will end. War is already here—it is already beginning. From the east, the Japanese, from the west, Poland. And we will leave here only then when our saviors deliver us from the enemy communists." "Because foreign governments delivered an ultimatum to the USSR and demanded our dispersal home, the Soviets will soon be forced to release us to our homes." "No one can free us but a foreign power." "In Uzbekistan, Soviet power is already no more. The Japanese are also in Siberia. Soon they will free us." "All Siberia is occupied by the Japanese."

These are a sampling of rumors collected by the OGPU in 1932, when the predominant political "mood" of the special settlers was to hope for foreign intervention.[1] If we are to trust the OGPU/NKVD sources, many special settlers spent ten years dreaming about war and planning to rise up against the "enemy communists" as soon as war broke out. "When the war begins, here in the localities we must make a war, beat and shoot up all communists so that nothing of them remains." "As soon as war begins, we must immediately seize the bosses and communists, not one will remain."[2] The collection, if not the reality, of such rumors and sentiments fueled Stalin's dread of a fifth column through the entirety of the 1930s.

When war finally broke out on 22 June 1941 with the onslaught of the Nazi blitzkrieg deep into Soviet territory, the OGPU/NKVD's nightmarish scenario of fifth column subversion largely failed to materialize.

Perhaps Molotov was correct when he said years later that "thanks to 1937," there was no fifth column in the Soviet Union during the war.[3] Or perhaps the withering repressive potential of the Soviet security forces forestalled any possibility of a fifth column rearing its head. Or perhaps any likely fifth column forces were, by this time, simply too atomized, isolated, and exhausted to act. Or they might have been a fabrication in the collective psyche of the Stalinist leadership to begin with.

In all probability, most people inside and outside of the gulag rallied around the flag, such as it was, in a quasi-atavistic national, if not entirely patriotic, response to intervention and the foreign foe. And the terrible atrocities of the Nazis during four long, hard years of war would only serve to cement such feelings. According to the NKVD, most of the kulaks responded to the outbreak of war in a "healthy" and "positive" manner.[4] Years later, the regime would use the wartime experience of the special settlers to argue that its efforts to reforge the kulak as a class had been successful, offering the ultimate proof of their transformation from "class enemy" to Soviet citizen.

From Terror to War

By the time World War II broke out in the Soviet Union, the Gulag of the labor camps, colonies, and prisons had begun to overshadow in importance the other archipelago of special settlements as the bloody mechanics of the Great Terror of 1937/38 channeled a new wave of victims into that part of the Gulag. In 1941, there were some 4 million inmates in the various domains of the Gulag: 1.5 million in labor camps, 429,000 in labor colonies, 488,000 in prisons, and another 1.5 million in special settlements.[5] In 1939/40, forced deportations from the Baltic countries and Poland had restocked the special settlements with new generations of exiles. Additional large-scale deportations of suspect national groups from within the Soviet Union during the war would ensure a steady supply of forced labor in the special settlements.[6]

In the years bridging the terror and the war, the tug-of-war between reform and reeducation, on the one hand, and repression and isolation, on the other, continued to characterize the Stalinist regime's treatment of the kulak. Could the kulak be transformed through reeducation and "honest" labor? Or would his "class" status permanently mark him? Was rehabilitation possible, or was isolation and physical elimination the only sure ways to "deal" with the kulak?

The Great Terror had not resolved these questions. In its wake, there would again be attempts to reform the system of special resettlement. To a great extent, these attempts flowed from the very system itself.

Repression and reform were two sides of a coin, the only possible ways of dealing with a system that had developed and continued to evolve in a mixture of illegality, chaos, and perpetual flux. When it was not terrorizing the special settler population, the regime attempted, in its words, to "normalize" the system of special resettlement.

In the aftermath of the Great Terror, the NKVD reverted to its earlier attempts to shed at least a part of the economic burden of the specifically kulak special settlements. The special settlement agricultural artels became, on 9 September 1938, regular, chartered collective farms, distinguished only by the maintenance of the commandant regimen, which continued to be necessary to keep the special settlers fixed in place.[7] The children of special settlers received the right, upon reaching the age of sixteen, to leave their settlements for work or study. They even received passports, although these had geographical restrictions.[8] Non-able-bodied elderly were allowed—indeed encouraged—to leave the settlements and could go anywhere to live except for Moscow and Leningrad, restricted cities due to their political and strategic importance.[9] From early 1938, the NKVD's earlier attempts to transfer a part of the burden of administration began to take root as some economic administrative functions were transferred to the regional authorities, and part of the commandant functions were handed off to the local militia.[10]

The most notable reform effort came in 1939 when Beria, the new NKVD chief, finally attempted to replace the "temporary" statutes of 1931 governing the special settlements with a permanent set of regulations. These reform efforts were intended more or less to "normalize" the special settlements, removing them entirely from the jurisdiction of the NKVD and the Gulag. Beria planned to establish rural soviets within the special settlements, transferring the supervisory-control functions of the commandants to what would be a numerically expanded local militia. Again, although the special settlers would have to remain in their place of exile, their children, upon reaching the age of sixteen, and settlers married to "free" citizens would have the right to move and settle anywhere within the Soviet Union except for certain strategically important large cities and industrial centers. Special settlers residing in the agricultural artels would be governed by the regular statutes of the collective farms as well as by the general laws of the Soviet Union. Settlers working in industry would be issued passports restricting them to residence in a given locale. In the end, Beria's reform plans came to naught. After two years of discussion and bureaucratic wrangling, in March 1941 the reform project was shelved as "not pressing."[11]

By this time, there were roughly 930,000 kulak settlers in about 1,750 settlements, with approximately one half working in industry, one fourth in forestry, and one fourth in agriculture.[12] Movement within the special settlements continued. In December 1939 the NKVD ordered the purge of a five-kilometer perimeter surrounding railroads. This order resulted in the forced relocation of some 93,794 families.[13] In Siberia dozens of special settlements with dwindling populations were merged in early 1941, their inhabitants uprooted yet again.[14] In the meantime, many special settlers worked outside their settlements. In the Arkhangel'skaia Region in early 1941, for example, some 20,000 of the 36,600 special settlers still registered with the NKVD lived and worked not in the special settlements but in nearby towns and cities.[15]

With the start of the war, the Gulag administration issued an order to halt all rehabilitations of special settlers (except youth).[16] In less than a year, however, there would be a sharp turnabout in policy. On 11 April 1942 the State Defense Committee issued a directive authorizing the mobilization of special settlers into the army.[17] Prior to this time, special settlers had been strictly forbidden to serve in the military or to engage in any type of military training activities in the schools.[18] But now the country was at war, with the enemy quite literally at the gates of Moscow. The army was in desperate need of manpower. In May 1942 it drafted 34,615 special settlers for the war effort; by 1 November 1942, this number had increased to over 60,000.[19]

World War II, or the "great war of the fatherland," as it was known to generations of Soviets, was a watershed in the history of the kulak special settlers. The war held out the possibility of official redemption. An NKVD directive of 22 October 1942 ordered the complete emancipation (that is, removal from police registries and the right to leave) of the families of special settlers serving in the military.[20] After more than a decade of suspicion, hostility, and inhuman treatment, the regime was prepared to liberate the kulak special settlers in return for their participation in the war effort. Had the special settlers finally succeeded in proving themselves in the eyes of Soviet power? Or was the NKVD again simply attempting to divest itself of the burden of the "kulaks," with the convenient excuse that the army was in desperate need of soldiers?

School Days

The special settlers, so the rhetoric went, were to be transformed from "former kulaks" and "enemies of socialism" into "conscious builders of socialism." They were to become "active participants" in socialist construction by taking part "in the process of production."[21] This rhetoric of reforging had served as one of the ideological justifications for the deportation of the kulaks, cloaking the reality that they had become little more than an exploitable resource, an army of unfree workers. In fact, if not in theory, the regime had little hope for the adult population of the special settlements. The "second dekulakization" of 1937 and 1938 had made that abundantly clear. The regime instead placed its main emphasis on youth—on the children who grew up in the other archipelago, toiling alongside their parents, studying in "special" schools, and fighting for the Soviet Union in World War II.

Officially, the regime emphasized nurture over nature.[22] Soviet education was to be the primary means to reforge youth. By the outbreak of war, there was a relatively well-developed network of schools within the special settlements: 1,106 elementary schools, 370 incomplete middle schools, and 136 middle schools in the special settlements, in addition to 12 technical schools (tekhnikumy) and 230 professional-technical schools (shkoly proftekhobrazovaniia). In all, the school network encompassed some 217,454 students and 8,280 teachers.[23] In 1938 the children of special settlers had gained the right, at age sixteen, to leave their place of exile in order to work or attend an institution of higher education or technical training. They received passports for internal travel, albeit with residence restrictions.[24] Many would indeed continue their education. They were expected to become teachers, agronomists, veterinarians, medics, and bookkeepers for the special settlements. In fact, by the end of the 1930s, according to reports from the Northern Territory, the majority of special settlement teachers were young people who had been exiled with their parents and "reeducated" in Soviet institutions.[25] Most, however, would not return to the special settlements once they had completed their education, resettling instead outside of the special settlements in the towns and cities of their exile zone.

The regime claimed that a Soviet education had provided the means with which to reforge the children of the kulak special settlers. The son would no longer answer for the father because he had become a new person—a Soviet person. It is impossible to judge with any degree of certainty the extent to which the regime succeeded in its endeavors given the difficulties of piercing through regime propaganda and delving into subjective experience. It is possible though to examine the lived experience of the children of the kulaks and to weigh that experience against regime rhetoric.

School represented possibilities—for a normal life, for a future. Education was a way out of the other archipelago. As Klavdia Petrovna Chudinova, who was exiled as a child from Voronezh to Komi, remembered "all the special settler children strove for an education."[26] Valentina Timofeevna Slipchenko, who was exiled from Ukraine to the Urals in 1930, remembered how, "With joy, [I] ran to school. There was an enormous stove there. One could warm up. . . . They gave me bread. . . . Here was happiness for me. Did I learn? I lived there." [27] Although the

regime touted Soviet education as transformative, it would be the realities of everyday life in the special settlements and the kulak stigma that
would have the greatest impact on young people.

Valentina Slipchenko's story brings these realities into sharp relief
and is worth recounting in full. Valentina was born in 1921 into a
Ukrainian-speaking family in Poltava. Her most vivid memories of
childhood before her family's deportation centered around school. She
remembered her village school in Poltava, how she finished two grades
in one year, and even won a prize (a pen and pencil). She remembered
her teachers. Then, suddenly and catastrophically, this part of her life
came to an end. They took her family away in carts and unloaded them
into a train where "everything was dark" and "everyone slept sitting on
the floor." Her mother died first: one day she simply failed to return
from work in the forest. By this time, her father had fled, and she was
alone to tend to her younger siblings. "Grisha and Masha [sat] on the stove
crying. What was I to do?" She settled the children as best she could and
then went out to search for her mother. "By evening, tired, hungry, and
blinded from tears, [I] returned home." Grisha and Masha had been
taken away, and Valentina found herself "alone in a cold home."

The only thing Valentina could do was to continue to go to school,
her only refuge from the realities of her life. One day when she was
returning to her empty home, some children ran up to her to tell her
that her mother had been found. "Fear and terror seized me." She
saw the blackened and partially decomposed body of her mother. A
neighbor took Valentina in for the night. "In the morning, I saw mama
on the floor. I saw her eyes. . . . The women said I should cut her hair.
I sat under mama's head and I was afraid. . . . Her hair was all tangled
in a wet mass. I was afraid that I would hurt my mother."

Soon her little brother Grisha died, and her sister Masha disappeared
forever into the state orphanage system. "This I absorbed without any
particular attention." Yet the trauma of her experience as well as malnutrition caught up with her: Valentina temporarily lost her eyesight. With
that, she could no longer go to school. She went to work as a nanny for
a family of woodcutters. She did well, her mistress was satisfied, but "I
talked badly and little [in Russian]." When she regained her sight, she
pleaded to go back to school. Her mistress wanted her to stay, promising
that she would be treated like a member of the family. Valentina instead
chose to return to school, this time in a neighboring village.

The school was poor—there were no pencils or paper. "We studied
in teams," Valentina recalled. "One answered and the grade went to
the entire brigade," a lucky break given Valentina's poor knowledge of
Russian. Within a short time, a commune for special settler children was
created. Valentina moved into its dormitories, but when summer came

she found herself alone again as the other students left to join their parents in the special settlements. Fortunately, a classmate left Valentina with a piece of soap, a rare commodity in that place and time, to trade for food. "I openly carried it in my hands to a village to exchange for a potato. A woman saw me and brought me home. She hurriedly opened her cellar. I was even frightened! She quickly went in and carried out a whole pail of potatoes. The woman did not want to take my soap."

Within no time, however, Valentina was at death's door, suffering from the effects of hunger. She was hospitalized and slowly recovered, thanks to the kindness of a nurse who fed her food from her own table and brought her back to health. When she was released, she went into an orphanage for special settler children. The orphanage was a two-story brick building with one room for girls and one for boys. The children did their best to care for each other. "The boys guarded the girls at night since the toilet was outside. In bed, the girls talked about all sorts of things." Yet the reality of their existence was never far away. Valentina remembered one night when a very small girl had to be restrained from jumping out of the second-story window. She cried, "Home! I want to go home." The other girls put her back into bed. She was dead by morning.

Valentina's only hope to pull herself out of this terrible abyss was school. She did well in her studies and became a prize pupil. In 1939 she finally received a passport and was allowed to leave for the city of Nizhnyi Tagil. There she studied first to be a cabinetmaker and then to work as a nursery teacher. During the war, she tended the wounded in a hospital. In 1947 she graduated from a teacher's training college and then worked steadily as a teacher until her retirement in 1977. Valentina Timofeevna lived long enough to become a member of Memorial, the Russian organization that arose in the waning days of the Gorbachev regime dedicated to the preservation of the memories of those who suffered repression during the Stalin years. Yet she never ceased to be haunted by her past: "For years, I saw my sister in every child."

Valentina Timofeevna's story clearly evokes the context in which special settler youth came to prize school and an education. Although she became a Soviet teacher and undoubtedly carried out her duties loyally and conscientiously, Valentina never forgot her past as a special settler, a kulak. Was she reforged? In her own words, "What I saw and lived, this is what I learned."[28]

Given these realities, school represented less an instrument of reforging than a place of refuge, hope, and possibility. Moreover and contrary to regime rhetoric, school was never a given for special settler youth, nor did it automatically erase the kulak stigma. Most had to struggle for an education, waiting long years for a school to open up in their vicinity and losing valuable time while working side by side with their parents. Some had to forego an education entirely, taking over household duties, caring for younger siblings, or working to supplement the household income. Those who succeeded in completing a seven-year school or a middle school had to struggle to continue their education outside the special settlements, even after 1938 when young people received passports and official permission to leave for work or study. The kulak marker set these young people apart.

The many letters that young people wrote to Soviet authorities illustrate these realities. Eighteen-year-old Vera Panasiuk, exiled to Siberia from Ukraine, wrote the following letter to E. P. Peshkova, the head of the Political Red Cross and the wife of the great socialist realist writer Maxim Gorky:

> Already it is three years since they exiled us to Siberia where we are at present. I finished a seven-year school at fourteen, that in 1930, I was the first pupil in all subjects, [I] was a pioneer and in all the clubs [*kruzhki*] . . . I now have three years of work experience. I began work at fifteen, and for a year and a half I was an unskilled laborer and now I work as an accountant in the central offices of a state farm. For some reason, they consider me an enemy, shun me and insult me. I am very hurt. I never had and don't have hostile thoughts to the Soviet country . . . I ask for the restoration of my rights and [permisson] to study. . . . In the seven-year school I was the first pupil in all subjects, although I have now forgotten a little. Allow me to study at night.[29]

Manefa Semenovna Gorokhova similarly petitioned Krupskaia, Lenin's widow and an authority on education:

> As a kulak's daughter who has graduated from a seven-year school, I have been deprived of the opportunity to continue my education. Feeling no guilt toward the Soviet government, because I was born in 1916 whereas my father had ended his commerce (1913), because I was absolutely uninvolved in my parents' actions, because my brother served in the Workers' and Peasants' Red Army in 1919, because our farm was considered a middle peasant's farm until 1933, I serenely graduated from the seven-year school upon reaching adolescence, firmly confident that I would receive further education, obtain a vocation, and work together with the toilers for the benefit of construction and Soviet power.
>
> All of this has been ruled out now. I am seventeen years old. I don't work anywhere, I am burning with shame in front of my girl friends, because they are continuing their education, while I am deprived of this because of the circumstances set forth above, although my young life demands an education.
>
> In view of the foregoing I ask you to put yourself in my position and give me assistance in continuing my studies and thereby fulfill V. I. Lenin's precepts (study, study, and study).[30]

Panasiuk justified her request by telling Peshkova about her exemplary school record, while Gorokhova attempted to prove her "social innocence" through a Soviet or sovietized autobiography (brother in the Red army, a middle peasant farm), not to mention by quoting Lenin ("study, study, and study"). It is clear from both letters that these young women viewed education as a desired goal and a necessity. Further, their petitions suggest that they also saw their continuing education as a normal and expected course of affairs unfairly denied them. In these respects, they were very much like other Soviet school children and youth for whom education had become a valued and necessary right, thanks to the revolution. What was different was that they faced an uphill struggle to attain their goals and that achieving them represented far greater stakes: a way out of the special settlements.

Panasiuk and Gorokhova's petitions, like Valentina's story, tell a story of nonbelonging. They are pleas for inclusion, for an end to discrimination, and, more generally, for consideration as part of the ideologically invented Soviet family. What little evidence exists hinting at the internal world of young special settlers suggests that they felt keenly their status as outsiders. Perhaps it is simply a universal truth of human existence that people, and especially young people, need to feel included in some larger, legitimating community. For many young special settlers, this community was the Soviet Union and they viewed their nonbelonging as insulting and unjust. A letter from special settler V. Bushmanov to Krupskaia illustrates these feelings:

> [We] are in our second year of living in the children's home . . . and have already been reeducated in the new way. . . . Soviet functionaries still call us these special migrants. Wherever we go it is always special migrants but we are very hurt that we all attend school together and we are called special migrants. What kind of special migrants are we when we have been reeducated in the new way?"

Young Bushmanov, who also pledged to "study and study," felt wronged that he could not shed his special settler status even after he had been reeducated in the "new way."[31]

Other young people described experiencing similar insults and discrimination as a result of special settler status. Vera Shkuropieva wrote a long letter to Krupskaia, documenting her life history while pleading for "parental help" in shedding her pariah status. "I am pinning all my hope on you," she wrote. "Why don't they let me have a normal life. . . . it is very painful for me why everybody is studying and I can't. Dear N. K. please show some concern for me, so that I can study and be a human being." Despite their rupture with an alcoholic father, Vera and her sister, Dusia, continued to encounter discrimination, thus losing work, the chance to study, and even their apartment ("I will not allow kulaks to live on the premises.") All Vera wanted was "to study and prove I am not an alien class element."[32] Like Bushmanov, she was highly sensitive to her alien status. She viewed the discrimination aimed at her as an injustice, given her break with her father, and simply hoped to "be a human being and bring benefit to the state."[33]

Like the other writers, Vera seamlessly incorporated a kind of Soviet speak into her letter, perhaps demonstrating implicitly how Soviet values had shaped her world and determined her view of *normalcy*. Young people's letters often made use of Soviet autobiographical conventions and terminology. They did not discuss their family background, they discussed their *class* background. They justified their requests by arguing that they were not kulaks or that they had been properly reeducated. It is difficult to say whether these formulations were simply politically correct ploys or sincere evidence of "reforging."[34] Many had already been to Soviet schools before being exiled, so that elements of a Soviet consciousness, to offer a crude shorthand, would inevitably have filtered into their mental world. The fact that these earlier experiences were so at odds with the actual lived experiences of special resettlement was likely of far greater significance. And the circumstances of their lives would impede the very possibility that they could live a "normal" life as equal members of the Soviet collective.

Young people branded with the kulak marker would continue to experience discrimination throughout their lives—in the form of denunciations, dismissal from school or work, and the fear of contagion that surrounded them at times in "normal" Soviet society. In school, they were restricted in their studies, in some cases forbidden to sing revolutionary songs, celebrate revolutionary holidays, or have portraits of Soviet leaders in their classrooms.[35] In one school, they were told, in response to questions about why they were exiled, "Soviet power needed labor; therefore [we] exiled your parents."[36] In an industrial complex in the Urals, special settler children were viewed as sources of "contagion" and forbidden admission to school; here the bosses believed that these children were intended exclusively for use as forced laborers "to the end of their days."[37] One nameless official, who advocated "tough measures" against even the children, rationalized his philosophy with the argument that it was necessary "to tear the evil from the root."[38]

Of course, these kinds of sentiments ran counter to the regime's stated aim of reeducation and reforging. Moscow had little real control over these realities of the special settlements. More important, Moscow's "concern" for the young people was, in the main, limited to the rhetoric of reforging and was contradicted at every stage by the more pressing demand for labor and the pervasive ideological prejudice, fear, and hatred that colored its relations to the kulaks. The prevailing realities for special settler youth continued to be poverty, backbreaking work, discrimination, and the overwhelming brutality of the special resettlement system.

Nowhere was the hypocrisy of the system more evident than in the special settler children's homes set up to foster orphaned children and to raise them in a "Soviet spirit." We have already seen evidence of the "happy childhood" Stalin bestowed upon special settler youth in the documentation on conditions in the children's homes during the famine years. Photographs of orphanages tell a similar story. A group photo of an orphanage in Narym shows some fifty orphans standing in front of the small, one-story building that served as their home. Many of the children are dressed in no more than sackcloth, standing barefoot in the mud, with stick-thin arms protruding from their sleeveless rags. The commandant and a female aide stand to the side, both dressed in three-quarter length coats with head coverings, indicating that the weather remained brisk. Meanwhile, the children are half-dressed. How many of these children and others like them survived into adulthood to be grateful to "beloved Stalin" is impossible to say, but clearly their "reforging" was nothing short of cruel travesty.

From time to time, there were reports of successful reforging. Northern Territory party chief Ivanov spoke of special settler children rendering a "positive influence" on their parents by informing on them in cases of planned escapes, pilfering, and work truancy.[39] Another report also noted "progress," calling attention to the creation of atheist circles among youth and proclaiming that "the children took part in the struggle for the timber export by putting pressure on shirkers, deserters, etc."—that is, on their parents.[40]

Reforging, then, could be tantamount to creating informers and overseers. This again was a travesty of reeducation, the effect of ignorance, cynicism, disdain, and neglect. Similar ingredients went into official initiatives designed to allow children to renounce their parents and change their names. Special settler children were encouraged to renounce their parents as "class enemies"; they often had no choice if they wanted to continue their education or secure employment. They also received official permission to change their names upon the restoration of their civil rights.[41] In order to move to Moscow, Anna Akimovna Dubova, whose family had been labeled kulaks while she managed to escape, recalled in an interview: "I had to write an official statement that I renounced my parents, that I no longer had any ties with them. That's what really happened! I had to do that in order to leave!" Elena Trofimovna Dolgikh was denounced as a daughter of kulaks in her teacher training college. In order to continue her education—albeit in another college— she too was forced to renounce her family. "But in fact, I went there every summer to help them with the farm work."[42] The renunciation of family—a cataclysmic act for someone born into a close-knit peasant family—was the ultimate degradation. In most cases, it represented little more than official reforging—superficial, hypocritical, and tantamount to a kind of cynical blackmail aimed, not necessarily successfully, at tearing families apart.

Special settler children were never entirely able to shed their ascribed status as class enemies. For this reason, most of the young people sent on to higher education to serve in the special settlements left at the first chance, using their training to re-create their lives elsewhere. The regime would never fully trust them, arguing that "the evaluation of the mood [of special settler youth] must be based not on oral declarations, but on deeds" and, in particular, deeds that aided the police—informing and denunciations.[43] Even the NKVD despaired at times of genuine reforging, noting in reports that in many cases the parents' influence had actually grown stronger, not weaker, while reforging had left no effect.[44] In the end, one special settler was very likely correct when she concluded that the cohesiveness of the special settler families was not broken: "The adults themselves served as models for their children." From this perspective, Soviet education was a means to an end for special settler youth. It represented a way out of the other archipelago but hardly constituted the reforging of kulak youth.

Stigma

Nonetheless the war would be a turning point in the lives of many special settlers. A little over a month following the October 1942 NKVD directive ordering the rehabilitation of the families of those serving in the military, 47,116 special settlers were crossed off the police registries (17,775 draftees and 29,341 family members).[45] Toward the end of the war, in January 1945, the government issued a decree granting the exiled kulaks "all rights of Soviet citizens," but this time with the notable caveat that the former special settlers must be occupied in "socially useful labor" and could not leave their place of exile without official permission.[46] If at the beginning of the war, there were 930,000 former kulaks living in exile, by October 1945, 606,808 remained (roughly 50 percent of whom had been exiled prior to 1933).[47]

Soviet historians later claimed that the heroic service of the kulaks in the war was proof of the successful transformation of the kulak as a class.[48] That the kulak special settlers served in the army in large numbers and that many were decorated veterans, some even achieving the highest honor of "hero of the Soviet Union," is not in doubt.[49] But that did not erase the memory of their experience or the reality of their status, nor did it prove the success of the regime's rhetoric of reforging.

Even during the war, the NKVD recorded hostile conversations among special settlers: "You see how the communists change their policies, they feel weak . . . and they begin to trust the kulaks." "For ten years they did not consider us human and now suddenly they call us to defend the motherland [*rodina*]." "There is nothing for us to defend." An informer in Vologda reported special settlers refusing to serve and secretly planning to go over to the Germans at the first opportunity.[50] At a 1943 meeting to discuss the war and its legal consequences for special settler families, the NKVD recorded several cases of special settler women casting doubt on new government promises to free the families of soldiers. One woman said, "My husband was killed at the front, for what do I need a certificate [of emancipation from the special settlement] when they killed my husband," while another groused, "I don't especially need your certificate taking me off the police registry, all the same there is nowhere to go."[51] It is impossible to say whether these sentiments were widespread. The NKVD claimed they were not. Still, the fact of their collection in official reports served as a reminder that kulaks remained kulaks.

The war did not serve as the ultimate school for the reforging of the kulaks. That role was reserved for the harsh realities of the special settlements. The regime's primary motivation in recruiting special settlers for wartime service was not based on ideological factors. Rather, as was the case through the 1930s, the regime needed manpower—in this case, cannon fodder. The war's main impact would be the simple fact of rehabilitation in return for military service. And not all kulaks would be redeemed with the victorious conclusion of the war. In 1947 there would still be 231,287 people living in the special settlements.[52] These numbers, however, declined drastically in the next four years as a result of large-scale rehabilitations enacted not by the center but by the regional authorities. As a result, by 1951, only about 24,300 special settlers remained on the police registries.[53]

It was only after the death of Stalin, on 13 August 1954, that the Central Committee of the Communist Party issued a directive lifting all restrictions on "former kulaks exiled in 1929–33 from the districts of wholesale collectivization," in effect, officially ending the exile of the kulaks.[54] By this time, only 17,348 former kulaks still held the formal status of special settler.[55] The justification for ending the exile of the kulaks was not based on humanitarian considerations. Rather, it was based on the special settlers' wartime service as well as the argument that removing restrictions would not harm the local economy because the kulak-special settlers who remained were now permanently settled in their exile zones. In fact, the directive was little more than a recognition of the status quo; the remaining special settlers were mostly elderly people, many of them women living alone in poverty, and most no longer lived under direct police supervision.[56]

The other archipelago of the peasant Gulag thus came to an official end just as Nikita Khrushchev was ushering in a "thaw" in post-Stalin Soviet politics.[57] In an extraordinary closed session of the Twentieth Congress of the Communist Party of the Soviet Union held on the night of 25/26 February 1956, Khrushchev delivered his now-famous speech on the "crimes of the Stalin era." He spoke of how Stalin abused his powers in the repression of tens of thousands of Communist Party members. He spoke of Stalin's incompetence at the outset of World War II. And he spoke of the injustice of the wartime deportations of entire nations. But he said not a word about the deportation of the kulaks. In part, this was because Khrushchev took pains to demonstrate Stalin's service in the struggle against political opponents within the party in the 1920s and in the "construction of socialism" "when the exploiting classes were generally liquidated." Here, according to Khrushchev, "Stalin played a positive role." In part, he ignored the fate of the kulaks because he could not condemn the entire legacy of Stalin and still maintain the hegemony of the Communist Party and the viability of the Soviet system.[58]

So the story of the kulak special settlers fell into official oblivion for the next thirty-odd years. The special settlers themselves, however, did not go away. An entire generation of by then middle-aged people who had survived the deportations continued to live and function within Soviet society. But their special status could not be so easily erased.

"I was afraid whenever I saw a policemen, because it seemed to me that they could tell that something about me wasn't right. . . . When Stalin died, I was working in a military organization. And I remember that they immediately called a meeting of our section and announced his death. When I heard the news, I got very frightened, thinking that they would be able to tell from the expression on my face that I was very happy. . . . And I forced myself to look sad, so they wouldn't notice that it didn't upset me."[59] "When I retired on pension, I became absolutely free. . . . It is really terrible to live under the weight of fear."[60] "As long as Yeltsin has not signed the laws, I'm not going to tell anyone I was dekulakized. . . . Before perestroika, I had not even told my son."[61]

These are voices of fear—fear of discovery, fear of officialdom. The three women quoted above, all elderly at the time of their statements, had grown up with the stigma of the kulak label, a central fact of their existence. Anna Akimovna Dubova, who was afraid whenever she saw a policeman, came from a family that owned a shop and, by her own admission, was relatively well-off. Her family escaped exile only because they promised her, then just thirteen years old, in marriage to a local Communist Party secretary. The family lost their farm all the same. Anna was forced to renounce her parents and could only remember her pre-exile childhood and peasant life as a "golden age."[62]

Elena Trofimovna Dolgikh who lived her life "under the weight of fear," had been the adopted daughter of rural school teachers. Her grandfather was dekulakized, and she herself was denounced as a "daughter of kulaks" while in teachers' college. Later she lost her position as a village teacher when she was again denounced. She continued to suffer discrimination, later even being rejected by a suitor after he discovered her class background.[63]

Anna R., who hadn't told her son about her past, was fourteen years old in a family of nine when they came for her family. Her elder sisters had been married off to poor peasants, so they were able to stay behind. Two of her other sisters died in the first few months of their exile. Her father was next. Anna and her brother worked, barefoot, in logging until her mother finally succeeded in leading them in an escape. They returned to their village and moved in with a widow. Anna worked as a nanny, going to school in the evenings. She eventually became a village teacher, later even serving as a rural soviet secretary during the war. She summed up her lifelong kulak status in the following way: "We never had any wealth and we suffered for nothing."[64]

The stories that these and other special settler survivors lived to tell are not necessarily reflective of all special settler children's experience. They are not exceptional either but for the fact that these women survived to tell their stories. What is clear is that their ascribed identity as kulaks could not easily be discarded. Like all Soviet citizens, they held multiple and sometimes contradictory identities, but the kulak identity was in many ways defining. They would not forget their status; nor would the regime allow them to forget it, proving the ultimate hypocrisy of reforging.[65] The kulak marker was indelible. The kulak— real, imaginary, ascribed—had ended up on the wrong side of the class divide of the revolution and could only cross the boundary through artifice and disguise.

Conclusion

It was all kept so dark, every stain so carefully scratched out, every whisper so swiftly choked.

—Aleksandr Solzhenitsyn, *The Gulag Archipelago*

The Silence and the Dark

After the fall of the Soviet Union, a local researcher in the Komi region discovered a small metal plaque on the grave of a peasant exiled as a kulak in the 1930s. On the plaque was an inscription that read, "The law is the taiga, the bear is our master."[1] That would, perhaps, be a fitting epitaph to the memory of the kulaks, were there a monument commemorating their suffering. But there are no national monuments to the kulaks. Their graves lie scattered and unmarked across the vast expanses of the former Soviet Union, the death toll through the 1930s roughly half a million people.[2] Most of their graves will remain forever unmarked in the depths of the taiga.

It was only in 1991 that the kulak special settlers were finally and fully "exonerated" for their nonexistent crimes. That year, the Yeltsin government, building on legislation from the late Gorbachev years, passed a series of laws "rehabilitating the victims of political repression." Although the kulaks were not mentioned by name—the law spoke, instead, of victims of the deprivation of freedom, forced labor, and the special settlements—the political repression of the Stalin regime was declared illegal.[3] The legislation condemned "the many-year terror and mass persecution of our people as incompatible with the ideas of law and justice," and ascribed them to the "arbitrariness [*proizvol*] of a totalitarian government."[4]

It was only then that survivors could be sure to the roots of their soul that they were safe to tell their stories. By that time, most had long since left the special settlements. The survivors, mainly women, were at the end of their long lives. Many lived alone and in abject poverty. With the encouragement of Memorial, the organization dedicated to preserving the memories of the victims of Stalin, they began to speak. They sat for interviews, they wrote long letters to the local and national branches of Memorial, and some, like Ivan Tvardovskii, wrote their autobiographies. With the Soviet Union gone, they came forward to testify.

The archives also began to open at this time, offering their own stories of the kulak special settlements. In a dissonance worthy of the Stalinist 1930s, there emerged a paper world of alternative truths and subjective realities, unrealized schemes resplendent with the most artful and intricate planning, endless litanies of irresolvable problems, and the individual tragedies voiced by the special settlers in countless and often desperate letters and complaints.

The regime had destroyed the farms and, in many cases, the families of the special settlers, but it did not erase the memories of the survivors; nor did it eliminate or, in most cases, even try to eliminate, the documentary records of the special settlers' saga. So the story of the special settlers was not so thoroughly "scratched out." It was hidden inside living memory and the vast Soviet secret archives. But why was it "all kept so dark" for so long?

The darkness that cloaked the story of the special settlers was maintained by a culture of secrecy, predating the revolution, but exaggerated beyond all measure and bolstered by unending fears and paranoia in the Stalinist 1930s. Yet there were other, perhaps more fundamental, reasons for the darkness. Simply put, the policy was an unmitigated disaster. Even from the point of view of the majority of Soviet leaders who cared nothing for the actual fate of the kulaks, the failure of the policy was glaringly evident. If only from an economic standpoint, the policy was, to paraphrase Danilov and Krasil'nikov, quintessentially irrational. On average, the regime spent 1,000 rubles per household for the costs of resettlement between 1930 and 1932; in the meantime, the state was able to extract on average only some 564 rubles per household in the process of dekulakization and property expropriations.[5] The economic situation hardly improved over time, clearly demonstrating the folly and wastefulness of forced labor and the unimaginable costs, financial and human, of the attempt to settle remote northern territories where the environment simply could not sustain such populations. The result would be a continual restocking of the special settlements with new waves of "enemies" in a criminal waste of lives through the duration of the Stalin era.

Perhaps the real question is why the regime preserved the archival records of kulak special resettlement. Within a culture of scapegoating and endless paper inspections, checks of policy fulfillment, and reports on "shortcomings," it was no doubt in the interests of individual officials to document thoroughly their activities in order to avoid personal responsibility. Moreover, the generation, processing, and preservation of papers was something that Soviet officialdom was generally good at. The regime, after all, was nothing if not an information hunter and gatherer; reality and the actual implementation of policy was another issue entirely. The preservation of documentation on the kulaks was also conditioned by an arrogant official confidence, still apparent even under Khrushchev, that the kulaks had indeed been *real* enemies, that they in some sense deserved what they got. Once the documents made it into the archives, they became untouchable—so heavily layered in classified status, so closely bound and locked with wax seals that almost no one dared to touch them before 1991.

The preservation of these documents by generations of archivists who served sometimes as the watchdogs of state secrets, sometimes as highly trained professionals dedicated to maintaining the records of the past, makes it possible to begin the process of excavating the history of the 1930s from layers of lies, propaganda, and "ideologized" conceit on both sides of the Cold War. And the voice of what Solzhenitsyn called the "silent people"—more accurately, the *silenced* people—allows a glimpse into the lived experience of Stalinist socialism and the other archipelago.

The Internal Colony

The other archipelago was both an emanation and a tragic emblem of the Stalinist path to modernity. The Soviet Union under Stalin was, in essence, an extraction state, characterized by extreme centralization and the total mobilization of resources (including labor) in the interests of state building and economic development. It was, at the same time, an agrarian nation. Under Stalin, the peasant majority served as the fulcrum of modernization in what was one of the most radical transformations in modern history.

The peasantry was as an internal resource for capital and human extraction to fuel Soviet development through the entirety of the Stalin era, if not the Soviet epoch as a whole. Stalin said as much in 1928, when he called for the peasantry to pay a "tribute" to finance Soviet industrialization, equating the peasantry with the overseas colonies he claimed financed British economic development. A continuing unequal and oppressive exchange between urban and rural economies served to deplete the countryside of its grain and other agricultural products. The labor power of the countryside was, in part, redeployed in the interests of Soviet industrial development—to the cities, to the giant construction projects of the First Five-Year Plan, in constant labor corvées for logging and road construction, and for the colonization of the Soviet hinterlands. Rural labor was also channeled into the military in order to stock the army with soldiers, the soldiers who would fight and win the "great war of the fatherland" at such enormous cost. The countryside served as the Soviet Union's "internal colony," to be tapped in the interests of Moscow.

The regime also exploited this internal colony in order to extract a legion of unfree laborers in what was one of the twentieth century's most expansive exercises in that oppressive and costly practice. Forced labor served as the foundation of the Gulag in all its manifestations, working to create a vast penal-economic empire within the empire. It was used in economic development, the extraction of raw materials for industrialization, and the colonization of the Soviet Union's vast and remote northern and eastern lands. An army of peasants—joined by a motley assortment of other, largely déclassé, social elements and political prisoners—would serve as the human (working) fodder for the Soviet Union's great leap over the centuries, its pharaonic enterprise of "building socialism."

The Soviet Union was an empire. The notion of the Soviet Union as an empire is generally associated either with its relations to the "satellite states" of Eastern Europe or its own internal national minorities. But the Soviet Union was an empire in another, equally important sense. The historian Ronald Grigor Suny has defined empire as "a composite state structure in which the metropole is distinct in some way from the periphery and the relationship between the two is conceived or perceived by metropolitan or peripheral actors as one of justifiable or unjustifiable inequity, subordination, and/or exploitation."[6] Moscow's relations with its peasantry, in and out of the Gulag, fits well within this definition. The peasantry became an exploitable resource used in the interests of state building and economic development. It was also relegated to a distinctly subordinate status.

In this sense, the Soviet empire exhibited commonalities with other empires, most notably with some of Europe's overseas colonial ventures. The Soviet internal colony similarly featured a dehumanization of peasantries, exploiting their labor under horrendous conditions and practicing the most brutalized forms of administration in the goal of limitless extraction of raw materials and natural resources. At the same time, the Soviet exercise in colonization departed from its European counterparts by way of a series of essential substitutions—the substitution of a native peasantry for foreign aboriginals, class for race, "socialist reeducation" for the "christian" enlightenment of "dark masses," and the curious phenomenon of the colonized being used as the colonizers in opening up the great expanses of the north. The Soviet Union was distinguished in other ways as well—in its status as an empire of peasantries and non-Russian nationalities, its relative underdevelopment and agrarian nature, its geographical breadth and seemingly endless possibilities for internal expansion, and the persistence of undergovernment in the countryside.

Like its European counterparts, the Soviet Union proclaimed a civilizing mission as it supposedly reached out to its own "dark masses" (*temnye liudi*, a term used for the Russian peasantry). The peasantry as a whole was largely reduced to stereotype as either "backwards" or "counterrevolutionary"—this, in spite of official Marxist-Leninist prognostication about the political attitudes and behavior ("consciousness") of peasants based on their class status (as poor peasants, middle peasants, or kulaks). In this sense, the kulak was little more than a symbol of and scapegoat for *all* peasants within an ideology that could not be explicitly antipeasant.

For the peasantry at large, the collective farm was to serve as the basis for socialist reeducation, for ridding peasants of their "individualistic, petit-bourgeois instincts" and transforming them into collective farmers. The other archipelago was to serve a similar purpose for kulaks, or at least for those who were still thought to be redeemable. In both cases collective, or so-called socialist labor was to provide the basis for reeducation. In reality, other more universal socializing agents like education, military training, and migration to the cities would play a greater role in transforming peasants into collective farmers and Soviet citizens than socialist labor.

For the kulak special settlers, there was in fact very little room for reeducation through labor, although perhaps somewhat more in the case of youth by way of school and later the army. In the main, however, the Soviet mission remained locked in a rhetoric that was seldom more than superficial in actual practice. Moreover, the punitive aspects of special resettlement would trump reeducation in any case. In the end, special resettlement was primarily about punishment, isolation, and the most brutal—and distinctly noneducational—exploitation of labor.

This brutality was furthered by the necessity for the center to rule from afar. This meant that Moscow had little real control over the day-to-day development of the special settlements. Moscow worked within the constraints of Russian rural undergovernment, a chronic problem that had been only partially addressed before the 1917 revolution resulted in the further weakening of the nation's governmental infrastructure. As a consequence, it was forced to rely on a weakly developed rural government often run by poorly educated individuals reared in civil war and class warfare, separated from the capital and even the provincial centers by vast distances, and at times lacking the most rudimentary forms of communication with the outside world. As a result of both rural undergovernment and the radical tempos with which policy was enacted, the center lacked local knowledge of terrain, ecology, labor conditions, and the workings of its industries. Therefore, the center resorted to rule by abstraction through avalanches of decrees, directives, resolutions, and orders. Actual enforcement, however, most often depended upon force or punishment. Rule by repression worked in tandem with rule by abstraction. Of course, this is not to say that Moscow would have created more humane conditions had administrative possibilities permitted; it is simply to point out the realities and limits of Moscow's rule as metropole ruling over a vast and unwieldy peasant empire.

Bast Leviathan

The Soviet state was not the Leviathan of Western cold-war lore. Despite its enormous repressive capabilities, the Soviet Union was an infrastructurally weak, agrarian state. Scholars and politicians alike often took Soviet rhetoric at its face value, assessing the Soviet state's strength solely on the basis of its ideology and totalizing policies. To fully understand Soviet state power, however, it is necessary to go beyond the Kremlin walls and to explore the reception of policy, its implementation, modification, and consequences. Persistent rural undergovernment and a weak provincial infrastructure, in concert with mass repression and radical policies, were central determining factors in the shape and outcome of policy as well as in the bloody contours that it all too often assumed.

Furthermore, Stalinist policy itself was often both contingent and reactive. From the late 1920s through the entirety of the 1930s, the Soviet Union existed in a state of almost perpetual crisis. In part, this was a crisis of the state's own making, erupting from the unintended consequences and politicized economic policies of the 1920s, the First Five-Year Plan industrialization drive, collectivization, and the terror. In part, the perpetual crisis was shaped and augmented by geopolitical realities, a dangerous international environment, and the much vaunted "capitalist encirclement" that was said to besiege the Soviet Union. And because crisis—a militarized warlike state— became a basic operating mode, and because totalizing visions and policies set off a chain of unintended (though perhaps easily anticipated) social, economic, and political consequences, Stalinist policies came to be more often than not reactive, following in the wake of and attempting to deal with new crises as they arose in a continuous chain reaction of policy outcomes.[7]

This phenomenon is evident throughout the history of kulak special resettlement. Concrete planning followed only in the wake of dekulakization; central coordinating commissions arose as the families were literally on the trains en route to exile. Fluidity and porousness characterized the supposedly intricately planned and controlled penal bastions of the other archipelago. And the center resorted to Potemkin inspections, scapegoating of local officials and economic managers, and repression intermixed with half-hearted reform to deal with what quickly became a human catastrophe and an economic boondoggle.

This is not to say that ideology played no role in the fate of the special settlers. Ideology was and remained the animus of policy on kulak special resettlement, and indeed the Gulag as a whole. However cynical Stalin and his coevals in the Politburo may have been, they operated within the confines of their ideological beliefs. The same could be said of the provincial party and police leadership that played such an important role in the enactment of special settler policy. On the local level, among the "company men" who ran the special settlements on a day-to-day basis, ideological prejudices were evident everywhere in the ways in which officials interacted with what they perceived to be an enemy class. Yet to understand the full meaning and at times terrible import of ideology, it must be contextualized within actual practice and local settings.

The same is true for planning. The special settlements were vast laboratories, replete with the most exquisitely detailed plans of control, regimentation, and order, designed to isolate enemies, to keep them under constant observation and surveillance, and to reeducate through labor those who could be reeducated. On paper, the special settlements exhibited all the traits of "scientific planning" from on high, ranging from centrally imposed schedules for everything from transportation to village construction, from detailed reporting to blueprints for homes, barns, and bathhouses, and intricately precise schedules for the "liquidation" of epidemic diseases.

Yet, the awful reality of the special settlements was anything but planned. Epidemic illnesses swept through the villages; exhaustion from hunger, neglect, and overwork took a continuing toll; brutal, corrupt, and drunken commandants exercised unlimited power; and tens of thousands of people died. The story of the special settlements, like so many of the grand utopian projects of those times, marked a radical, if predictable, disjuncture between "scientific" planning and actual practice. In the case of the special settlements, Moscow planners not only had to execute their plans with the bluntest of instruments—the

Soviet Union's underdeveloped rural administration—but under the conditions of an emergency state that grafted secrecy, excessive haste, and military procedure on to all plans. To make matters worse, the tempos of collectivization outpaced dekulakization and even the deportation operation, making a reactive planning—however "scientific" it may have appeared on paper—an essential feature of this process. And the more the operation developed beyond the control of Moscow, the more Moscow responded with its endless plans, directives, orders, and threats, in an attempt to paper over reality and to "ideologize" existing practice in order to bring it under the umbrella of "building socialism."

The all-mighty and omnipresent blueprints that characterized every detail of Soviet life represented a *vision* of control and rational order projected onto the chaos of Russia by an urban state determined to transform and control a largely agrarian administration and peasant economy. Stalinist planning was more state aesthetic than totalitarian reality.[8] Planning represented reality as it was imagined and intended, more often than not in a lofty and terrible isolation from actuality. It was both a denial of and a compensation for reality. Planning was super-imposed onto reality, enduring as a mere facade grafted onto a complex society and bureaucracy that resisted order and instead simply continued on in more "normal," messy human ways, translating in the case of the special settlements into utopian quagmire and distopian nightmare. The disjunctures between planning and reality, almost of necessity, continually rebounded in excesses, violence, and terror. This phenomenon was an essential feature of Stalinism, imposed as it was from outside on subject populations, operating in a void of local knowledge, and enforced within the context of an illiberal, weak and nonunitary state polity.[9]

In the end, the Stalinist state of the 1930s was capable of ruling its vast dominions only by repression—force, coercion, threats, penalties, arrests. The combination of an infrastructurally weak state, an interventionist state bent on a totalizing vision of societal transformation (all too often in the abstract), and an ideological Weltanschauung of prejudice, fear, and limitless hatreds were at the roots of Stalinist repression and the Gulag. What on paper began as a penal utopia for isolating and reforging social enemies became in fact little more than a carelessly constructed institution of forced labor that was meant to be self-sufficient and self-sustaining. By 1931, any remaining visions of the penal utopia would evaporate in the face of local realities and the economic-penal desiderata of the Gulag. The idea of settlers opening up new territories, participating in "honorable" labor, and being reeducated became little more than a hollow facade for a system that most settlers viewed as no more than an unwarranted penal, if not death, sentence.

The Peasants' Tribute

The centrality of the peasant experience in shaping, perhaps predetermining the subsequent course of Soviet historical development has been glaringly overlooked in the historical literature of the 1930s. The policies of collectivization and the "liquidation of the kulak as a class" played a crucial role in the solidification of Stalin's dictatorship—through emergency measures and the grain procurement crisis of the late 1920s, the battle with the Right Opposition, and the emergence of the secret police as a state within a state. From the time of the grain procurement crisis on, the secret police assumed an ever increasing role both in the rural economy and in politics more generally while simultaneously evolving into Stalin's power base and cudgel of control.

The Gulag itself was built upon the edifice of the war with the peasantry. This is not to contest those who date the emergence of concentration camps to Lenin's time, but rather to point to the obvious—the enormous expansion of the Gulag from 1930 based on the massive influx of peasants into both the special settlements and the labor camps. Moreover, peasants in one form or another (as kulaks, counterrevolutionaries charged under Article 58, class aliens, member of "enemy nations," or nationalist opponents) would continue to stock the Gulag with their labor power over the next two decades, serving in a very real way as the foundation of the Gulag. They would provide the human fodder for the Gulag's empire of forced labor which increasingly came to be central to the powers of the secret police, the functioning of the Gulag, and the Soviet economy as a whole.

The social and political consequences of the rural policies of the First Five-Year Plan were equally insidious. The great demographic flux sparked by collectivization led to massive population movement, voluntary and forced, throughout the country. This social flux—in particular that associated with kulak escapes from the village and the special settlements—proved profoundly disturbing to Stalin and the secret police, as they sought desperately to gain control of the social chaos unleashed by the First Five-Year Plan. In the eyes of the regime, this uncontrolled movement provided the cadres of crime, banditry, and counterrevolution. It was an essential reason for the introduction of internal passports in late 1932, as well as a major factor in the police actions waged against "social aliens" in the mid-1930s and the "mass operations" of 1937/38.

Collectivization and dekulakization were central to the history of the 1930s in other ways as well. These policies had immense, unintended consequences—consequences that should have been anticipated but for the political lens through which they were refracted and the state of emergency that colored so much of the 1930s. The economic costs of the policies are, of course, the most obvious: collectivization and draconian grain levies depleted the countryside of its sustenance leading to a devastating famine in 1932/33. And "socialized" agriculture remained throughout the Soviet period the Achilles heel of the Soviet economy.

For millions of former Soviet citizens, collectivization was one of the major turning points in their lives, second only to the experience of World War II. Collectivization served as a profound rupture in the lives of the majority of the population, catapulting an agrarian nation through decades of Western economic development within the confines of a five-year plan. The peasantry paid the highest price for the Soviet experiment—in the extraction of Stalin's "tribute," in the "Great War of the Fatherland," and in the Gulag. The Soviet superpower was built upon the poverty of the village, artificially fueled by an economy and a society that could not in the end sustain its growth and power. Long before 1991, to those who could see, it was evident that the Soviet Union was a Leviathan in bast shoes. Soviet modernity always remained moored to its agrarian legacy.

Legacies

The consequences of these policies remain to the present day, providing, as it were, a case study of what happens when the metropolitan center attempts to carry out a reengineering of the society and economy without real knowledge of the local, without consideration of ecological consequences, and in complete disregard for human costs, driven only by political, ideological, and misconstrued economic rationale. The impact on agriculture and on millions of lives profoundly altered by the effects of migration, urbanization, and repression are evident. The legacies of the Gulag and Soviet colonization are only beginning to emerge, as the costs of "building socialism" in the remote and forbidding regions of the far north become clear.

In the last decades of Soviet rule, the government resorted to bonuses and higher wages to entice free labor to work in these territories. The "geography of penality" remained the same, with prisons and camps situated largely in areas without a permanent labor force. This situation continues today, with (the far smaller population of) penal labor still tied to the timber industry in the far north. These territories, moreover, remain remote and inaccessible. In some places, the old special settlements are still operative as penal settlements.[10] The northern towns and cities that arose on the basis of Gulag labor witnessed a rapid depopulation through the 1990s as the Russian government realized the futility of trying to maintain urban populations in these remote territories without the artificial economic prop of the Gulag. In recent years, the

Russian government has launched an initiative to relocate citizens southward in what would amount to a reversal of Gulag demographics and the largest state-initiated mass migration since the Stalin years.[11] The problem of how to extract the rich natural resources of these territories has not been solved. The burden and futility of Stalin's attempt to colonize the far north remain present-day legacies.

Memory is also a legacy. But memory is an amorphous vessel, subject to contestation, alteration, and exploitation in the service of the present. In the heady days of *perestroika* and the Yeltsin 1990s when Stalinist history was being dismantled, memory was awash in the tragedy of the Stalin era as special settler survivors and other victims of those times came forth to testify at the court of history. In today's Russia, this side of memory has diminished as Vladimir Putin searches for a useable past on which to rebuild a nation, a past based not on Stalinist tragedy but on Russian triumph. Paralleling Putin's efforts, public interest in the crimes of the Stalin era has also declined. This occurred in part because popular culture emerged in the 1990s to push out and stifle an interest in the past, in part because the critical intelligentsia became exhausted to the point of despair by the revelations of the horrors of the past that saturated the media. History once denied through lies is now threatened by obscurity; forgetting has taken the place of falsification. It will take time and distance before collective memory can absorb the Stalinist legacy. In the meantime, the survivors' stories are now part of the public record. They cannot be erased.

The story of the special settlers is only one among many of the human costs of Soviet state aggrandizement, economic development, and perhaps twentieth-century social engineering in general. Because all of the rationalization in the world, all of the historical description, will not resurrect those whose lives were wasted, it is worth concluding with the sage words of a survivor of a contemporaneous human catastrophe. Primo Levi, asked in reference to the Holocaust, "Were we witnessing the rational development of an inhuman plan or a manifestation . . . of collective madness? Logic intent on evil or the absence of logic?" In answer to his own question, Levi wrote, "As so often in human affairs, the two alternatives coexisted."[12]

And the price was paid most often by ordinary people, people like the special settlers whose voices have largely told this story—people like Varvara Stepanovna who "remember[ed] a lot and [could] tell the truth"; people like Valentina Slipchenko who "for years" saw "her sister in every child"; and people like Ivan Tvardovskii who lived into old age to write eloquently and passionately of his life and to tend the Smolensk house museum of his famous brother, the poet Aleksandr Tvardovskii, the same brother who renounced him so long ago as a kulak and a class enemy.

Appendix

Table 1. Deportations in 1930 and 1931*

Region of Origin	Number of Families	Region of Destination
Ukraine	63,720⁺	North (19,658), Urals (32,127), W. Siberia (6,556), E. Siberia (5,056), Iakutiia (97), Far East (323)
North Caucasus	38,404	Urals (25,995), N. Caucasus (12,409)
Lower Volga	30,933	North (10,963), Urals (1,878), Kazakhstan (18,092)
Middle Volga	23,006†	North (5,566), Urals (663), E. Siberia (620), Kazakhstan (11,477)
Central Black Earth	26,006	North (10,236), Urals (1,408), E. Siberia (2,367), Kazakhstan (10,544), Far East (1,097), Iakutiia (354)
Belorussia	15,724	North (4,763), Urals (9,113), Far East (1,561), Iakutiia (287)
Crimea	4,325	North (1,553), Urals (2,772)
Tatariia	9,424	Urals (7,810), Far East (1,614)
Central Asia	6,944	Kazakhstan (159), N. Caucasus (2,213), Ukraine (3,444), Central Asia (1,128)
Nizhegorodskii	9,169#	North (2,471), Urals (5,201), Kazakhstan (50), Nizhegorodskii (1,497)
Western	7,038	Urals (7,038)
IPO	3,655	Urals (3,655)
Bashkiriia	12,820	W. Siberia (5,305), E. Siberia (1,515), Bashkiriia (6,000)

Moscow	10,813	Urals (3,112), W. Siberia (4,729), Kazakhstan (2,972)
North	3,061	North (3,061)
Leningrad Military Region	8,604	Urals (337), W. Siberia (1,269), E. Siberia (929), Iakutiia (725), Leningrad Military Region (5,344)
Urals	28,394	Urals (26,854), Leningrad Military Region (1,540)
Western Siberia	52,091	W. Siberia (52,091)
Eastern Siberia	16,068	E. Siberia (16,068)
Far East	2,922	Far East (2,922)
Kazakhstan	6,765	Kazakhstan (6,765)
Transcaucasia	870	Kazakhstan (870)
Total	381,026$^\nabla$	376,223

* *GARF*, f. 9479, op. 1, d. 89, l. 205. (Date of document is 1 January 1932)
+ The actual total based on the figures in the third column is 63,817.
† The actual total based on the figures in the third column is 18,326.
# The actual total based on the figures in the third column is 9,219.
$^\nabla$ The correct total is 380,756.

Table 2. Regional Destinations of Kulaks Deported in 1930 and 1931*

Region	1930		1931		Total	
	Families	People	Families	People	Families	People
North	46,623	230,370	11,648	55,239	58,271	285,609
Urals	32,689	153,181	95,544	438,908	128,233	592,089
W. Siberia	15,590	76,130	54,360	241,313	69,960	317,443
E. Siberia	12,047	55,792	14,508	73,111	26,555	128,903
Kazakhstan	1,424	7,590	49,455	253,637	50,879	261,227
Far East	3,919	20,901	5,778	28,002	9,697	48,903
Iakutiia	287	2,007	1,079	5,150	1,366	7,157
Leningrad	2,140	11,110	4,744	20,356	6,884	31,466
Nizhegorodskii	512	2,451	985	3,865	1,497	6,316
Middle Volga	—	—	2,500	12,500	2,500	12,500
N. Caucasus	—	—	14,622	61,028	14,622	61,028
Bashkiriia	—	—	6,000	30,000	6,000	30,000
Ukraine	—	—	3,444	15,111	3,444	15,111
Central Asia	—	—	1,128	5,640	1,128	5,640
Total	115,231	559,532	265,795	1,243,860	381,036+	1,803,392

* *GARF*, f. 374, op. 28, d. 4055, ll. 33–48.
+ The total should be 381,026; there is a mistake in the column.

Table 3. Results of the Bergavinov Commission's Work*

Exiled from	Incorrect		Correct		Questionable		Totals
	Numbers	Percentages	Numbers	Percentages	Numbers	Percentages	
Ukraine	943	9	8,644	82.4	908	8.6	10,495
L. Volga	321	9.2	2,720	77.6	462	13.2	3,503
Central Black Earth	751	16.5	2,888	63	938	10.5	4,577
			2,880			20.5	
M. Volga	192	6.1	2,614	82.8	349	11.1	3,155
Belorussia	134	8.3	1,290	79.1	206	12.6	1,630

* *RGASPI*, f. 17, op. 120, d. 26, l. 10; *GAOPDF AO*, f. 290, op. 1, d. 385, l. 13. (In the case of double figures, the top figure is from *RGASPI* and the bottom figure is from *GAOPDF AO*.)

Table 4. Employment of Special Settlers*

Industrial Sector	Families	Individuals
Forestry	135,636	565,754
Coal and Peat	29,080	141,846
Nonferrous Metals and Gold	23,708	121,038
Iron Ore and Steel	21,893	98,886
Railroad and Road Construction	15,000	75,000
Industrial Crops	9,262	56,320
Agricultural Colonies	63,787	255,763
Construction	9,577	44,985
Fishing	4,344	20,141
Livestock Farming	4,000	20,000
Misc.	8,378	27,806
Total	324,665	1,427,539

* A. Berelovich and V. P. Danilov, *Sovetskaia derevnia glazami VChK-OGPU-NKVD, 1918–1939. Dokumenty i materialy v 4 tomakh* (Moscow, 1998–), vol. 3 (1), p. 726.

Notes

Introduction

1. Cited in A. Bazarov, *Kulak i agrogulag* (Cheliabinsk, 1991), pp. 222–23. The lines in the epigraph are cited in Kornei Chukovsky, *Diary, 1901–1969*, ed. Victor Erlich, trans. Michael Henry Heim (New Haven: Yale University Press, 2005), pp. 46, 94.
2. Bazarov, *Kulak i agrogulag*, pp. 222–23.
3. The statistics vary. See *GARF* (*Gosudarstvennyi arkhiv Rossiiskoi Federatsii*), f. 9479, op. 1, d. 89, l. 205 for a total of 1,803,392 people exiled in 1930 and 1931. A report in *RGASPI* (*Rossiiskii gosudarstvennyi arkhiv sotsial'no-politicheskoi istorii*), f. 17, op. 120, d. 56, l. 59, offers the lower figure of 1,679,258.
4. The terminology changed over time. The word *spetspereselentsy* was in use through 1933. From 1934, the official term changed to *trudposelentsy* ("labor settlers"). From 1944, *spetspereselentsy* was in use again for deported kulaks. And after 1949 the term *spetsposelentsy* ("special settlers") makes an appearance. I will use "special settlers" throughout to designate the kulak deportees. On the etymology of the term, see V. P. Danilov and S. A. Krasil'nikov, eds., *Spetspereselentsy v Zapadnoi Sibiri*, 4 vols. (Novosibirsk, 1992–96), vol. 3, p. 13; and T. I. Slavko, *Kulatskaia ssylka na Urale, 1930–1936* (Moscow, 1995), p. 77.
5. Pavel Polian, *Ne po svoei vole . . . Istoriia i geografiia prinuditel'nykh migratsii v SSSR* (Moscow, 2001), p. 68. According to Danilov and Krasil'nikov, there were 1,861 special settlements in mid-1939. (Danilov and Krasil'nikov, eds., *Spetspereselentsy v Zapadnoi Sibiri*, vol. 4, pp. 40–41). A report on the special settlements, dated 1 January 1938, gives a figure of 1,751 settlements in 1937. (*GARF*, f. 9479, op. 1, d. 47, ll. 12–22).
6. See, for example, Jan Plamper, "Abolishing Ambiguity: Soviet Censorship Practices in the 1930s," *Russian Review*, vol. 60, no. 4 (2001): 530; and Jeffrey Brooks, *Thank You, Comrade Stalin! Soviet Public Culture from Revolution to Cold War* (Princeton: Princeton University Press, 2000), p. 133.
7. A. I. Kokurin and N. V. Petrov, eds., *GULAG, 1917–1960: Dokumenty* (Moscow, 2000), lists the names of 476 individual camps and complexes.
8. S. V. Mironenko and N. Werth, eds., *Istoriia Stalinskogo gulaga. Konets 1920-kh-pervaia polovina 1950-kh godov. Sobranie dokumentov*, 7 vols. (Moscow, 2004–5), vol. 4, pp. 38–39, 54–56. (The statistics on mortality are highly problematic and should be considered a minimal figure only.)

9.   Alexander I. Solzhenitsyn, *The Gulag Archipelago*, trans. Thomas P. Whitney and Harry Willetts, 3 vols. (New York: Harper and Row, 1973).

10. Ibid., vol. 1, p. 24.

11. Anne Applebaum, *Gulag: A History* (New York: Doubleday, 2003). The literature on the gulag that has been published since the fall of the Soviet Union is voluminous. My bibliography lists the main reference works and document collections on the topic. Two works in English by Russian historians are well worth noting: Galina Mikhailovna Ivanova, *Labor Camp Socialism: The Gulag in the Soviet Totalitarian System*, trans. Carol Flath (Armonk, NY: M. E. Sharpe, 2000); and Oleg V. Khlevniuk, ed., *The History of the Gulag*, trans. Vadim A. Staklo (New Haven: Yale University Press, 2004).

12. For a discussion of the regional studies and document collections that have appeared on this topic, see the Research Note in this book, pp. 249–51.

13. S. A. Krasil'nikov, *Na izlomakh sotsial'noi struktury: marginaly v poslerevoliutsion- nom Rossiiskom obshchestve* (Novosibirsk, 1998), p. 54; Mironenko and Werth, eds., *Istoriia Stalinskogo gulaga*, vol. 5, p. 90. (The numbers of special settlers of all categories reached 2,819,776 in 1953.)

14. Ivanova, *Labor Camp Socialism*, pp. 10, 18, 69–72, 186; S. A. Krasil'nikov, "Rozhdenie GULAGa: diskussii v verkhnikh eshelonakh vlasti: postanovleniia Politbiuro TsK VKP (b), 1929–1930," *Istoricheskii arkhiv*, no. 4 (1997): 142–46, 152–53.

15. Iagoda was formally the deputy secret police chief from 1924 to 1934. Because V. R. Menzhinskii, the actual head of the OGPU from 1926 to 1934, was frequently ill, Iagoda was the de facto chief.

16. A. N. Dugin, *Neizvestnyi GULAG: Dokumenty i fakty* (Moscow, 1999), pp. 7–8.

17. The official estimates of the numbers of kulak households varied wildly, reaching as high as 5–6 million in some calculations. See Moshe Lewin, "Who Was the Soviet Kulak?" in Lewin, ed., *The Making of the Soviet System* (New York: Pantheon, 1985), pp. 128–29. Also see R. W. Davies, *The Socialist Offensive: The Collectivisation of Soviet Agriculture, 1929–1930* (Cambridge, MA: Harvard University Press, 1980), pp. 6, 23–28.

18. Lynne Viola, *Peasant Rebels Under Stalin: Collectivization and the Culture of Peasant Resistance* (New York: Oxford University Press, 1996), pp. 80–84; Sheila Fitzpatrick, *Stalin's Peasants: Resistance and Survival in the Russian Village after Collectivization* (New York: Oxford University Press, 1994), pp. 70–71; 131–32; 154–55.

19. For information on these other deportations, see Robert Conquest, *The Nation Killers: The Soviet Deportation of Nationalities* (London: MacMillan, 1970); Terry Martin, *The Affirmative Action Empire: Nations and Nationalism in the Soviet Union, 1923–1939* (Ithaca: Cornell University Press, 2001); Norman Naimark, *Fires of Hatred: Ethnic Cleansing in Twentieth-Century Europe* (Cambridge, MA: Harvard University Press, 2001), chap. 3; Aleksandr M. Nekrich, *The Punished Peoples: The Deportation and Tragic Fate of Soviet Minorities at the End of the Second World War*, trans. George Saunders (New York: Norton, 1978); N. L. Pobol' and P. M. Polian, eds., *Stalinskie deportatsii, 1928–1953* (Moscow, 2005); Polian, *Ne po svoei vole . . .* ; and Amir Weiner, "Nature, Nurture, and Memory in a Socialist Utopia: Delineating the Soviet Socio-Ethnic Body in the Age of Socialism," *American Historical Review*, vol. 104, no. 4 (October 1999): 1114–55.

20. *Istochnik*, no. 4 (1998): 76.

21. The best discussion of the term is by Moshe Lewin, "Who Was the Soviet Kulak?" pp. 121–41. Also see Lynne Viola, "The Second Coming: Class Enemies in the

Soviet Countryside, 1927–1935," in J. Arch Getty and Roberta T. Manning, eds., *Stalinist Terror: New Perspectives* (New York: Cambridge University Press, 1993), pp. 65–98; and Lynne Viola, "The Peasants' Kulak: Social Identities and Moral Economy in the Soviet Countryside in the 1920s," *Canadian Slavonic Papers*, vol. 42 (December 2000): 431–60.

22. V. P. Popov, "Gosudarstvennyi terror v Sovetskoi Rossii. 1923–1953 gg.," *Otechestvennye arkhivy*, no. 2 (1992): 28–29.

23. *GARF*, f. 9479, op. 1, d. 89, l. 205; d. 949, ll. 75–79.

24. E. A. Zaitsev, ed., *Sbornik zakonodatel'nykh i normativnykh aktov o repressiiakh i reabilitatsii zhertv politicheskikh repressii* (Moscow, 1993), pp. 187–89, 194–204. (Gorbachev initiated this process with legislation in 1990.)

25. For more on this issue, see Danilov and Krasil'nikov, eds., *Spetspereselentsy v Zapadnoi Sibiri*, vol. 2, p. 8; vol. 3, pp. 7–8.

26. Solzhenitsyn, *Gulag Archipelago*, vol. 1, p. 24.

27. See Davies, *The Socialist Offensive*; and Lewin, *Russian Peasants and Soviet Power*, for discussions of the economic background to collectivization.

28. The term, "domestic other," is from Stephen P. Frank, "Confronting the Domestic Other: Rural Popular Culture and Its Enemies in Fin-De-Siecle Russia," in *Culture in Flux*, ed. Stephen P. Frank and Mark D. Steinberg (Princeton: Princeton University Press, 1994), pp. 74–107.

29. This argument is developed in Viola, *Peasant Rebels under Stalin*.

30. In addition to the documentary publications cited throughout this work and discussed in the Research Note at the end of the book, I would like to note several important scholarly works that have appeared since I began my work: N. A. Ivnitskii, *Sud'ba raskulachennykh v SSSR* (Moscow, 2004), a largely institutional history of the fate of the dekulakized peasants; S. A. Krasil'nikov, *Serp i molokh: Krest'ianskaia ssylka v Zapadnoi Sibiri v 1930-e gody* (Moscow, 2003), a regional study based on Siberia; V. N. Zemskov, whose seminal statistical work has appeared in *Spetsposelentsy v SSSR, 1930–1960* (Moscow, 2003); the important contribution of Nicolas Werth, who explored this topic in "A State Against Its People," in *The Black Book of Communism*, ed. Stephane Courtois et al., trans. Jonathan Murphy and Mark Kramer (Cambridge, MA: Harvard University Press, 1999); and Viktor Berdinskikh, *Spetsposelentsy: Politicheskaia ssylka narodov Sovetskoi Rossii* (Moscow, 2005).

Chapter 1

1. The epigraph is from *Trudy pervoi vsesoiuznoi konferentsii agrarnikov-marksistov*, 2 vols. (Moscow, 1930), vol. 1, p. 446.

2. Iagoda used the Russian word *ochistka*, which is translated here as "purge." V. P. Danilov, R. T. Manning, and L. Viola, eds., *Tragediia Sovetskoi derevni: Kollektivizatsiia i raskulachivanie. Dokumenty i materialy, 1927–1939*, 5 vols. (Moscow, 1999–2006), vol. 2, pp. 103–4. (Further, *TSD*; documents from earlier drafts of this document collection and subsequently not published, are cited as "*TSD*," followed by the archival citation numbers.)

3. A. Berelovich and V. Danilov, eds., *Sovetskaia derevnia glazami VChK-OGPU-NKVD, 1918–1939. Dokumenty i materialy*, 4 vols. (Moscow, 1998–), vol. 2, pp. 1016–21. (Further, cited as *DGO*.)

4. See the report from the Northern Territory soviet executive committee in *GARF*, f. 393, op. 43a, d. 1796, ll. 2–18. The Russian phrase is *na khodu*, which would become a veritable refrain to describe the practice of resettlement.

5. This phrase comes from V. P. Danilov and S. A. Krasil'nikov, eds., *Spetspereselentsy v Zapadnoi Sibiri*, 4 vols. (Novosibirsk, 1992–96), vol. 1, p. 14.

6. Lynne Viola, V. P. Danilov, N. A. Ivnitskii, and Denis Kozlov, eds., *The War Against the Peasantry, 1927–1930*, trans. Steven Shabad (New Haven: Yale University Press, 2005), pp. 98–99. (Vol. 1 of 4 vol. series, *The Tragedy of the Soviet Countryside*, a part of the *Annals of Communism* and *Yale Agrarian Studies* series.)

7. James Millar conclusively disproved the notion that collectivization "paid" for industrialization in the short term. See the classic debate between James R. Millar and Alec Nove, "A Debate on Collectivization: Was Stalin Really Necessary?" *Problems of Communism*, vol. 25 (July/Aug. 1976): 49–62.

8. See Lynne Viola, *Peasant Rebels under Stalin: Collectivization and the Peasant Culture of Resistance* (New York: Oxford University Press, 1996), chap. 1, for further discussion.

9. *TSD*, vol. 1, pp. 136, 231.

10. N. Ia. Gushchin, *Raskulachivanie v Sibiri (1928–1934 gg.)* (Novosibirsk, 1996), p. 51; *TSD*, vol. 1, pp. 390–92.

11. *TSD*, vol. 1, pp. 74–77, 136–37; *TSD: TsA FSB (Tsentral'nyi arkhiv federal'noi sluzhby bezopasnosti)*, f. 2, op. 7, d. 523, ll. 1–8.

12. *TSD*, vol. 1, pp. 612–18, p. 659. See also the discussion in James Hughes, *Stalinism in a Russian Province: Collectivization and Dekulakization in Siberia* (New York: St. Martin's Press, 1996).

13. According to official statistics, in the Russian Republic, the number of kulak farms declined from 3.9 percent of the peasant population in 1927 to 2.2 percent in 1929; in Ukraine, the decline was from 3.8 percent to 1.4 percent. Kulaks reduced their sown acreage by at least 40 percent between 1927 and 1929. By late 1929 and early 1930, kulak farms had sold 60–70 percent of their livestock and up to 50 percent of their agricultural machinery in many parts of the countryside. The weight of the gross output of kulak farms in grain producing regions declined from 10.2 percent in 1927 to 5.7 percent in 1929. See Viola, *Peasant Rebels*, pp. 79–80.

14. For a detailed discussion of this complicated process, see Lynne Viola, "The Case of Krasnyi Meliorator *or* 'How the Kulak Grows into Socialism,'" *Soviet Studies*, vol. 38, no. 4 (October 1986): 508–29; and Viola, "The Campaign to Eliminate the Kulak as a Class, Winter 1929–1930: A Reevaluation of the Legislation," *Slavic Review*, vol. 45, no. 3 (fall 1986): 503–24.

15. *RGASPI*, f. 17, op. 162, d. 7, ll. 22–23.

16. Ibid., ll. 158, 171.

17. *TSD*, vol. 1, pp. 713–14.

18. Viola, "Campaign," p. 508; *RGASPI*, f. 17, op. 32, d. 184, ll. 8, 16, 18–19.

19. *RGAE (Rossiiskii gosudarstvennyi arkhiv ekonomiki)*, f. 7486, op. 37, d. 40, l. 190.

20. The operation to deport "socially-dangerous elements" from the border zones of Belorussia, Ukraine, the Leningrad Region, and the Western Region has not received serious attention from historians and remains relatively archivally opaque. The existence of this operation begs the question of its operational relevance to the subsequent nation-wide campaign against the kulak. For a brief discussion, see S. A. Krasil'nikov, ed., *Marginaly v sotsiume. Marginaly kak sotsium. Sibir' (1920–1930-e gody)* (Novosibirsk, 2004), pp. 318–19. Also see the Ukrainian Council of People's Commissars decree in *RGAE*, f. 5675, op. 1, d. 23a, ll. 42–41.

21. Viola, "Campaign," pp. 508–9.
22. *Sobranie uzakonenii i rasporiazhenii raboche-krest'ianskogo pravitel'stva RSFSR*, no. 5 (25 February 1930): 74–75.
23. I. Stalin, *Sochineniia*, 13 vols. (Moscow, 1946–52), vol. 12, p. 132.
24. See Viola et al., eds., *War Against the Peasantry*, p. 122; and R. W. Davies, *The Socialist Offensive: The Collectivization of Soviet Agriculture, 1929–1930* (Cambridge, MA: Harvard University Press, 1980), pp. 112, 147.
25. Davies, *Socialist Offensive*, pp. 112, 147.
26. Ibid., p. 442.
27. *RGAE*, f. 260, op. 1, d. 6, ll. 163–64.
28. M. A. Vyltsan, N. A. Ivnitskii, and Iu. A. Poliakov, "Nekotorye problemy istorii kollektivizatsii v SSSR," *Voprosy istorii*, no. 3 (1965): 4–7; M. Lewin, *Russian Peasants and Soviet Power: A Study of Collectivization*, trans. Irene Nove (New York: Norton, 1975), chap. 15.
29. Lynne Viola, *The Best Sons of the Fatherland: Workers in the Vanguard of Soviet Collectivization* (New York: Oxford University Press, 1987), chap. 1.
30. See Viola et al., eds., *War Against the Peasantry*, ch. 4, for a detailed discussion of this commission.
31. *RGASPI*, f. 17, op. 2, d. 441, vol. 1: ll. 32, 69–70, 72, 104; vol. 2: ll. 3–18, 33, 40, 42, 50, 56, 61, 64–72.
32. *TSD*, vol. 2, pp. 85–86. For a discussion of the radicalizing initiatives of Stalin, see Viola et al., eds., *War Against the Peasantry*, chap. 4.
33. See Viola et al., eds., *War Against the Peasantry*, pp. 177–78.
34. Ibid., pp. 207–8.
35. See *TSD*, vol. 2, pp. 126–30. The Politburo also issued a special decree ordering that the 30 January directives not be published, after reprimanding the North Caucasus and Lower Volga Regional party committees for practically publishing the secret directives. (*TSD: RGASPI*, f. 17, op. 3, d. 776, l. 14.) At the same time, the USSR Central Executive Committee and Council of People's Commissars published a short decree "On the Measures for Strengthening the Socialist Transformation of Agriculture in Regions of Wholesale Collectivization and the Struggle with the Kulaks" on 1 February, followed by detailed, unpublished accompanying "secret instructions" on 4 February. (*Sobranie zakonov i rasporiazhenii raboche-krest'ianskogo pravitel'stva SSSR*, no. 9 [24 February 1930]: 187–88; *RGAE*, f. 7486, op. 37, d. 38, ll. 4–2.)
36. This ruling against disposal of property had already been legislated on 16 January 1930 in the Central Executive Committee-Council of People's Commissars decree, "On Measures against the Willful Destruction of Livestock." *Sobranie zakonov*, no. 6 (13 February 1930): 137–38. The ruling forbidding kulaks from leaving their villages applied to *all* kulaks, not just those in districts of wholesale collectivization, and was issued in a Central Executive Committee-Council of People's Commissars decree of 1 February. *TSD*, vol. 2, p. 161.
37. See Viola et al., eds., *War Against the Peasantry*, pp. 208–9, for a discussion of the expropriation process.
38. Regional quotas were as follows: Middle Volga (3,000–4,000), North Caucasus and Dagestan (6,000–8,000), Ukraine (15,000), Central Black Earth (3,000–5,000), Lower Volga (4,000–6,000), Belorussia (4,000–5,000), Urals (4,000–5,000), Siberia (5,000–6,000), and Kazakhstan (5,000–6,000).
39. The control figures for the numbers of kulak households to be deported from each region were as follows: Middle Volga (8,000–10,000), North Caucasus and Dagestan (20,000), Ukraine (30,000–35,000), Central Black Earth (10,000–15,000),

Lower Volga (10,000–12,000), Belorussia (6,000–7,000), Urals (10,000–15,000), Siberia (25,000), and Kazakhstan (10,000–15,000).

40. The Politburo decree is reprinted in *TSD*, vol. 2, pp. 126–30.

41. Dates of dekulakization decisions taken by regional party committees were as follows: 20 January: Transcaucasia, Middle Volga; 21 January: Urals; 24 January: Lower Volga; 20 January: Central Black Earth Region; 28 January: Ukraine; 29 January: North Caucasus. Viola, "Campaign," p. 508; A. A. Bazarov, *Kulak i agrogulag* (Cheliabinsk, 1991), p. 193.

42. "*Luchshe perekulachit' chem nedokulachit.*" I. E. Plotnikov, "Kak likvidirovali kulachestvo na Urale," *Otechestvennaia istoriia*, no. 4 (1993): 159.

43. Lynne Viola, Sergei Zhuravlev, Tracy McDonald, and Andrei Mel'nik, eds., *Riazanskaia derevnia v 1929–1930 gg. Khronika golovokruzheniia. Dokumenty i materialy* (Moscow, 1998), pp. 161–69.

44. *GAMO (Gosudarstvennyi arkhiv Moskovskoi oblasti)*, f. 7121, op. 1, d. 1, ll. 301–4, 321, 322–28, 329. Elsewhere, from as early as late December (Ukraine) and early January (Siberia and the North Caucasus), decisions were taken to remove kulaks to the worst land. (*RGASPI*, f. 17, op. 32, d. 184, ll. 18, 28–29.)

45. V. P. Danilov and N. A. Ivnitskii, eds., *Dokumenty svidetel'stvuiut: Iz istorii derevni nakanune i v khode kollektivizatsii, 1927–1932 gg.* (Moscow, 1989), pp. 318, 321–22.

46. The center shared these concerns. In a draft statement by a member of the Iakovlev subcommittee (a part of the Molotov Politburo commission on dekulakization), it was written, "It is necessary to take into account that the kulak is already reacting in all districts to our policy with *razbazarivanie....*" The draft therefore recommended working out plans for dekulakization in districts without wholesale collectivization. *RGAE*, f. 7486, op. 37, d. 78, l. 25.

47. *GARO (Gosudarstvennyi arkhiv Riazanskoi oblasti)*, f. 2, op. 1, d. 236, ll. 6–16. This document is published in Viola et al., eds., *Riazanskaia derevnia*, pp. 161–70.

48. Italics in the original. *TSD*, vol. 2, pp. 137–38. Iagoda also called for the beginning of arrests of first category kulaks here. Later, on 30 January, the Politburo would revoke the Moscow regional party committee decision. *TSD: RGASPI*, f. 17, op. 3, d. 775, ll. 15–16.

49. See the reference to this request in *GARF*, f. 9414, op. 1, d. 1943, l. 27.

50. Evdokimov was head of the Secret Operations Department of the OGPU. Messing was the head of the Foreign Department of the OGPU and a deputy chairman of OGPU. Prokof'ev was the head of the Economic Department of the OGPU. Blagonravov was a member of the OGPU collegium and a deputy commissar of the Commissariat of Transportation. Bokii was the deputy head of the Special Section of the OGPU. For further biographical information, see *Kto rukovodil NKVD, 1934–1941. Spravochnik* (Moscow, 1999) and the biographical entries in *TSD*, vol. 2.

51. *TSD*, vol. 2, pp. 103–4. See Viola et al., eds., *War Against the Peasantry*, p. 206, for the detailed instructions.

52. *TSD: TsA FSB*, f. 2, op. 8, d. 337, ll. 5. Also see the North Caucasus regional party decree on the administrative exile of the kulak in *TSD*, vol. 2, pp. 100–103.

53. On 16 January, a conference of regional OGPU workers took place in the North Caucasus to work out further plans on dekulakization, and on the same day Andreev telegraphed Stalin with a request for Central Committee sanction of their detailed plan for exile. *TSD: TsA FSB*, f. 2, op. 8, d. 337, ll. 148–49; N. A.

Ivnitskii, *Kollektivizatsiia i raskulachivanie (nachalo 30-kh godov)* (Moscow, 1994), p. 123.

54. Northern Territory party committee first secretary Bergavinov, for example, noted in a 14 January telegram to L. M. Kaganovich, one of Stalin's closest associates, that the OGPU had inquired with the Northern OGPU about the possibility of receiving up to 100,000 kulak families (to which the Northern OGPU countered with an offer to take 50–70,000 by May). *GAOPDF AO* (*Gosudarstvennyi arkhiv obshchestvenno-politicheskikh dvizhenii i formirovanii Arkhangel'skoi oblasti*), f. 290, op. 1, d. 386, l. 24 (undated). The date is given in Ivnitskii, *Kollektivizatsiia i raskulachivanie*, p. 122. Also see Lynne Viola, "The Other Archipelago: Kulak Deportations to the North in 1930," *Slavic Review*, vol. 60, no. 4 (2001): 734, n. 17.

55. *GARF*, f. 9414, op. 1, d. 1944, l. 15.

56. See Viola et al., eds., *War Against the Peasantry*, pp. 206–11, for a detailed discussion.

57. *TSD: TsA FSB*, f. 2, op. 8, d. 504, ll. 16–18.

58. *TSD*, vol. 2, pp. 143–47.

59. Ibid., pp. 163–67. On 31 January at 5:00 pm, the OGPU collegium held a meeting with its regional bosses and responsible workers involved in the kulak question, which Molotov was scheduled to address. The protocols to this meeting indicate the formation of three commissions to work out plans of arrest and exile. These three commissions were likely in the background of the OGPU's own directive on dekulakization. (Ibid., pp. 151–55.)

60. Ibid. See also *GARF*, f. 9414, op. 1, d. 1943, ll. 28–29.

61. *TSD*, vol. 2, pp. 163–67. (The regional-level OGPU was to create operative troikas, with analogous groups on the county and district levels to implement the operation. The district operative groups would participate directly in the operation along with maneuverable OGPU troops.)

62. *TSD*, vol. 2, pp. 169–75; and Ivnitskii, *Kollektivizatsiia i raskulachivanie*, p. 99.

63. *GARF*, f. 9414, op. 1, d. 1944, ll. 65–66.

64. Several foreign embassies attempted to intervene on behalf of their nationals. See *GARF*, f. 9414, op. 1, d. 1944, l. 67; and V. A. Kozlov et al., eds., *Neizvestnaia Rossiia. XX vek* (Moscow, 1992), vol. 2, pp. 324–36.

65. *GARF*, f. 9414, op. 1, d. 1944, ll. 72–77.

66. Ibid., l. 80.

67. Bergavinov sent a copy of the protocols of this meeting to Molotov, with a copy to Iagoda. *GAOPDF AO*, f. 290, op. 1, d. 378, ll. 11–12, 15–17, 30–32. (On Bergavinov's whereabouts, see Rudol'f Khantalin, *Nevol'niki i bonzy* [Arkhangel'sk, 1998], p. 54.) Stalin's letter is in *TSD: TsA FSB*, f. 2, op. 8, d. 204, l. 468.

68. *GARF*, f. 9414, op. 1, d. 1944, l. 98.

69. Danilov and Ivnitskii, eds., *Dokumenty svidetel'stvuiut*, pp. 350–55. Given the costs of resettlement, especially of "native" kulaks resettled within their own regions, the types of regional initiatives in the competition for labor which James Harris has investigated for the Urals, do not seem to have come into play yet. As long as the regional soviets were required to play a central financial and administrative role in special resettlement, kulak labor seems not to have been much of an immediate benefit and, in some cases, an extremely onerous burden to bear. I would hypothesize that the economic advantages of kulak labor became more practically apparent—and real—to some regions only when the Andreev Politburo commission and the OGPU took full charge of special resettlement

in 1931, releasing the hard-pressed regions from their heavy obligations to special settlers. I would also question whether this experience was uniform for all regions. My guess is that the Urals benefited in later years much more than, for example, the Northern Territory where the number of "imported" kulaks was drastically lowered in the second year of the deportations. See the important and pioneering article by James Harris, "The Growth of the Gulag: Forced Labor in the Urals Region, 1929–31," *Russian Review*, vol. 56 (April 1997): 265–80.

70. *GARF*, f. 9414, op. 1, d. 1944, ll. 88–89, 189; *TSD*, vol. 2, pp. 195–96.

71. Viola, *Peasant Rebels*, p. 80.

72. *TSD*, vol. 2, p. 167.

73. Ibid.; *RGASPI*, f. 17, op. 162, d. 8, ll. 109–10; *GARF*, f. 9414, op. 1, d. 1944, l. 82. The Ukrainian Council of People's Commissars had already passed a decree on 13 November 1929 on exiling "socially dangerous" elements from border areas. *RGAE*, f. 5675, op. 1, d. 23, ll. 42–41.

74. *"Ni v koem sluchae."*

75. *TSD*, vol. 2, p. 166. This directive was violated at times. See the collection of documents, edited by Andrea Romano and Nonna Tarkhova, *Krasnaia armiia i kollektivizatsiia derevni v SSSR (1928–1933 gg.)* (Naples, 1996). In addition to the use of OGPU internal security troops, the OGPU would mobilize its reserve and retired "chekists." Ibid., pp. 154, 182–84, 189–90. For information on the numbers and use of OGPU troops, see ibid., pp. 405–9. On the participation of the militia, see *GARF*, f. 393, op. 43a, d. 1798, ll. 56–59; d. 1870, ll. 274–81.

76. *TSD*, vol. 2, p. 167. K. E. Voroshilov (Commissar of Military and Naval Affairs) was involved in discussions about the effects of repression in the countryside on soldiers from at least 30 January. See *RGASPI*, f. 17, op. 162, d. 8, l. 84.

77. *TSD*, vol. 2, p. 310.

78. *GARF*, f. 9414, op. 1, d. 1944, l. 69. (Similar directives were issued on 5 March [l. 85] and on 20 March [l. 86].)

79. *Partiinoe stroitel'stvo*, no. 9 (May 1932): 48. Over one-third of rural party members were illiterate or self-educated and about half were relatively inexperienced, having joined the party after 1924. Peasants constituted only a tiny minority among party members. *Sotsial'nyi i natsional'nyi sostav VKP(b). Itogi vsesoiuznoi partiinoi perepisi 1927 g.* (Moscow, 1928), pp. 33, 41, 85, 87; A. S. Bubnov, "Statisticheskie svedeniia o VKP(b)," *Bol'shaia Sovetskaia entsiklopediia*, 1st ed. (Moscow, 1930), vol. 11, pp. 532–33, 541; I. N. Iudin, *Sotsial'naia baza rosta KPSS* (Moscow, 1973), p. 164; T. H. Rigby, *Communist Party Membership in the USSR, 1917–1961* (Princeton: Princeton University Press, 1968), p. 134.

80. A. I. Lepeshkin, *Mestnye organy vlasti Sovetskogo gosudarstva* (Moscow, 1959), pp. 59–60, 232, 237; *Sovetskoe stroitel'stvo*, no. 12 (December 1929): 7, 11; no. 2 (February 1930): 38–40; Bubnov, "Statisticheskie svedeniia," pp. 541–42; I. K. Ozol, "Obzor zakonodatel'stva i sostoianiia mestnykh biudzhetov RSFSR za 1929/30 g.," *Ezhegodnik Sovetskogo stroitel'stva i prava na 1931 god* (Moscow-Leningrad, 1931), p. 163.

81. In 1928, on the eve of a general party purge, seven regional party organizations were purged of an average of 13 percent of their membership, a large percent of them from the rural party apparatus. In the 1929–30 general party purge, the rural party lost some 14 percent (47,753) of its membership. An additional 47,137 members received party reprimands, and some 3,857 were removed from responsible positions. Rigby, *Communist Party Membership*, pp. 176–77, 181, 187; *Derevenskii kommunist*, nos. 11–12 (21 June 1930): 46. High turnover rates

for chairmen and secretaries of rural soviets caused widespread instability; in many areas, there were from eight to ten different chairmen in one year. In early 1930 the government scheduled extraordinary elections in a large number of rural soviets; in some parts of the countryside, as many as 82 percent of rural soviet chairmen were replaced. *Derevenskii kommunist*, nos. 23–24 (25 December 1929): 51; *Put' sovetov* (North Caucasus), no. 14 (31 July 1930): 23–24; *Sovetskoe stroitel'stvo*, no. 2 (February 1930): 58; *Izvestiia*, 26 January 1930, p. 1; *Put' sovetov* (Middle Volga), no. 10 (May 1930): 1; B. Levin and I. Suvorov, "Sovety i stroitel'stvo sotsializma," in *15 let Sovetskogo stroitel'stva*, ed. E. Pashukanis (Moscow, 1932), pp. 465–66.

82. For more on the problems of rural administration, see Lynne Viola, "'L'ivresse du succes': les cadres russe et le pouvoir sovietique durant les campagnes de collectivisation de l'agriculture," *Revue des etudes Slaves*, vol. 64, no. 1 (Paris, 1992): 75–101.

83. Davies, *Socialist Offensive*, pp. 442–43.

84. See Viola, *Peasant Rebels*, chaps. 4 and 5, for further information on the peasant rebellion against collectivization.

85. Stalin, *Sochineniia*, vol. 12, pp. 191–99.

86. Davies, *Socialist Offensive*, pp. 442–43. Between 1 March and 1 May, percentages of collectivized households fell in the Moscow Region from 74.2 percent to 7.5 percent; in the Central Black Earth Region, from 83.3 percent to 18.2 percent; in the Urals, from 75.6 percent to 31.9 percent; in the Lower Volga, from 70.1 percent to 41.4 percent; in the Middle Volga, from 60.3 percent to 30.1 percent; and in the North Caucasus, from 79.4 percent to 63.2 percent.

87. The "overfulfillment" was more than fourfold (283,717) if we add the total figures and over twofold (124,889) if we count only those actually designated as kulaks. *TSD: TsA FSB*, f. 2, op. 8, d. 329, l. 202; *DGO*, 3, pp. 313–14.

88. The statistics vary according to the source consulted. *TSD*, vol. 2, pp. 809–10; V. P. Popov, "Gosudarstvennyi terror v sovetskoi Rossii. 1923–1953 gg.," *Otechestvennye arkhivy*, no. 2 (1992): 28–29.

89. *TSD*, vol. 2, p. 415. Also see *GARF*, f. 9414, op. 1, d. 1943, l. 54 for slightly higher figures.

90. *TSD*, vol. 2, p. 746; *RGASPI*, f. 17, op. 120, d. 52, l. 59; *GARF*, f. 374, op. 28, d. 4055, ll. 33–48; and f. 9479, op. 1, d. 89, l. 205 for the range of available statistics.

91. *TSD*, vol. 2, p. 746. The overwhelming majority fell into the third category. Removal of third-category kulak families, if begun at all, ceased after the March retreat in most places, postponed until after the end of the spring sowing. Data from August 1930 demonstrates that only 26,033 families had been moved, with further plans to relocate an additional 4,500 Ukrainian families and 20,756 North Caucasus families by 1 October. Impediments to the campaign were mainly inertia and bureaucratic overload as well as continued village resistance to the removal of these families. In late December, the OGPU complained that the operation was "*bezsistemno*" (unsystematic), with each region taking its own approach. As of early February 1931, numbers of third-category kulaks resettled outside the collective farm fields were still only about 44,000. After 1931, this category falls out of the records. The majority of families affected were either administratively dekulakized through taxation, left for the cities, or were simply deported when dekulakization resumed in fall 1930 and in 1931. For further information, see *GARF*, f. 9414, op. 1, d. 1943, ll. 81–82, 117–18, 135–48, 152–53; and Ivnitskii, *Kollektivizatsiia i raskulachivanie*, pp. 183–85, 222–23.

92. *RGAE*, f. 7733, op. 8, d. 162, ll. 5–6.
93. *TSD*, vol. 2, p. 773.
94. *RGASPI*, f. 17, op. 162, d. 9, ll. 138, 161. Postyshev (a senior member of the Ukrainian Communist Party leadership and a Central Committee secretary) acted as chair in Andreev's absence. From October 1931 through the end of 1932, Ia. E. Rudzutak (from 1931 to 1934, chairman of the Central Control Commission and commissar of the Workers' and Peasants' Inspectorate) took over as the head of the commission.
95. *RGASPI*, f. 17, op. 162, d. 10, ll. 51–54; d. 9, ll. 175–78; *GARF*, f. 9479, op. 1, d. 3, ll. 2–3.
96. *RGASPI*, f. 17, op. 120, d. 52, l. 59; *GARF*, f. 374, op. 28, d. 4055, l. 47; *GARF*, f. 9479, op. 1, d. 89, l. 205.
97. Popov, "Gosudarstvennyi terror v sovetskoi Rossii," p. 28.
98. *RGASPI*, f. 17, op. 162, d. 10, ll. 126, 180–81. Also see *RGASPI*, f. 17, op. 162, d. 12, ll. 104–6, 134.
99. Ivnitskii, *Kollektivizatsiia i raskulachivanie*, pp. 183, 188–89.
100. *TSD*, vol. 3, pp. 746–50. The decree still allowed for the exile of some 12,000 families.
101. *GARF*, f. 374, op. 28, d. 4055, l. 47; *RGASPI*, f. 17, op. 120, d. 52, l. 59. V. P. Danilov discovered a higher figure for the numbers of kulaks deported in 1930 and 1931 in the Central Registry of the OGPU. The figure—517,665 families or 2,437,062 people—refers specifically to special settlers. See *TSD*, vol. 5, book 1, p. 8, for a discussion of these numbers.
102. Pavel Polian, *Ne po svoei vole . . . Istoriia i geografiia prinuditel'nykh migratsii v SSSR* (Moscow, 2001), p. 74.
103. On the political basis of class, see E. H. Carr, *Socialism in One Country, 1924–1926*, 3 vols. (London: MacMillan, 1958), vol. 1, p. 99.

Chapter 2

1. The epigraph is from Maurice Hindus, *Red Bread: Collectivization in a Russian Village* (Bloomington: Indiana University Press, 1988), pp. 255–58.
2. *RGAE*, f. 7486, op. 37, d. 61, l. 110.
3. T. I. Slavko, ed., *Kulatskaia ssylka na Urale, 1930–1936* (Moscow, 1995), pp. 153–57.
4. I. E. Plotnikov, ed., *Sploshnaia kollektivizatsiia i raskulachivanie v Zaural'e (Materialy po istorii Kurganskoi oblasti)* (Kurgan, 1995), pp. 108–9.
5. V. A. Kozlov, et al., eds., *Neizvestnaia Rossiia. XX vek. Arkhivy, pis'ma, memuary* (Moscow, 1992), vol. 1, p. 214.
6. Olga Litinenko and James Riordan, eds., *Memories of the Dispossessed: Descendants of Kulak Families Tell Their Stories* (Nottingham, UK: Bramcote Press, 1998), pp. 27–39. (In some parts of the country, village officials ordered boycotts of kulak farms before the center issued its decrees on dekulakization.)
7. Kozlov et al., eds., *Neizvestnaia Rossia*, vol. 1, p. 214.
8. Ibid., pp. 198–99.
9. Ibid., p. 214.
10. Novoselova's hardworking father was arrested as a first-category kulak and carted off to the Solovetskii Island prison camp in the White Sea. He would return home blind. *Zabveniiu ne podlezhit. Neizvestnye stranitsy Nizhegorodskoi istorii (1918–1984 gody)* (Nizhnyi Novgorod, 1994).

11. Lynne Viola, *Peasant Rebels Under Stalin: Collectivization and the Culture of Peasant Resistance* (New York: Oxford University Press, 1996), p. 37.

12. V. P. Danilov and S. A. Krasil'nikov, eds., *Spetspereselentsy v Zapadnoi Sibiri, 1930–1945*, 4 vols. (Novosibirsk, 1992–96), vol. 1, p. 86.

13. V. P. Danilov and N. A. Ivnitskii, eds., *Dokumenty svidetel'stvuiut. Iz istorii derevni nakanune i v khode kollektivizatsii, 1927–1932 gg.* (Moscow, 1989), p. 313; *GARF*, f. 9414, op. 1, d. 1943, l. 19.

14. *RGAE*, f. 7446, op. 5, d. 87, l. 2; f. 7486, op. 37, d. 122, ll. 174.

15. Ibid., l. 5; f. 7486, op. 37, d. 122, l. 176.

16. Viola, *Peasant Rebels*, pp. 103–4, 110, 136–37, 140, 181–204.

17. Ibid., pp. 145–54.

18. *TSD: TsA FSB*, f. 2, op. 9, d. 572, ll. 311–26; *DGO*, vol. 3, book 1, p. 712.

19. *TSD: TsA FSB*, f. 2, op. 8, d. 793, ll. 221–31.

20. Ibid., op. 9, d. 45, ll. 12–18.

21. *RGAE*, f. 7446, op. 1, d. 87, l. 17; *GARF*, f. 393, op. 43a, d. 1874, ll. 46–47.

22. Viola, *Peasant Rebels*, pp. 81–82, 199–200.

23. *TSD: TsA FSB*, f. 2, op. 9, d. 20, l. 52–95.

24. *GARF*, f. 393, op. 43a, d. 1876, l. 289.

25. *RGAE*, f. 7446, op. 5, d. 87, l. 21.

26. *TSD: TsA FSB*, f. 2, op. 9, d. 539, ll. 209–18.

27. I. E. Plotnikov, "Krest'ianskie volneniia i vystupleniia na Urale v kontse 20-kh—nachale 30-kh godov," *Otechestvennaia istoriia*, no. 2 (1998): 80; *TSD: TsA FSB*, f. 2, op. 8, d. 793, ll. 221–31.

28. *TSD*, vol. 2, p. 127.

29. *GARF*, f. 9414, op. 1, d. 1944, ll. 148–49; *VOANPI* (*Vologodskii oblastnoi arkhiv noveishei politicheskoi istorii*), f. 1855, op. 1, d. 10, ll. 253–57.

30. *GARF*, f. 9414, op. 1, d. 1944, ll. 26–30; *VOANPI*, f. 1855, op. 1, d. 10, ll. 253–57.

31. E.g., *RGAE*, f. 7486, op. 37, d. 122, l. 77.

32. Working members of families were serviced by the economic enterprise employing them.

33. *TSD: GARF*, f. 353s, op. 16a, d. 9, ll. 12–13. (The axes and other sharp instruments were to be transported separately, in baggage cars.)

34. The collection points assembled all families from a given county. Operational groups under the county department of the OGPU orchestrated the collections unless the collection points served more than one county in which case the OGPU regional troika took charge. *GARF*, f. 9414, op. 1, d. 1944, ll. 26–30, 34–35.

35. Ibid.

36. Ibid., ll. 31–32, 34–35.

37. Ivan Tvardovskii, "Stranitsy perezhitogo," *Iunost'*, no. 3 (1988): 13. Also see Kozlov et al., eds., *Neizvestnaia Rossiia*, vol. 1, pp. 214–16; V. N. Maksheev, ed., *Narymskaia khronika, 1930–1945: Tragediia spetspereselentsev. Dokumenty i vospominaniia* (Moscow, 1997), pp. 18–19, 36–37; and V. M. Kirillova, ed., *Kniga pamiati: posviashchaetsia Tagil'chanam—zhertvam repressii, 1917–1980-kh godov* (Ekaterinburg, 1994), pp. 134–41.

38. *GARF*, f. 9414, op. 1, d. 1943, ll. 17–18.

39. Kozlov et al., eds., *Neizvestnaia Rossiia*, vol. 1, pp. 214–16.

40. Litinenko and Riordan, eds., *Memories of the Dispossessed*, p. 40.

41. Slavko, ed., *Kulatskaia ssylka na Urale*, p. 154.

42. I thank Jon Bone for alerting me to this possibility.

43. *GARF*, f. 9414, op. 1, d. 1944, ll. 42–50.

44. Ibid., d. 1943, l. 52.
45. Ibid., d. 1944, ll. 51–60, 92.
46. Ibid., ll. 51–60, 61–64.
47. *TSD: TsA FSB*, f. 2, op. 8, d. 35, ll. 25–28.
48. Ibid. d. 840, l. 109; *GARF*, f. 9414, op. 1, d. 1943, l. 20.
49. *GARF*, f. 9414, op. 1, d. 1944, l. 118.
50. Echelon #401 from the Lower Volga carried more than 190 people over seventy years of age alongside fathers and small children without mothers. *TSD: TsA FSB*, f. 2, op. 8, d. 840, l. 109.
51. This was in fact a contradiction to stated policy in regard to the fate of category one kulak families who explicitly were to be deported without their arrested heads of households. *GARF*, f. 9414, op. 1, d. 1944, l. 148.
52. Ibid., l. 149.
53. Ibid., l. 126.
54. Ibid., l. 121. Data on 189 echelons indicated that 390 people (173 children, 168 women, and 49 men) were removed from trains due to illness, while 58 (47 children, 10 men, 1 woman) died en route. Doubtless these numbers say little about actual cases of illness given the likelihood of families hiding illness to prevent separation. Ibid., f. 9414, op. 1, d. 1943, ll. 20–21.
55. Litinenko and Riordan, eds., *Memories of the Dispossessed*, p. 41. A *burzhuika* was a small, jerry-rigged stove.
56. Slavko, ed., *Kulatskaia ssylka na Urale*, pp. 153–57; Kirillova, ed., *Kniga pamiati*, pp. 134–41.
57. A. A. Bazarov, *Kulak i agrogulag* (Cheliabinsk, 1991), p. 230.
58. *GAOPDF AO*, f. 290, op. 1, d. 380, l. 21. A 28 February 1930 telegram from the deputy head of the OGPU Transport Department to local OGPU officials noted cases of kulaks throwing "anti-Soviet" notes from the trains and stipulated that those guilty of such actions were to be transferred to the labor camps. Further, the telegram noted that all letters were to go through the OGPU Transport Department and those with "anti-Soviet content" were to be destroyed. This document is from N. N. Pokrovskii, ed., *Politbiuro i krest'ianstvo: vysylka, spetsposelenie, 1930–1940*, 2 vols. (Moscow, 2005–6), vol. 2: P-212/TsA FSB fond 2, op. 8, d. 2: forthcoming.
59. *GARF*, f. 9414, op. 1, d. 1943, l. 47a.
60. *TSD: TsA FSB*, f. 2, op. 8, d. 504, ll. 187–88; *GARF*, f. 9414, op. 1, d. 1943, ll. 47–48. Bergavinov spoke of a kulak insurrection (*vosstanie*) in Kotlas at a late March meeting of the regional party committee, probably referring to this one. He claimed that up to 2,500 people were involved and that they burned down the OGPU offices.
61. *TSD: TsA FSB*, f. 2, op. 8, d. 504, l. 262; *GARF*, f. 9414, op. 1, d. 1943, ll. 47–48.
62. *GARF*, f. 9414, op. 1, d. 1943, l. 48.
63. *TSD: TsA FSB*, f. 2, op. 8, d. 504, ll. 200–218, 224–25.
64. *GAOPDF AO*, f. 290, op. 1, d. 387, l. 9.
65. This was in the summer of 1931. Kirillova, ed., *Kniga pamiati*, p. 45.
66. *GARF*, f. 1235, op. 141, d. 786, ll. 4–2.
67. Ibid., f. 9414, op. 1, d. 1944, ll. 30, 51–60, 126, 135, 139; *GARF*, f. 393, op. 43a, d. 1796, ll. 230–31. *TSD: TsA FSB*, f. 2, op. 8, d. 840, l. 109. Able-bodied were defined as men and women over sixteen. Non-able–bodied included children under sixteen with their mothers, the ill, and the elderly.
68. *GARF*, f. 9414, op. 1, d. 1944, ll. 34–36.
69. *TSD: TsA FSB*, f. 2, op. 8, d. 504, l. 308.
70. *GARF*, f. 393, op. 43a, d. 1796, ll. 230–31.

71. A. A. Petrushin, ed., *My ne znaem poshchady ... Izvestnye, maloizvestnye, i neizvestnye sobytiia iz istorii Tiumenskogo kraia po materialam VChK-GPU-NKVD-KGB* (Tiumen, 1999), p. 133.

72. *GAOPDF AO*, f. 290, op. 1, d. 386, l. 1.

73. Ibid., d. 379, l. 5. In some areas, the kulak exile population would exceed that of the local population. See, for example, V. V. Alekseev and T. I. Slavko, eds., *Raskulachennye spetspereselentsy na Urale (1930–1936 gg.). Sb. dokumentov* (Ekaterinburg, 1993), p. 211, n. 13.

74. *GAOPDF AO*, f. 290, op. 1, d. 440, l. 15. (Bergavinov ended the letter, saying "So you see, I now have 'happy' [*veselaia*] work, but when I'm free of it (in the middle of March) [I] will come to Piter [Leningrad].")

75. Petrushin, ed., *My ne znaem poshchady ...*, p. 133.

76. *GAOPDF AO*, f. 290, op. 1, d. 387, l. 8.

77. Ibid., d. 384, l. 1. Also see *GARF*, f. 9414, op. 1, d. 1943, ll. 35–7. (The objection came from Mizinov, the secretary of the Arkhangel'skii County party committee.)

78. *GAOPDF AO*, f. 290, op. 1, d. 384, ll. 4–6.

79. Ibid., d. 378, ll. 11–12.

80. Ibid., d. 387, l. 8.

81. *GARF*, f. 9414, op. 1, d. 1944, l. 98.

82. A 10 April 1930 Russian Council of People's Commissars decree called on OGPU to pay for the expenses of the resettlement of native kulaks. *GARF*, f. 393, op. 43a, d. 1796, ll. 230–31.

83. *GARF*, f. 9414, op. 1, d. 1944, ll. 80, 128–29, 135; ibid., f. 9414, op. 1, d. 1943, ll. 28–29; ibid., f. 5446, op. 11a, d. 560, l. 5.

84. Ibid., f. 1235, op. 141, d. 786, ll. 4–2.

85. *RGAE*, f. 5675, op. 1, d. 23a, ll. 60–59.

86. *GAOPDF AO*, f. 290, op. 1, d. 386, ll. 97–104.

87. *GARF*, f. 393, op. 43a, d. 1796, l. 308.

88. G. F. Dobronozhenko and L. S. Shabarova, eds., *Spetsposelki v Komi oblasti: sbornik dokumentov* (Syktyvkar, 1997), pp. 10–11.

89. *GARF*, f. 1235, op. 141, d. 786, ll. 23–22.

90. Kozlov et al., eds., *Neizvestnaia Rossiia*, vol. 1, pp. 221–22.

91. *Rossiiskaia gazeta*, 22 January 1993, p. 6. An OGPU telegram to regional chiefs in the Urals, Siberia, and the North ordered that letters about the difficult conditions of exile should not be allowed to get through to their addressees. Pokrovskii, ed., *Politbiuro i krest'ianstvo*, vol. 2: P-221/TsA FSB, fond 2, op. 8, d. 2, l. 210: forthcoming.

92. Maksheev, ed., *Narymskaia khronika*, pp. 34–35.

93. *And the Past Seems But a Dream* (Sverdlovsk, 1987), a film based on the stories of the children of Igarki.

94. *GAOPDF AO*, f. 290, op. 1, d. 386, l. 7.

95. Ibid., d. 378, l. 12.

96. *GARF*, f. 9414, op. 1, d. 1944, l. 119. The OGPU told the head of the Northern OGPU that because of frost, no potatoes were possible, so the North would have to rely on local resources. USLON (*Upravlenie Solovetskikh lagerei osobogo naznacheniia*, or the Administration of Solovetskii Special Designation Camps) was to provide eighty tons of cabbage and twenty-five tons of onions.

97. *TSD*, vol. 2, pp. 346–47.

98. *RGASPI*, f. 17, op. 162, d. 8, l. 139.

99. *GAOPDF AO*, f. 290, op. 1, d. 386, ll. 125, 146.

100. *GARF*, f. 393, op. 43a, d. 1796, l. 396.
101. *RGASPI*, f. 17, op. 162, d. 8, l. 173.
102. For examples, see *TSD: TsA FSB*, f. 2, op. 8, d. 840, ll. 243–60; *GAAO* (*Gosudarstvennyi arkhiv Arkhangel'skoi oblasti*), f. 621, op. 3, d. 25, ll. 12–11; *RGASPI*, f. 17, op. 162, d. 8, l. 39; *GARF*, f. 9414, op. 1, d. 1944, l. 107; Danilov and Krasil'nikov, eds., *Spetspereselentsy v Zapadnoi Sibiri*, vol. 1, p. 258.
103. *VOANPI*, f. 5, op. 1, d. 277, ll. 36–40; *GARF*, f. 393, op. 43a, d. 1796, l. 392. ("*Tif*" is sometimes identified as "*sypnoi tif*" or "*briushnoi tif*," meaning typhus or spotted fever, and typhoid fever, but sometimes only the word "*tif*" appears.)
104. *GARF*, f. 393, op. 43a, d. 1796, ll. 184–90.
105. Ibid., f. 9414, op. 1, d. 1944, l. 115.
106. *GAOPDF AO*, f. 290, op. 1, d. 387, l. 9.
107. *GARF*, f. 1235, op. 141, d. 786, ll. 4–2.
108. Dobronozhenko and Shabarova, *Spetsposelki v Komi oblasti*, pp. 8–9.
109. *GAAO*, f. 621, op. 3, d. 19, l. 11.
110. *GAOPDF AO*, f. 290, op. 1, d. 425, ll. 5–6.
111. *TSD: GARF*, f. R-393sz, op. 43a, d. 1796, ll. 306–7.
112. *GAAO*, f. 621, op. 3, d. 25, ll. 6–1.
113. *GARF*, f. 393, op. 1a, d. 292, l. 48.
114. *GAAO*, f. 621, op. 3, d. 19, l. 17.
115. *RGASPI*, f. 17, op. 162, d. 8, l. 163.
116. *GARF*, f. 393, op. 43a, d. 1796, l. 388. (19 June letter to S. I. Syrtsov)
117. Ibid., f. 9414, op. 1, d. 1944, l. 115; f. 393, op. 43a, d. 1796, ll. 229, 231, 388, 408–9; f. 393, op. 1a, d. 292, l. 48; f. 1235, op. 141, d. 786, ll. 4–2; *RGASPI*, f. 17, op. 162, d. 8, l. 163.
118. *GAAO*, f. 621, op. 3, d. 19, ll. 23–22.
119. *GARF*, f. 1235, op. 141, d. 786, ll. 4–2.
120. Lynne Viola, "'Tear the Evil From the Root': The Children of the *Spetspereselentsy* of the North," *Studia Slavica Finlandensia*, tom. 17 (Helsinki, 2000): 34–35.
121. *GARF*, f. 393, op. 43a, d. 1796, ll. 408–9; *GAAO*, f. 621, op. 3, d. 19, ll. 23–22. Also see *TSD: TsA FSB*, f. 2, op. 8, d. 504, ll. 200–218, 224–25.
122. *GAAO*, f. 621, op. 3, d. 25, ll. 12–11.
123. *GAOPDF AO*, f. 290, op. 1, d. 386, l. 110. On 16 April, Tolmachev wrote that between 29 March and 15 April, 677 children had died in Vologodskii county and, by 12 April, 734 exiles (634 of them children) had died in Severo-Dvinskii county. A Russian Central Executive Committee commission on children later sent inspector M. I. Morgunov to report on exile children in the Northern Territory. He wrote that between 24 March and 1 August, 1,277 children in the Northern Territory—mostly those under five to seven years of age—had died in temporary residence in Makarikha, which had a total exile population of 45,000, half under the age of sixteen. In the town of Sol'vychegodsk, between 19 March and 21 July, 468 children died from an exile population of 5,110 people, 2,170 of them children. One self-described "coincidental witness" of this disaster wrote in early May to the Russian Central Executive Committee children's commission that up to 30 children a day were dying in the town of Kotlas. Ibid., l. 98; *VOANPI*, f. 5, op. 1, d. 277, ll. 62–67; *GARF*, f. 1235, op. 141, d. 786, l. 23.
124. *RGASPI*, f. 17, op. 162, d. 8, l. 65.
125. Ibid., f. 17, op. 165, d. 16, ll. 48–49.
126. *GARF*, f. 9414, op. 1, d. 1944, l. 148.

127. Ibid., f. 393, op. 43a, d. 1796, ll. 230–31. In 1931, during the second round of dekulakization, Iagoda and Evdokimov issued a memo to the regional OGPU chief in Rostov reminding him that children under ten and the elderly over sixty-five years of age were allowed to stay with relatives or friends in the village when their families were exiled. This memo may have been an attempt to alleviate the financial burden of supporting the families and was likely issued to other OGPU regional chiefs, although the actual effect appears minimal (ibid., f. 9479, op. 1, d. 3, ll. 10–11).

128. This document is from Pokrovskii, ed., *Politbiuro i krest'ianstvo*, vol. 1, p. 231. (Emphasis in the original.)

129. *RGASPI*, f. 17, op. 120, d. 126, l. 192.

130. E.g., *GARF*, f. 393, op. 43a, d. 1796, l. 231; ibid., f. 1235, op. 141, d. 786, ll. 4–2; *RGASPI*, f. 17, op. 162, d. 8, l. 139.

131. Dobronozhenko and Shabarova, *Spetsposelki v Komi oblast*, p. 11.

132. *VOANPI*, f. 1855, op. 1, d. 10, ll. 169–71.

133. *GARF*, f. 9414, op. 1, d. 1944, l. 152.

134. *TSD: TsA FSB*, f. 2, op. 8, d. 504, ll. 494–96.

135. *GARF*, f. 1235, op. 141, d. 786, ll. 23–22.

136. Ibid., f. 374, op. 28, d. 4055, ll. 16–14.

137. Ibid., f. 9479, op. 1, d. 3, ll. 132–39; f. 9479, op. 1, d. 5, l. 44. This, despite a 29 December 1931 Gulag administration ruling not to permit further transfers of children or the elderly to their native villages in view of the supposed improvement of conditions. Such transfers were to be allowed only in individual and exceptional cases and only with the permission of the OGPU regional boss. Ibid., d. 11, l. 92.

138. Ibid., f. 374, op. 28, d. 4055, l. 16–14. (10 August 1931 Northern Territory Party Committee decree calling on the OGPU to "force" the transfer of elderly over sixty to relatives back in the villages.) Ibid., f. 9479, op. 1, d. 11, l. 92. (29 December 1931 order to end transfer of elderly to relatives, supposedly in view of improved living conditions.) Ibid. d. 5, l. 44 (24 August 1931 OGPU telegram indicating children under fourteen and elderly over sixty could be sent home to friends or relatives.)

139. Kozlov et al., eds., *Neizvestnaia Rossia*, vol. 1, p. 207.

Chapter 3

1. The epigraph is from *GAOPDF AO*, f. 290, op. 1, d. 379, l. 6.

2. A. N. Dugin, *Neizvestnyi gulag: Dokumenty i fakty* (Moscow, 1999), pp. 8–9. (Italics in original.)

3. See Viola, "The Role of the OGPU in Dekulakization, Mass Deportations, and Special Resettlement in 1930," *The Carl Beck Papers in Russian and East European Studies*, no. 1406 (2000).

4. See, for example, *GAOPDF AO*, f. 290, op. 1, d. 356, ll. 27–84, for protocols of the Northern Territory commission on dekulakization. In the North, OGPU chief Austrin was the chair of the commission. See *GAOPDF AO*, f. 290, op. 1, d. 384, l. 15.

5. According to the Russian historian, N. A. Ivnitskii, the Molotov Politburo commission on dekulakization called for the creation of another subcommission at the end of January to work out concrete issues of exile resettlement and employment. No documentary evidence is accessible to evaluate this conclusion further or to

follow the work of this subcommission. N. A. Ivnitskii, *Repressivnaia politika Sovetskoi vlasti v derevne (1928–1932 gg.)* (Moscow, 2000), p. 115.

6. *GARF*, f. 393, op. 43a, d. 1796, ll. 264–65.

7. Ibid., d. 1797, ll. 75–76; ibid., d. 1796, ll. 230–31.

8. Ibid., f. 393, op. 43a, d. 1796, l. 232. The Shmidt commission consisted of the following members: S. A. Messing (head of the Foreign Department of OGPU and a deputy chairman of OGPU), V. N. Tolmachev (Commissar of Internal Affairs RSFSR), Ia. A. Teumin (head of the Budget Administration and member of the Commissariat of Finance SSSR), G. F. Grin'ko (Deputy Commissar of Agriculture), A. I. Muralov (Commissar of Agriculture RSFSR), Ia. K. Ol'skii (head of the Special Department of the OGPU), S. S. Lobov (chairman of the Supreme Council of the National Economy RSFSR), and F. P. Griadinskii (Deputy Commissar of Trade SSSR).

9. *GAOPDF AO*, f. 290, op. 1, d. 386, l. 102. This sentiment was echoed in the provinces. See the complaint of the Siberian resettlement agency in *RGAE*, f. 5675, op. 1, d. 23a, l. 121.

10. *GARF*, f. 393, op. 1a, d. 292, ll. 82, 450; ibid., f. 9479, op. 1, d. 1, l. 1; ibid., f. 9414, op. 1, d. 1944, l. 110. Behind the scenes, there was a struggle over whether the Commissariat of Agriculture of the RSFSR or of the SSSR should hold primary responsibility for special settler affairs in the North. Tolmachev was against the delegation of responsibilities to the RSFSR-level, apparently because of inadequate funding and personnel in the provinces. *GAAO*, f. 621, op. 3, d. 49, ll. 30–33; *GARF*, f. 393, op. 1a, d. 291, l. 4.

11. *GARF*, f. 9414, op. 1, d. 1944, l. 107.

12. Ibid., d. 1943, ll. 74–75. A "Temporary Charter on the Rights and Responsibilities of the Special Settlers" appeared only in late October 1931. (V. P. Danilov and S. A. Krasil'nikov, eds., *Spetspereselentsy v Zapadnoi Sibiri, 1930–1945*, 4 vols. [Novosibirsk, 1992–96], vol. 2, pp. 68–76. Also see *GARF*, f. 9479, op. 1, d. 3, ll. 132–39.)

13. *GARF*, f. 9414, op. 1, d. 1944, ll. 100, 107; f. 393, op. 43a, d. 1796, ll. 2–18.

14. *GAVO* (*Gosudarstvennyi arkhiv Vologodskoi oblasti*), f. 399, op. 1, d. 192, l. 54; *GARF*, f. 393, op. 43a, d. 1797, l. 35.

15. *GARF*, f. 393, op. 43a, d. 1797, ll. 35–36.

16. Ibid., f. 9414, op. 1, d. 1944, l. 100; f. 393, op. 43a, d. 1797, ll. 39a, 44; f. 1235, op. 144, d. 776, l. 2; *TSD: TsA FSB*, f. 2, op. 8, d. 204, l. 545.

17. *GARF*, f. 393, op. 43a, d. 1796, ll. 2–18; f. 1235, op. 141, d. 776, l. 66. Also see O. V. Artemova, "Spetspereselentsy v Vozhegodskom raione (1930-e gody)," *Vozhega: Kraevedcheskii al'manakh* (Vologda, 1995), pp. 172–94.

18. *GARF*, f. 1235, op. 141, d. 776, l. 6.

19. Ibid., f. 393, op. 1a, d. 292, l. 90.

20. *GAAO*, f. 621, op. 3, d. 19, l. 58; *RGAE*, f. 5675, op. 1, d. 23, l. 233.

21. *GARF*, f. 393, op. 43a, d. 1796, ll. 2–18.

22. Ibid., l. 389.

23. For discussions of the earlier history of penal servitude, see Abby M. Schrader, "Branding the Exiles 'Other': Corporal Punishment and the Construction of Boundaries in mid-Nineteenth-Century Russia," in *Russian Modernity*, ed. David L. Hoffmann and Yanni Kotsonis (London: MacMillan, 2000), pp. 24–25; and Richard Hellie, "Migration in Early Modern Russia, 1480s–1780s," in *Coerced and Free Migration: Global Perspectives*, ed. David Eltis (Stanford: Stanford University Press, 2002), pp. 292–323.

24. Galina Mikhailovna Ivanova, *Labor Camp Socialism: The Gulag in the Soviet Totalitarian System*, trans. Carol Flath (Armonk, NY: M. E. Sharpe, 2000), pp. 10, 18, 69–72; Peter H. Solomon, Jr., *Soviet Criminal Justice Under Stalin* (Cambridge: Cambridge University Press, 1996), p. 29. For the 1922 legislation on administrative exile, see E. A. Zaitsev, ed., *Sbornik zakonodatel'nykh i normativnykh aktov o repressiiakh i reabilitatsii zhertv politicheskikh repressii* (Moscow, 1993), p. 12.

25. Ivanova, *Labor Camp Socialism*, p. 186.

26. S. A. Krasil'nikov, "Rozhdenie GULAGa: diskussii v verkhnikh eshelonakh vlasti: postanovleniia Politbiuro TsK VKP (b), 1929–1930," *Istoricheskii arkhiv*, no. 4 (1997): 142; E. A. Rees, "The People's Commissariat of the Timber Industry," in Rees, ed., *Decision-Making in the Stalinist Command Economy, 1932–37* (London: MacMillan, 1997), pp. 126–31; Solomon, *Soviet Criminal Justice*, part 1.

27. Krasil'nikov, "Rozhdenie GULAGa," pp. 143–44.

28. Ibid., pp. 144–46, 152–53. For the Politburo's June decree, see A. I. Kokurin and N. V. Petrov, eds., *GULAG, 1917–1960: Dokumenty* (Moscow, 2000), pp. 62–63.

29. *RGASPI*, f. 17, op. 21, d. 2542, ll. 312–17.

30. *TSD: TsA FSB*, f. 2, op. 9, d. 21, ll. 393–94.

31. *GARF*, f. 9414, op. 1, d. 1944, l. 80.

32. *RGASPI*, f. 17, op. 21, d. 192, l. 3.

33. *GARF*, f. 393, op. 43a, d. 1796, ll. 184–90; *TSD: TsA FSB*, f. 2, op. 9, d. 20, ll. 52, 95.

34. T. I. Slavko, ed., *Kulatskaia ssylka na Urale, 1930–1936* (Moscow, 1995), p. 89.

35. *GAOPDF AO*, f. 290, op. 1, d. 379, l. 15.

36. Ibid., ll. 2–4; *GARF*, f. 393, op. 43a, d. 1796, ll. 2–18. (Unchartered collective farms were farms lacking the charter that defined the "rights and responsibilities" of ordinary collective farmers.)

37. *GARF*, f. 9479, op. 1, d. 1, l. 1.

38. Ibid., f. 393, op. 43a, d. 1796, ll. 163–64; *GAVO*, f. 399, op. 1, d. 219, ll. 163–64.

39. *RGAE*, f. 5675, op. 1, d. 23a, l. 201.

40. *GAOPDF AO*, f. 290, op. 1, d. 379, l. 15.

41. Ibid., d. 331, l. 45.

42. *GARF*, f. 3316, op. 64, d. 1207, ll. 5–8.

43. Danilov and Krasil'nikov, eds., *Spetspereselentsy v Zapadnoi Sibiri*, vol. 3, p. 5.

44. S. A. Krasil'nikov, *Na izlomakh sotsial'noi struktury: marginaly v poslerevoliutsion- nom Rossiiskom obshchestve* (Novosibirsk, 1998), p. 53. While the special settlers provided the largest source of unfree labor in the Soviet Union through the mid- 1930s, they also played a large role in the colonization of the hinterlands. In 1930, for example, special settlers made up 19 percent of the population of the Komi Republic, even constituting the majority of the population within some districts. In the same year, it was estimated that the special settlers would account for some 17 percent of the Northern Territory's total population. By 1934, according to the Russian historian Tatiana Slavko, special settlers made up anywhere from 40 to 80 percent of the work force in Urals industry, and between 50 and 90 percent in the forestry industry. (Slavko, ed., *Kulatskaia ssylka na Urale*, p. 124.) See also G. F. Dobronozhenko and L. S. Shabalova, eds., *Spetsposelki v Komi oblasti po materialam sploshnogo obsledovaniia. Iiun' 1933. Sb. dokumentov* (Syktyvkar, 1997), p. 16; N. D. Sapozhnikova and A. G. Sapozhnikov, "Nekotorye aspekty otnosheniia vlasti k raskulachennym krest'ianam na Urale v kontse 20-kh–nachale 30-kh gg.," *Totalitarizm i lichnost'* (Perm, 1994), p. 83; *GAOPDF AO*, f. 290, op. 1, d. 379, l. 5; *GARF*, f. 393, op. 43a, d. 1796, ll. 2–18.

45. *GAOPDF AO*, f. 290, op. 1, d. 379, l. 5; d. 425, ll. 5–6.

46. For a sample of the petitions used in the North, see *GAOPDF AO*, f. 833, op. 1, d. 82, ll. 6–12.
47. *RGASPI*, f. 17, op. 3, d. 781, l. 3. In the Politburo protocols, Iagoda and D. Z. Lebed', deputy chairman of the Russian Republic Council of People's Commissars, are listed as commission members. It is unclear whether these last two were brought in to attempt a compromise. They are not listed as commission members in any other source that I have seen; nor were either in the North at this time. (*RGASPI*, f. 17, op. 162, d. 8, l. 152). Similar commissions would be created in other regions by order of a Council of People's Commissars decree of 10 April that enlisted Tolmachev to instruct these commissions as to their duties. (*GARF*, f. 393, op. 43a, d. 1796, ll. 230–31.)
48. *GAOPDF AO*, f. 290, op. 1, d. 385, ll. 1–3. (Also see *VOANPI*, f. 1855, op. 1, d. 10, ll. 169–71.) A Northern Territory party committee decree of 11 April had already ordered the creation of county subcommissions. See *VOANPI*, f. 1855, op. 1, d. 10, l. 99.
49. *GAOPDF AO*, f. 290, op. 1, d. 385, ll. 1–3; *VOANPI*, f. 1855, op. 1, d. 10, ll. 169–71.
50. *RGASPI*, f. 17, op. 120, d. 26, l. 1; f. 17, op. 162, d. 8, ll. 152–53.
51. Ibid., op. 120, d. 26, ll. 8–10; *GAOPDF AO*, f. 290, op. 1, d. 385, ll. 9–10, 13.
52. Ibid.
53. *GAOPDF AO*, f. 290, op. 1, d. 385, ll. 22–28, 31, 34–35. Another document (*svodka rezul'tatov rassmotrennykh zaiavlenii*) from the Arkhangel'sk County subcommission indicated that 22 percent of families had been exiled incorrectly and 8.5 were classified as "doubtful." (*GAOPDF AO*, f. 833, op. 1, d. 69, l. 59.)
54. Ibid., f. 290, op. 1, d. 385, l. 36.
55. Ibid., l. 30.
56. *VOANPI*, f. 5, op. 1, d. 275, ll. 8–15.
57. See Viola, "The Role of the OGPU in Dekulakization."
58. *GARF*, f. 9414, op. 1, d. 1944, ll. 140–42. In actuality, the OGPU would find its work complicated even by the relatively small numbers of returns. Although its regional bosses were in charge of issuing travel documents for returnees, by 27 May it had become so unclear as to who was returning legally and who illegally that Iagoda ordered the creation of standardized documents. (Ibid., ll. 142, 145.) By 1 June 1930, there were 14,123 escapes of special settlers from the North. (*TSD: TsA FSB*, f. 2, op. 8, d. 35, ll. 30–37.)
59. *GARF*, f. 9414, op. 1, d. 1944, ll. 143–44. The "incorrectly exiled" would be settled as "free citizens" with what were called "special privileges" and put to work in agriculture and industry. See *GARF*, f. 9414, op. 1, d. 1944, ll. 140, 143–44; *RGASPI*, f. 17, op. 162, d. 8, ll. 152–53. According to a September 1930 report from the Northern OGPU chief, Austrin, some 12,425 "incorrectly dekulakized" peasants had been set up in work in factories in the North. *GAAO*, f. 621, op. 3, d. 15, l. 291. In fact, the legal status of these peasants would never be clarified. In practice, the fate of the "incorrectly exiled" settled as "free citizens" remained unclear. On 19 October 1930, the OGPU wrote to its regional chiefs that in view of queries about how to return incorrect exiles, these issues should be decided by provincial-level commissions. (*GARF*, f. 9414, op. 1, d. 1944, l. 146). A 12 August 1931 Vologda city soviet note to the deputy chairman of the Northern Territory soviet executive committee noted that 576 incorrect exiles worked at a local brick factory and were, at present, "in a unique situation outside the law," with no documents and no right to join the trade unions or obtain housing. The city soviet asked for "clarity" in this "clearly abnormal situation." (*GAAO*, f. 621, op. 3, d. 49, l. 286). By September 1931, according to a Western Siberian Regional soviet executive com-

mittee directive, only the regional soviet executive committees had the right to determine if an incorrectly exiled peasant could return home. (Danilov and Krasil'nikov, eds., *Spetspereselentsy v Zapadnoi Sibiri*, vol. 2, p. 112.) A February 1932 report from the Commissariat of Justice to the Northern Territory soviet executive committee noted that these peasants were still deprived of their civil rights. *GAAO*, f. 621, op. 3, d. 98, l. 24.

60. *RGASPI*, f. 17, op. 162, d. 8, ll. 152–53.
61. Ibid., f. 17, op. 120, d. 26, ll. 1–5; *GAOPDF AO*, f. 290, op. 1, d. 385, ll. 6–8.
62. Ibid.; G. F. Dobronozhenko and L. S. Shabalova, eds., *Pokaianie. Komi respublikanskii martirolog zhertv massovykh politicheskikh repressii*, vol. 4 (book 1) (Syktyvkar, 2001), p. 45. On 30 April 1930, Bergavinov wrote to Molotov that "If these figures are allowed to get out, then this will play into the hands of people wanting to see only excesses." N. N. Pokrovskii, ed., *Politbiuro i krest'ianstvo: vysylka, spetsposelenie, 1930–1940*, 2 vols. (Moscow, 2005–6), vol. 1, p. 223.
63. *RGASPI*, f. 17, op. 162, d. 8, ll. 152–53.
64. *GAOPDF AO*, f. 290, op. 1, d. 385, ll. 6–8; *RGASPI*, f. 17, op. 120, d. 26, l. 5.
65. Bergavinov was also a Central Committee member from 1930 to 1934. Rudol'f Khantalin, *Nevol'niki i bonzy* (Arkhangel'sk, 1998), pp. 48, 52, 79; R. W. Davies et al., eds., *Soviet Government Officials, 1922–41: A Handlist* (Birmingham: CREES, University of Birmingham, 1989), p. 268.
66. Khantalin, *Nevol'niki*, p. 52.
67 On Bergavinov's ambitions for the North, see *GAOPDF AO*, f. 290, op. 1, d. 379, ll. 2–4, 5–30; and *RGAE*, f. 5675, op. 1, d. 23a, ll. 1–7, 201–2.
68. Khantalin, *Nevol'niki*, p. 52; *TSD: TsA FSB* (15 January 1930 Politburo protocol), no archival citation numbers.
69. (*iz ruk von plokho*). *GAOPDF AO*, f. 290, op. 1, d. 380, ll. 34–35; ibid., f. 290, op. 1, d. 356, l. 203.
70. *GARF*, f. 393, op. 43a, d. 1796, ll. 264–65, 450; *TSD: TsA FSB*, f. 2, op. 9, d. 760, l. 6; also see *GARF*, f. 393, op. 1a, d. 292, ll. 34, 82.
71. *GARF*, f. 393, op. 43a, d. 1796, ll. 229, 230–31.
72. See Viola, "The Role of the OGPU in Dekulakization," for further information. (Although V. V. Shmidt led a similar coordinating commission to Tolmachev's, under the USSR Council of People's Commissars, he does not seem to have taken such an active, or at least visible role, as Tolmachev.)
73. Khantalin, *Nevol'niki*, p. 59; V. A. Kozlov et al., eds., *Neizvestnaia Rossiia. XX vek. Arkhivy, pis'ma, memuary* (Moscow, 1992), vol. 1, p. 71.
74. (All capital lettering is in the original document.) *GAOPDF AO*, f. 290, op. 1, d. 386, ll. 97–104; Khantalin, *Nevol'niki*, pp. 61–63. (According to Khantalin, Lebed' almost immediately sent 100,000 rubles to the North, in part for children's food and medicines [Ibid., p. 66].)
75. (See the postscript in his letter to Lebed'.) *GAOPDF AO*, f. 290, op. 1, d. 386, ll. 95–96; Khantalin, *Nevol'niki*, p. 64.
76. *GAOPDF AO*, f. 290, op. 1, d. 386, ll. 69–80.
77. Ibid.
78. This is suggested in Khantalin, *Nevol'niki*, pp. 70–73, 76.
79. See above.
80. Khantalin, *Nevol'niki*, p. 63.
81. Ronald Grigor Suny, "Stalin and His Stalinism: Power and Authority in the Soviet Union, 1930–53," in *Stalinism and Nazism: Dictatorships in Comparison*, ed. Ian Kershaw and Moshe Lewin (Cambridge: Cambridge University Press, 1997), p. 34.
82. Kozlov et al., eds., *Neizvestnaia Rossiia*, vol. 1, p. 59.

83. Derek Watson, *Molotov and Soviet Government: Sovnarkom, 1930–41* (New York: St. Martin's Press, 1996), pp. 9, 13, 30–31, 37–38; R. W. Davies, "The Syrtsov-Lominadze Affair," *Soviet Studies*, vol. 33, no. 1 (January 1981): 30. Khantalin, *Nevol'niki*, (p. 59) points to a Syrtsov-Tolmachev connection dating back to the civil war. Tolmachev, Smirnov, and Eismont would be accused of antiparty activity in late 1932–early 1933.

84. Unfortunately, Ivnitskii provides no reference for this remark. See his introduction to *TSD*, vol. 2, p. 28, n. 27.

85. Oleg V. Khlevniuk, *The History of the Gulag*, trans. Vadim Staklo (New Haven: Yale University Press, 2004), p. 28; and Lars T. Lih, Oleg V. Naumov, and Oleg V. Khlevniuk, eds., *Stalin's Letters to Molotov*, trans. Catherine A. Fitzpatrick (New Haven: Yale University Press, 1995), p. 212.

86. As early as 22 February, Russian Republic Council of People's Commissars chairman Syrtsov was instructing the Karelian Council of People's Commissars chairman, Guilling, to report any plans on special resettlement "to the RSFSR Commissar of Internal Affairs Tolmachev, I repeat—to Tolmachev." (N. A. Ivnitskii and V. G. Makurov, eds., *Iz istorii raskulachivaniia v Karelii, 1930–1931* [Petrozavodsk, 1991], p. 36.) The OGPU and the People's Commissariat of Internal Affairs competed throughout 1930 for prison labor. The latter held some 60,000 inmates as of 1 May versus about 166,000 in the OGPU's corrective labor camps. (Danilov and Krasil'nikov, *Spetspereselentsy v Zapadnoi Sibiri*, vol. 1, pp. 14–15; and Krasil'nikov, *Na izlomakh sotsial'noi struktury*, pp. 24, 39.) For more information on the Commissariat of Internal Affairs, see T. P. Korzhikhina, *Sovetskoe gosudarstvo i ego uchrezhdeniia. Noiabr' 1917 g.–dekabr' 1991 g.* (Moscow: RGGU, 1994), pp. 176–79. See also John L. Scherer and Michael Jakobson, "The Collectivisation of Agriculture and the Soviet Prison Camp System," *Europe-Asia Studies*, vol. 45, no. 3 (1993): 540–41.

87. E.g., see *TSD: TsA FSB*, f. 2, op. 9, d. 45, ll. 120–34.

88. *GARF*, f. 5446, op. 12a, d. 14, ll. 26–27ob. Syrtsov appears to have agreed with Tolmachev. In a 29 July 1930 letter to various economic agencies, he noted the "increased and unconditionally abnormal tendency" of economic enterprises to use special settlers as a working force. (Both of these sources are from Pokrovskii, ed., *Politbiuro i krest'ianstvo*, vol. 2, *GARF*, f. A-259, op. 40, d. 2537, l. 2: forthcoming.)

89. E.g., *GARF*, f. 393, op. 43a, d. 1796, ll. 388, 389, 391.

90. Khantalin, *Nevol'niki*, pp. 48, 52, 79; Davies et al., eds., *Soviet Government Officials, 1922–24*, p. 268; Yuri Slezkine, *Arctic Mirrors* (Ithaca: Cornell University Press, 1994), p. 284; Kozlov et al., eds., *Neizvestnaia Rossiia*, vol. 1, pp. 67, 71. (Tolmachev was rehabilitated posthumously in 1962. See Kozlov et al., eds., *Neizvestnaia Rossiia*, vol. 1, p. 128.)

Chapter 4

1. *VOANPI*, f. 5, op. 1, d. 275, l. 3. (The epigraph is from *GAOPDF AO*, f. 290, op. 1, d. 380, l. 26.)

2. *VOANPI*, f. 5, op. 1, d. 275, l. 3.

3. Ibid., ll. 3–7.

4. *GAOPDF AO*, f. 290, op. 1, d. 378, l. 11; f. 833, op. 1, d. 70, ll. 29–31, 33, 45.

5. *TSD: TsA FSB*, f. 2, op. 8, d. 653, ll. 176–79.

6. *GARF*, f. 1235, op. 141, d. 786, ll. 4–2.

7. *GAOPDF AO*, f. 290, op. 1, d. 380, l. 22.

8. Ibid., l. 25. Another man warned, however, "Don't send me personal documents in a letter because they have begun to open letters, so one must not put anything into letters." Ibid., l. 21.

9. Ibid., ll. 22, 25–26.

10. Ibid., l. 22.

11. Ibid., ll. 97–104.

12. N. A. Ivnitskii, *Repressivnaia politika v Sovetskoi derevne (1928–1933 gg.)* (Moscow, 2000), p. 115.

13. *GAOPDF AO*, f. 290, op. 1, d. 378, l. 10; f. 290, op. 1, d. 384, l. 15.

14. *GARF*, f. 393, op. 43a, d. 1796, ll. 230–31, 264–65; f. 393, op. 43a, d. 1797, ll. 75–76.

15. Ibid., ll. 163–64; *GAVO*, f. 399, op. 1, d. 121, l. 16.

16. *GAVO*, f. 399, op. 1, d. 192, l. 54; *GARF*, f. 393, op. 43a, d. 1797, l. 35.

17. *RGAE*, f. 5675, op. 1, d. 23a, l. 21.

18. Ibid.; *GAVO*, f. 399, op. 1, d. 182, ll. 5–9.

19. *RGAE*, f. 5675, op. 1, d. 23a, ll. 96–94.

20. *GAVO*, f. 399, op. 1, d. 219, ll. 163–64.

21. *GARF*, f. 393, op. 43a, d. 1796, ll. 2–18. The numbers of families to be sent to this area was soon scaled back to 6,000. Ibid., f. 9414, op. 1, d. 1943, l. 41.

22. According to a 7 July 1930 report from the head of the Migration Agency, 89 land tracts for 11,125 families were planned for Arkhangel'skii County; 124 for 14,852 families for Vologodskii County; 42 for 5,250 families for Severo-Dvinskii County; 47 for 6,344 families for Niandomskii County; and 32 for 4,800 families for Komi. *GAAO*, f. 621, op. 3, d. 27, ll. 117–109.

23. *GAVO*, f. 399, op. 1, d. 182, ll. 5–9.

24. *VOANPI*, f. 5, op. 1, d. 275, ll. 3–7; *GAVO*, f. 399, op. 1, d. 213, ll. 163–64.

25. *VOANPI*, f. 1855, op. 1, d. 10, ll. 11–13.

26. Ibid., f. 5, op. 1, d. 277, ll. 36–40.

27. An explanatory note on "special colonization" in Siberia from April 1930 and addressed to the Migration Administration under the All-Union Commissariat of Agriculture noted that it took about four years to prepare land for settlers as opposed to months (which the current situation dictated), thus leaving the land completely unprepared for the settlers. *RGAE*, f. 5675, op. 1, d. 23, ll. 50–49.

28. *GARF*, f. 393, op. 43a, d. 1796, ll. 2–18.

29. See *GAVO*, f. 907, op. 5, d. 10, on the slow progress of land clearance.

30. *GARF*, f. 393, op. 43a, d. 1796, ll. 230–31.

31. *GAVO*, f. 399, op. 1, d. 219, ll. 131–34.

32. *GARF*, f. 393, op. 43a, d. 1796, l. 450.

33. *VOANPI*, f. 5, op. 1, d. 277, ll. 28–29.

34. *GAVO*, f. 395, op. 1, d. 40, ll. 166–70; *VOANPI*, f. 329, op. 1, d. 97, l. 3; f. 5, op. 1, d. 277, ll. 28–29.

35. E.g., *GARF*, f. 1235, op. 141, d. 776, l. 66; f. 1235, op. 141, d. 786, ll. 4–2; f. 393, op. 43a, d. 1796, ll. 184–90; *GAVO*, f. 399, op. 1, d. 219, ll. 15, 23; f. 399, op. 1, d. 218, ll. 26–27, 52; *VOANPI*, f. 5, op. 1, d. 274, ll. 63–64, 114–18. Road construction represented one of the most formidable tasks. In Vologodskii County, the resettlement operation necessitated the repair or construction of 455 kilometers of roads. (*GAVO*, f. 399, op. 1, d. 182, ll. 80–83.) In Severo-Dvinskii County, it was estimated that up to 600 kilometers of roads were needed, requiring some 153,000 labor days. (*VOANPI*, f. 5, op. 1, d. 274, ll. 114–18.) "Labor days," in this context, represented some combination of the number of workers and the

number of days required. In some places, road construction was described as the crux of the resettlement problem. (*VOANPI*, f. 5, op. 1, d. 277, ll. 36–38.)

36. See *GARF*, f. 393, op. 43a, d. 1796, ll. 2–18; *GAVO*, f. 399, op. 1, d. 182, ll. 5–9. At one point, expenses were estimated at 75 million rubles. (*GARF*, f. 9414, op. 1, d. 1914, l. 115.)

37. *RGAE*, f. 5675, op. 1, d. 23a, ll. 8–26.

38. *GAVO*, f. 395, op. 1, d. 39, l. 7.

39. *GAOPDF AO*, f. 833, op. 1, d. 70, ll. 35–36.

40. *TSD: TsA FSB*, f. 2, op. 8, d. 267, l. 9.

41. *GAOPDF AO*, f. 290, op. 1, d. 379, ll. 2–4, 5–30. For a discussion of regional variations in village population, see V. P. Danilov, "Sel'skoe naselenie soiuza SSR nakanune kollektivizatsii," *Istoricheskie zapiski*, no. 74 (1963): 70–71. The average size of a village population in the Northern Territory was 22 farms. (*GARF*, f. 393, op. 43a, d. 1796, ll. 2–18). The OGPU wanted village populations kept small based on a fear of rebellion. *GARF*, f. 9414, op. 1, d. 1944, l. 99. The fact that most special settlements were far larger than the average peasant village did not seem, inexplicably, to register in the OGPU documents.

42. *GAVO*, f. 399, op. 1, d. 219, ll. 3–9; f. 395, op. 1, d. 39, l. 22; f. 399, op. 1, d. 219, ll. 3–9, 18; *GAOPDF AO*, f. 290, op. 1, d. 379, ll. 4–2; *GARF*, f. 393, op. 43a, d. 1796, ll. 2–18; *VOANPI*, f. 1855, op. 1, d. 86, ll. 32–33.

43. *RGASPI*, f. 17, op. 120, d. 52, ll. 171–74. The actual size of the allotments tended to be far less in reality; moreover, the families faced the daunting task of clearing this land, so that the actual amount under cultivation was far less at least for the first years. See T. I. Slavko, ed., *Kulatskaia ssylka na Urale, 1930–1936* (Moscow, 1995), p. 89, on the issue of the forced economic dependency of the Urals kulaks on industry. (Parenthetically, one could note that the exiled kulaks officially received far larger allotments than the private plots the collective farmers would receive in 1935 after the publication of the Collective Farm Charter. Plot size was between one-quarter and one-half of a hectare, in some regions going up to one hectare [one hectare is equal to 2.47 acres]. See *Istoriia kolkhoznogo prava: Sbornik zakonodatel'nykh materialov SSSR i RSFSR, 1917–1958*, tom 1 [Moscow, 1959], p. 427.)

44. *GARF*, f. 393, op. 43a, d. 1796, ll. 199–201, 203–7; also see ibid., f. 5446, op. 57, d. 13, l. 37.

45. Ibid., f. 393, op. 43a, d. 1796, ll. 208–9.

46. *GAAO*, f. 621, op. 3, d. 19, l. 11.

47. *GARF*, f. 393, op. 43a, d. 1796, ll. 163–64.

48. Ibid., f. 9414, op. 1, d. 1945, ll. 1–2.

49. Ibid., f. 393, op. 43a, d. 1796, ll. 203–6; f. 9479, op. 1, op. 21, l. 22.

50. V. P. Danilov and S. A. Krasil'nikov, eds., *Spetspereselentsy v Zapadnoi Sibiri, 1930–1945*, 4 vols. (Novosibirsk, 1992–96), vol. 1, p. 32.

51. Ibid., vol. 2, pp. 49–53; *GARF*, f. 9479, op. 1, d. 5, ll. 9–11.

52. *GARF*, f. 9414, op. 1, d. 1944, l. 100; f. 9414, op. 1, d. 1945, l. 8. The amount deducted from wages would decrease over time, to 15 percent in August 1931 and to 5 percent in February 1932. Slavko, ed., *Kulatskaia ssylka na Urale*, p. 75.

53. *VOANPI*, f. 1855, op. 1, d. 86, ll. 43–46.

54. Danilov and Krasil'nikov, eds., *Spetspereselentsy v Zapadnoi Sibiri*, vol. 1, p. 175.

55. "*Iz ruk von plokho.*" *GAOPDF AO*, f. 290, op. 1, d. 331, l. 45.

56. *VOANPI*, f. 5, op. 1, d. 275, ll. 1–2.

57. *RGAE*, f. 5675, op. 1, d. 23a, l. 51.

58. *GAVO*, f. 395, op. 1, d. 39, ll. 9–15, 16–21.

59. *GARF*, f. 393, op. 43a, d. 1796, ll. 280–81, 286. A 10 April 1930 Russian Republic Council of People's Commissars decree called on the OGPU to pay for the expenses of the resettlement of native kulaks. Ibid., ll. 230–31.
60. *VOANPI*, f. 5, op. 1, d. 278, ll. 13–14, 35.
61. Ibid., d. 276, l. 28.
62. Ibid., d. 274, ll. 1, 6–8, 15–16, 27–31, 36–39, 63–64, 92–95.
63. Ibid., d. 279, ll. 9–11.
64. Ibid., f. 5, op. 1, d. 277, ll. 28–29.
65. *GAOPDF AO*, f. 290, op. 1, d. 426, ll. 39–56; *GAVO*, f. 399, op. 1, d. 219, l. 172.
66. The Northern Territory soviet estimated that sixty percent of able-bodied settlers were needed for construction work. *GARF*, f. 393, op. 43a, d. 1796, ll. 2–18.
67. *GAVO*, f. 399, op. 1, d. 219, ll. 131–34.
68. *TSD: TsA FSB*, f. 2, op. 8, d. 504, ll. 443–45.
69. *GAOPDF AO*, f. 290, op. 1, d. 380, ll. 34–35.
70. Ibid., f. 833, op. 1, d. 70, ll. 95–96.
71. *RGAE*, f. 5675, op. 1, d. 23a, ll. 96–94; *GAOPDF AO*, f. 290, op. 1, d. 386, l. 25.
72. *GAOPDF AO*, f. 290, op. 1, d. 378, ll. 30–32.
73. *RGAE*, f. 5675, op. 1, d. 23a, ll. 60–59; *GARF*, f. 393, op. 43a, d. 1796, ll. 2–18; *GAAO*, f. 621, op. 3, d. 27, l. 95; f. 621, op. 3, d. 49, ll. 22–25; *GARF*, f. 1235, op. 141, d. 776, ll. 4–1, 13–12, 11–10.
74. *GAOPDF AO*, f. 290, op. 1, d. 378, l. 11.
75. See Lynne Viola, "The Other Archipelago: Kulak Deportations to the North in 1930," *Slavic Review*, vol. 60, no. 4 (2001): 737.
76. *GAVO*, f. 395, op. 1, d. 140, l. 163.
77. *VOANPI*, f. 5, op. 1, d. 278, l. 12; *GAVO*, f. 399, op. 1, d. 219, l. 51.
78. *GAAO*, f. 621, op. 3, d. 49, l. 13.
79. *GARF*, f. 393, op. 43a, d. 1796, ll. 2–18; *GAVO*, f. 399, op. 1, d. 182, l. 223; *VOANPI*, f. 329, op. 1, d. 97, l. 9.
80. *GARF*, f. 9414, op. 1, d. 1944, l. 98.
81. Ibid., f. 9414, op. 1, d. 1944, ll. 128–29, 135; f. 5446, op. 11a, d. 560, l. 5.
82. *GAVO*, f. 399, op. 1, d. 182, l. 105.
83. *GARF*, f. 393, op. 43a, d. 1796, ll. 2–18; *GAAO*, f. 621, op. 3, d. 27, l. 40.
84. *GARF*, f. 393, op. 43a, d. 1796, l. 396.
85. *RGASPI*, f. 17, op. 162, d. 8, l. 173.
86. *GAOPDF AO*, f. 290, op. 1, d. 386, ll. 147–49; Danilov and Krasil'nikov, eds., *Spetspereselentsy v Zapadnoi Sibiri*, vol. 1, p. 32; *GARF*, f. 9414, op. 1, d. 1944, l. 102.
87. Danilov and Krasil'nikov, eds., *Spetspereselentsy v Zapadnoi Sibiri*, vol. 1, pp. 240–42; *VOANPI*, f. 1855, op. 1, d. 10, l. 222; *GARF*, f. 393, op. 43a, d. 1796, ll. 2–18.
88. *GAVO*, f. 395, op. 1, d. 40, ll. 155–59; f. 399, op. 1, d. 182, l. 127; *VOANPI*, f. 5, op. 1, d. 278, l. 12.
89. For examples, see *VOANPI*, f. 5, op. 1, d. 278, ll. 13–14; *GAVO*, f. 399, op. 1, d. 182, l. 127; *TSD: TsA FSB*, f. 2, op. 8, d. 504, ll. 498–507.
90. *GAVO*, f. 395, op. 1, d. 40, ll. 155–56.
91. Ibid., f. 399, op. 1, d. 182, ll. 53, 127; f. 399, op. 1, d. 380, l. 80; *GARF*, f. 393, op. 43a, d. 1798, ll. 239–47; *TSD: TsA FSB*, f. 2, op. 8, d. 204, ll. 368–86; *DGO*, vol. 3, pp. 376–82.
92. *GAVO*, f. 395, op. 1, d. 40, ll. 180–82.
93. *TSD: TsA FSB*, f. 2, op. 8, d. 653, ll. 167–69.
94. *GAOPDF AO*, f. 290, op. 1, d. 380, l. 22.
95. Ibid., d. 426, l. 114; also see ll. 116–21.

96. *GARF*, f. 9414, op. 1, d. 1943, ll. 104–14.

97. Ibid., d. 1944, l. 113; f. 393, op. 43a, d. 1798, ll. 239–47.

98. *VOANPI*, f. 1855, op. 1, d. 86, ll. 43–46; *GARF*, f. 1235, op. 141, d. 463, ll. 9–3; f. 393, op. 43a, d. 1796, l. 118.

99. Initially, families in the Urals were sent directly into the interior. *GARF*, f. 9414, op. 1, d. 1944, ll. 30, 51–60, 126, 135, 139; f. 393, op. 43a, d. 1796, ll. 230–31. *TSD: TsA FSB*, f. 2, op. 8, d. 840, l. 109.

100. E.g., *VOANPI*, f. 5, op. 1, d. 274, ll. 4–18; *GARF*, f. 393, op. 43a, d. 1796, ll. 2–18, 184–90.

101. S. A. Krasil'nikov and O. M. Mamkin, eds., "Vosstanie v Parbigskoi komendature: Leto 1931 g.," *Istoricheskii arkhiv*, no. 3 (1994): 128.

102. *GARF*, f. 9414, op. 1, d. 1943, l. 42.

103. Ibid., f. 393, op. 43a, d. 1796, l. 391.

104. *GAVO*, f. 399, op. 1, d. 182, ll. 33–34; *GARF*, f. 9414, op. 1, d. 1943, l. 72.

105. V. N. Maksheev, ed., *Narymskaia khronika, 1930–1945: Tragediia spetspereselentsev. Dokumenty i vospominaniia* (Moscow, 1997), pp. 18–19.

106. Ibid., pp. 36–37.

107. Ibid., pp. 34–35.

108. *And the Past Seems But a Dream* (Sverdlovsk, 1987), a film based on the stories of the children of Igarki.

109. *GAOPDF AO*, f. 290, op. 1, d. 386, ll. 69–80.

110. *GARF*, f. 9414, op. 1, d. 1944, l. 150.

111. O. A. Nikitina, *Kollektivizatsiia i raskulachivanie v Karelii* (Petrozavodsk, 1997), p. 92; Danilov and Krasil'nikov, eds., *Spetspereselentsy v Zapadnoi Sibiri*, vol. 2, pp. 62–63, 315–16, n. 23; *GARF*, f. 9479, op. 1, d. 11, l. 36.

112. *RGASPI*, f. 17, op. 162, d. 9, l. 38; *GARF*, f. 9414, op. 1, d. 1944, l. 178.

113. *Zabveniiu ne podlezhit. Neizvestnye stranitsy Nizhegorodskoi istorii (1918–1984 gody)* (Nizhnyi Novgorod, 1994), pp. 236–37.

114. Olga Litinenko and James Riordan, eds., *Memories of the Dispossessed: Descendants of Kulak Families Tell Their Stories* (Nottingham, UK: Bramcote Press, 1998), pp. 43–45.

115. Slavko, ed., *Kulatskaia ssylka na Urale*, pp. 155–56.

116. *GAVO*, f. 399, op. 1, d. 219, ll. 259–60.

117. *GARF*, f. 393, op. 43a, d. 1798, l. 224.

118. Slavko, ed., *Kulatskaia ssylka na Urale*, p. 155.

119. *GAAO*, f. 621, op. 3, d. 49, ll. 30–33.

120. *GAOPDF AO*, f. 290, op. 1, d. 426, ll. 116–21.

121. Ibid., f. 833, op. 1, d. 71, l. 37.

122. *GARF*, f. 393, op. 43a, d. 1796, l. 296; *VOANPI*, f. 5, op. 1, d. 277, ll. 36–40.

123. *GAVO*, f. 395, op. 1, d. 40, ll. 157–59.

124. *GAOPDF AO*, f. 290, op. 1, d. 380, ll. 52–71. On the Urals, see V. V. Alekseev and T. I. Slavko, eds., *Raskulachennye spetspereselentsy na Urale (1930–1936 gg.). Sb. dokumentov* (Ekaterinburg, 1993), p. 16.

125. *VOANPI*, f. 5, op. 1, d. 277, ll. 36–40, also see ll. 72–73.

126. *GAVO*, f. 399, op. 1, d. 219, ll. 259–60.

127. *GARF*, f. 9414, op. 1, d. 1943, ll. 104–14.

128. E.g., Maksheev, ed., *Narymskaia khronika*, pp. 17–18; I. E. Plotnikov, "Ssylka krest'ian na Urale v 1930-e gody," *Otechestvennaia istoriia*, no. 1 (1995): 163.

129. *RGASPI*, f. 17, op. 120, d. 52, ll. 20–21; *GAOPDF AO*, f. 290, op. 1, d. 404, ll. 1–3, 43, 64–65; *GARF*, f. 393, op. 43a, d. 1798, ll. 145–46.

Chapter 5

1. T. I. Slavko, ed., *Kulatskaia ssylka na Urale, 1930–1936* (Moscow, 1995), p. 152. (The epigraph is from *Vecherniaia Moskva*, 19 November 1998, p. 6.)
2. *TSD: TsA FSB*, f. 2, op. 9, d. 45, ll. 42–46; *RGASPI*, f. 17, op. 42, d. 23, ll. 72–88.
3. *RGASPI*, f. 17, op. 42, d. 23, ll. 72–88.
4. *GAOPDF AO*, f. 290, op. 1, d. 386, ll. 97–104; Rudol'f Khantalin, *Nevol'niki i bonzy* (Arkhangel'sk, 1998), pp. 61–63.
5. *GARF*, f. 9414, op. 1, d. 1943, ll. 74–75.
6. See V. P. Danilov and S. A. Krasil'nikov, eds., *Spetspereselentsy v Zapadnoi Sibiri*, 4 vols. (Novosibirsk, 1992–96), vol. 1, p. 11, setting the date for the appearance of the term in April/May of 1930; and Sergei Krasil'nikov, *Serp i molokh: Krest'ianskaia ssylka v Zapadnoi Sibiri v 1930-e gody* (Moscow, 2003), p. 23, who sets the date as the beginning of summer 1930.
7. Socialist realism was the official doctrine that guided all Soviet art from 1934. According to the historian Sheila Fitzpatrick, socialist realism represented the "tendency to view the present through the promise of an imagined future." See Sheila Fitzpatrick, "Becoming Cultured: Socialist Realism and the Representation of Privilege and Taste," in *The Cultural Front: Power and Culture in Revolutionary Russia*, ed. Sheila Fitzpatrick (Ithaca: Cornell University Press, 1992), p. 217.
8. *GARF*, f. 393, op. 43a, d. 1797, ll. 120–21. (Tolmachev continued to argue that the use of special settlers as a labor force was secondary to the goal of political isolation and reeducation, an argument that would evaporate by 1931.)
9. N. A. Ivnitskii, "Spetspereselentsy—zhertvy Stalinskikh repressii (1930–1941 gg.)," in *Kniga pamiati zhertv politicheskikh repressii Kalininskoi oblasti*, ed. E. I. Kravtsova et al. (Tver', 2001), vol. 2, p. 406; N. A. Ivnitskii, *Sud'ba raskulachennykh v SSSR* (Moscow, 2004), pp. 112–16; Krasil'nikov, *Serp i molokh*, pp. 71–77; G. F. Dobronozhenko and L. S. Shabalova, eds., *Pokaianie. Komi respublikanskii martirolog zhertv massovykh politicheskikh repressii* (Syktyvkar, 2001), vol. 4 (1), pp. 71–72, 250–54.
10. *GARF*, f. 393, op. 1a, d. 290, ll. 4–7; f. 1235, op. 141, d. 776, ll. 4–1; f. 5446, op. 12, d. 144, l. 124. "Temporary statutes" were in force in the regions. In late April 1930, the Urals Regional soviet executive committee had issued "Thoughts" (*soobrazheniia*) on the administration of the kulak villages and, on 19 June 1930, both the Siberian and Northern soviet executive committees issued temporary statutes on the administration of the settlements. *GARF*, f. 1235, op. 141, d. 786, ll. 19–16; f. 393, op. 43a, d. 1797, ll. 35–36, 81–86; Dobronozhenko and Shabalova, eds., *Pokaianie*, vol. 4 (1), pp. 215–18.
11. On the eve of the war, in 1939, Beria was working on plans to reform the special or labor settlements as they were then called. The plans never went into affect and a new regulation for the settlements only came into being in 1944. See Danilov and Krasil'nikov, eds., *Spetspereselentsy v Zapadnoi Sibiri*, vol. 4, pp. 7–8, 34–35, 42–47.
12. See Lynne Viola, "The Aesthetic of Stalinist Planning and the World of the Special Villages," *Kritika*, vol. 4, no. 1 (winter 2003): 116; *GARF*, f. 9414, op. 1, d. 1944, l. 99; f. 1235, op. 141, d. 776, ll. 13–12; and *GAOPDF AO*, f. 290, op. 1, d. 379, ll. 5–30.
13. Michel Foucault, *Discipline and Punish: The Birth of the Prison*, trans. Alan Sheridan, 2nd ed. (New York: Vintage, 1995), pp. 195–228.
14. The following discussion on the statutes is based on a summary of both the 1930 and 1931 statutes. *GARF*, f. 1235, op. 141, d. 776, ll. 4–1, 11–10; f. 9479, op. 1,

d. 3, ll. 132–39; Danilov and Krasil'nikov, eds., *Spetspereselentsy v Zapadnoi Sibiri*, vol. 2, pp. 68–76; Viola, "The Aesthetic of Stalinist Planning," pp. 118–19.

15. *GARF*, f. 1235, op. 141, d. 776, ll. 4–1, 11–10, 13–12; f. 1235, op. 1, d. 786, ll. 19–16; f. 9414, op. 1, d. 1944, l. 100; f. 9479, op. 1, d. 3, ll. 132–39.

16. Ibid., f. 9414, op. 1, d. 1944, l. 168; *TSD*, vol. 2, pp. 526–29.

17. E.g., *GARF*, f. 1235, op. 141, d. 776, ll. 11–10.

18. Danilov and Krasil'nikov, eds., *Spetspereselentsy v Zapadnoi Sibiri*, vol. 2, pp. 71–72.

19. Ibid., pp. 73–74.

20. *GASO* (*Gosudarstvennyi arkhiv Sverdlovskoi oblasti*), f. 88r, op. 21, ed. khr. 63, ll. 45–79. (I am indebted to Dr. James Harris for sharing several documents with me from this archive.)

21. Danilov and Krasil'nikov, eds., *Spetspereselentsy v Zapadnoi Sibiri*, vol. 2, pp. 70–71.

22. *GARF*, f. 9479, op. 1, d. 5, l. 43.

23. Ibid., f. 9479, op. 1, d. 11, l. 39.

24. Danilov and Krasil'nikov, eds., *Spetspereselentsy v Zapadnoi Sibiri*, vol. 2, pp. 152–58.

25. Ibid., vol. 2, pp. 132–39; *GARF*, f. 1235, op. 141, d. 776, ll. 4–1.

26. *GARF*, f. 9479, op. 1, d. 3, ll. 32–39.

27. Ibid., f. 1235, op. 141, d. 776, ll. 4–1; Danilov and Krasil'nikov, eds., *Spetspereselentsy v Zapadnoi Sibiri*, vol. 2, pp. 132–39.

28. Ibid.; *RGASPI*, f. 17, op. 120, d. 26, l. 232.

29. *GARF*, f. 1235, op. 141, d. 776, ll. 4–1; f. 9479, op. 1, d. 10, l. 47; Danilov and Krasil'nikov, eds., *Spetspereselentsy v Zapadnoi Sibiri*, vol. 2, pp. 68–72; Slavko, ed., *Kulatskaia ssylka na Urale*, p. 75.

30. E.g., Danilov and Krasil'nikov, eds., *Spetspereselentsy v Zapadnoi Sibiri*, vol. 2, p. 70.

31. *DGO*, vol. 3, p. 727.

32. *RGASPI*, f. 17, op. 162, d. 10, ll. 116–18. For more information on the Andreev Commission, see chaps. 1 and 6, and *RGASPI*, f. 17, op. 162, d. 9, ll. 138, 161.

33. Ivnitskii, *Sud'ba raskulachennykh v SSSR*, pp. 198, 210; *GARF*, f. 374, op. 28, d. 4055, l. 2.

34. *DGO*, vol. 3, pp. 601–2; *TSD: TsA FSB*, f. 2, op. 9, d. 20, ll. 52–95; Ivnitskii, *Sud'ba raskulachennykh v SSSR*, chaps. 4 and 5; Krasil'nikov, *Serp i molokh*, p. 15; Slavko, ed., *Kulatskaia ssylka na Urale*, p. 89.

35. Danilov and Krasil'nikov, eds., *Spetspereselentsy v Zapadnoi Sibiri*, vol. 3, p. 13; Slavko, ed., *Kulatskaia ssylka na Urale*, p. 77. (The change in nomenclature was a result of the influx of new categories of exiles, mainly city people, as a result of the urban purges of "social aliens," starting in 1933.)

36. Ivnitskii, *Sud'ba raskulachennykh v SSSR*, p. 219.

37. Danilov and Krasil'nikov, eds., *Spetspereselentsy v Zapadnoi Sibiri*, vol. 2, pp. 42–46.

38. V. V. Alekseev and T. I. Slavko, eds., *Raskulachennye spetspereselentsy na Urale (1930–1936 gg.)* (Ekaterinburg, 1993), p. 40.

39. *GARF*, f. 9479, op. 1, d. 3, ll. 132–39.

40. Danilov and Krasil'nikov, eds., *Spetspereselentsy v Zapadnoi Sibiri*, vol. 2, pp. 42–46; *RGASPI*, f. 17, op. 120, d. 26, l. 323; f. 17, op. 42, d. 23, ll. 17–88; *GARF*, f. 9479, op. 1, d. 2, ll. 28–29.

41. E.g., *GASO*, f. 88r, op. 21, ed. khr. 74a, ll. 92–101; Krasil'nikov, *Serp i molokh*, pp. 135–46.

42. Alekseev and Slavko, eds., *Raskulachennye spetspereselentsy na Urale*, p. 23; *RGASPI*, f. 17, op. 120, d. 26, l. 215.

43. *RGASPI*, f. 17, op. 120, d. 26, l. 217.

44. *GARF*, f. 1235, op. 141, d. 463, ll. 9–3.
45. I. E. Plotnikov, "Ssylka krest'ian na Urale v 1930-e gody," *Otechestvennaia istoriia*, no. 1 (1995): 167–71.
46. V. M. Samosudov and L. V. Rachek, *Sud'by liudskie* (Omsk, 1998), p. 140.
47. John Harder, ed. and trans., *From Kleefeld with Love* (Kitchener, Ontario: Pandora Press, 2003), p. 172. (I am very grateful to my former student, Andrew Harder, who brought this book of his family's letters to my attention.)
48. *RGASPI*, f. 17, op. 120, d. 52, ll. 188–200.
49. *GAVO*, f. 395, op. 1, d. 40, ll. 155–56.
50. *TSD: TsA FSB*, f. 2, op. 9, d. 45, ll. 120–34.
51. Danilov and Krasil'nikov, eds., *Spetspereselentsy v Zapadnoi Sibiri*, vol. 2, p. 57.
52. *RGASPI*, f. 17, op. 120, d. 52, ll. 273–80; see also *TSD: TsA FSB*, f. 2, op. 9, d. 45, ll. 120–34.
53. *GARF*, f. 9479, op. 1, d. 3, ll. 81–85.
54. *RGASPI*, f. 17, op. 120, d. 26, ll. 215–16; also see *TSD: TsA FSB*, f. 2, op. 9, d. 45, ll. 42–46; *GAVO*, f. 399, op. 1, d. 218, l. 73; *GAAO*, f. 621, op. 3, d. 201, l. 103.
55. *RGASPI*, f. 17, op. 42, d. 23, ll. 72–88.
56. *GAOPDF AO*, f. 290, op. 1, d. 947, ll. 172–88; *GARF*, f. 374, op. 28, d. 4055, ll. 21–19. Also see *RGASPI*, f. 17, op. 120, d. 26, ll. 203–8, 214–24; f. 17, op. 120, d. 52, ll. 214–31; *TSD: TsA FSB*, f. 2, op. 9, d. 45, ll. 34–37.
57. *GARF*, f. 1235, op. 141, d. 463, ll. 9–3. In terms of actual purchasing power, a kilogram of flour cost anywhere from 3 to 5 rubles; a kilogram of sugar, 4 to 9; a kilogram of meat, 4.68 to 6.84; a kilogram of fish, 2.69 to 3.14, according to average price variations across the Soviet Union in the first half of 1932. See Elena Osokina, *Our Daily Bread: Socialist Distribution and the Art of Survival in Stalin's Russia, 1927–1941* (Armonk, NY: M. E. Sharpe, 2001), p. 208. (My thanks to Dr. Osokina for a discussion of these issues.)
58. *GARF*, f. 3316, op. 64, d. 1207, l. 2.
59. *TSD: TsA FSB*, f. 2, op. 9, d. 45, ll. 34–37; Dobronozhenko and Shabalova, eds., *Pokaianie*, vol. 4 (1), pp. 63–64.
60. Alekseev and Slavko, eds., *Raskulachennye spetspereselentsy na Urale*, p. 16.
61. V. A. Kozlov et al., eds., *Neizvestnaia Rossiia. XX vek* (Moscow, 1992), vol. 1, p. 231.
62. *GAOPDF AO*, f. 290, op. 1, d. 947, ll. 172–88; *RGASPI*, f. 17, op. 42, d. 23, ll. 72–88; *TSD: TsA FSB*, f. 2, op. 9, d. 45, ll. 120–34.
63. *TSD: TsA FSB*, f. 2, op. 9, d. 45, ll. 120–34.
64. *RGASPI*, f. 17, op. 42, d. 23, ll. 72–88.
65. Ibid., f. 17, op. 120, d. 52, ll. 214–31, 273–80; *TSD: TsA FSB*, f. 2, op. 9, d. 45, ll. 100–105, 120–34; *GARF*, f. 393, op. 43a, d. 1798, ll. 239–47; Dobronozhenko and Shabalova, eds., *Pokaianie*, vol. 4 (1), p. 105.
66. E.g., *GARF*, f. 374, op. 28, d. 4055, l. 31; f. 1235, op. 141, d. 776, ll. 86–83.
67. *RGASPI*, f. 17, op. 42, d. 23, ll. 72–88.
68. Ibid., f. 17, op. 120, d. 52, ll. 188–200. (Underlining in original.)
69. *TSD: TsA FSB*, f. 2, op. 9, d. 539, ll. 293–99.
70. *RGASPI*, f. 17, op. 120, d. 52, ll. 273–80; *TSD: TsA FSB*, f. 2, op. 9, d. 45, ll. 100–105.
71. Krasil'nikov, *Serp i molokh*, pp. 90–91.
72. *GARF*, f. 374, op. 28, d. 4055, ll. 12–2.
73. *RGASPI*, f. 17, op. 120, d. 26, l. 37.
74. Siberia and Kazakhstan were both reluctant to take in deported kulaks in 1930, citing underfunding and lack of preparation. See chaps. 1 and 3. See also *DGO*,

vol. 3, p. 726, where the OGPU writes that the industrial organs viewed the special settlers as a "burden," as well as a "working force without any rights obliged to work irrespective of their living conditions." In 1932 and 1933, as a result of the famine, a series of regional party organizations would again attempt to block the "import" of large numbers of special settler families. See chap. 7.

75. Dobronozhenko and Shabalova, eds., *Pokaianie*, vol. 4 (2), p. 197.

76. *GAVO*, f. 907, op. 5, d. 11, ll. 20–27.

77. V. M. Kirillova, ed., *Kniga pamiati: Posviashchaetsia Tagil'chanam zhertvam repressii 1917–1980-kh godov* (Ekaterinburg, 1994), pp. 48–50. See also Dobronozhenko and Shabalova, eds., *Pokaianie*, vol. 4 (2), p. 199.

78. *RGASPI*, f. 17, op. 42, d. 42, ll. 131–32.

79. S. A. Krasil'nikov, ed., *Marginaly v sotsiume: Marginaly kak sotsium. Sibir' (1920–1930-e gody)* (Novosibirsk, 2004), pp. 356–57.

80. *GARF*, f. 393, op. 43a, d. 1797, l. 6.

81. Ibid., f. 9414, op. 1, d. 1945, l. 5.

82. Ibid., l. 3. (The provincial offices of the Commissariat of Education took charge in cases when special settlers worked exclusively in agriculture.)

83. They did so in 1931 with the aid of a five-million-ruble grant from the government along with what would be a continuing 2-percent wage deduction from the special settlers to cover the cost of "cultural-educational servicing." *GARF*, f. 9414, op. 1, d. 1945, l. 48; S. V. Mironenko and N. Werth, eds., *Istoriia Stalinskogo Gulaga: konets 1920-kh—pervaia polovina 1950-kh godov*, 7 vols. (Moscow, 2004), vol. 5, p. 166.

84. *GARF*, f. 9414, op. 1, d. 1945, ll. 1–2. (Seven-year schools included children from the ages of 7 to 14.)

85. *TSD: TsA FSB*, f. 2, op. 10, d. 379a, ll. 70–91. The statistics on the numbers of children in school are inconsistent and unreliable. On December 1931, a Commissariat of Justice report noted that only 25 percent of children were in school in the Urals, adding that this was the best situation anywhere. *GARF*, f. 3316, op. 64, d. 1207, l. 3.

86. Olga Litinenko and James Riordan, eds., *Memories of the Dispossessed: Descendents of Kulak Families Tell Their Stories* (Nottingham: Bramcote Press, 1998), p. 49.

87. V. N. Maksheev, *Narymskaia khronika, 1930–1945. Tragediia spetspereselentsev. Dokumenty i vospominaniia* (Moscow, 1997), pp. 34–35.

88. Dobronozhenko and Shabalova, eds., *Pokaianie*, vol. 4 (2), p. 201; *GAAO*, f. 621, op. 3, d. 118, ll. 35–30; *GARF*, f. 3316, op. 64, d. 1207, ll. 5–8; f. 9479, op. 1, d. 12, l. 6; *GAOPDF AO*, f. 290, op. 1, d. 1200, ll. 1–26.

89. Mironenko and Werth, eds., *Istoriia Stalinskogo Gulaga*, vol. 5, p. 173.

90. N. N. Pokrovskii, ed., *Politbiuro i krest'ianstvo: Vysylka, Spetsposelenie, 1930–1940*, 2 vols. (Moscow, 2005–6), vol. 1, pp. 693–94.

91. *GARF*, f. 9414, op. 1, d. 1945, l. 2.

92. See Lynne Viola, "'Tear the Evil from the Root': The Children of the *Spetspereselentsy* of the North," *Studia Slavica Finlandensia*, tom. 17 (Helsinki, 2000): 68, nn. 95–96, 100–102.

93. Alekseev and Slavko, eds., *Raskulachennye spetspereselentsy na Urale*, p. 20; *GAOPDF AO*, f. 290, op. 1, d. 1200, ll. 1–26; and Krasil'nikov, *Serp i molokh*, p. 168.

94. *GARF*, f. 9479, op. 1, d. 11, l. 35.

95. Dobronozhenko and Shabalova, eds., *Pokaianie*, vol. 4 (2), pp. 202–3.

96. Alekseev and Slavko, eds., *Raskulachennye spetspereselentsy na Urale*, p. 108; Danilov and Krasil'nikov, eds., *Spetspereselentsy v Zapadnoi Sibiri*, vol. 2, pp. 85–87.

97. *GAAO*, f. 621, op. 3, d. 118, ll. 35–30.

98. Here, twelve of sixteen teachers were special settlers. Ibid., d. 201, ll. 273–67.

99. Dobronozhenko and Shabalova, eds., *Pokaianie*, vol. 4 (2), p. 202.

100. *GAOPDF AO*, f. 290, op. 1 d. 1200, l. 54.

101. In 1935, in the North, some 320 special settler children graduated from middle schools; most were subsequently sent on to teacher training colleges. Dobronozhenko and Shabalova, eds., *Pokaianie*, vol. 4 (2), pp. 202–3. As early as 1934, the Commissariat of Education was calling for the mobilization of the best special settlers for teacher training colleges. Danilov and Krasil'nikov, eds., *Spetspereselentsy v Zapadnoi Sibiri*, vol. 3, p. 57.

102. Dobronozhenko and Shabalova, eds., *Pokaianie*, vol. 4 (2), pp. 236–37; Krasil'nikov, *Serp i molokh*, p. 128.

103. Kirillova, ed., *Kniga pamiati*, p. 136. For a similar description of a commandant with lash always in hand, see Slavko, ed., *Kulatskaia ssylka na Urale*, p. 152.

104. Dobronozhenko and Shabalova, eds., *Pokaianie*, vol. 4 (1), p. 717. The tongue twister, absolutely untranslatable, was as follows:

       Pystin Petr Petrovich poimal ptitsu-perepelitsu,
       polozhil na polovitsu,
       polovitsa prognila,
       ptitsa poletela.

105. Samosudov and Rachek, *Sud'by liudskie*, p. 141.

106. Ibid., p. 140.

107. Dobronozhenko and Shabalova, eds., *Pokaianie*, vol. 4 (2), p. 303.

108. Ivan Tvardovskii, "Stranitsy perezhitogo," *Iunost'*, no. 3 (1988): 17. (The use of the word "comrade" was reserved for the politically pure of heart.)

109. Maksheev, ed., *Narymskaia khronika*, pp. 36–37.

110. Slavko, ed., *Kulatskaia ssylka na Urale*, p. 151.

111. Alekseev and Slavko, eds., *Raskulachennye spetspereselentsy na Urale*, pp. 55–56.

112. Krasil'nikov, *Serp i molokh*, pp. 188, 191–92.

113. *TSD: TsA FSB*, f. 2, op. 8, d. 204, l. 545; *VOANPI*, f. 5, op. 1, d. 276, l. 16.

114. E.g., see *GAAO*, f. 621, op. 3, d. 49, l. 221, for a list of commandants in this region.

115. Krasil'nikov, *Serp i molokh*, pp. 187–88.

116. *GAOPDF AO*, f. 290, op. 1, d. 388, l. 77.

117. Krasil'nikov, *Serp i molokh*, p. 192. See also *GAOPDF AO*, f. 290, op. 1, d. 1200, ll. 25–26; and *GAAO*, f. 621, op. 3, d. 118, l. 82.

118. Krasil'nikov, *Serp i molokh*, p. 173.

119. Plotnikov, "Ssylka krest'ian na Urale v 1930-e gody," p. 161.

120. *VOANPI*, f. 329, op. 1, d. 97, ll. 16–18; *GARF*, f. 1235, op. 141, d. 463, ll. 9–3.

121. Krasil'nikov, *Serp i molokh*, p. 189.

122. Cited in ibid., p. 201.

123. See *GARF*, f. 1235, op. 141, d. 776, ll. 11–10 for the Russian Republic Central Executive Committee-Council of People's Commissars decree laying out the rights and responsibilities of commandants.

124. In Siberia, approximately 10 percent of commandants could expect to be fired or arrested. Krasil'nikov, *Serp i molokh*, p. 189. In the Urals in 1931, forty-eight commandants were arrested; in the first half of 1932, an additional seventeen were arrested and eighty-four fired. See Slavko, ed., *Kulatskaia ssylka na Urale*, pp. 87–88.

125. E.g., *GAOPDF AO*, f. 290, op. 1, d. 1448, l. 21; Alekseev and Slavko, eds., *Raskulachennye spetspereselentsy na Urale*, p. 25; O. V. Artemova, "Spetspereselentsy v Vozhegodskom raione," *Vozhega: Kraevedcheskii al'manakh* (Vologda, 1995), pp. 203–7.

126. Krasil'nikov, *Serp i molokh*, p. 189; *GAOPDF AO*, f. 290, op. 1, d. 426, ll. 116–21; *TSD: TsA FSB*, f. 2, op. 9, d. 45, ll. 120–34.

127. See, for example, J. Arch Getty, *Origins of the Great Purges* (New York: Cambridge University Press, 1985), p. 46; Lynne Viola, *The Best Sons of the Fatherland* (New York: Oxford University Press, 1987), pp. 21, 222, n. 45.

128. *GARF*, f. 9479, op. 1, d. 11, l. 34; f. 3316, op. 64, d. 1207, ll. 3, 7; *TSD: TsA FSB*, f. 2, op. 10, d. 513, ll. 93–103; f. 2, op. 9, d. 45, ll. 120–34; *VOANPI*, f. 5, op. 1, d. 278, l. 17; *GAAO*, f. 621, op. 3, d. 339, ll. 28–27; *GAOPDF AO*, f. 290, op. 1, d. 1448, l. 21; Dobronozhenko and Shabalova, eds., *Pokaianie*, vol. 4 (1), p. 619; Alekseev and Slavko, eds., *Raskulachennye spetspereselentsy na Urale*, p. 25; Plotnikov, "Ssylka krest'ian na Urale v 1930-e gody," pp. 167–71; Maksheev, ed., *Narymskaia khronika*, p. 25; Danilov and Krasil'nikov, eds., *Spetspereselentsy v Zapadnoi Sibiri*, vol. 3, pp. 201–2.

129. *VOANPI*, f. 5, op. 1, d. 278, l. 17; *GAAO*, f. 621, op. 3, d. 49, l. 77; *GAOPDF AO*, f. 290, op. 1, d. 948, ll. 141–42; *TSD: TsA FSB* f. 2, op. 9. d. 45, ll. 120–34; *RGASPI*, f. 17, op. 42, d. 23, ll. 72–88; f. 17, op. 120, d. 26, ll. 214–24; Plotnikov, "Ssylka krest'ian na Urale v 1930-e gody," pp. 167–71; Alekseev and Slavko, eds., *Raskulachennye spetspereselentsy na Urale*, p. 25.

130. *GAAO*, f. 621, op. 3, d. 49, l. 77.

131. *GAOPDF AO*, f. 290, op. 1, d. 948, ll. 63–65.

132. Dobronozhenko and Shabalova, eds., *Pokaianie*, vol. 4 (1), p. 619.

133. *TSD: TsA FSB*, f. 2, op. 9, d. 45, ll. 120–34.

134. *GAOPDF AO*, f. 290, op. 1, d. 1448, l. 21.

135. *GARF*, f. 9479, op. 1, d. 11, l. 34.

136. Danilov and Krasil'nikov, eds., *Spetspereselentsy v Zapadnoi Sibiri*, vol. 3, p. 10. (In fact, it would turn out that the state's "planned loss" was a modest estimate.)

137. *GARF*, f. 9479, op. 1, d. 27, ll. 43–51; Plotnikov, "Ssylka krest'ian na Urale v 1930-e gody," pp. 167–71.

138. Maksheev, ed., *Narymskaia khronika*, p. 76.

139. *RGASPI*, f. 17, op. 42, d. 23, ll. 72–88; *TSD: TsA FSB*, f. 2, op. 9, d. 45, ll. 120–34.

140. Cited in Lynne Viola, *Peasant Rebels Under Stalin: Collectivization and the Culture of Peasant Resistance* (New York: Oxford University Press, 1996), p. 16.

141. Danilov and Krasil'nikov, eds., *Spetspereselentsy v Zapadnoi Sibiri*, vol. 2, pp. 152–58.

142. Plotnikov, "Ssylka krest'ian na Urale v 1930-e gody," pp. 167–71.

143. Danilov and Krasil'nikov, eds., *Spetspereselentsy v Zapadnoi Sibiri*, vol. 1, p. 86.

144. *TSD: TsA FSB*, f. 2, op. 9, d. 45, ll. 120–34.

145. *RGASPI*, f. 17, op. 42, d. 23, ll. 72–88.

146. Kirillova, ed., *Kniga pamiati*, p. 149.

147. *GARF*, f. 1235, op. 141, d. 786, ll. 26–26 ob.

148. E.g., *GAVO*, f. 395, op. 1, d. 40, ll. 180–82; *VOANPI*, f. 5, op. 1, d. 278, l. 35.

Chapter 6

1. *RGASPI*, f. 17, op. 162, d. 10, ll. 51–54. The epigraph is from *GARF*, f. 1235, op. 141, d. 776, l. 6.
2. *RGASPI*, f. 17, op. 120, d. 52, l. 119.
3. Ibid., f. 17, op. 120, d. 52, ll. 188–200.
4. *TSD: TsA FSB*, f. 2, op. 8, d. 35, ll. 30–37.
5. *GARF*, f. 9479, op. 1, d. 1, l. 1; f. 9414, op. 1, d. 1944, l. 110.
6. *TSD: TsA FSB*, f. 2, op. 8, d. 267, ll. 37–38.
7. *GARF*, f. 9414, op. 1, d. 1944, l. 112.
8. In October 1930, a commission was formed to rework special resettlement policies. It included representatives from both the commissariat of internal affairs (Tolmachev) and OGPU (Messing). The documentary opacity of this commission suggests that the commission had little effect. *GARF*, f. 1235, op. 141, d. 776, l. 8.
9. *RGASPI*, f. 17, op. 162, d. 9, l. 138; *GARF*, f. 9414, op. 1, d. 1944, ll. 188, 191; *DGO*, vol. 3, pp. 510–11, 514–15.
10. *RGASPI*, f. 17, op. 162, d. 9, ll. 138, 161. In Andreev's absence, the OGPU was to work through Molotov in its dealings with the Politburo. From October 1931, Rudzutak took over as the chair of the commission.
11. Depending on the source, the statistics for 1931 range from 243,531 to 265,795 families. See *GARF*, f. 374, op. 28, d. 4055, ll. 40–45, 47; and *RGASPI*, f. 17, op. 120, d. 52, l. 59.
12. *GARF*, f. 1235, op. 141, d. 776, l. 59.
13. From the beginning, conflict had existed between the OGPU and the commissariat of internal affairs over the administration of the kulak settlements, a continuation of a long history of institutional rivalry over jurisdiction of prisoners and forced labor. The liquidation of the Tolmachev commission on special resettlement in August 1930 was not coincidental. Tolmachev was the head of the commissariat of internal affairs (through the end of 1930), had devised the system of administration and supervision of the special settlements, and had announced in late May 1930 that the OGPU's role must end once the kulaks arrived at their final destinations from which time the soviet apparatus and the commissariat of internal affairs were to take over. Tolmachev, it should be recalled, had also emerged in April as a critic of the OGPU exile operation in the course of the Bergavinov commission proceedings.
14. *TSD: TsA FSB*, f. 2, op. 8, d. 504, ll. 498–507.
15. Ibid.
16. Ibid.
17. E.g., ibid., f. 2, op. 9, d. 45, ll. 120–34; f. 2, op. 9, d. 539, ll. 293–99; *GARF*, f. 393, op. 43a, d. 1798, ll. 239–47.
18. *GARF*, f. 363, op. 43a, d. 1798, l. 152.
19. Ibid., f. 9414, op. 1, d. 1943, l. 103. Also see *DGO*, vol. 3, pp. 612, 739, 772–73. See *GARF*, f. 9479, op. 1, d. 89, l. 217, for statistics on flight through the 1930s. (According to the February 1931 statistics, among the 33,110 kulaks recaptured, 17,590 were returned to their place of exile and 3,100 were sent on to labor camps.)
20. John A. Harder, ed. and trans., *From Kleefeld with Love* (Kitchener, Ontario: Pandora Press, 2003), p. 123. My thanks to Andrew Harder for sharing this amazing collection of letters with me.
21. *GARF*, f. 9414, op. 1, d. 1943, ll. 56–58.

22. *RGAE*, f. 7486, op. 37, d. 122, ll. 191–90. As of mid-January 1930, there were only eighty-one people working for the OGPU in the entire Northern Region. *GAOPDF AO*, f. 290, op. 1, d. 386, l. 28.

23. *GARF*, f. 9414, op. 1, d. 1943, ll. 56–58; f. 9414, op. 1, d. 1944, ll. 170–72; f. 393, op. 43a, d. 1798, l. 152; *TSD: TsA FSB*, f. 2, op. 8, d. 35, ll. 30–37.

24. T. I. Slavko, ed., *Kulatskaia ssylka na Urale, 1930–1936* (Moscow, 1995), pp. 153–57.

25. V. A. Kozlov, et al., eds., *Neizvestnaia Rossiia. XX vek* (Moscow, 1992), vol. 1, pp. 214–16.

26. *Zabveniiu ne podlezhit. Neizvestnye stranitsy Nizhegorodskoi istorii (1918–1984 gg.)* (Nizhnyi Novgorod, 1994), pp. 236–37.

27. Although Aleksandr was pressured to renounce his family by the Smolensk party organization and later helped them come back to Smolensk, he remained permanently estranged from them. See Denis Kozlov, "The Readers of *Novyi Mir*: Twentieth-Century Experience and Soviet Historical Consciousness" (PhD diss., University of Toronto, 2005), chap. 4.

28. Ivan Tvardovskii, "Stranitsy perezhitogo," *Iunost'*, no. 3 (1988): 10–30. Also see *Vecherniaia Moskva*, 19 November 1998, p. 19. Ivan Tvardovskii died in 2003.

29. A member of a religious sect that had broken away from the Russian Orthodox Church in the late seventeenth century.

30. S. S. Vilenskii et al., eds., *Deti Gulaga, 1918–1956: Dokumenty* (Moscow, 2002), pp. 124–36.

31. For reference to the arrests of visitors, see *GARF*, f. 9479, op. 1, d. 11, l. 79; *GAOPDF AO*, f. 290, op. 1, d. 386, ll. 69–80.

32. *TSD: TsA FSB*, f. 2, op. 8, d. 204, ll. 368–86; *DGO*, vol. 3, pp. 368–96. An exile in the Northern Territory wrote, "The bread we brought with us had been taken and now they give us nothing. We are hungry and tortured. Up to thirty-five souls die a day. Share our letter with all the villagers and write to the newspapers about how we live." *TSD: TsA FSB*, f. 2, op. 8, d. 653, ll. 176–77. An able-bodied settler in the Northern Territory, already at work in the interior, wrote, "Dear spouse [*supruga*], I will write Zina to ask her to get personal documents for me and send them to you" while another warned his brother, "Don't send me personal documents in a letter because they have begun to open letters so one must not put anything in letters." *GAOPDF AO*, f. 390, op. 1, d. 380, l. 21.

33. *TSD: TsA FSB*, f. 2, op. 8, d. 653, ll. 311–26.

34. *GAOPDF AO*, f. 290, op. 1, d. 386, ll. 69–80; *TSD: TsA FSB*, f. 2, op. 8, d. 35, ll. 30–37.

35. *TSD: TsA FSB*, f. 2, op. 8, d. 35, ll. 30–37; *GARF*, f. 9414, op. 1, d. 1944, ll. 170–72. From this time on, the exiles could only receive postcards, telegrams, money, and packages to ease the censor's work. *GARF*, f. 9414, op. 1, d. 1944, l. 171.

36. *GARF*, f. 393, op. 43a, d. 1870, l. 474.

37. Ibid., ll. 4–5.

38. Ibid., d. 1796, l. 117.

39. V. P. Danilov and S. A. Krasil'nikov, eds., *Spetspereselentsy v Zapadnoi Sibiri*, 4 vols. (Novosibirsk, 1992–96), vol. 1, pp. 167–68.

40. *GARF*, f. 393, op. 43a, d. 1796, l. 114.

41. E.g., *RGASPI*, f. 17, op. 120, d. 52, ll. 273–80; *DGO*, vol. 3, pp. 772–73; G. F. Dobronozhenko and L. S. Shabalova, eds., *Spetsposelki v Komi oblasti: Po materialam sploshnogo obsledovaniia. Iiun' 1933 g. Sb. dokumentov.* (Syktyvkar, 1997), p. 16.

42. "Dobrye liudi, podaite khrista radi." Slavko, ed., *Kulatskaia ssylka na Urale*, p. 156. (Also see ibid., pp. 151–53.)

43. I. E. Plotnikov, ed., *Sploshnaia kollektivizatsiia i raskulachivanie v Zaural'e (Materialy po istorii Kurganskoi oblasti)* (Kurgan, 1995), pp. 108–9.

44. *TSD: TsA FSB*, f. 2, op. 8, d. 840, ll. 243–69.

45. Ibid., f. 2, op. 8, d. 653, l. 176.

46. E.g., *GARF*, f. 1235, op. 141, d. 786, ll. 23–22. Also see Barbara Alpern Engel and Anastasia Posadskaya-Vanderbeck, eds., *A Revolution of their Own: Voices of Women in Soviet History* (Boulder: Westview Press, 1998), pp. 28–29.

47. G. F. Dobronozhenko and L. S. Shabalova, eds., *Pokaianie: Komi respublikanskii martirolog zhertv massovykh politicheskikh repressii* (Syktyvkar, 2001), vol. 4 (2), pp. 287–89.

48. *GARF*, f. 1235, op. 141, d. 776, ll. 4–1, 11–10; f. 9479, op. 1, d. 3, ll. 132–39; Danilov and Krasil'nikov, eds., *Spetspereselentsy v Zapadnoi Sibiri*, vol. 2, pp. 68–72.

49. *GARF*, f. 9414, op. 1, d. 1944, l. 168; *TSD*, vol. 2, pp. 526–29.

50. See chap. 2.

51. *TSD: TsA FSB*, f. 2, op. 8, d. 840, ll. 243–69.

52. Ibid., f. 2, op. 10, d. 513, ll. 93–103.

53. Ibid., f. 2 op. 9, d. 45, ll. 120–34.

54. Danilov and Krasil'nikov, eds., *Spetspereselentsy v Zapadnoi Sibiri*, vol. 1, pp. 186–88; *GARF*, f. 9414, op. 1, d. 1944, ll. 111–12; and V. M. Kirillova, *Kniga pamiati: Posviashchaetsia Tagil'chanam zhertvam repressii 1917–1980-kh godov* (Ekaterinburg, 1994), pp. 42–43. (According to an OGPU report of 23 November 1930, 23 percent of Siberian criminal bands were made up of escaped kulaks.)

55. *GARF*, f. 9414, op. 1, d. 1944, ll. 65–66, 154–58; *TSD*, vol. 2, p. 130.

56. *GARF*, f. 393, op. 43a, d. 1796, l. 114.

57. *TSD: TsA FSB*, f. 2, op. 8, d. 504, ll. 454–60.

58. *GARF*, f. 9414, op. 1, d. 1944, ll. 65–66, 154–58; *TSD*, vol. 2, p. 130.

59. *GARF*, f. 9414, op. 1, d. 1944, ll. 164–65.

60. *TSD: TsA FSB*, f. 2, op. 8, d. 35, ll. 30–37.

61. *GARF*, f. 9414, op. 1, d. 1944, ll. 168, 171; *TSD: TsA FSB*, f. 2, op. 8, d. 840, ll. 243–69. (In the Urals, local peasants received thirty rubles for the capture of escapees.)

62. *GARF*, f. 9414, op. 1, d. 1944, ll. 69, 163, 170; *TSD: TsA FSB*, f. 2, op. 8, d. 35, ll. 30–37.

63. In later years, those with escape attempts on their records would be denied legal rehabilitation.

64. By 15 October 1930, the OGPU had recorded 29,035 escapes from the Northern Territory (16,368 recaptured); 6,000 from the Urals (1,365 recaptured); 12,000 from Siberia (3,807 recaptured), 1,400 from Kazakhstan (8 recaptured); and 50 from the Far Eastern Region (12 recaptured). *TSD: TsA FSB*, f. 2, op. 8, d. 329, l. 209.

65. Ibid., f. 2, op. 8, d. 504, ll. 454–56.

66. *GARF*, f. 9414, op. 1, d. 1944, l. 168; *TSD: TsA FSB*, f. 2, op. 8, d. 504, ll. 454–60; *TSD: TsA FSB*, f. 2, op. 8, d. 35, ll. 30–37.

67. *TSD: TsA FSB*, f. 2, op. 10, d. 514, ll. 208–28.

68. Ibid.

69. Ibid., f. 2, op. 8, d. 35, ll. 30–37.

70. Ibid., d. 329, l. 208.

71. Ibid., f. 2, op. 10, d. 514, ll. 208–28.
72. *GARF*, f. 9414, op. 1, d. 1943, l. 103.
73. *TSD: TsA FSB*, f. 2, op. 10, d. 378a, ll. 96–97.
74. *GARF*, f. 9479, op. 1, d. 89, l. 217. The OGPU's statistics for flight from the special settlements were as follows:

	1932	1933	1934	1935	1936	1937	1938	1939	1940
Fled	207,010	215,856	87,617	43,070	26,193	27,809	9,712	7,345	4,430
Captured	37,978	54,211	45,443	33,238	23,075	17,384	10,939	8,290	4,562

The table indicates that in 1938 and 1939, more special settlers were captured than escaped. This seeming anomaly most likely points to the increased activity of the security forces during the "kulak operation" of 1937 (operation 00447) in catching kulaks who escaped in earlier years.

75. On the dangerous social fluidity of these years and its consequences in terms of police repressive activities and elite fears, see Paul M. Hagenloh, "'Socially Harmful Elements' and the Great Terror," in *Stalinism: New Directions*, ed. Sheila Fitzpatrick (London and New York: Routledge, 2000), pp. 286–308; and David Shearer, "Crime and Social Disorder in Stalin's Russia: A Reassessment of the Great Retreat and the Origins of Mass Repression," *Cahiers du Monde Russe*, vol. 39, nos. 1–2 (Jan.–June 1998): 119–48; and Shearer, "Social Disorder, Mass Repression, and the NKVD during the 1930s," in *Stalin's Terror*, ed. Barry McLoughlin and Kevin McDermott (London: Palgrave, 2003), pp. 85–117.

76. *RGASPI*, f. 17, op. 120, d. 26, ll. 214–24.

77. *TSD: TsA FSB*, f. 2, op. 9, d. 45, ll. 120–34.

78. S. A. Krasil'nikov and O. M. Mamkin, "Vosstanie v Parbigskoi komendatura. Leto 1931 g.," *Istoricheskii arkhiv*, no. 3 (1994): 128–38; *RGASPI*, f. 17, op. 120, d. 52, ll. 238–39; *TSD: TsA FSB*, f. 2, op. 10, d. 379a, ll. 10–11, 19–20.

79. *DGO*, vol. 3, pp. 706–8, 832, n. 132.

80. Danilov and Krasil'nikov, eds., *Spetspereselentsy v Zapadnoi Sibiri*, vol. 2, pp. 68–69, 309–10, n. 2; Dobronozhenko and Shabalova, eds., *Pokaianie*, vol. 4 (1), pp. 369–72; and *DGO*, vol. 3, pp. 689–90. At the end of 1932, the OGPU's Gulag administration was divided into two separate sections, one for the administration of the camps and one for the administration of the special settlements, the first under the direction of M. D. Berman, and the second under S. G. Firin. (Danilov and Krasil'nikov, eds., *Spetspereselentsy v Zapadnoi Sibiri*, vol. 3, p. 15.) On 20 April 1933, the Council of People's Commissars enacted a decree changing the nomenclature of Gulag from Glavnoe upravlenie lagerei OGPU (Main Administration of Camps of the OGPU) to Glavnoe upravlenie lagerei i trudovykh poselenii OGPU (Main Administration of the Camps and Labor Settlements of the OGPU). M. D. Berman was the head of Gulag, with deputies Ia. D. Rapoport and S. G. Firin in charge of, respectively, the camps and special/labor settlements. (Danilov and Krasil'nikov, eds., *Spetspereselentsy v Zapadnoi Sibiri*, vol. 3, p. 15.) In 1936, the NKVD (*Narodnyi komissariat vnutrennykh del*, or the People's commissariat of internal affairs, the OGPU's successor) began to transfer the "economic aspects" of administration of the settlers to the provincial administrations, leaving NKVD with the tasks of political administration. In 1938, the settlement commandants were transferred to the jurisdiction of the regular police (*militsiia*). *GARF*, f. 9479, op. 1, d. 47, ll. 1–2, 18, 31.

81. *RGASPI*, f. 17, op. 162, d. 10, l. 126. Exiles of kulaks from national areas would continue according to the directive, and in spite of the directive, exiles would continue from Russian areas of wholesale collectivization: 71,236 people were exiled in 1932; 268,081 in 1933, 111,459 in 1934, 117,270 in 1935, and 77,182 in 1936. See N. A. Ivnitskii, *Sud'ba raskulachennykh v SSSR* (Moscow, 2004), pp. 44–50; and V. N. Zemskov, *Spetsposelentsy v SSSR, 1930–1960* (Moscow, 2003), pp. 20–25.

82. *RGASPI*, f. 17, op. 162, d. 10, ll. 132–33. (Five members of the Central Control Commission were sent to the regions to inspect the special settlements, one each to the Urals, Siberia, the Northern Region, Kazakhstan, and the Far East.)

83. *RGASPI*, f. 17, op. 62, d. 10, ll. 144–48.

84. Ibid., l. 147.

85. Ibid., ll. 154–59,

86. Ibid., ll. 144–48; also see *GARF*, f. 9479, op. 1, d. 5, l. 53 (for Berman's circular on reducing pay deductions).

87. *RGASPI*, f. 17, op. 62, d. 10, ll. 154–59.

88. Ibid.

89. *GARF*, f. 9479, op. 1, d. 7, ll. 5–12. (Rudzutak headed the commission until its apparent demise at the end of 1932. *TSD*, vol. 3, p. 10.)

90. *GARF*, f. 9479, op. 1, d. 6, ll. 7–10; f. 1235, op. 141, d. 776, l. 66; f. 9479, op. 1, d. 2, ll. 38, 40; *GAAO*, f. 621, op. 3, d. 49, ll. 413–14.

91. *GARF*, f. 9414, op. 1, d. 1945, l. 5.

92. Ibid., ll. 1–2.

93. Ibid., l. 48. (See *TSD: TsA FSB*, f. 2, op. 10, d. 379a, ll. 70–91, for further information on the number of special settlers in schools.)

94. *GARF*, f. 9479, op. 1, d. 5, ll. 5–8.

95. *RGASPI*, f. 17, op. 120, d. 52, ll. 119–21, 122–27. (See also *TSD: TsA FSB*, f. 2, op. 9, d. 45, ll. 104–7 for further information on hospitals.)

96. Danilov and Krasil'nikov, eds., *Spetspereselentsy v Zapadnoi Sibiri*, vol. 2, p. 71.

97. *GARF*, f. 9479, op. 1, d. 11, l. 92.

98. *TSD: TsA FSB*, f. 2, op. 10, d. 379a, ll. 70–91.

99. Ibid. ll. 164–65; Danilov and Krasil'nikov, eds., *Spetspereselentsy v Zapadnoi Sibiri*, vol. 2, pp. 62–63, 315–16, n. 23; *GARF*, f. 9479, op. 1, d. 3, ll. 127–28; f. 9479, op. 1, d. 11, l. 27. (See *GARF*, f. 9479, op. 1, d. 11, l. 36 on actual difficulties of finding kulaks in the labor camps in order to reunite them with their families.)

100. *GARF*, f. 9414, op. 1, d. 1944, l. 146; Danilov and Krasil'nikov, eds., *Spetspereselentsy v Zapadnoi Sibiri*, vol. 2, p. 112. Although kulak families that were deemed "incorrectly dekulakized" were supposed to be settled in the exiled regions as "free" citizens, their actual situation was complicated. See chap. 3, n. 59.

101. *GARF*, f. 9479, op. 1, d. 3, ll. 132–39; also in Danilov and Krasil'nikov, eds., *Spetspereselentsy v Zapadnoi Sibiri*, vol. 2, pp. 68–72.

102. *GARF*, f. 3316, op. 64, d. 1207, ll. 2–4; f. 1235, op. 141, d. 776, ll. 76–75.

103. *DGO*, vol. 3, p. 663.

104. Ibid., pp. 689–90.

Chapter 7

1. The epigraph is from T. I. Slavko, ed., *Kulatskaia ssylka na Urale, 1930–1936* (Moscow, 1995), p. 153.

2. G. F. Dobronozhenko and L. S. Shabalova, eds., *Spetsposelki v Komi oblasti. Po materialam sploshnogo obsledovaniia. Iiun' 1933 g. Sb. dokumentov* (Syktyvkar, 1997), p. 259.

3. On the famine, see Robert Conquest, *Harvest of Sorrow: Soviet Collectivization and the Terror-Famine* (Oxford: Oxford University Press, 1986); *TSD*, vol. 3; and, in particular, R. W. Davies and Stephen G. Wheatcroft, *Industrialisation of Soviet Russia: Years of Hunger* (London: Palgrave, 2003).

4. V. V. Alekseev and T. I. Slavko, eds., *Raskulachennye spetspereselentsy na Urale (1930–1936 gg.)* (Ekaterinburg, 1993), p. 157.

5. *TSD: TsA FSB*, f. 2, op. 10, d. 514, ll. 208–28.

6. *GAAO*, f. 621, op. 3, d. 201, l. 261.

7. *GAOPDF AO*, f. 290, op. 1, d. 1446, ll. 20–23.

8. V. P. Danilov and S. A. Krasil'nikov, eds., *Spetspereselentsy v Zapadnoi Sibiri, 1930–1945*, 4 vols. (Novosibirsk, 1992–96), vol. 2, pp. 231–32.

9. *GAAO*, f. 621, op. 3, d. 201, ll. 90–89.

10. For a discussion of the history of denial of the famine (prior to the 1990s), see Conquest, *Harvest of Sorrow*, introduction and epilogue. For discussions of the end of official denial and the beginning of a more accurate documentation, see R. W. Davies, *Soviet History in the Gorbachev Revolution* (Bloomington: Indiana University Press, 1989), pp. 47–58; Hiroshi Okuda, "Recent Rethinking of Collectivization in the Soviet Union," in *Facing Up To the Past: Soviet Historiography under Perestroika*, ed. Takayuki Ito (Sapporo: Hokkaida University, 1989), pp. 177–81; Alec Nove, *Glasnost' in Action* (Boston: Unwin Hyman, 1989), pp. 74–78; Nove, "Victims of Stalinism: How Many?" in *Stalinist Terror: New Perspectives*, ed. J. Arch Getty and Roberta T. Manning (Cambridge: Cambridge University Press, 1993), pp. 261–74; and Stephen G. Wheatcroft, "More Light on the Scale of Repression and Excess Mortality in the Soviet Union in the 1930s," in Getty and Manning, pp. 278–90. One of the very best discussions of the issue of genocide and the famine is in Terry Martin, *The Affirmative Action Empire: Nations and Nationalism in the Soviet Union, 1923–1939* (Ithaca: Cornell University Press, 2001), p. 305.

11. *TSD: TsA FSB*, f. 2, op. 10, d. 379a, ll. 70–91. (Other statistics, from late 1931, for the percentage of completed housing in the Urals are lower. See chap. 5.)

12. Cited in proceedings from the Andreev Commission. N. N. Pokrovskii, ed., *Politbiuro i krest'ianstvo: vysylka, spetsposelenie, 1930–1940*, 2 vols. (Moscow, 2005–6), vol. 1, pp. 411–12.

13. Ibid., pp. 412–13; *RGASPI*, f. 17, op. 42, d. 23, ll. 100–103.

14. Pokrovskii, ed., *Politbiuro i krest'ianstvo*, vol. 1, p. 415.

15. *GARF*, f. 1235, op. 141, d. 776, ll. 76–75.

16. *TSD: TsA FSB*, f. 2, op. 10, d. 379a, ll. 70–91.

17. *RGASPI*, f. 17, op. 42, d. 42, ll. 62–65.

18. Ibid., f. 17, op. 162, d. 11, ll. 167–69.

19. Ibid., f. 17, op. 42, d. 42, ll. 33, 93–96; *GAAO*, f. 621, op. 3, d. 118, ll. 111–81.

20. *RGASPI*, f. 17, op. 162, d. 11, ll. 167–69; f. 17, op. 42, d. 42, l. 33; *GAAO*, f. 621, op. 3, d. 118, l. 77; *GARF*, f. 9479, op. 1, d. 11, ll. 9–10.

21. *RGASPI*, f. 17, op. 42, d. 42, ll. 93–96.

22. Alekseev and Slavko, eds., *Raskulachennye spetspereselentsy na Urale*, pp. 80–81.

23. Ibid., pp. 84–103.

24. *GAAO*, f. 621, op. 3, d. 118, l. 84.

25. *GARF*, f. 5446, op. 14, d. 543, l. 12.

26. Ibid., f. 9479, op. 1, d. 12, l. 16.

27. *RGASPI*, f. 17, op. 162, d. 11, ll. 167–69; *GARF*, f. 9479, op. 1, d. 11, ll. 9–10; *TSD: TsA FSB*, f. 2, op. 10, d. 379a, ll. 39–42; *GAOPDF AO*, f. 290, op. 1, d. 1200, ll. 18–20.

28. *GARF*, f. 9479, op. 1, d. 11, l. 44.
29. Ibid., l. 55.
30. Pokrovskii, ed., *Politbiuro i krest'ianstvo*, vol. 1, pp. 552–53.
31. Ibid., pp. 554–56.
32. Ibid., p. 555.
33. Ibid., pp. 556–58.
34. *TSD*, vol. 2, pp. 844, 868; N. V. Petrov, K. V. Skorkin, N. G. Okhotin, and A. B. Roginskii, eds., *Kto rukovodil NKVD, 1934–1941. Spravochnik* (Moscow, 1999), pp. 94–95. (In 1937, Austrin was first transferred to the Kirovsk NKVD, then arrested and shot. Shiiron simply disappears from the documentary record after his appointment to the Belorussian NKVD in 1937.)
35. *GAAO*, f. 621, op. 3, d. 116, l. 143.
36. Ibid., l. 88.
37. Ibid., l. 143.
38. *GAOPDF AO*, f. 290, op. 1, d. 1196, ll. 114–19.
39. Ibid., f. 290, op. 1, d. 1200, l. 59.
40. Ibid., ll. 60–62.
41. Ibid., l. 63.
42. *RGASPI*, f. 17, op. 42, d. 42, l. 219.
43. *GAOPDF AO*, f. 290, op. 1, d. 1446, ll. 6–7.
44. *GAAO*, f. 621, op. 3, d. 201, ll. 83–81
45. *GAOPDF AO*, f. 290, op. 1, d. 1446, ll. 82–87.
46. *GAAO*, f. 621, op. 3, d. 201, l. 84.
47. Ibid., f. 621, op. 3, d. 201, ll. 93–91.
48. *GAOPDF AO*, f. 290, op. 1, d. 1446, ll. 19–23; *GAAO*, f. 621, op. 3, d 201, ll. 98–94.
49. *GAOPDF AO*, f. 290, op. 1, d. 1446, l. 24–28; *GAAO*, f. 621, op. 3, d. 201, ll. 128–24.
50. *GAOPDF AO*, f. 290, op. 1, d. 1447, ll. 11–16.
51. *GAAO*, f. 621, op. 3, d. 187, l. 86.
52. E.g., ibid., f. 621, op. 3, d. 201, ll. 251–49.
53. *GAOPDF AO*, f. 290, op. 1, d. 1446, ll. 39–43.
54. Ibid., ll. 44–48.
55. *GAAO*, f. 621, op. 3, d. 269, ll. 10–15.
56. *GARF*, f. 9479, op. 1, d. 17, l. 31. See chap. 4 for the official size of the allotments allowed according to a Gulag memo of 7 August 1931. The necessity of "raising" the size of the allotments indicates that the official amounts of land intended for special settlers' allotments had never been fulfilled in the first place.
57. *RGASPI*, f. 17, op. 42, d. 70, l. 65.
58. Ibid., l. 69.
59. V. N. Zemskov, *Spetsposelentsy v SSSR, 1930–1960* (Moscow, 2003), pp. 22–25 (based on statistics from *GARF*, f. 9479, op. 1, d. 89, ll. 206–7). N. A. Ivnitskii has estimated that 51,000 special settlers in the Urals and 26,709 in Western Siberia died in 1933. N. A. Ivnitskii, *Sud'ba raskulachennykh v SSSR* (Moscow, 2004), p. 276.
60. *GARF*, f. 9479, op. 1, d. 89, l. 217. Also see chap. 6.
61. *GAAO*, f. 621, op. 3, d. 198, ll. 189, 187.
62. E.g., ibid., f. 621, op. 3, d. 200, ll. 328–23; *RGAE*, f. 7480, op. 2, d. 1, ll. 41–45; *GAOPDF AO*, f. 290, op. 1, d. 1446, ll. 44–48; *GARF*, f. 9479, op. 1, d. 22, ll. 23–24, 39–49; f. 9479, op. 1, d. 23, ll. 7–11.

63. G. F. Dobronozhenko and L. S. Shabalova, eds., *Pokaianie: Komi Respublikanskii martirolog zhertv massovykh politicheskikh repressii* (Syktyvkar, 2001), vol. 4, book 1, p. 461.

64. Dobronozhenko and Shabalova, eds., *Spetsposelki v Komi oblasti*, p. 259.

65. *TSD: TsA FSB*, f. 2, op. 10, d. 514, ll. 208–28. (On the crisis in Ivanovo-Voznesensk, see Jeffrey J. Rossman, *Worker Resistance Under Stalin: Class and Revolution on the Shop Floor* (Cambridge, MA: Harvard University Press, 2005).

66. E.g., *TSD: TsA FSB*, f. 2, op. 10, d. 513, ll. 163–71.

67. *GAAO*, f. 621, op. 3, d. 187, l. 86; f. 621, op. 3, d. 201, ll. 98–94; *GAOPDF AO*, f. 290, op. 1, d. 1446, ll. 19–23.

68. Slavko, ed., *Kulatskaia ssylka na Urale*, p. 153.

69. S. S. Vilenskii, A. I. Kokurin, G. V. Atmashkina, I. Iu. Novichenko, eds., *Deti GULAGa, 1918–1956* (Moscow, 2002), p. 121.

70. Alekseev and Slavko, eds., *Raskulachennye spetspereselentsy na Urale*, pp. 18–19.

71. Dobronozhenko and Shabalova, eds, *Pokaianie*, p. 437.

72. *GARF*, f. 3316, op. 64, d. 1207, ll. 10–11; *GAAO*, f. 621, op. 3, d. 187, l. 86.

73. *GAOPDF AO*, f. 290, op. 1, d. 947, l. 79.

74. *GAAO*, f. 621, op. 3, d. 200, ll. 328–23; *TSD: TsA FSB*, f. 2, op. 10, d. 514, ll. 208–28.

75. V. N. Maksheev, *Narymskaia khronika, 1930–1945. Tragediia spetspereselentsev. Dokumenty i vospominaniia* (Moscow, 1997), pp. 36–37.

76. Slavko, *Kulatskaia ssylka na Urale*, pp. 161–64.

77. Ibid., pp. 151–53.

78. Maksheev, *Narymskaia khronika*, p. 76.

79. Danilov and Krasil'nikov, eds., *Spetspereselentsy v Zapadnoi Sibiri*, vol. 3, pp. 122–23.

80. Slavko, *Kulatskaia ssylka na Urale*, pp. 151–53.

81. See above; and, e.g., *GARF*, f. 3316, op. 64, d. 1207, ll. 10–11.

82. *GARF*, f. 9479, op. 1, d. 10, l. 1; f. 9479, op. 1, d. 11, l. 43.

83. Ibid., d. ll. 51–52, 92.

84. *GAAO*, f. 621, op. 3, d. 118, l. 42; f. 621, op. 3, d. 100, l. 59; *RGASPI*, f. 17, op. 42, d. 70, ll. 49–51.

85. *GARF*, f. 9479, op. 1, d. 11, ll. 51–52.

86. Ibid., l. 26; *GAOPDF AO*, f. 290, op. 1, d. 1200, ll. 1–26; *RGASPI*, f. 17, op. 162, d. 11, ll. 167–69; *TSD: TsA FSB*, f. 2, op. 10, d. 379a, ll. 39–42; *GAAO*, f. 621, op. 3, d. 118, l. 77.

87. Vilenskii, et al., eds., *Deti GULAGa*, pp. 123–24.

88. *TSD: TsA FSB*, f. 2, op. 10, d. 379a, ll. 70–91.

89. For a history of *besprizornost'*, see Alan M. Ball, *And Now My Soul Is Hardened: Abandoned Children in Soviet Russia, 1918–1930* (Berkeley: University of California Press, 1994).

90. Danilov and Krasil'nikov, eds., *Spetspereselentsy v Zapadnoi Sibiri*, vol. 3, pp. 45–46; *GARF*, f. 9479, op. 1, d. 17, l. 36.

91. Vilenskii, et al., eds., *Deti GULAGa*, p. 123; *GAAO*, f. 621, op. 3, d. 201, ll. 242–47.

92. E.g., Vilenskii, et al., eds., *Deti GULAGa*, p. 161; *GAAO*, f. 621, op. 3, d. 201, ll. 242–37; f. 621, op. 3, d. 187, ll. 137–22.

93. Dobronozhenko and Shabalova, eds., *Pokaianie*, pp. 642–45, 656–58.

94. Ibid., pp. 603–4.

95. *GAOPDF AO*, f. 290, op. 2, d. 38, ll. 14–15.

96. Dobronozhenko and Shabalova, eds., *Spetsposelki v Komi oblasti*, pp. 267–68.

97. Maksheev, *Narymskaia khronika*, pp. 43–44. (*Vozhd'* was a term for the leader, similar to the German, *führer*.)
98. *GARF*, f. 9479, op. 1, d. 24, l. 4.
99. Danilov and Krasil'nikov, eds., *Spetspereselentsy v Zapadnoi Sibiri*, vol. 3, p. 15; Sergei Krasil'nikov, *Serp i molokh: krest'ianskaia ssylka v Zapadnoi Sibiri v 1930-e gody* (Moscow, 2003), pp. 24–25.
100. Zemskov, *Spetsposelentsy v SSSR*, pp. 20–23; *GARF*, f. 9479, op. 1, d. 89, ll. 206–7, 217.
101. Krasil'nikov, *Serp i molokh*, p. 24; *GAOPDF AO*, f. 290, op. 1, d. 1441, ll. 27–36; *TSD: TsA FSB*, f. 2, op. 10, d. 514, ll. 402–6; f. 2, op. 11, d. 1310, ll. 28–29; *RGASPI*, f. 81, op. 3, d. 232, l. 27; f. 17, op. 162, d. 14, ll. 13, 16, 44–45, 48, 51, 64, 99, 108, 124. Also see R. W. Davies, Oleg V. Khlevniuk, E. A. Rees, Liudmila P. Kosheleva, and Larisa A Rogovaya, eds., *The Stalin-Kaganovich Correspondence, 1931–1936*, tr. Steven Shabad (New Haven: Yale University Press, 2003), pp. 10, 291.
102. *TSD*, vol. 3, pp. 746–50.
103. For discussion of the ethnic deportations, see Robert Conquest, *The Nation Killers: The Soviet Deportation of Nationalities* (London: MacMillan, 1970); Terry Martin, *The Affirmative Action Empire: Nations and Nationalism in the Soviet Union, 1923–1939* (Ithaca: Cornell University Press, 2001); Norman M. Naimark, *Fires of Hatred: Ethnic Cleansing in Twentieth-Century Europe* (Cambridge, MA: Harvard University Press, 2001); Aleksandr M. Nekrich, *The Punished Peoples: The Deportation and Tragic Fate of Soviet Minorities at the End of the Second World War*, trans. George Saunders (New York: Norton, 1978); Pavel Polian, *Ne po svoei vole . . . Istoriia i geografiia prinuditel'nyikh migratsii v SSSR* (Moscow, 2001); Amir Weiner, "Nature, Nurture, and Memory in a Socialist Utopia: Delineating the Soviet Socio-Ethnic Body in the Age of Socialism," *American Historical Review*, vol. 104, no. 4 (October 1999).
104. V. N. Khaustov, V. P. Naumov, N. S. Plotnikova, eds., *Lubianka: Stalin i VChK-GPU-OGPU-NKVD. Ianvar' 1922–dekabr' 1936* (Moscow, 2003), p. 406 (see Stalin's handwritten comments on Iagoda's 1933 report); Krasil'nikov, *Serp i molokh*, pp. 95–96.
105. Pokrovskii, ed., *Politbiuro i krest'ianstvo*, vol. 1, pp. 575–76.
106. Krasil'nikov, *Serp i molokh*, pp. 95–96, 106–7. See his discussion of the statistics on exiles in 1933. Iagoda's plan to deport an additional two million new exiles is in Khaustov, et al., eds., *Lubianka: Stalin i VChK-GPU-OGPU-NKVD. Ianvar' 1922–dekabr' 1936*, pp. 398–406.
107. Oleg Khlevniuk writes: "In late 1932 and early 1933 the OGPU leadership secured the government's approval of new plans for development of the Gulag. These plans called for the special settlements in particular . . . to be turned into the foundation of the Gulag." The plans collapsed, however, as a result of the crisis in resources, especially during the famine. In consequence, the labor camps became the foundation of the Gulag from 1933. See Oleg Khlevniuk, "The Economy of the Gulag," in *Behind the Facade of Stalin's Command Economy*, ed. Paul R. Gregory (Stanford, CA: Hoover Institution Press, 2001), p. 116.

Chapter 8

1. The epigraph is from Veronique Garros, Natalia Korenevskaya, and Thomas Lahusen, eds., *Intimacy and Terror*, trans. Carol A. Flath (New York: New Press, 1995), p. 158 (For the reference to Arzhilovskii as a special settler, see A. A. Petrushin, ed., *My ne znaem poshchady* [Tiumen, 1999], pp. 149–60.)

2. Although the official terminology had changed to "labor settlers," I shall continue to employ the term "special settlers" in order to distinguish kulak settlers from the increasing numbers of other categories joining the labor settlements.

3. *GARF*, f. 9479, op. 1, d. 29, l. 10. The May 1934 decree is in ibid., f. 3316, op. 64, d. 1221, ll. 4–5.

4. Ibid., f. 9479, op. 1, d. 29, ll. 12–14. See also S. A. Krasil'nikov, ed., *Marginaly v sotsiume: Marginaly kak sotsium. Sibir' (1920–1930-e gody)* (Novosibirsk, 2004), p. 306.

5. Oleg V. Khlevniuk, *The History of the Gulag*, trans. Vadim Staklo (New Haven: Yale University Press, 2004), p. 131.

6. *GARF*, f. 9479, op. 1, d. 25, l. 1.

7. Ibid., d. 54, ll. 1–2.

8. Ibid., d. 89, ll. 205, 216 (data for 1 January); and N. A. Ivnitskii, *Sud'ba raskulachennykh v SSSR* (Moscow, 2004), p. 143. Data from 1 September 1936 gives the figure of 1,845 special settlements with a population of 979,017 people (278,700 families). This document also indicates that an additional 77,616 rehabilitated kulaks were still living in the settlements, thus bringing the total to 1,056,633. See N. N. Pokrovskii, ed., *Politbiuro i krest'ianstvo: vysylka, spetsposelenie, 1930–1940*, 2 vols. (Moscow, 2005–6), vol. 2, forthcoming: P-383, 31 October 1936.

9. *GARF*, f. 9479, op. 1, d. 89, l. 216.

10. Ibid., l. 217.

11. Ibid., ll. 211, 216.

12. Ibid., d. 29, ll. 58–60.

13. A pud is a Russian measure, equal to approximately 16.38 kilograms or 36 pounds.

14. *GARF*, f. 9479, op. 1, d. 30, ll. 18–25; also see ibid., d. 29, ll. 61–63 for similar requests from Iagoda that would have freed special settlers living in unchartered agricultural collectives from state requisitions for two to three years and extended debt repayment to the end of 1937 for those exiled in 1930–31.

15. *GAOPDF AO*, f. 290, op. 2, d. 59, ll. 13–15.

16. *GAAO*, f. 621, op. 3, d. 269, ll. 118–13.

17. Ibid., ll. 81–77; *GARF*, f. 9479, op. 1, d. 22, ll. 14–15.

18. *GAAO*, f. 621, op. 3, d. 269, ll. 81–77; *GARF*, f. 9479, op. 1, d. 29, ll. 58–60, 64–65.

19. *GARF*, f. 9479, op. 1, d. 29, ll. 12–13.

20. Ibid., l. 59. For further information on these deportations, see Terry Martin, *The Affirmative Action Empire: Nations and Nationalism in the Soviet Union, 1923–1939* (Ithaca: Cornell University Press, 2001), pp. 296–307.

21. *GAAO*, f. 621, op. 3, d. 269, ll. 81–77.

22. *GARF*, f. 9479, op. 1, d. 27, ll. 2–3. (The Sverdlovsk Region was a newly organized administrative-territorial zone within what was formerly designated the Urals Region.)

23. Ibid., d. 29, ll. 2–6; d. 22, ll. 39–49. Also see V. N. Zemskov, *Spetsposelentsy v SSSR, 1930–1960* (Moscow, 2003), p. 34.

24. *GARF*, f. 9479, op. 1, d. 22, ll. 23–24.

25. *GAAO*, f. 621, op. 3, d. 269, ll. 122–24.

26. Ibid., d. 342, ll. 14, 19; d. 270, l. 24; d. 268, ll. 1–3, d. 204, l. 1.

27. *GARF*, f. 9479, op. 1, d. 27, ll. 24–26.

28. Ibid., d. 35, l. 23.

29. Ibid., d. 29, l. 60.

30. Ibid., f. 5446, op. 18a, d. 620, ll. 1–3, 12–15, 22. See also S. A. Krasil'nikov, *Serp i molokh: Krest'ianskaia ssylka v Zapadnoi Sibiri v 1930-e gody* (Novosibirsk, 2003), pp. 183–84.

31. *GARF*, f. 9479, op. 1, d. 35, l. 23. Eikhe's letter is published (in English) in full in Khlevniuk, *History of the Gulag*, pp. 132–34.

32. Krasil'nikov, *Serp i molokh*, pp. 183–84. (I thank Sergei Krasil'nikov for clarifying some aspects of these attempts in an e-mail of 19 October 2004.)

33. *RGASPI*, f. 17, op. 162, d. 10, ll. 53–54.

34. *GARF*, f. 9479, op. 1, d. 2, l. 19.

35. *RGASPI*, f. 17, op. 162, d. 10, ll. 154–59. (This was a part of Iagoda's attempts to stem escapes and tie down the special settlers to their places of exile. See ibid., ll. 144–48.)

36. R. W. Davies, Oleg V. Khlevniuk, and E. A. Rees, eds., *The Stalin-Kaganovich Correspondence, 1931–1936*, trans. Steven Shabad (New Haven: Yale University Press, 2003), p. 69. From the Russian edition, Oleg V. Khlevniuk, R. W. Davies, L. P. Kosheleva, E. A. Rees, L. A. Rogovaia, eds., *Stalin i Kaganovich: Perepiska, 1931–1936 gg.* (Moscow, 2001), pp. 72–73.

37. Alexander I. Solzhenitsyn, *The Gulag Archipelago*, trans. Thomas P. Whitney and Harry Willets, 3 vols. (New York: Harper and Row, 1973), vol. 3, p. 359.

38. In 1935, at a conference of combine-harvester operatives, Stalin uttered his now-famous quote, "A son is not responsible for his father," while discussing plans for a new constitution. See Davies et als., eds. *Stalin-Kaganovich Correspondence*, p. 295.

39. *DGO*, vol. 3, pp. 725–29.

40. *GARF*, f. 393, op. 43a, d. 1798, l. 213; Krasil'nikov, *Serp i molokh*, p. 128. In the Urals, between January and March 1932, there were twenty-three cases of special settlers marrying "free" citizens. See V. V. Alekseev and T. I. Slavko, eds., *Raskulachennye spetspereselentsy na Urale (1930–1936 gg.). Sb. dokumentov* (Ekaterinburg, 1993), pp. 106–29. See T. I. Slavko, ed., *Kulatskaia ssylka na Urale, 1930–1936* (Moscow, 1995), p. 144, who writes that male special settlers who married free citizens were subsequently freed, while female special settlers who married free citizens were not. See V. P. Danilov and S. A. Krasil'nikov, eds., *Spetspereselentsy v Zapadnoi Sibiri*, 4 vols. (Novosibirsk, 1992–96), vol. 2, pp. 60–61 for the August 1931 Gulag administration circular on marriages.

41. Pokrovskii, ed., *Politbiuro i krest'ianstvo*, vol. 1, pp. 498–500.

42. Danilov and Krasil'nikov, eds., *Spetspereselentsy v Zapadnoi Sibiri*, vol. 2, p. 310, n. 3.

43. Ibid.; and *GARF*, f. 9479, op. 1, d. 13, l. 4.

44. *GARF*, f. 9479, op. 1, d. 11, ll. 76–78.

45. Danilov and Krasil'nikov, eds., *Spetspereselentsy v Zapadnoi Sibiri*, vol. 3, p. 14.

46. *GARF*, f. 9479, op. 1, d. 17, l. 32.

47. Golfo Alexopoulos, *Stalin's Outcasts: Aliens, Citizens, and the Soviet State, 1926–1936* (Ithaca: Cornell University Press, 2003), p. 148.

48. *GARF*, f. 3316, op. 64, d. 1221, ll. 4–5.

49. Ibid., f. 9479, op. 1, d. 29, ll. 12–13.

50. Ibid., d. 943, ll. 75–79; d. 57, l. 42. (From December 1932, all Soviet citizens, with the exception of the collective farm peasantry, were forced to carry internal passports.)

51. Danilov and Krasil'nikov, eds., *Spetspereselentsy v Zapadnoi Sibiri*, vol. 2, p. 112.

52. *GARF*, f. 9479, op. 1, d. 17, l. 32.

53. Danilov and Krasil'nikov, eds., *Spetspereselentsy v Zapadnoi Sibiri*, vol. 4, pp. 51–55. (In some places, they were even allowed to join the collective farms.)

54. *GARF*, f. 9479, op. 1, d. 25, l. 1.

55. Ivnitskii, *Sud'ba raskulachennykh v SSSR*, p. 141. See also Khlevniuk, *History of the Gulag*, p. 138, for instances in which escaped special settlers could be treated more leniently.

56. Zemskov, *Spetsposelentsy*, p. 64. The data on rehabilitation varies. See also *GARF*, f. 9479, op. 1, d. 62, ll. 6–7; d. 59, ll. 1–3. (Note the new designations for regions within the Urals and Siberia, following a reshuffling of some administrative-territorial zones.)

57. *GARF*, f. 9479, op. 1, d. 10, l. 4.

58. *GAAO*, f. 621, op. 3, d. 392, l. 236.

59. See the discussion in Sheila Fitzpatrick, *The Russian Revolution*, 2nd ed. (New York: Oxford University Press, 1994), pp. 154–56.

60. *TSD*, vol. 5 (book 1), pp. 84–86.

61. Ibid., p. 83.

62. Danilov and Krasil'nikov, eds., *Spetspereselentsy v Zapadnoi Sibiri*, vol. 4, pp. 166–67.

63. *TSD*, vol. 5 (1), pp. 80–81.

64. *GARF*, f. 9479, op. 1, d. 89, l. 217.

65. Alekseev and Slavko, eds., *Raskulachennye spetspereselentsy na Urale*, p. 202.

66. Such passports were then marked with residence restrictions. See *GARF*, f. 9479, op. 1, d. 54, l. 22; d. 57, ll. 42–43; Danilov and Krasil'nikov, eds., *Spetspereselentsy v Zapadnoi Sibiri*, vol. 4, pp. 4, 17.

67. Danilov and Krasil'nikov, eds., *Spetspereselentsy v Zapadnoi Sibiri*, vol. 3, pp. 70–72.

68. *GARF*, f. 9479, op. 1, d. 54, ll. 1–2.

69. V. N. Maksheev, ed., *Narymskaia khronika, 1930–1945. Tragediia spetspereselent-sev. Dokumenty i vospominaniia* (Moscow, 1997), pp. 36–37.

70. V. A. Kozlov et al., eds., *Neizvestnaia Rossiia. XX vek. Arkhivy, pis'ma, memuary* (Moscow, 1992), vol. 1, pp. 214–16.

71. *And the Past Seems But a Dream* (Sverdlovsk, 1987), a film based on the stories of the children of Igarki.

72. *Kotlovan (Khibinskoe obshchestvo "Memorial")*, March 1991, p. 8. (My thanks to Kathleen Smith for very kindly sharing this source with me.) During the Khrushchev years and the first rehabilitations of the terror's victims, officials routinely gave families false information about the fate of their relatives. Officials withheld the true date of death and did not disclose if a person had been executed. See R. W. Davies, *Soviet History in the Yeltsin Era* (New York: St. Martin's Press, 1997), pp. 160–61; and Kathleen E. Smith, *Remembering Stalin's Victims: Popular Memory and the End of the USSR* (Ithaca: Cornell University Press, 1996), p. 136.

73. J. Arch Getty and Oleg V. Naumov, eds., *The Road to Terror: Stalin and the Self-Destruction of the Bolsheviks, 1932–1939* (New Haven: Yale University Press, 1999), pp. 588, 590 (from *GARF*, f. 9401, op.1, d. 4157, ll. 201–5.) It is important to note that these figures pertain only to the work of the troikas, excluding the arrests and sentencing that came through the courts and other legal institutions. For a discussion, see Stephen G. Wheatcroft, "Victims of Stalinism and the Soviet Secret Police: The Comparability and Reliability of the Archival Data—Not the Last Word," *Europe-Asia Studies*, vol. 51, no. 2 (1999): 315–45, who gives a total of 686,000 executions and 1,365,000 camp and prison sentences in these two years once the sentences from other institutions are added in (p. 327). (My thanks to Professor Wheatcroft for discussing these data with me.) For statistics on the camp population, see Khlevniuk, *History of the Gulag*, pp. 178–79, 328. He indicates a population of 1,126,000 prisoners in labor camps on 1 February 1938. By 1 January 1939, 1,317,195 were in the camps, 355,243 in labor colonies, and 352,508 in prisons. Khlevniuk sees these figures as incomplete, suggesting they are at most minimal.

74. The order was first published in *Trud*, 4 June 1992. See also *TSD*, vol. 5 (book 1), pp. 330–37.

75. See Robert C. Tucker and Stephen F. Cohen, eds., *The Great Purge Trial* (New York: Grosset and Dunlap, 1965). See also Ezhov's accusations against the former Right Opposition at the February 1937 Central Committee Plenum. L. P. Kosheleva, O. V. Naumov, and L. A. Rogovaia, eds., "Materialy fevral'sko-martovskogo plenuma TsK VKP (b) 1937 goda," *Voprosy istorii*, nos. 4–5 (1992): 5, 14–15.

76. *Molotov Remembers: Inside Kremlin Politics. Conversations with Felix Chuev* (Chicago: Ivan R. Dee, 1991), p. 254.

77. Lynne Viola, *Peasant Rebels Under Stalin: Collectivization and the Culture of Peasant Resistance* (New York: Oxford University Press, 1996), p. 80.

78. The total number of escapes in the years between 1932 and 1940 was 629,042 (of which 235,140 were caught and returned). *TSD*, vol. 5 (book 1), p. 15. (Data is calculated from *GARF*, f. 9479, op. 1, d. 89, l. 217.)

79. The upcoming elections for the USSR Supreme Soviet also may have served as a stimulus to the terror since the Stalin constitution had given the franchise to an army of former enemies. Some scholars speculate that the great terror may have been at least partially motivated by the need to ensure that these "enemies" never actually exercised their right to vote. Getty and Naumov, eds., *Road to Terror*, pp. 468–69; Marc Jansen and Nikita Petrov, *Stalin's Loyal Executioner: People's Commissar Nikolai Ezhov, 1895–1940* (Stanford: Hoover Institution Press, 2002), pp. 106–8.

80. Some historians suggest that Iagoda was under suspicion since the 1934 assassination of Kirov and may even have attempted to mitigate some of the attacks on former oppositionists. See Getty and Naumov, eds., *Road to Terror*, pp. 274–76; and Robert Conquest, *The Great Terror: Stalin's Purge of the Thirties* (New York: Collier, 1973), pp. 217–19. The most interesting and persuasive discussion of Iagoda's fall is in David Shearer, *Policing Stalin's Socialism: Social Order and Mass Repression in the Soviet Union, 1928–1953* (Ithaca: Cornell University Press, forthcoming), chap. 9. Also see what Molotov had to say about Iagoda in *Molotov Remembers*, pp. 257–58, where he calls him a "filthy nobody" and a "reptile."

81. See the discussion in Getty and Naumov, eds., *Road to Terror*, pp. 491–92.

82. *TSD*, vol. 5 (book 1), pp. 256–58.

83. According to Getty and Naumov, the troikas handed down 87 percent of all criminal sentences in 1937, and 75 percent in 1938. The troikas were responsible for 92.6 percent of all executions in 1937 and 1938. Getty and Naumov, eds., *Road to Terror*, pp. 469–70.

84. *TSD*, vol. 5 (book 1), p. 319.

85. Ibid.

86. Ibid., pp. 328–29.

87. Ibid., p. 330.

88. Ibid., p. 334.

89. Ibid., pp. 331–33.

90. Ibid., pp. 330–31.

91. Ibid., p. 331.

92. Getty and Naumov, eds., *Road to Terror*, pp. 478–79.

93. Zemskov, *Spetsposelentsy v SSSR*, pp. 20–21, presents data for the population of kulaks in the special villages on 1 January 1937 (916,787) and 1 January 1938 (877,651). These figures do not include rehabilitated special settlers. If we add them to these figures, the total for 1937 is 1,053,137 and for 1938, 1,010,749. See ibid., pp. 19, 60.

94. This did not mean that the special settlements would disappear. They would continue to serve as a place of isolation for suspect categories of the population in cases when entire families were involved. Furthermore, the labor camps would prove to be almost as costly and economically ineffective as the special settlements. See Oleg Khlevnyuk, "The Economy of the OGPU, NKVD, and MVD of the USSR, 1930–1953," in *The Economics of Forced Labor: The Soviet Gulag*, ed. Paul R. Gregory and Valery Lazarev (Stanford: Hoover, 2003), pp. 54–56, 59–66.

95. By January 1938, the NKVD could boast of a total of 573,541 arrests. which yielded 553,362 convictions—far higher numbers than those in the original 00447 quotas. The total convictions were in turn divided between category 1 (239,252) and category 2 (314,110). Roughly 44 percent of each category (105,124 and 138,588) was made up of "kulaks." *TSD*, vol. 5 (book 1), p. 393. The data is necessarily incomplete given that the operation continued well beyond its original term of four months. (Khlevniuk, *History of the Gulag*, p. 162.) Moreover, the term kulak continued to be an arbitrary designation. Nevertheless, these data offer an accurate picture of the high proportion of officially designated kulaks among the repressed. The total percentage of officially designated kulaks would in fact grow among the 00447 contingents as the overall numbers of all categories arrested increased in later months to as many as 700,000. *TSD*, vol. 5, book 2, forthcoming. (From a total of 699,929 people arrested in operation 00447, 376,206 were cited as "kulaks" as of July of 1938. The total percentage of kulaks thus grew to roughly 54 percent.)

96. For data on the numbers arrested from within the camps (14,600), see *TSD*, vol. 5, book 1, p. 393.

97. Zemskov, *Spetsposelentsy v SSSR*, pp. 20–21, 60. (17,385 special settlers were convicted in 1937 and 28,830 in 1938.)

98. Ibid., p. 55; *GARF*, f. 9479, op. 1, d. 54, ll. 4–12. Also see *TSD*, vol. 5, book 1, for information on the purges in the agricultural and forestry commissariats, which were also hit hard, though somewhat earlier.

Chapter 9

1. *TSD: TsA FSB*, f. 2, op. 10, d. 514, ll. 208–28. The epigraph is from V. M. Kirillova, ed., *Kniga pamiati. Posviashchaetsia Tagil'chanam zhertvam repressii 1917–1980-kh godov* (Ekaterinburg, 1994), p. 122.

2. *TSD: TsA FSB*, f. 2, op. 10, d. 514, ll. 208–28.

3. *Molotov Remembers: Inside Kremlin Politics. Conversations with Felix Chuev* (Chicago: Ivan R. Dee, 1991), p. 254.

4. *GARF*, f. 9479, op. 1, d. 77, ll. 221–34; d. 113, l. 33; V. P. Danilov and S. A. Krasil'nikov, eds., *Spetspereselentsy v Zapadnoi Sibiri*, 4 vols. (Novosibirsk, 1992–96), vol. 4, pp. 179–82, 202–5.

5. Oleg V. Khlevniuk, *The History of the Gulag*, trans. Vadim Staklo (New Haven: Yale University Press, 2004), pp. 273, 328.

6. Ibid., pp. 273, 320; and Norman Naimark, *Fires of Hatred: Ethnic Cleansing in Twentieth-Century Europe* (Cambridge, MA: Harvard University Press, 2001), chap. 3. For a thorough discussion and analysis of the prewar ethnic deportations, see Terry Martin, *The Affirmative Action Empire: Nations and Nationalism in the Soviet Union, 1923–1939* (Ithaca: Cornell University Press, 2001), p. 311.

7. Danilov and Krasil'nikov, eds., *Spetspereselentsy v Zapadnoi Sibiri*, vol. 4, p. 40.

8. (Rulings of 22 October 1938 and 19 February 1939). Ibid., pp. 4, 17, 45–47. Passports were marked *goden dlia prozhivaniia v takom-to raione* (intended for residence in a given district).

9. *GARF*, f. 9479, op. 1, d. 33, ll. 4–5. Elderly "invalids" without family were transferred to special settler invalid homes. A 5 February 1937 report from Northern NKVD chief Austrin described what he called the "outrages" in such homes in the North. He reported outbreaks of lice among residents, noting that many had no change of underwear or bed linens. Only 15–20 percent had any outer clothes, leaving the rest to walk around half dressed. Residents received only 200 grams of bread per day (vs. the suggested norm of 600 grams), and ate out of jars because there were no dishes. *GAAO*, f. 621, op. 3, d. 412, l. 11.

10. This was most notably the case in the agricultural sectors. *GARF*, f. 9479, op. 1, d. 47, ll. 1–2, 31.

11. Danilov and Krasil'nikov, eds., *Spetspereselentsy v Zapadnoi Sibiri*, vol. 4, pp. 7, 42–47.

12. Khlevniuk, *History of the Gulag*, pp. 272, 320. (The population in 1939 was 988,000; in 1940, 998,000.) These figures do not include nonkulak categories of inhabitants in the special settlements. Also see *GARF*, f. 9479, op. 1, d. 47, ll. 12–22; Danilov and Krasil'nikov, eds., *Spetspereselentsy v Zapadnoi Sibiri*, vol. 4, pp. 42–44.

13. *GARF*, f. 9479, op. 1, d. 65, l. 209; *GAOPDF*, f. 296, op. 1, d. 749, l. 14; Danilov and Krasil'nikov, eds., *Spetspereselentsy v Zapadnoi Sibiri*, vol. 4, p. 57.

14. Danilov and Krasil'nikov, eds., *Spetspereselentsy v Zapadnoi Sibiri*, vol. 4, p. 31.

15. Khlevniuk, *History of the Gulag*, pp. 270–71.

16. Danilov and Krasil'nikov, eds., *Spetspereselentsy v Zapadnoi Sibiri*, vol. 4, p. 108.

17. *GARF*, f. 9479, op. 1, d. 949, l. 78; d. 113, l. 48. (According to the NKVD, 100,000 special settlers were eligible to be drafted. Ibid., d. 949, ll. 1–2; d. 113, ll. 1. 48. The regime first called for 35,000 special settlers, aged eighteen to forty, to be drafted; then in July, the figure rose to 50,000. Danilov and Krasil'nikov, eds., *Spetspereselentsy v Zapadnoi Sibiri*, vol. 4, pp. 112–14, 137–38. At about this same time, the regime halted the military recruitment of all Chechens and Ingush, "enemy nations" now subject to wholesale deportation. See Naimark, *Fires of Hatred*, p. 94.)

18. *GARF*, f. 9479, op. 1, d. 11, l. 39; Danilov and Krasil'nikov, eds., *Spetspereselentsy v Zapadnoi Sibiri*, vol. 4, pp. 23–24. (Rehabilitated kulaks were eligible to be conscripted.)

19. Danilov and Krasil'nikov, eds., *Spetspereselentsy v Zapadnoi Sibiri*, vol. 4, pp. 137–38.

20. Ibid., p. 115; *GARF*, f. 9479, op. 1, d. 113, ll. 190, 192.

21. G. F. Dobronozhenko and L. S. Shabalova, eds., *Pokaianie: Komi respublikanskii martirolog zhertv massovykh politicheskikh repressii* (Syktyvkar, 2001), vol. 4 (2), p. 197.

22. See the brilliant discussion of this problematic in Amir Weiner, "Nature, Nurture, and Memory in a Socialist Utopia: Delineating the Soviet Socio-Ethnic Body in the Age of Socialism," *American Historical Review*, vol. 104, no. 4 (Oct. 1999): 1114–155.

23. N. A. Ivnitskii, *Sud'ba raskulachennyh v SSSR* (Moscow, 2004), pp. 281–82. (The statistics are for 1937, the latest date for which they are available.)

24. Prior to this, from 1936, only individuals among the special settler youth had succeeded in earning that privilege. By this time, special settler children were also permitted to form Pioneer organizations in their schools and could apply for permission to join the Komsomol. S. A. Krasil'nikov, ed., *Marginaly v sotsiume: Marginaly kak sotsium* (Novosibirsk, 2004), pp. 307–8; Danilov and Krasil'nikov, eds., *Spetspereselentsy v Zapadnoi Sibiri*, vol. 4, p. 4; *GAOPDF AO*, f. 296, op. 1, d. 468, ll. 39–41.

25. *GAOPDF AO*, f. 296, op. 1, d. 542, l. 51.
26. Dobronozhenko and Shabalova, eds., *Pokaianie*, vol. 4 (1), p. 729.
27. Kirillova, ed., *Kniga pamiati*, pp. 118–34.
28. Ibid.
29. S. S. Vilenskii et al., eds., *Deti Gulaga, 1918–1956: Dokumenty* (Moscow, 2002), p. 161.
30. Lewis Siegelbawm and Andrei Sokolov, eds., *Stalinism as a Way of Life*, trans. Thomas Hoisington and Steven Shabad (New Haven: Yale University Press, 2000), pp. 408–9.
31. Ibid., p. 403.
32. Ibid., pp. 409–11.
33. Ibid., p. 411.
34. On conventions of Soviet autobiography, see Sheila Fitzpatrick, "Supplicants and Citizens: Public Letter-Writing in Soviet Russia in the 1930s," *Slavic Review*, vol. 55, no. 1 (1996).
35. *GARF*, f. 9479, op. 1, d. 22, l. 11; d. 12, l. 6.
36. Ibid., d. 12, l. 6.
37. *TSD: TsA FSB*, f. 2, op. 9, d. 45, ll. 42–46.
38. Lynne Viola, "'Tear the Evil from the Root': The Children of the *Spetspereselentsy* of the North," *Studia Slavica Finlandensia*, tom. 17 (2000): 63.
39. *Kollektivizatsiia sel'skogo khoziaistva v Severnom raione* (Vologda, 1964), p. 601.
40. *GAAO*, f. 621, op. 3, d. 201, ll. 273–67.
41. *GARF*, f. 9479, op. 1, d. 33, l. 6.
42. Barbara Alpern Engel and Anastasia Posadskaya-Vanderbeck, eds., *A Revolution of their Own: Voices of Women in Soviet History* (Boulder: Westview Press, 1998), pp. 46, 164–66.
43. Krasil'nikov, ed., *Marginaly v sotsiume*, p. 358.
44. *GARF*, f. 9414, op. 1, d. 1949, ll. 7–10.
45. Dobronozhenko and Shabalova, eds., *Pokaianie*, vol. 4 (2), p. 26.
46. Danilov and Krasil'nikov, eds., *Spetspereselentsy v Zapadnoi Sibiri*, vol. 4, pp. 121–22.
47. *GARF*, f. 9479, op. 1, d. 949, ll. 75–79.
48. E.g., N. A. Ivnitskii, *Klassovaia bor'ba v derevne i likvidatsiia kulachestva kak klassa* (Moscow, 1972); and I. Ia. Trifonov, *Likvidatsiia ekspluatatorskikh klassov v SSSR* (Moscow, 1975).
49. See, for example, *GARF*, f. 9479, op. 1, d. 327, l. 64.
50. Ibid., d. 113, ll. 33, 200; Danilov and Krasil'nikov, eds., *Spetspereselentsy v Zapadnoi Sibiri*, vol. 4, pp. 179–82.
51. Danilov and Krasil'nikov, eds., *Spetspereselentsy v Zapadnoi Sibiri*, vol. 4, pp. 202–5.
52. *GARF*, f. 9479, op. 1, d. 327, l. 64.
53. I thank Professor Sergei Krasil'nikov for clarifying this steep numerical decline for me in an e-mail of 6 July 2005.
54. Nikolai Bougai, *The Deportation of Peoples in the Soviet Union* (New York: Nova Science Publishers, 1996), pp. 162–63, n. 12; G. F. Dobronozhenko and L. S. Shabalova, eds., *Spetsposelki v Komi oblasti: Sbornik dokumentov po materialam sploshnogo obsledovaniia. Iiun' 1933 g.* (Syktyvkar, 1997), p. 19; T. I. Slavko, ed., *Kulatskaia ssylka na Urale, 1930–1936* (Moscow, 1995), p. 146.
55. *GARF*, f. 9479, op. 1, d. 949, ll. 75–79 (data for 1 January 1954); and e-mail communication with Professor Sergei Krasil'nikov (5 July 2005) regarding the age of those remaining on police registries. For other, different numbers of former kulaks still holding the status of special settler, see Slavko, ed., *Kulatskaia ssylka na*

Urale, p. 146 (17,321); and A. Artizov et al., eds., *Reabilitatsiia: Kak eto bylo: Mart 1953–fevral' 1956. Dokumenty* (Moscow, 2000), p. 99 (24,686, data from 4 March 1954); and S. V. Mironenko and N. Werth, eds., *Istoriia Stalinskogo Gulaga: Konets 1920-kh—pervaia polovina 1950-kh godov*, 7 vols. (Moscow, 2004–5), vol. 5, p. 715 (21,305, data from 1 July 1953).

56. Again, I thank Professor Krasil'nikov for this information. On the basis of his work in the Tomsk archives, he has established that the special settlers in this vicinity no longer reported to the police after the spring of 1951. Prior to that, they were required to appear once a month at the *komandatura*.

57. It would take longer for the regime to release the "suspect" national categories held in the special settlements.

58. "The Crimes of the Stalin Era: Special Report to the 20th Congress of the Communist Party of the Soviet Union by Nikita S. Khrushchev," annotated by Boris I. Nicolaevsky, *The New Leader* (1962).

59. Engel and Posadskaya-Vanderbeck, eds., *A Revolution of their Own*, pp. 31, 35.

60. Ibid., pp. 158–59.

61. Olga Litinenko and James Riordan, eds. *Memories of the Dispossessed: Descendants of Kulak Families Tell Their Stories* (Nottingham, UK: Bramcote Press, 1998), pp. 62–63.

62. Engel and Posadskaya-Vanderbeck, eds., *A Revolution of their Own*, pp. 19–20, 27.

63. Ibid., pp. 157–59.

64. Litinenko and Riordan, eds., *Memories of the Dispossessed*, pp. 53–63.

65. O. Burova, who was exiled from Rostov-on-Don to the Urals in 1930, wrote that employers hired the children of kulaks "at their own risk." *Kotlovan (Khibinskoe obshchestvo "Memorial")*, March 1991, p. 8.

Conclusion

1. Fedor Liushenko, "Pamiatniki zhertvam politicheskikh repressii sovetskogo gosudarstva na territorii Respubliki Komi," in *Mir posle gulaga: reabilitatsiia i kul'tura pamiati*, ed. Irina Flige (St. Petersburg, 2004), p. 63. The epigraph is from Alexander I. Solzhenitsyn, *The Gulag Archipelago*, trans. Thomas P. Whitney and Harry Willetts, 3 vols. (New York: Harper and Row, 1973), vol. 3, p. 350.

2. According to Khlevniuk, some 389,521 people died in kulak exile between 1932 and 1940. Ivnitskii has estimated that 100,000 died in 1930. See Oleg. V. Khlevniuk, *The History of the Gulag*, trans. Vadim Staklo (New Haven: Yale University Press, 2004), pp. 17, 327; and *TSD*, vol. 2, pp. 26–27. The figure would surely be higher if we had numbers for 1931.

3. E. A. Zaitsev, ed., *Sbornik zakonodatel'nykh i normativnykh aktov o repressiiakh i reabilitatsii zhertv politicheskikh repressii* (Moscow, 1993), p. 186–206. (Gorbachev's legislation did refer to those who were exiled as a consequence of collectivization. Ibid., p. 189.)

4. Ibid., p. 194.

5. V. P. Danilov and S. A. Krasil'nikov, eds., *Spetspereselentsy v Zapadnoi Sibiri*, 4 vols. (Novosibirsk, 1992–96), vol. 1, p. 12.

6. Ronald Grigor Suny, "The Empire Strikes Out: Imperial Russia, 'National Identity,' and Theories of Empire," in *A State of Nations: Empire and Nation-Making in the Age of Lenin and Stalin*, ed. Ronald Grigor Suny and Terry Martin (New York: Oxford University Press, 2001), p. 26.

7. My thanks to Donald Filtzer for raising the issue of the reactive nature of Stalinism in a discussion at a conference titled, "Labour History of Russia and the Soviet

Union: Work in Progress," held at the International Institute of Social History in the spring of 2005.

8. In this context, it is worth quoting Boris Groys: "When the entire economic, social, and everyday life of the nation was totally subordinated to a single planning authority commissioned to regulate, harmonize, and create a single whole out of even the most minute details, this authority—the Communist party leadership— was transformed into a kind of artist whose material was the entire world and whose goal was to 'overcome the resistance' of this material and make it plaint, malleable, capable of assuming any desired form." From *The Total Art of Stalinism: Avant-Garde, Aesthetic Dictatorship, and Beyond*, trans. Charles Rougle (Princeton: Princeton University Press, 1992), p. 3.

9. Soviet development under Stalin had much in common with what James Scott has dubbed "high modernism"—that is, the state's desire for "the mastery of nature (including human nature), and, above all, the rational design of social order commensurate with the scientific understanding of natural laws." Scott adds, "The carriers of high modernism tended to see rational order in remarkably visual aesthetic terms. For them, an efficient, rationally organized city, village, or farm was a city that *looked* regimented and orderly." See James C. Scott, *Seeing Like a State: How Certain Schemes to Improve the Human Condition Have Failed* (New Haven: Yale University Press, 1998), pp. 4–5. See also Lynne Viola, "The Aesthetic of Stalinist Planning and the World of the Special Villages," *Kritika*, vol. 4, no. 1 (winter 2003). For a discussion of the nonunitary nature of the state as well as the world of Soviet planning in relation to city planning, see Heather Dehaan, "From Nizhnii to Gor'kii: The Reconstruction of a Russian Provincial City in the Stalinist 1930s" (PhD diss., University of Toronto, 2005).

10. The term "geography of penality" belongs to Judith Pallot, who is carrying out brilliant research on the aftereffects of the gulag and the current state of penal institutions in Russia. See, for example, Judith Pallot, "Forced Labour for Forestry: The Twentieth Century History of Colonization and Settlement in the North of Perm Oblast'," *Europe-Asia Studies*, vol. 54, no. 6 (2002). Also see Alan Barenberg, "From Prisoners to Miners: The Gulag and Its Legacy in Vorkuta" (PhD diss., University of Chicago, forthcoming).

11. Steven Lee Myers, "Siberians Tell Moscow: Like It or Not, It's Home," *New York Times*, 28 January 2004, p. 1.

12. Primo Levi, *The Drowned and the Saved*, trans. Raymond Rosenthal (New York: Vintage, 1989), p. 106.

Research Note

1. The best of these works was published only ten years later: N. A. Ivnitskii, *Klassovaia bor'ba v derevne i likvidatsiia kulachestva kak klassa* (Moscow, 1972), which covered well the story of dekulakization. Other notable works include the many publications of N. Ia. Gushchin, most especially "Likvidatsiia kulachestva kak klassa v Sibirskoi derevne," *Sotsial'naia struktura naseleniia SSSR* (Novosibirsk, 1970); and I. Ia. Trifonov, *Likvidatsiia ekspluatatorskikh klassov v SSSR* (Moscow, 1975). In general, Soviet historians produced better work on the history of collectivization, especially in the provinces. The most notable accomplishment was the publication of the multivolume documentary series on collectivization. For a description and a bibliography, see Lynne Viola, "Guide to Document Series on Collectivization," in *A Researcher's Guide to Sources on Soviet Social History in the 1930s*, ed. Sheila Fitzpatrick and Lynne Viola (Armonk, NY: Sharpe, 1990).

2. For some early scholarly western works on these topics, see Robert Conquest, *Kolyma* (New York: Viking Press, 1978); Conquest, *The Great Terror: Stalin's Purges of the Thirties* (New York: MacMillan, 1968); Conquest, *The Nation Killers: The Soviet Deportation of Nationalities* (London: MacMillan, 1970); David J. Dallin and Boris I. Nikolaevsky, *Forced Labor in Soviet Russia* (New Haven: Yale University Press, 1955); J. Arch Getty, *Origins of the Great Purges* (New York: Cambridge University Press, 1985); Roy Medvedev, *Let History Judge*, trans. George Shriver, rev. ed. (New York: Columbia University Press, 1989); Aleksandr M. Nekrich, *The Punished Peoples: The Deportation and Tragic Fate of Soviet Minorities at the End of the Second World War*, trans. George Saunders (New York: Norton, 1978); Robert C. Tucker and Stephen F. Cohen, eds., *The Great Purge Trial* (New York: Grosset and Dunlap, 1965).

3. For further information, see V. P. Kozlov and P. K. Grimsted, eds., *Arkhivy Rossii: Moskva i Sankt-Peterburg. Spravochnik-obozrenie i bibliograficheskii ukazatel'* (Moscow, 1997), pp. 9–12.

4. V. P. Danilov, R. T. Manning, L. Viola, eds., *Tragediia Sovetskoi derevni: Kollektivizatsiia i raskulachivanie. Dokumenty i materialy, 1927–1937*, 5 vols. (Moscow, 1999–2006); A. Berelovich and V. Danilov, eds., *Sovetskaia derevnia glazami VChK-OGPU-NKVD, 1918–1939. Dokumenty i materialy*, 3 vols. (Moscow, 1998–2003).

5. N. N. Pokrovskii, ed., *Politibiuro i krest'ianstvo: Vysylka, spetsposelenie, 1930–1940*, 2 vols. (Moscow, 2005–6).

6. E.g., V. P. Danilov and S. A. Krasil'nikov, eds., *Spetspereselentsy v Zapadnoi Sibiri*, 4 vols. (Novosibirsk, 1992–96); V. N. Maksheev, ed., *Narymskaia khronika, 1930–1945. Tragediia spetspereselentsev: Dokumenty i vospominaniia* (Moscow, 1997); V. A. Il'inykh and O. K. Kavtsevich, eds., *Politika raskrest'ianivaniia v Sibiri* (Novosibirsk, 2000), vyp. 1; V. M. Samosudov and L. V. Rachek, eds., *Sud'by liudskie: Istoriko-dokumental'nyi ocherk* (Omsk, 1998); V. V. Alekseev and T. I. Slavko, eds., *Raskulachennye spetspereselentsy na Urale (1930–1936 gg.)* (Ekaterinburg, 1993); V. I. Pervukhina, ed., *Sud'ba raskulachennykh spetspereselentsev na Urale (1930–1936 gg.)*, vyp. 2 (Ekaterinburg, 1994); T. I. Slavko, ed., *Kulatskaia ssylka na Urale, 1930–1936* (Moscow, 1995); I. E. Plotnikov, ed., *Sploshnaia kollektivizatsiia i raskulachivanie v Zaural'e (Materialy po istorii Kurganskoi oblasti)* (Kurgan, 1995); N. A. Ivnitskii and V. G. Makurov, eds., *Iz istorii raskulachivaniia v Karelii, 1930–1931 gg.* (Petrozavodsk, 1991); V. G. Makurov, ed., *Gulag v Karelii, 1930–1941: Sbornik dokumentov i materialov* (Petrozavodsk, 1992); V. G. Makurov, ed., *Neizvestnaia Kareliia, 1921–1956*, 2 vols. (Petrozavodsk, 1997–99). In addition to the documentary publications, a series of articles and monographs based on regional research have appeared. The most notable is S. A. Krasil'nikov, *Serp i molokh: Krest'ianskaia ssylka v Zapadnoi Sibiri v 1930-e gody* (Moscow, 2003).

7. A number of interesting documentary collections on the North have appeared since I began my work on this topic: O. V. Artemova, "Spetspereselentsy v Vozhegodskom raione," *Vozhega: Kraevedcheskii al'manakh* (Vologda, 1995); G. F. Dobronozhenko and L. S. Shabalova, *Spetsposelki v Komi oblasti po materialm sploshnogo obsledovaniia iiunia 1933 g. Sbornik dokumentov* (Syktyvkar, 1997); and, perhaps most importantly, G. F. Dobronozhenko and L. S. Shabalova, eds., *Pokaianie: Komi Respublikanskii martirolog zhertv massovykh politicheskikh repressii* (Syktyvkar, 2001), vol. 4 in two books.

8. See the discussion in Lynne Viola, ed., *Contending With Stalinism: Soviet Power and Popular Resistance in the 1930s* (Ithaca: Cornell University Press, 2002), pp. 27–28.

Research Note

The subject of the special settlers was taboo to Soviet researchers for decades. In the Khrushchev era, when there was a slight thaw in historical writing, several researchers were permitted to begin work on dekulakization. The issue of what happened to the kulaks after dekulakization, though, was reduced to a relatively benign socialist reeducation in undescribed settings and the resurrection of the occasional ex-kulak World War II hero.[1] While samizdat (books published illegally in the Soviet Union) and Western histories began to uncover the history of the Stalinist terror, the concentration camps, and to a lesser extent the ethnic deportations of the late 1930s and 1940s, the story of the special settlers remained terra incognita.[2] There was no diaspora in exile to champion their memory; nor did the small professional army of Western intellectuals embittered by cold war hatreds of the "evil empire" or motivated by Marxist leanings inquire further into their fate. It was as if the kulaks had simply vanished after dekulakization.

Although the absence of peasant historical advocacy and the political (and perhaps class) motivations of scholars were doubtless a part of the reason for this state of affairs, the primary reason for the long silence was official Soviet policy. From the very beginning in 1930, the state decreed that this would be an un-topic, appearing neither in the press nor in published records. All the documentation on the special settlers was subject to the highest order of archival classification and remained "top secret" until the early 1990s.

Soon after the inglorious demise of the Soviet Union in 1991, the new government of the Russian Federation under Boris Yeltsin took the first steps toward reforming what had been the Soviet archival system. In 1992 and 1993, a series of new laws eased researchers' access to the archives and initiated a partial process of declassification.[3] Russian and foreign researchers alike were among the beneficiaries of this process. Formerly inaccessible materials like the protocols of Politburo meetings and the personal archives of many top Communist Party leaders stored at the Russian State Archive of Social and Political History (RGASPI), the repository of the Communist Party archives; the GULAG files at the State Archive of the Russian Federation (GARF); and the secret files of the People's Commissariat of Agriculture at the Russian State Archive of the Economy (RGAE) were completely or partially opened. These and other files contain an endless variety of previously classified materials, including unpublished legislation, policy commission papers, official protocols, numerous genres of reports, statistical materials, budgets, and communications from all branches of party and government at all regional levels as well as a wealth of materials—letters, petitions, complaints—from the special settlers themselves. I spent all or parts of each summer from 1993 to 2004 working in these central archives in Moscow. Two important central archives remain persistently less accessible: the archives of the Federal Security Bureau (FSB), which stores the greater part of the secret police's records, and the Presidential or Kremlin archives, the innermost sanctum of archival secrecy for state records of the Soviet period. I benefited from participation in the multivolume Russian documentary history of the Soviet peasantry, *The Tragedy of the Soviet Countryside (Tragediia Sovetskoi derevni)*, which, along with the Russian-French project, *The Soviet Countryside Through the Eyes of the VChK-OGPU-NKVD (Sovetskaia derevnia glazami VChK-OGPU-NKVD)*, has had some access to materials on the special settlers in those archives.[4] My work in the two-volume documentary collection, *The Politburo and the Peasantry (Politbiuro i krest'ianstvo)*, has also allowed me to access the thematic files on dekulakization held in the Presidential archives.[5] Unless otherwise indicated (by reference to these projects), however, all of the archival work for this book is based on my own work directly in the archives.

Some of the most important work on resurrecting the history of the special settlers comes from the provinces. Russian researchers have produced a series of documentary collections covering key regions of exile and, in particular, Siberia, the Urals, and Karelia.[6] I was able to rely on these publications, along with my own work in the central archives, for coverage of Siberia and the Urals, the areas (along with the Northern Territory) that I chose to highlight (intentionally slighting, in the process, Kazakhstan and the Far East.) When I began my research on this topic, there were no published documents on the Northern Territory, the region that took in the single largest contingent of special settlers in 1930.[7] With that in mind, I decided to focus my provincial archival field work on the North, journeying to Vologda and Arkhangel'sk to investigate the holdings of regional party and government archives. The wealth of materials in these archives, which include sizeable collections of secret police documents, is impressive and, in many ways, comparable to the accessible collections on the topic in Moscow. My work in these archives has allowed me not only to research the history of the special settlers in the North but also to complement and compare the published collections on Siberia and the Urals.

Needless to say, the archives are not a repository of "truth." Official documents can be highly tendentious, molded in form and content to reflect authorial intent. The bureaucratic author was, moreover, constrained by his or her audience, in our case, a hierarchy of superiors extending all the way to the Kremlin. This was an audience existing in dangerously thin air. It could be expected, assumed, or inferred by a document's author that a certain kind of reporting was necessary, replete with exaggeration, understatement, or cover-up depending on concrete circumstances and fears. Documents are further shaped, or distorted, by stilted bureaucratic language and a highly charged political vocabulary often designed, whether consciously or not, to present a black-and-white world of communism and counterrevolution, good and evil.[8] It is therefore necessary to approach Soviet documents with extreme caution, reading against the grain. By carefully comparing different types of documents and documents of differing institutional provenance, as well as paying especially close attention to documentation arising at times when policy or personnel were changed thereby allowing for more or less frank criticism of previous policy or disgraced personnel, one can build a reasonably accurate picture of the history of the special settlements. The sources do thin out over time. The available documentary coverage is the most dense in the first half of the 1930s, less so in the second half of the 1930s, and relatively sparse in the 1940s and first half of the 1950s.

It would have been impossible to write this book without access to the archives. The archives, however, tell only a part—albeit a major part—of the story. The documentary foundations of this book are reinforced by the voices of the special settlers themselves, some long confined to the archives, most of recent vintage appearing in widely scattered published sources. Beginning in the late 1980s, countless survivors have stepped forward—or have been tracked down by enterprising researchers—to tell their stories in letters, interviews, and memoirs. I make use of these stories whenever I can, inserting the voices of the special settlers directly into the narrative allowing them to counter the official narrative.

Archival documentary sources together with first-hand accounts form the evidentiary foundation of this book. All references cited in the book are listed in the bibliography that follows this note.

Bibliography

Primary Sources

Archives

Citations of archival materials are by *fond, opis', delo, list(y)* and abbreviated: f., op., d., l. (ll. if plural)

GAAO (*Gosudarstvennyi arkhiv Arkhangel'skoi oblasti*)
    f. 621. Arkhangel'skii oblastnoi ispolkom

GAMO (*Gosudarstvennyi arkhiv Moskovskoi oblasti*)
    f. 7121. Leninskii RIK

GARF (*Gosudarstvennyi arkhiv Rossiiskoi Federatsii*)
    f. R-374. Tsentral'naia kontrol'naia komissiia VKP (b)-Narodnyi komissariat raboche-krest'ianskoi inspektsii SSSR
    f. R-393. Narodnyi komissariat vnutrennikh del RSFSR
    f. R-1235. Vserossiiskii tsentral'nyi ispolnitel'nyi komitet sovetov rabochikh, krest'ianskikh i krasnoarmeiskikh deputatov
    f. R-3316. Tsentral'nyi ispolnitel'nyi komitet sovetov rabochikh, krest'ianskikh i krasnoarmeiskikh deputatov SSSR
    f. R-5446. Sovet narodnykh komissarov SSSR
    f. R-9401. Narodnyi komissariat vnutrennikh del SSSR
    f. R-9414. Glavnoe upravlenie mest zakliucheniia NKVD SSSR
    f. R-9479. 4-i Spetsotdel NKVD

GAOPDF AO (*Gosudarstvennyi arkhiv obshchestvenno-politicheskikh dvizhenii i formirovanii Arkhangel'skoi oblasti*)
    f. 290. Sevkraikom VKP (b)
    f. 296. Arkhangel'skii obkom VKP (b)
    f. 833. Arkhangel'kii okruzhkom VKP (b)

GAVO (*Gosudarstvennyi arkhiv Vologodskoi oblasti*)
  f. 395. Vologodskii okruzhnoi Rabkrin
  f. 399. Vologodskoe okruzhnoe zemupravlenie
  f. 903. Totemskii RIK
  f. 907. Vozhegodskii RIK

RGAE (*Rossiiskii gosudarstvennyi arkhiv ekonomiki*)
  f. 260. Vsesoiuznyi nauchno-issledovatel'skii institut ekonomiki sel'skogo khoziaistva
  f. 3983. Soiuz soiuzov sel'skokhoziaistvennoi kooperatsii RSFSR-SSSR
  f. 5675. Glavnoe pereselencheskoe upravlenie pri NKZ SSSR
  f. 7446. Vsesoiuznyi soiuz sel'skokhoziaistvennykh kollektivov SSSR i RSFSR (Kolkhoztsentr)
  f. 7480. Vsesoiuznyi sel'skokhoziaistvennyi bank SSSR
  f. 7486. Narodnyi komissariat zemledeliia SSSR
  f. 7733. Narodnyi komissariat finansov SSSR

RGASPI (*Rossiiskii gosudarstvennyi arkhiv sotsial'no-politicheskoi istorii*)
  f. 17. Tsentral'nyi komitet VKP (b)
  f. 78. Mikhail Ivanovich Kalinin

TsA FSB (*Tsentral'nyi arkhiv federal'noi sluzhby bezopasnosti*)

VOANPI (*Vologodskii oblastnoi arkhiv noveishei politicheskoi istorii*)
  f. 5. Severo-Dvinskii okruzhkom VKP (b)
  f. 329. Vozhegodskii raikom VKP (b)
  f. 399. Vologodskoe okruzhnoe zemupravlenie
  f. 1855. Vologodskii okruzhkom VKP (b)

Russian and Soviet Periodicals

Bednota
Bol'shevik
Derevenskii kommunist
Istoricheskii arkhiv
Izvestiia
Kotlovan (Khibinskoe obshchestvo "Memorial")
Krest'ianskaia gazeta
Otechestvennaia istoriia
Otechestvennye arkhivy
Partiinoe stroitel'stvo
Pravda
Sotsiologicheskie issledovaniia
Sovetskaia iustitsiia
Sovetskoe stroitel'stvo
Vecherniaia Moskva
Voprosy istorii

Reference Works

Davies, R. W., M. J. Ilic, H. P. Jenkins, C. Merridale, and S. G. Wheatcroft, eds. *Soviet Government Officials, 1922–41: A Handlist*. Birmingham: CREES, University of Birmingham, 1989.

Garniuk, S. D., ed. *Sovet narodnykh komissarov SSSR. Sovet ministrov SSSR. Kabinet ministrov SSSR. 1923–1991. Entsiklopedicheskii spravochnik.* Moscow, 1999.

Istoriia kolkhoznogo prava: Sbornik zakonodatel'nykh materialov SSSR i RSFSR, 1917–1958. 2 vols. Moscow, 1959.

Ivkin, V. I. ed. *Gosudarstvennaia vlast' SSSR: Vysshie organy vlasti i upravleniia i ikh rukovoditeli, 1923–1991. Istoriko-biograficheskii spravochnik.* Moscow, 1999.

Kokurin, A. I., and N. V. Petrov, eds. *Lubianka. VChK-OGPU-NKVD-NKGB-MGB-MVD-KGB, 1917–1960. Spravochnik.* Moscow, 1997.

———, eds. *Lubianka. Organy VChK-OGPU-NKVD-NKGB-MGB-MVD-KGB, 1917–1991. Spravochnik.* Moscow, 2003.

Korzhikhina, T. P. *Sovetskoe gosudarstvo i ego uchrezhdeniia. Noiabr' 1917 g.–dekabr' 1991 g.* Moscow, 1994.

Kozlov, V. P., and P. K. Grimsted, eds. *Arkhivy Rossii: Moskva i Sankt-Peterburg. Spravochnik-obozrenie i bibliograficheskii ukazatel'.* Moscow, 1997.

Okhotin, N. G., and A. B. Roginskii, eds. *Sistema ispravitel'no-trudovykh lagerei v SSSR. Spravochnik.* Moscow, 1998.

The Penal Code of the Russian Socialist Federal Soviet Republic. Text of 1926 (with Amendments up to December 1, 1932). London, 1934.

Petrov, N. V., K. V. Skorkin, N. G. Okhotin, and A. B. Roginskii, eds. *Kto rukovodil NKVD, 1934–1941. Spravochnik.* Moscow, 1999.

Rigby, T. H. *Communist Party Membership in the USSR, 1917–1961.* Princeton: Princeton University Press, 1968.

Sobranie uzakonenii i rasporiazhenii raboche-krest'ianskogo pravitel'stva RSFSR.

Sobranie zakonov i rasporiazhenii raboche-krest'ianskogo pravitel'stva SSSR.

Sostav VKP (b) na 1 ianvaria 1930 goda (Moscow, 1930). (Manuscript marked "na pravakh rukopisi")

Sotsial'nyi i natsional'nyi sostav VKP(b). Itogi vsesoiuznoi partiinoi perepisi 1927 g. Moscow, 1928.

Spravochnik partiinogo rabotnika. Vol. 8. Moscow, 1934.

I. Stalin. *Sochineniia.* 13 vols. Moscow, 1946–52.

Torchinov, V. A., and A. M. Liontiuk, ed. *Vokrug Stalina: Istoriko-biograficheskii spravochnik.* St. Petersburg, 2000.

Viola, Lynne. "Guide to Document Series on Collectivization." In *A Researcher's Guide to Sources on Soviet Social History in the 1930s,* edited by Sheila Fitzpatrick and Lynne Viola. Armonk, NY: M. E. Sharpe, 1990.

Published Archival Documents, Memoirs, and Other Primary Materials

Alekseev V. V., and T. I. Slavko, eds. *Raskulachennye spetspereselentsy na Urale (1930–1936 gg.).* Ekaterinburg, 1993.

Artemova, O. V., ed. "Spetspereselentsy v Vozhegodskom raione." *Vozhega: Kraevedcheskii al'manakh.* Vologda, 1995.

Artizov, A., et al., eds. *Reabilitatsiia: Kak eto bylo. Dokumenty.* 3 vols. Moscow, 2000–2004.

Berelovich, A., and V. Danilov, eds. *Sovetskaia derevnia glazami VChK-OGPU-NKVD, 1918–1939. Dokumenty i materialy.* 3 vols. Moscow, 2000–2003.

Danilov, V. P., and N. A. Ivnitskii, eds. *Dokumenty svidetel'stvuiut: Iz istorii derevni nakanune i v khode kollektivizatsii, 1927–1932 gg.* Moscow, 1989.

Danilov, V. P., O. V. Khlevniuk, and A. Iu. Vatlin, eds. *Kak lomali NEP. Stenogrammy plenumov TsK VKP (b), 1928–1929.* 5 vols. Moscow, 2000.

Danilov, V. P., and S. A. Krasil'nikov, eds. *Spetspereselentsy v Zapadnoi Sibiri*. 4 vols. Novosibirsk, 1992–96.

Danilov, V. P., R. T. Manning, L. Viola, eds. *Tragediia Sovetskoi derevni: Kollektivizatsiia i raskulachivanie. Dokumenty i materialy, 1927–1937*. 5 vols. Moscow, 1999–2006.

Davies, R. W., Oleg V. Khlevniuk, E. A. Rees, Liudmila P. Kosheleva, and Larisa A Rogovaya, eds. *The Stalin-Kaganovich Correspondence, 1931–1936*. Trans. Steven Shabad. New Haven: Yale University Press, 2003.

Dobronozhenko, G. F., and L. S. Shabalova, eds. *Pokaianie. Komi Respublikanskii martirolog zhertv massovykh politicheskikh repressii*. Syktyvkar, 2001. Vol. 4 (in two books).

———. *Spetsposelki v Komi oblasti po materialam sploshnogo obsledovaniia iiunia 1933 g. Sbornik dokumentov*. Syktyvkar, 1997.

Dobrovol'skii, I. V., ed. *Gulag: eto stroiteli, obitateli i geroi*. Frankfurt a. M./Moscow, 2001.

Dugin, A. N., ed. *Neizvestnyi GULAG: Dokumenty i fakty*. Moscow, 1999.

Engel, Barbara Alpern, and Anastasia Posadskaya-Vanderbeck, eds. *A Revolution of their Own: Voices of Women in Soviet History*. Trans. Sona Hoisington. Boulder: Westview Press, 1998.

Garros, Veronique, Natalia Korenevskaya, and Thomas Lahusen, eds. *Intimacy and Terror*. Trans. Carol A. Flath. New York: New Press, 1995.

Gvozdkova, L. I., ed. *Prinuditel'nyi trud: Ispravitel'no-trudovye lageria v Kuzbasse (30–50 gg.)*. 2 vols. Kemerevo, 1994.

Harder, John, ed. and trans. *From Kleefeld with Love*. Kitchener, Ontario: Pandora Press, 2003.

Hindus, Maurice. *Red Bread: Collectivization in a Russian Village*. Bloomington: Indiana University Press, 1988.

Il'inykh, V. A., and O. K. Kavtsevich, eds. *Politika raskrest'ianivaniia v Sibiri*. Novosibirsk, 2000.

Ivnitskii, N. A., and V. G. Makurov, eds. *Iz istorii raskulachivaniia v Karelii, 1930–1931 gg*. Petrozavodsk, 1991.

Khaustov, V. N., V. P. Naumov, and N. S. Plotnikova, eds. *Lubianka: Stalin i VChK-GPU-OGPU-NKVD. Ianvar' 1922–dekabr' 1936*. Moscow, 2003.

Khlevniuk, Oleg V. *The History of the Gulag*. Trans. Vadim Staklo. New Haven: Yale University Press, 2004.

Khlevniuk, Oleg V., R. W. Davies, L. P. Kosheleva, E. A. Rees, and L. A. Rogovaia, eds. *Stalin i Kaganovich: Perepiska, 1931–1936 gg*. Moscow, 2001.

Khlusov, M. I., ed. *Ekonomika GULAGa i ee rol' v razvitii strany. 1930-e gody. Sbornik dokumentov*. Moscow, 1998.

Khrushchev, N. S., "The Crimes of the Stalin Era: Special Report to the 20th Congress of the Communist Party of the Soviet Union by Nikita S. Khrushchev." Annotated by Boris I. Nicolaevsky. *The New Leader* (1962).

Kirillova, V. M., ed. *Kniga pamiati: posviashchaetsia Tagil'chanam—zhertvam repressii, 1917–1980-kh godov*. Ekaterinburg, 1994.

Kokurin, A. I., and N. V. Petrov, eds. *GULAG, 1917–1960: Dokumenty*. Moscow, 2000.

Kollektivizatsiia sel'skogo khoziaistva v Severnom raione. Vologda, 1964.

Kollektivizatsiia sel'skogo khoziaistva v Zapadnom raione RSFSR. Smolensk, 1968.

Kosheleva, L. P., O. V. Naumov, and L. A. Rogovaia, eds. "Materialy fevral'sko-martovskogo plenuma TsK VKP (b) 1937 goda." *Voprosy istorii*, nos. 4–5 (1992).

Kozlov, V. A., et al., eds. *Neizvestnaia Rossiia: XX vek. Arkhivy, pis'ma, memuary*. 4 vols. Moscow, 1992–94.

Krasil'nikov, S. A. "Rozhdenie GULAGa: diskussii v verkhnikh eshelonakh vlasti: postanovleniia Politburo TsK VKP (b), 1929–1930." *Istoricheskii arkhiv*, no. 4 (1997).

Krasil'nikov, S. A., and O. M. Mamkin, eds. "Vosstanie v Parbigskoi komendature: Leto 1931 g." *Istoricheskii arkhiv*, no. 3 (1994).

Litinenko, Olga, and James Riordan, eds. *Memories of the Dispossessed: Descendants of Kulak Families Tell Their Stories*. Nottingham, UK: Bramcote Press, 1998.

Maksheev, V. N., ed. *Narymskaia khronika, 1930–1945. Tragediia spetspereselentsev. Dokumenty i vospominaniia*. Moscow, 1997.

Makurov, V. G., ed. *Gulag v Karelii, 1930–1941: Sbornik dokumentov i materialov*. Petrozavodsk, 1992.

———, ed. *Neizvestnaia Kareliia, 1921–1956*. 2 vols. Petrozavodsk, 1997–1999.

Mironenko, S. V., and N. Werth, eds. *Istoriia Stalinskogo gulaga: konets 1920-kh–pervaia polovina 1950-kh godov*. 7 vols. Moscow, 2004–5.

Molotov Remembers: Inside Kremlin Politics. Conversations with Felix Chuev. Chicago: Ivan R. Dee, 1991.

XV s"ezd VKP (b). Sten. otchet. 2 vols. Moscow, 1961–62.

Plotnikov, I. E., ed. *Sploshnaia kollektivizatsiia i raskulachivanie v Zaural'e (Materialy po istorii Kurganskoi oblasti)*. Kurgan, 1995.

———, ed. "Ssylka krest'ian na Urale v 1930-e gody." *Otechestvennaia istoriia*, no. 1 (1995).

Pobol', N. L., and P. M. Polian, eds. *Stalinskie deportatsii, 1928–1956: Dokumenty*. Moscow, 2005.

Pokrovskii, N. N., ed. *Politbiuro i krest'ianstvo: Vysylka, spetsposelenie, 1930–1940*. 2 vols. Moscow, 2005–6.

Put' trudovykh pobed. Volgograd, 1967.

Romano, Andrea, and Nonna Tarkhova, eds. *Krasnaia armiia i kollektivizatsiia derevni v SSSR (1928–1933 gg.)*. Naples, 1996.

Samosudov, V. M., and L. V. Rachek, eds. *Sud'by liudskie: Istoriko-dokumental'nyi ocherk*. Omsk, 1998.

XVI konferentsiia VKP (b). Sten. Otchet. Moscow and Leningrad, 1929.

XVI s"ezd VKP (b). Sten. otchet. 2 vols. Moscow, 1930.

Slavko, T. I., ed. *Kulatskaia ssylka na Urale, 1930–1936*. Moscow, 1995.

———, ed. *Sud'ba raskulachennykh spetspereselentsev na Urale (1930–1936 gg.)*. Ekaterinburg, 1994.

Trudy pervoi vsesoiuznoi konferentsii agrarnikov-marksistov. 2 vols. Moscow, 1930.

Tucker, Robert C., and Stephen F. Cohen, eds. *The Great Purge Trial*. New York: Grosset and Dunlap, 1965.

Tvardovskii, Ivan. "Stranitsy perezhitogo." *Iunost'*, no. 3 (1988).

Vilenskii, S. S., A. I. Kokurin, G. V. Atmashkina, and I. Iu. Novichenko, eds. *Deti GULAGa, 1918–1956*. Moscow, 2002.

Viola, Lynne, Sergei Zhuravlev, Tracy McDonald, and Andrei Mel'nik, eds. *Riazanskaia derevnia v 1929–1930 gg: Khronika golovokruzheniia. Dokumenty i materialy*. Moscow, 1998.

Viola, Lynne, V. P. Danilov, N. A. Ivnitskii, and Denis Kozlov, eds. *The War Against the Peasantry, 1927–1930*. Vol. 1 of *The Tragedy of the Soviet Countryside*. 4 vols. Trans. Steven Shabad. New Haven: Yale University Press, 2005.

Zabveniiu ne podlezhit: Neizvestnye stranitsy Nizhegorodskoi istorii (1918–1984 gody). Nizhnyi Novgorod, 1994.

Zaitsev, E. A., ed. *Sbornik zakonodatel'nykh i normativnykh aktov o repressiiakh i reabilitatsii zhertv politicheskikh repressii*. Moscow, 1993.

Secondary Sources

Adler, Nanci. *The Gulag Survivor: Beyond the Soviet System.* New Brunswick, NJ: Transaction Publishers, 2002.

Alexopoulos, Golfo. *Stalin's Outcasts: Aliens, Citizens, and the Soviet State, 1926–1936.* Ithaca: Cornell University Press, 2003.

Arendt, Hannah. *Eichman in Jerusalem: A Report on the Banality of Evil.* Rev. ed. New York: Penguin, 1977.

Ball, Alan M. *And Now My Soul Is Hardened: Abandoned Children in Soviet Russia, 1918–1930.* Berkeley: University of California Press, 1994.

Bazarov, A. A. *Kulak i agrogulag.* Cheliabinsk, 1991.

Bell, Wilson T. "One Day in the Life of Educator Khrushchev: Labour and Kul'turnost' in the Gulag Newspapers." *Canadian Slavonic Papers,* vol. 46, nos. 3–4 (2004).

Bougai, Nikolai. *The Deportation of Peoples in the Soviet Union.* New York: Nova Science Publishers, 1996.

Brooks, Jeffrey. *Thank You, Comrade Stalin! Soviet Public Culture from Revolution to Cold War.* Princeton: Princeton University Press, 2000.

Bubnov, A. S. "Statisticheskie svedeniia o VKP(b)." *Bol'shaia Sovetskaia entsiklopediia.* Vol. 11. Moscow, 1930.

Carr, E. H. *Socialism in One Country, 1924–1926.* 3 vols. London: MacMillan, 1958.

Conquest, Robert. *The Great Terror: Stalin's Purges of the Thirties.* New York: MacMillan, 1968.

———. *Harvest of Sorrow: Soviet Collectivization and the Terror-Famine.* Oxford: Oxford University Press, 1986.

———. *Kolyma.* New York: Viking Press, 1978.

———. *The Nation Killers: The Soviet Deportation of Nationalities.* London: MacMillan, 1970.

Dallin, David J., and Boris I. Nikolaevsky. *Forced Labor in Soviet Russia.* New Haven: Yale University Press, 1955.

Danilov, V. P. "Sel'skoe naselenie soiuza SSR nakanune kollektivizatsii." *Istoricheskie zapiski,* no. 74 (1963).

Davies, R. W. *The Socialist Offensive: The Collectivization of Soviet Agriculture, 1929–1930.* Cambridge, MA: Harvard University Press, 1980.

———. *Soviet History in the Gorbachev Revolution.* Bloomington: Indiana University Press, 1989.

———. *Soviet History in the Yeltsin Era.* New York: St. Martin's Press, 1997.

———. "The Syrtsov-Lominadze Affair." *Soviet Studies,* vol. 33, no. 1 (1981).

Davies, R. W., and Stephen G. Wheatcroft. *Industrialisation of Soviet Russia: Years of Hunger.* London: Palgrave, 2003.

Druzhnikov, Yuri. *Informer 001: The Myth of Pavlik Morozov.* New Brunswick, NJ: Transaction Publishers, 1997.

Fitzpatrick, Sheila. "Becoming Cultured: Socialist Realism and the Representation of Privilege and Taste." In *The Cultural Front: Power and Culture in Revolutionary Russia,* ed. Sheila Fitzpatrick. Ithaca: Cornell University Press, 1992.

———. *The Russian Revolution.* Oxford: Oxford University Press, 1994.

———. "Supplicants and Citizens: Public Letter-Writing in Soviet Russia in the 1930s." *Slavic Review,* vol. 55, no. 1 (1996).

Foucault, Michel. *Discipline and Punish: The Birth of the Prison.* Trans. Alan Sheridan. 2nd ed. New York: Vintage, 1995.

Frank, Stephen P. "Confronting the Domestic Other: Rural Popular Culture and Its Enemies in Fin-De-Siecle Russia." In *Culture in Flux: Lower-Class Values, Practices, and Resistance in Late Imperial Russia*, ed. Stephen P. Frank and Mark D. Steinberg. Princeton: Princeton University Press, 1994.

Getty, J. Arch. *Origins of the Great Purges*. New York: Cambridge University Press, 1985.

———, and Oleg V. Naumov, eds. *The Road to Terror: Stalin and the Self-Destruction of the Bolsheviks, 1932–1939*. New Haven: Yale University Press, 1999.

Gregory, Paul R., ed. *Behind the Facade of Stalin's Command Economy: Evidence from the Soviet State and Party Archives*. Stanford: Hoover Institution Press, 2001.

———. *The Political Economy of Stalinism: Evidence from the Soviet Secret Archives*. Cambridge: Cambridge University Press, 2004.

Gregory, Paul R., and Valery Lazarev, eds. *The Economics of Forced Labor: The Soviet Gulag*. Stanford: Hoover Institution Press, 2003.

Groys, Boris. *The Total Art of Stalinism: Avant-Garde, Aesthetic Dictatorship, and Beyond*. Trans. Charles Rougle. Princeton: Princeton University Press, 1992.

Gushchin, N. Ia. "Likvidatsiia kulachestva kak klassa v Sibirskoi derevne." In *Sotsial'naia struktura naseleniia SSSR*. Novosibirsk, 1970.

———. *Raskulachivanie v Sibiri (1928–1934 gg.)*. Novosibirsk, 1996.

Hagenloh, Paul M. "'Socially Harmful Elements' and the Great Terror." In *Stalinism: New Directions*, ed. Sheila Fitzpatrick. London: Routledge, 2000.

Harris, James R. *The Great Urals: Regionalism and the Evolution of the Soviet System*. Ithaca: Cornell University Press, 1999.

———. "The Growth of the Gulag: Forced Labor in the Urals Region, 1929–31." *Russian Review*, vol. 56 (April 1997).

Hellie, Richard. "Migration in Early Modern Russia, 1480s–1780s." In *Coerced and Free Migration: Global Perspectives*, ed. David Eltis. Stanford: Stanford University Press, 2002.

Holquist, Peter. "The Logic of Violence in Soviet Totalitarianism." In *Landscaping the Human Garden*, ed. Amir Weiner. Stanford: Stanford University Press, 2003.

———. *Making War, Forging Revolution: Russia's Continuum of Crisis, 1914–1921*. Cambridge, MA: Harvard University Press, 2002.

Hughes, James. *Stalinism in a Russian Province: Collectivization and Dekulakization in Siberia*. London, 1996.

Iudin, I. N. *Sotsial'naia baza rosta KPSS*. Moscow, 1973.

Ivanova, Galina Mikhailovna. *Labor Camp Socialism: The Gulag in the Soviet Totalitarian System*. Trans. Carol Flath. Armonk, NY: M. E. Sharpe, 2000.

Ivnitskii, N. A. *Klassovaia bor'ba v derevne i likvidatsiia kulachestva kak klassa*. Moscow, 1972.

———. *Kollektivizatsiia i raskulachivanie (nachalo 30-kh godov)*. Moscow, 1994.

———. *Repressivnaia politika Sovetskoi vlasti v derevne (1928–1932 gg.)*. Moscow, 2000.

———. "Spetspereselentsy—zhertvy Stalinskikh repressii (1930–1941 gg.)." In *Kniga pamiati: Zhertvy politicheskikh repressii Kalininskoi oblasti*, ed. E. I. Kravtsova et al. Tver', 2001.

———. *Sud'ba raskulachennykh v SSSR*. Moscow, 2004.

Jansen, Mark, and Nikita Petrov. *Stalin's Loyal Executioner: People's Commissar Nikolai Ezhov, 1895–1940*. Stanford: Hoover Institution Press, 2002.

Khantalin, Rudol'f. *Nevol'niki i bonzy*. Arkhangel'sk, 1998.

Khlevniuk, Oleg. "The Economy of the Gulag." In *Behind the Facade of Stalin's Command Economy*, ed. Paul R. Gregory. Stanford: Hoover Institution Press, 2001.

———. "The Economy of the OGPU, NKVD, and MVD of the USSR, 1930–1953." In *The Economics of Forced Labor: The Soviet Gulag*, ed. Paul R. Gregory and Valery Lazarev. Stanford: Hoover Institution Press, 2003.

Krasil'nikov, S. A., ed. *Marginaly v sotsiume. Marginaly kak sotsium. Sibir' (1920–1930-e gody)*. Novosibirsk, 2004.

———. *Na izlomakh sotsial'noi struktury: marginaly v poslerevoliutsionnom Rossiiskom obshchestve*. Novosibirsk, 1998.

———. *Serp i molokh: Krest'ianskaia ssylka v Zapadnoi Sibiri v 1930-e gody*. Moscow, 2003.

Lepeshkin, A. I. *Mestnye organy vlasti Sovetskogo gosudarstva*. Moscow, 1959.

Levi, Primo. *The Drowned and the Saved*. Trans. Raymond Rosenthal. New York: Vintage, 1989.

———. *The Reawakening*. Trans. Stuart Woolf. New York: Simon and Schuster, 1965.

Levin, V., and I. Suvorov "Sovety i stroitel'stvo sotsializma." In *15 let Sovetskogo stroitel'stva*, ed. E. Pashukanis. Moscow, 1932.

Lewin, Moshe. *Russian Peasants and Soviet Power: A Study of Collectivization*. Trans. Irene Nove. New York: Norton, 1975.

———. "Who Was the Soviet Kulak?" In *The Making of the Soviet System*, ed. Moshe Lewin. New York: Pantheon, 1985.

Martin, Terry. *The Affirmative Action Empire: Nations and Nationalism in the Soviet Union, 1923–1939*. Ithaca: Cornell University Press, 2001.

Medvedev, Roy. *Let History Judge*. Trans. George Shriver. Rev. ed. New York: Columbia University Press, 1989.

Myers, Steven Lee. "Siberians Tell Moscow: Like It or Not, It's Home." *New York Times*. 28 January 2004, 1.

Naimark, Norman M. *Fires of Hatred: Ethnic Cleansing in Twentieth-Century Europe*. Cambridge, MA: Harvard University Press, 2001.

Nekrich, Aleksandr M. *The Punished Peoples: The Deportation and Tragic Fate of Soviet Minorities at the End of the Second World War*. Trans. George Saunders. New York: Norton, 1978.

Nikitina, O. A. *Kollektivizatsiia i raskulachivanie v Karelii*. Petrozavodsk, 1997.

Nove, Alec. *Glasnost' in Action*. Boston: Unwin Hyman, 1989.

———. "Victims of Stalinism: How Many?" In *Stalinist Terror: New Perspectives*, ed. J. Arch Getty and Roberta T. Manning. Cambridge: Cambridge University Press, 1993.

Okuda, Hiroshi. "Recent Rethinking of Collectivization in the Soviet Union." In *Facing Up to the Past: Soviet Historiography under Perestroika*, ed. Takayuki Ito. Sapporo: Hokkaida University, 1989.

Ozol, I. K. "Obzor zakonodatel'stva i sostoianiia mestnykh biudzhetov RSFSR za 1929/30 g." *Ezhegodnik Sovetskogo stroitel'stva i prava na 1931 god*. Moscow-Leningrad, 1931.

Pallot, Judith. "Forced Labour for Forestry: The Twentieth Century History of Colonization and Settlement in the North of Perm' Oblast'." *Europe-Asia Studies*, vol. 54, no. 6 (2002).

Petrushin, A. A., ed. *My ne znaem poshchady . . . Izvestnye, maloizvestnye, i neizvestnye sobytiia iz istorii Tiumenskogo kraia po materialam VChK-GPU-NKVD-KGB*. Tiumen, 1999.

Plamper, Jan. "Abolishing Ambiguity: Soviet Censorship Practices in the 1930s." *Russian Review*, vol. 60, no. 4 (2001).

Plotnikov, I. E. "Kak likvidirovali kulachestvo na Urale." *Otechestvennaia istoriia*, no. 4 (1993).

———. "Krest'ianskie volneniia i vystupleniia na Urale v kontse 20-kh—nachale 30-kh godov." *Otechestvennaia istoriia*, no. 2 (1998).

Polian, Pavel. *Ne po svoei vole . . . Istoriia i geografiia prinuditel'nyikh migratsii v SSSR*. Moscow, 2001.

Popov, V. P. "Gosudarstvennyi terror v Sovetskoi Rossii. 1923–1953 gg." *Otechestvennye arkhivy*, no. 2 (1992).

Rees, E. A. "The People's Commissariat of the Timber Industry." In *Decision-Making in the Stalinist Command Economy, 1932–37*, ed. E. A. Rees. London: MacMillan, 1997.

Rossman, Jeffrey J. *Worker Resistance Under Stalin: Class and Revolution on the Shop Floor*. Cambridge, MA: Harvard University Press, 2005.

Sapozhnikova, N. D., and A. G. Sapozhnikov. "Nekotorye aspekty otnosheniia vlasti k raskulachennym krest'ianam na Urale v kontse 20-kh—nachale 30-kh gg." *Totalitarizm i lichnost'*. Perm, 1994.

Scherer, John L., and Michael Jakobson "The Collectivisation of Agriculture and the Soviet Prison Camp System." *Europe-Asia Studies*, vol. 45, no. 3 (1993).

Schrader, Abby M. "Branding the Exiles 'Other': Corporal Punishment and the Construction of Boundaries in Mid-Nineteenth-Century Russia." In *Russian Modernity*, ed. David L. Hoffmann and Yanni Kotsonis. London: MacMillan, 2000.

Scott, James C. *Seeing Like a State: How Certain Schemes to Improve the Human Condition Have Failed*. New Haven: Yale University Press, 1998.

Shearer, David. "Crime and Social Disorder in Stalin's Russia: A Reassessment of the Great Retreat and the Origins of Mass Repression." *Cahiers du Monde Russe*, vol. 39, nos. 1–2 (January–June 1998).

———. "Social Disorder, Mass Repression, and the NKVD during the 1930s." In *Stalin's Terror*, ed. Barry McLoughlin and Kevin McDermott. London: Palgrave, 2003.

Siegelbawm, Lewis, and Andrei Sokolov, eds. *Stalinism as a Way of Life*. New Haven: Yale University Press, 2000.

Slezkine, Yuri. *Arctic Mirrors*. Ithaca: Cornell University Press, 1994.

Smith, Kathleen E. *Remembering Stalin's Victims: Popular Memory and the End of the USSR*. Ithaca: Cornell University Press, 1996.

Solomon, Peter H., Jr. *Soviet Criminal Justice under Stalin*. Cambridge: Cambridge University Press, 1996.

Solzhenitsyn, Alexander I. *The Gulag Archipelago*. Trans. Thomas P. Whitney and Harry Willetts. 3 vols. New York: Harper and Row, 1973.

Suny, Ronald Grigor. "Stalin and His Stalinism: Power and Authority in the Soviet Union, 1930–53." In *Stalinism and Nazism: Dictatorships in Comparison*, ed. Ian Kershaw and Moshe Lewin. Cambridge: Cambridge University Press, 1997.

Suny, Ronald Grigor, and Terry Martin, eds. *A State of Nations: Empire and Nation-Making in the Age of Lenin and Stalin*. New York: Oxford University Press, 2001.

Trifonov, I. Ia. *Likvidatsiia ekspluatatorskikh klassov v SSSR*. Moscow, 1975.

Viola, Lynne. "The Aesthetic of Stalinist Planning and the World of the Special Villages." *Kritika*, vol. 4, no. 1 (2003).

———. *The Best Sons of the Fatherland: Workers in the Vanguard of Soviet Collectivization*. New York: Oxford University Press, 1987.

———. "The Campaign to Eliminate the Kulak as a Class, Winter 1929–1930: A Reevaluation of the Legislation." *Slavic Review*, vol. 45, no. 3 (1986).

———. "The Case of Krasnyi Meliorator *or* 'How the Kulak Grows into Socialism.'" *Soviet Studies*, vol. 38, no. 4 (1986).

———. "'L'ivresse du succes': les cadres russe et le pouvoir sovietique durant les campagnes de collectivisation de l'agriculture." *Revue des études Slaves*, vol. 64, no. 1 (1992).

———. "The Other Archipelago: Kulak Deportations to the North in 1930." *Slavic Review*, vol. 60, no. 4 (2001).

——. *Peasant Rebels Under Stalin: Collectivization and the Culture of Peasant Resistance.* New York: Oxford University Press, 1996.

——. "The Peasants' Kulak: Social Identities and Moral Economy in the Soviet Countryside in the 1920s." *Canadian Slavonic Papers*, vol. 42 (2000).

——. "The Role of the OGPU in Dekulakization, Mass Deportations, and Special Resettlement in 1930." *Carl Beck Papers in Russian and East European Studies*, no. 1406 (2000).

——. "The Second Coming: Class Enemies in the Soviet Countryside, 1927–1935." In *Stalinist Terror: New Perspectives*, ed. J. Arch Getty and Roberta T. Manning. New York: Cambridge University Press, 1993.

——. "A Tale of Two Men: Bergavinov, Tolmachev and the Bergavinov Commission." *Europe-Asia Studies*, vol. 52, no. 8 (2000).

——. "'Tear the Evil from the Root': The Children of the *Spetspereselentsy* of the North." *Studia Slavica Finlandensia*, Tom. 17 (2000).

Vyltsan, M. A., N. A. Ivnitskii, and Iu. A. Poliakov, "Nekotorye problemy istorii kollektivizatsii v SSSR." *Voprosy istorii*, no. 3 (1965).

Walicki, Andrzej. *The Controversy over Capitalism: Studies in the Social Philosophy of the Russian Populists.* Reprint. Notre Dame, IN: University of Notre Dame Press, 1989.

Watson, Derek. *Molotov and Soviet Government: Sovnarkom, 1930–41.* New York: St. Martin's Press, 1996.

Weiner, Amir, ed. *Landscaping the Human Garden.* Stanford: Stanford University Press, 2003.

——. "Nature, Nurture, and Memory in a Socialist Utopia: Delineating the Soviet Socio-Ethnic Body in the Age of Socialism." *American Historical Review*, vol. 104, no. 4 (October 1999).

Werth, Nicolas. "A State against Its People." In *The Black Book of Communism*, ed. Stephane Courtois et al. Trans. Jonathan Murphy and Mark Kramer. Cambridge, MA: Harvard University Press, 1999.

Wheatcroft, Stephen G. "More Light on the Scale of Repression and Excess Mortality in the Soviet Union in the 1930s." In *Stalinist Terror: New Perspectives*, ed. J. Arch Getty and Roberta T. Manning. Cambridge: Cambridge University Press, 1993.

——. "Victims of Stalinism and the Soviet Secret Police: The Comparability and Reliability of the Archival Data—Not the Last Word." *Europe-Asia Studies*, vol. 51, no. 2 (1999).

Zemskov, V. N. "'Kulatskaia ssylka' nakanune i v gody velikoi otechestvennoi voiny." *Sotsiologicheskie issledovaniia*, no. 2 (1992).

——. "'Kulatskaia ssylka' v 30-e gody." *Sotsiologicheskie issledovaniia*, no. 10 (1991).

——. "Spetsposelentsy (po dokumentatsii NKVD-MVD SSSR)." *Sotsiologicheskie issledovaniia*, no. 11 (1990).

——. *Spetsposelentsy v SSSR, 1930–1960.* Moscow, 2003.

——. "Sud'ba 'kulatskoi ssylki' (1930–1954 gg.)." *Otechestvennaia istoriia*, no. 1 (1994).

——. "Sud'ba 'kulatskoi ssylki' v poslevoennoe vremia." *Sotsiologicheskie issledovaniia*, no. 8 (1992).

Dissertations

Barenberg, Alan. "From Prisoners to Miners: The Gulag and Its Legacy in Vorkuta." PhD diss., University of Chicago, forthcoming.

Dehaan, Heather. "From Nizhnii to Gor'kii: The Reconstruction of a Russian Provincial City in the Stalinist 1930s." PhD diss., University of Toronto, 2005.

Kozlov, Denis. "The Readers of *Novyi Mir*: Twentieth-Century Experience and Soviet Historical Consciousness." PhD diss., University of Toronto, 2005.

McDonald, Tracy. "Face to Face with the Peasant: Village and State in Riazan, 1921–1930." PhD diss., University of Toronto, 2002.

Rossman, Jeffrey J. "Worker Resistance under Stalin: Class and Gender in the Textile Mills of the Ivanovo Industrial Region, 1928–1932." PhD diss., University of California–Berkeley, 1997.

Acknowledgments

I have been very fortunate in receiving support for this project. It is a great pleasure to express my gratitude to the John Simon Guggenheim Foundation and the Killam Program of the Canada Council for the Arts for awarding research fellowships to me in order to complete this project. The Canadian Social Science and Humanities Research Council has provided generous support for the project from its inception. Two successive chairs of the history department at the University of Toronto, Ronald Pruessen and Jane Abray, have tolerated my frequent leaves and offered collegial encouragement and good cheer.

I would also like to take this opportunity to thank the editors of *Kritika* and *Slavic Review* and the American Association for the Advancement of Slavic Studies for permission to use parts of previously published articles in this book. A series of institutions sponsored seminars where I was able to preview portions of the book before insightful audiences. For this, I am grateful to Amir Weiner, Norman Naimark, Terry Emmons, and their graduate students at Stanford University's Center for Russian and East European Studies; Yuri Slezkine, the late Reginald Zelnik, and the Berkeley Slavic Center seminar; and Sheila Fitzpatrick, Richard Hellie, Ronald Suny, and the University of Chicago Russian History Workshop. I also presented a series of lectures derived from the research for this book. For their generous invitations, I am grateful to Heather Coleman and the University of Calgary's history department; William Husband and Oregon State University's Holocaust Memorial Week organizing committee; William Smaldone, Mark Conliffe, Jeffrey Rossman, David Schimmelpenninck van der Oye, Olga Andriewsky, and their students at (respectively) Willamette University, University of Virginia, Brock University, and Trent University. I thank the organizers and attendants of two conferences at which I presented research findings for this book, one sponsored by the Finnish Institute for Russian and East European Studies, the Aleksanteri Institute of Helsinki University, and Helsinki University Library in 1999; and the other by the International Institute of Social History, Carnegie Mellon University, and the University of East London in 2005. I am also grateful to the organizing committee and lively audience of the Annual Ukrainian Famine Lecture at the University of Toronto where I spoke in 2005.

In Russia, V. P. Danilov and N. A. Ivnitskii served as my mentors. I am forever grateful to them as well as to my other colleagues in the *Tragedy of the Soviet Countryside* project: Roberta Manning, M. A. Vyltsan, Liubov' Denisova, L. Dvoinykh, E. Khandurina, E. Kirillova, V. Kondrashin, M. Kudiukina, Sergei Miakin'kov, Iu. Moshkov, Vera Mikhaleva, N. Murav'eva, Nona Tarkhova, Tat'iana Tsarevskaia, V. Vinogradov, M. A. Vyltsan, and the late I. E. Zelenin. E. A. Tiurina, the director of RGAE, provided an ideal work environment for the project and for my own research. I am grateful to her fine staff, as well as to the many wonderful archivists at RGASPI and GARF in Moscow, at GAVO and VOANPI in Vologda, and at GAAO and GAOPDF in Arkhangel'sk. I am also indebted to Oleg Khlevniuk, E. V. Kodin, S. A. Krasil'nikov, and Sergei Zhuravlev for their friendship and generosity in sharing their vast expertise with me.

Wilson Bell, Auri Berg, Elspeth Cameron, Svitlana Frunchak, J. Arch Getty, Steven Maddox, Alex Mel'nyk, Douglas Northrop, and Jennifer Polk read a draft of the manuscript and offered invaluable criticism. I am especially grateful to Marci Shore for her thorough reading of the manuscript. Denis Kozlov helped me in countless ways, providing a series of expert translations and insightful feedback. My greatest debt is to Ron Suny who has been an inspiration throughout and unfailingly kind. For assistance in a variety of ways, I would like to acknowledge Golfo Alexopoulos, Jeff Burds, Bill Chase, Stephen F. Cohen, Mark Cornwall (for the coffee cup), Monty Craig, Heather Dehaan, Michael Gelb, Tom Gleason, Wendy Goldman, Maya Haber, Mark von Hagen, Andrew and John Harder, James Harris, Dan Healey, Peter Holquist, Desi Hopkins, Diane Koenker, Jean Levesque, Elena Osokina, Jorg Schendel (for the Greek lesson), Sharik Sharikov, Kathleen E. Smith, Peter Solomon, Pam Thomson Verrico, and Amir Weiner. I would also like to thank Glen Hartley and Lynn Chu at Writers Representatives, along with their assistant Catharine Sprinkel. For years of friendship, support, and emotional sustenance in Moscow, I thank Zoia Orlova, Liuda Kipnis, Galia and Masha Runkevich, and Aaron and Esfir Luskin. And I thank Marina Khazanova for being Marina Khazanova.

Susan Ferber of Oxford University Press has been an ideal editor; her work on this manuscript has improved it in innumerable ways. I am delighted to be able to express my gratitude to her and her fine staff at OUP, especially Helen Mules and Mary Sutherland.

Last but not least, I thank Colleen Craig, without whom this work could even have been imagined. Her love, friendship, and wisdom sustain me.

Index